7-07

# Genrefied Classics

# Genreflecting Advisory Series

**Diana Tixier Herald, Series Editor**

Make Mine a Mystery: A Reader's Guide to Mystery and Detective Fiction
*Gary Warren Niebuhr*

Teen Genreflecting: A Guide to Reading Interests, Second Edition
*Diana Tixier Herald*

Blood, Bedlam, Bullets, and Badguys: A Reader's Guide to Adventure/
Suspense Fiction
*Michael B. Gannon*

Rocked by Romance: A Guide to Teen Romance Fiction|
*Carolyn Carpan*

Jewish American Literature: A Guide to Reading Interests
*Rosalind Reisner*

African American Literature: A Guide to Reading Interests
*Edited by Alma Dawson and Connie Van Fleet*

Historical Fiction: A Guide to the Genre
*Sarah L. Johnson*

Canadian Fiction: A Guide to Reading Interests
*Sharron Smith and Maureen O'Connor*

Genreflecting: A Guide to Popular Reading Interests, 6th Edition
*Diana Tixier Herald, Edited by Wayne A. Wiegand*

The Real Story: A Guide to Nonfiction Reading Interests
*Sarah Statz Cords, Edited by Robert Burgin*

Read the High Country: A Guide to Western Books and Films
*John Mort*

Graphic Novels: A Genre Guide to Comic Books, Manga, and More
*Michael Pawuk*

# Genrefied Classics

## A Guide to Reading Interests in Classic Literature

Tina Frolund

**Genreflecting Advisory Series**

**Diana Tixier Herald, Series Editor**

**LIBRARIES**
U N L I M I T E D
A Member of the Greenwood Publishing Group

Westport, Connecticut • London

**Library of Congress Cataloging-in-Publication Data**

Frolund, Tina.
    Genrefied classics : a guide to reading interests in classic literature / Tina Frolund.
        p. cm. — (Genreflecting advisory series)
    Includes bibliographical references and index.
    ISBN 1-59158-172-9 (alk. paper)
    1. Literature—Bibliography. I. Title.
Z6511.F76   2007
[PN6013]
016.8093—dc22      2006033740

British Library Cataloguing in Publication Data is available.

Library of Congress Catalog Card Number: 2006033740
ISBN: 1-59158-172-9

First published in 2007

Libraries Unlimited, 88 Post Road West, Westport, CT 06881
A Member of the Greenwood Publishing Group, Inc.
www.lu.com

Printed in the United States of America

∞™

The paper used in this book complies with the
Permanent Paper Standard issued by the National
Information Standards Organization  (Z39.48–1984).

10   9   8   7   6   5   4   3   2   1

*To Harry Holton and Catherine Rotter, my Uncle Harry
and Auntie Frau, the people who taught me to love books.*

# Contents

# Acknowledgments

The collections of the Las Vegas Clark County Library District supplied all the materials needed to complete this volume. This is truly a world-class library district where you least expect it.

My colleague John Faria contributed enthusiasm and annotations for the Horror, Fantasy, and Science Fiction chapters. His commitment to the project was steadfast, and I have appreciated his participation.

Barbara Ittner has been a patient but persistent editor who guided this project from the very beginning.

Ron Sande provided me with meals, a beautiful home and the moral support I needed to complete this volume.

# Introduction

## Genrefied Classics: Reader's Advisory for the Books That Endure

## The Classics

Some readers feel all cozy when they hear those words. They imagine sitting in front of a roaring fire on a winter's night, snuggling under a lap robe in a gleaming leather club chair, being led by a master craftsman, the author, on a moving literary exploration of the inner workings of humankind.

Other readers have a different response.

"The classics" conjures up images of nodding readers chained to books that are too big to lift, books that shoot out puffs of dust with every page turn. Enduring the same sentence over and over and over again, the reader is trapped in a wasteland of dense, boring books filled with impossible-to-understand language and remote unbelievable stories.

Both images are justified, for the classics offer both experiences. The classics, in fact, offer every experience.

## What Makes a Book a Classic?

Everyone sort of knows which books are the classics. They are the books that Penguin and Bantam publish. They are the books continually reissued in new editions with new cover art and fresh introductions. They are books that have won the big awards, the Pulitzer, Nobel, and Newbery and that appear consistently on college-bound reading lists.

What makes a book a classic?

- **Longevity**—a classic must endure through time. Classics are the books that have been around, in print and still read, for fifty years, two hundred years, two thousand years. These books say something to us across time.

- **Age**—age contributes to classic status. A new book, although it can be a predicted classic (think *Harry Potter*), isn't a classic until it proves its staying power. Generally twenty to fifty years of staying power are needed for reader's to consider a book a "classic." Only books published before 1985 are included in this volume.

- **Universality**—classics explicate our shared human experience. They are stories from diverse geographic regions and different historical eras. Odysseus was a Greek warrior, Elizabeth Bennet a nineteenth-century English girl, yet their stories address something enduringly human that modern readers can still connect with. Authors of the classics provide us with something that transcends time and culture; these writers speak to the human condition. Dickens, Tolstoy, and Hemingway wrote about their times but wrote about all times, too.

- **Multiple levels of meaning**—Classics speak to readers on several levels. These books can be read many times throughout a lifetime and will offer a new experience with each reading. *Wuthering Heights* read at age forty is a different experience from *Wuthering Heights* read at age eighteen. *Peter Pan* is as delightful at six as at fifty, but different things in the story delight us at those very different life stages.

- **A great story**—every classic that endures is, at its inner core, a wonderful story—engaging, rousing, ripping, moving, tender, intriguing, haunting, compelling, or otherwise splendid. Humans love and need story. These stories accomplish their mission across generations. None of these books would still be read today if they didn't engage readers as entertainment.

- **Memorable characters**—the characters in the classics become part of our common heritage. You know what I mean when I say, "he's a real Scrooge" or "Okay, Pollyanna, now let's get serious." Classic fictional characters inhabit our mind and give us a constellation of human patterns to learn from, be entertained by, laugh at, feel sorrow with. The people in these books stay with us.

- **An emotional or thought-provoking experience**—classic fiction, really all fiction, lets readers try on different experiences; it helps us feel things. Through fiction we can explore experiences we will all encounter—such as love and death—and experiences we may never undergo—such as exploration or physical heroism. The field of bibliotherapy exists because we acknowledge that fiction can help readers explore and understand experiences, behavior, and emotions. Narrative orders our world for us and helps us to learn what it is to be human. Fiction provides readers with an emotional experience; it helps us make sense of the world.

- **Great writing and language at its best**—well, usually. Great literary style, although a definite plus, is not always present in the classics. Many authors demonstrate the highest standards of literary style and usage—E. L. Doctorow, E. B. White, Ernest Hemingway, and Jane Austen, for example. And some authors are so stylistically excellent and important that they are a challenge to read, like Henry James or Virginia Woolf. But not all classics exemplify the best writing. Theodore Dreiser wrote important books with memorable characters and thought-provoking situations, but many critics consider him a clumsy writer. Dickens is called uneven and sentimental, and because he was writing for serial publication, his writing is, at times, padded. But these authors gave us a view of the world that engages us and helps us grow. Because their stories and characters shine through, we forgive them any literary awkwardness.

- **Stories that transcend their original format**—Ballets, theatrical plays, films, operas, television series, the stories from classic novels show up again and again in formats other than print. The stories endure across media. Adaptations are listed in the Film/Video/DVD section of each annotation.

- **Awards**—winning an award indicates that a book achieved recognized excellence. Books that have won awards stay in print. Remember, though, that many of the books we consider classics never won any awards.

- **Enduring critical acclaim**—the people who spend their days thinking about books and literature acknowledge certain books as the hallmarks of literary effort.

- **Popular appeal**—the bottom line is that people like these books and turn to them again and again. The best sellers of yesterday are often, but not always, today's classics. *The Sorrows of Young Werther* was a sensation in its day, as was *Gone with the Wind* in its. The majority of best sellers don't linger on as classics, but many classics were the popular and topical literary works of their times.

## Why Read the Classics? Or Do You Really Like Those Big, Old Books?

The classics entertain. In fact, the classics permeate contemporary media. In fall 2005, there was a new *Masterpiece Theatre* television broadcast of Robert Louis Stevenson's 1886 adventure tale *Kidnapped*; *The Color Purple,* Alice Walker's powerful 1984 book, recently opened as a Broadway musical; new film versions of *Pride and Prejudice* (Jane Austen, 1813*), Oliver Twist* (Charles Dickens, 1839), and *The Lion, the Witch and the Wardrobe* (C. S. Lewis, 1950) were released in 2005; and that same year Oprah Winfrey turned to the classics when she revived her book club and had America choosing William Faulkner as their summer beach read that summer. Flipping through television movies on a windy Sunday afternoon there was *The Man in the Iron Mask*, *The Autobiography of Miss Jane Pittman,* and the *The Big Sleep*. Clearly, the classics still have something to say to audiences.

Reading the classics stretches our minds, too—they challenge our intellects, build reading comprehension and language skills, and open us to new experiences. This is why classics are assigned to students.

They connect us with great minds and great thoughts from other places and times, enlarging our experience as humans.

Reading the classics encourages a common cultural heritage. An acquaintance with the Bible, Greek mythology, the characters of Dickens, and the journey of Huck Finn gives Western readers common intellectual ground and readers from other cultures an insight into the Western world.

Reading classic works from around the world gives Western readers greater cultural empathy and understanding as well. Happily, in recent years the literary canon, that is, the books considered to exemplify our common culture, has expanded to include books from traditions, cultures, races, genders, and experiences other than the upper-class white male perspective that dominated the list for previous generations.

## Why Are the Classics Hard to Read?

The classics present several difficulties to modern readers. For one thing, these books are old. They were written in different times, and the language is different from that we use today. The classics put us into a realm of arcane syntax and unfamiliar vocabulary. For some readers, this is the charm of the classic; for others, it is very disturbing to be confronted with unfamiliar usage and words. This creates a barrier to the story and ideas contained in the work. To younger readers still mastering reading skills and vocabulary, this can be an unwelcome and overwhelming intellectual challenge.

Because the stories are old, they refer to activities and objects that have lost meaning. Getting water at a well or riding "in a fly" are not things with which modern readers are familiar. Willing readers see this as the allure of the books. Fans of historical fiction seek out these old-time experiences. But many contemporary readers find these references confusing—and a major barrier to their enjoyment of a book. Footnotes and annotations can help, but they disturb the flow of the fictional experience.

Pacing is also an issue with older books. The pace of most classic novels is different from the pace of current fiction and our contemporary lives; to modern readers, the leisurely unfolding of events, lengthy detailed descriptions, or intrusion of a philosophizing omniscient narrator create a reading experience that seems excruciatingly slow. In pre-television days readers were willing to take more time in their reading to explore a setting or a mood. Today, readers are accustomed to the four-second cut of a movie that instantly establishes place, weather, mood, time of day, and so on. The classics sometimes require patience and intellectual endurance that modern readers are less accustomed, and perhaps less willing, to muster.

Along with older language, reference to lost activities and slower pacing, some of the classics portray the racism, sexism, and anti-Semitism that went unquestioned in past ages. Modern readers find the inclusion of these attitudes startling and upsetting.

## Genrefying the Classics

Because "classics" can be read on multiple levels, they lend themselves nicely to genre classification. On the most basic level, a classic is a good read—a tense mystery, a thrilling adventure, a passionate romance. Only secondarily is it an allegory of man's struggle in society or an expose of the impersonal cruelty of nature.

In recent years, one of the hottest topics of discussion in library service is Reader's Advisory work based on the appeals of genre fiction. We all read for entertainment—at least some of the time. Many of us like to read the same story with variations over and over again. A fan of horror stories wants to read other horror stories; romance readers want to feel the thrill of a love story when they read.

The classics too can be arranged under these categories to provide readers with genre access to them. This is not to say that Mary Shelley's *Frankenstein* is simply a horror story or that Poe's *Murders on the Rue Morgue* is just a mystery. They are more than that; but noting the genre aspects of classic literature helps you link it to other titles in that genre. Genrefying the classics offers readers and reader's advisors yet another way to approach a large body of fiction, and bring readers together with books they will enjoy.

# Teens and the Classics

There has always been a love-hate relationship between teens and the classics. These are, after all, the books teens are made to read, think about, write papers about, take tests on.

However, remember that teen readers like intensity, and that is what the classics are about—intensity—passion, rage, terror, and obsession. Consider *Wuthering Heights, Dracula, Madam Bovary*. Human experience ratcheted up to a fevered pitch, that's the classics. Like most readers, young adults want an emotional experience. The books listed in this bibliography deliver!

The twentieth century, and particularly its last forty years, saw the creation of an entire category of books for young adults. Classic adult books about young protagonists such as *Huckleberry Finn, Anne of Green Gables*, and *The Yearling* are no longer the only reading option for teens. Accomplished writers are crafting excellent books written specifically with the maturity of the teenager in mind. With so many wonderful stories available to younger readers, should we still bother with classics? I would say yes. The right book for the right reader at the right time demands we offer these stories. Some of these novels are too good to miss; and the teen years are the perfect time to experience many of them. The intention of this volume isn't to insist classic fiction be recommended to the exclusion of contemporary fiction but that classics be recommended as well.

# How to Recommend a Classic

Many teens love to read, and what they love about it is good stories. One way to ease young adult readers into the classics is to motivate them to read a good story.

When it comes to recommending books to young adults, librarians are often in a friendlier position than teachers. Librarians can recommend and then step back, always available later to chat about a book but seldom in a position to force the material on the reader. Teachers often play a stricter role, being tied to a curriculum or having to work through a required reading list.

For librarians, however, the freedom to recommend any book ever written may actually be too much freedom. The brain of the librarian typically locks up as soon as someone asks for "a good book to read." What to do?

Start a conversation with the reader. Find out what he or she is interested in. The key question to ask is, "Tell me about a book that you liked." The answer will give you clues to areas of interest as well as reading ability. Someone who likes Terry Pratchett may like Douglas Adams, a fan of Stephen King should definitely try *Dracula*.

It is helpful to walk and talk, move the conversation toward the stacks or the paperback rack, that way you will be reminded of titles as you see the books and you can recommend what is actually on the shelf and waiting to be checked out.

Offer several books. The books can be similar or radically different, but give the patron three or four. Tell a little about each book. Point out what is exciting and intriguing, share an anecdote you know about the author, mention that there is a great movie version, share your enthusiasm for the book (without gushing or overdoing it), and you may gain it a new reader. Don't be ashamed to admit you haven't read it. Say honestly, "I haven't read this, but I hear it is great," or "lots of readers like this, but I haven't read it yet. Come back and tell me what you think of it." No one likes a phony intellectual and honestly admitting you have not read every book in the library can make you more approachable to teens

Remember that some readers missed the classics of childhood. Not everyone read *Kidnapped, The Secret Garden, The Wind in the Willows,* or *Little Women* when they were younger. Others love to revisit these stories that they adored as children. When approached the right way, you can give an older reader a younger book. Let them know it isn't a baby book, it is a book for everyone—a story too good to miss—and if they missed it when they were younger they might like reading it now.

Young adults are sensitive, and giving a teen reader a book that appears "too young" is more mortifying than giving them one that is too advanced. But consider that a classic children's book written a hundred years ago may be a challenging read, and because it is a classic, it will appeal on multiple levels. This is a valid reason to include in a library's collection mass-market paperback editions of childhood classics such as *Peter Pan, The Wizard of Oz,* or *Alice in Wonderland.* It is less embarrassing for a young adult reader to check out a paperback than an illustrated children's edition. Also new paperback editions (from Bantam, Signet, or Modern Library, for example) often include essays and introductory material interesting to the older reader.

Never be afraid to encourage a young adult to read up a level. Interest is definitely the key when encouraging readers to challenge themselves. A book with high interest appeal may inspire a reader to push through a difficult text. Moving a reader from Annette Klause's *Silver Kiss* to Bram Stoker's *Dracula* is easier when vampires are the motivating factor, not when you suggest, "this is a more challenging book." A complimentary "you seem like a mature enough reader to handle this" can be the motivation a reader needs.

Finally, ask for follow-up. When you are sincerely interested in the opinions of the young people to whom you recommend books, they will repay you by becoming thoughtful readers interested in discussing their reading with you because you are interested in their opinions.

## Reading Level

Assessing the reading skill level of YA readers is part science, part art. Often students can't or won't tell you their reading level. Reading ability is highly individual, and grade level does not always equate to reading level—students may read above or below their grade level. Asking students what books they have read recently often tells you more about their reading comfort zone than asking their grade.

Don't fall into the trap of recommending a thin book thinking it is an easy book. Size does not equate to complexity in the classics. A book can be very thin but still have a complex and mature story or convoluted language, thus being difficult to comprehend or inappropriate for less mature readers, Conrad's *Heart of Darkness* or Steinbeck's *Of Mice and Men* are two skinny examples.

The same can be true for the fat books. Not every big book is difficult. *A Tree Grows in Brooklyn, King Solomon's Mines,* and *Lonesome Dove* are thick volumes that read with ease.

# The Classics and the Movies

Young people, maybe all people, love movies. Watching the film version of a classic book can create a more complete experience for a reader. One way to whet the appetite of a reluctant reader and enrich the experience of every reader is to suggest a film version. But the movie is never a substitute for the reading experience. Watching a movie and reading a book are two distinctly different activities; neither can replace the other.

Relying on a film instead of actually reading the book is not good policy for students. Hollywood has no investment in an accurate translation of books from page to screen. Consequently, many film adaptations do not accurately reflect the book on which they are based. Often major characters and subplots are cut. *Gone with the Wind* is a classic example. Although it is considered a very fine adaptation of a book to a film, several of Scarlett's children are not in the movie; and Will Benteen, a major character at Tara after the war ("Undoubtedly, as Mammy frequently declared, Will was something the Lord had provided and Scarlett often wondered how Tara could have lived through the last few months without him.") isn't in the movie at all.

The lesson is clear, the movie may be fantastic and yet tell a very different story from the book. Plots, settings, time periods, and characters and their motivations may change in the migration to the screen. The standard phrase used by authors who still want to encourage ticket sales but not totally betray their original creative work is "Well, the movie is not the book." In other words, it may be a great thing, but it's a different thing.

# Audio Books

Literacy starts when we read aloud to little children. Audio books are a way to extend that experience into the teen and adult years. When you listen to an audio book, a sensitive, intelligent, and involved reader is reading the book to you! Full cast recordings and audio books that use music and sound effects create an even richer experience.

Audio books, in cassette, CD, or downloaded formats, are a form of literary enrichment. They give students an example of fluent and expressive reading, and often hearing a classic makes it a more enjoyable and understandable text. They offer entertainment, can improve listening and concentration skills, are an exercise for the imagination, give the listener the proper pronunciation of words and names, and can contribute to comprehension and expand vocabulary. Unabridged versions are preferred; why miss anything? These are listed in the "Audio" section of each annotation.

Audio books appeal to a different learning style, the style of auditory learners. They make it easier to share the classics with people who are not necessarily "readers." Audio books can also be invaluable for introducing classics to reluctant readers and to readers with vision problems or with reading disabilities.

Active teens can download an entire book to their iPod and go. Busy parents can pop a disc into the car CD player and run errands with the kids. Teachers can offer audio book excerpts as a supplement to classroom reading.

# Purpose

*Genrefied Classics* has many goals. Among them are the following:

Reader's Advisory source—libraries have always been in the business of recommending good books. The art and science of guiding the reader has become a library specialty in recent years. This volume will give the library staff charged with that role one more tool to use when suggesting the best and most appropriate fiction to readers, both teens and adult.

Ready Reference source—readers looking for specific information about a publication date, an author or a plot can turn here.

Suggestions for further reading—readers looking for "read-alikes" to an author or title will find suggestions in the "Similar Read" section of each annotation. Also similar books are grouped together in their chapter subgenres. Because this guide organizes classics according to genres, subgenres and reading interests, it helps you identify read-alikes. If your teen reader loves Tom Clancy, you're more likely to find a classic he or she enjoys in the Adventure chapter than in the Romance chapter. Using the subject index will further expand the recommendations.

Collection Development tool—middle school, high school, community college, undergraduate, and public libraries wanting to develop or maintain their Classics collections can refer to this volume for suggestions.

# Intended Audience

This is a book about books. It is intended for readers. Forcing the classics on unwilling teens or convincing anyone that classics make better reading than other types of fiction is not the goal. The intention has been to present the classics from a new point of view, offering the reader a chance to revisit these grand older books from the access points offered by genre classification and reader's advisory service.

School and public librarians and teachers who work with young adults are the primary audience for this book. Homeschoolers will also appreciate the recommendations in this volume. Those who work with adult readers will also find the classifications helpful.

Young adult readers will find the book useful for browsing, learning about the classics, and making their own reading selections. They will find it a valuable complement to college-bound and advanced placement reading lists.

Book groups will also appreciate this volume. Every book included would generate lively discussions and multiple interpretations, making them great choices for book clubs.

This is a good browsing tool for anyone interested in literature and classic books. Interested adult readers wanting to revisit the classics can benefit from this volume. Adult readers can also gain insight into YA literature using this book. Not only does this book offer adult books for teen consumption, it offers teen books for adult consumption, too.

# Scope

This book is an annotated bibliography of classic literary works arranged within genre classifications. This is an international and multicultural bibliography. Every book is available in English, and all but a handful are still in print. More than four hundred titles are annotated; more titles and authors are recommended as "Similar Reads."

For the purpose of this guide, "classic" is defined as a work that has endured over time and transcended the scene of its creation. A classic is a great story with multiple levels of meaning, literary merit, and popular appeal. When it comes to today's teen readers, twenty years is enough time to qualify a book as a classic. Only books published before 1985 are included.

In this volume, you will find prose fiction, epics, and longer forms of poetry—*The Canterbury Tales, Paradise Lost, The Divine Comedy,* sort of the novels of their day. Not included are short stories (except for a few must-read collections such as Poe and Conan Doyle), short poetry and nonfiction. Fictional works written from 800 B.C. through 1985 are included. Missing from this volume are recent classics like *Fallen Angels* (Myers, 1988), *The Joy Luck Club* (Tan, 1989), *The Giver* (Lowry, 1993), *Holes* (Sachar, 1998), and that instant classic, *Harry Potter* (Rowlings, 1999). If these books have the predicted staying power, look for them in subsequent editions.

Listed in this book are classic works of particular interest to young adult readers. These are books that have a teen protagonist, explore an issue of particular interest during the teen years, or provide a glimpse into adult reality that will engage, entertain, and enlighten a young adult reader. Some of the books were written specifically with teen readers in mind. These titles are indicated with the word **Teen.** Also included are adult works suitable for young adult readers and classic children's books with appeal for older readers.

# Selection of Titles

All of the books in this volume are recommended for teen readers, although not all are Young Adult books. Children's classics and adult classics are included. Many children's classics have enduring appeal, and teens have always taken for their own adult books that portray a young person stepping into adulthood—*David Copperfield, A Tree Grows in Brooklyn, To Kill a Mockingbird, The Yearling, The Catcher in the Rye.*

Titles included in this guide have been drawn from publisher's lists (think Penguin, renowned for their editions of classics and Cliff's Notes, the go-to source for explication of the classics), the Young Adult Library Services Association (YALSA) recommendations, and lists for college-bound students.

Two very valuable sources used for selecting titles were *Reading Lists for College-Bound Students,* by Doug Estell with Michele L. Satchwell and Patricia S. Wright, 3rd edition, published by Arco 2000; and *Outstanding Books for the College Bound; Choices for a Generation,* YALSA, American Library Association, 1996 and 2006 editions.

Advanced placement English reading lists have also been a treasure trove of titles. Reading lists from schools across America can easily be found online now. It is a fascinating expedition to see who is reading what and to note similarities and variations in lists.

Books published before 1985 that appear on school reading lists again and again (*The Scarlet Letter, A House on Mango Street*) have been selected for this bibliography.

## Awards

Titles have also been drawn selectively from literary award lists. Every award winner has literary merit for its time, but not all have endured as classics.

Awards include the following:

The Newbery is awarded every year to the author of a distinguished contribution to American literature suitable for children up to and including the age of fourteen. The Newbery winners and honor books selected for inclusion here have appeal for readers at the higher end of that age range. Many Newbery books are for younger readers and were not selected for inclusion in this volume.

The Scott O'Dell award is given for historical fiction.

The Pulitzer Prize is an award for adult books. Only those books with a young protagonist or with issues and stories appealing to young adults have been included

The Nobel is an international award given to an author for a body of work, not a specific title. Again, selected titles with young adult appeal were chosen.

Margaret A. Edwards Award given for lifetime achievement to an author of young adult books

Genre awards like the Hugo or Nebula for science fiction, the Damon Knight Memorial Grand Master Award (formerly the Nebula Grand Master award) for lifetime contribution to Science Fiction, the Spur for Western literature, the Rita for romance are also listed.

Award winners are indicated with a ♣ before the title. The award is then listed in the Subject section of the annotation.

## Methodology

After the basic list of titles from the resources mentioned, was compiled, standard print sources were consulted, *Something about the Author, Masterplots, What Do Young Adults Read Next, Teen Genreflecting,* online library catalogs from around the country, and online sources such as *Novelist* and *Reader's Advisor Online* to help determine genre, subject headings, and reading levels.

I also reacquainted myself with each book. A degree in English literature, graduate studies in comparative literature, and twenty years involvement with libraries have positioned me to be familiar with the books that are deemed classics. I have, at one time or another, read most of these titles. In the past two years, I have revisited them all.

Annotations were written by myself and by my colleague John Faria, who contributed to the Science Fiction, Horror, and Fantasy chapters.

# Arrangement

Books are arranged under broad genre headings. Books are further arranged by subgenres or thematic groupings within each chapter. Titles are then arranged alphabetically by the author's name.

# Entry Anatomy

Each entry includes name of author and the author's birth and death dates, then the title of the book. In parenthesis after the title is the original country and original date of publication. A currently available edition of the work is recommended. Award winners are indicated with 🏵 preceding the title. The specific award is listed with the subject headings.

Suggested reading level is indicated with a letter following the bibliographic information. Reading levels are: **M** = Middle School, grades 5–7, ages 10 to 12; **J** = Junior High School, grades 7–9, ages 12 to 14; **S** = Senior High School, grades 10–12, ages 15 to 18. Use your own judgment along with the designated reading levels, keeping in mind that these are simply suggestions, and every reader is different. All of the books in this volume are recommended for young adult readers, but books that were written specifically for YA readers are indicated with the word "**Teen**."

The final symbol, **Q**, indicates a book that is a quick and easy classic. The kind of book a teen reader can grab the afternoon before a paper is due and start and finish reading before midnight. These books are the shortest (under 250 pages) and easiest to read.

Following the bibliographic information is the annotation.

If the book is readily available in an unabridged audio version this is indicated under **Audio** and film versions or other adaptations are listed in the **Film/Video/DVD** section. **New Media** includes recommendations for games, graphic novels; or pertinent Web sites to consult for further information. **Similar Reads** includes other works by the same author, other titles in the series, and read-alike recommendations. Not all Similar Reads recommended are annotated in this volume; all are indexed.

Please note that books suitable for book clubs are not identified as such, because virtually every title in this volume fits that category.

**Subjects** complete the annotations. This is where the setting and time period of the story, subject headings, thematic indicators, and awards are listed. You will also find several descriptors used here to give a fuller understanding of the book:

"Childhood Classic" indicates a title suitable for the youngest readers (fifth grade and under) but highly recommended for all readers. These books are included because today's young adults, distracted as they are with many forms of media and entertainment, may have missed reading them as children. These classic books can be read (and reread) at any age. Reading these classics of world literature contributes to a reader's overall literary education; they are entertaining, thought provoking, and typically contain multiple levels of meaning. They are terrific read-aloud selections and all are family friendly.

"Gentle Reads" are partly defined by what they don't include: overt sex and graphic violence. They also contain "old-fashioned" qualities such as courage, loyalty, family, and honesty. They are filled with strong and sometimes eccentric characters. Often humorous, they depict deep emotions and are sometimes heartbreakingly sad. These books treat the reader gently.

"Mature Reads" contain more thematically complex stories about the human condition. They may use strong language, depict complex relationships, and contain overt sex or explicit violence. These books treat the reader as an open-minded adult who is able to look at the darker side of humanity. They are the most challenging reads and generally the longest books.

"Frequently Challenged" books are those that perpetually attract controversy; the books whose inclusion in libraries and curricula is often questioned. The American Library Association's Office of Intellectual Freedom publishes "The 100 Most Frequently Challenged Books" list. Titles with the subject designation of "Frequently Challenged" were drawn from the 1990–2000 list.

# Appendices

**Publication Chronology** and an appendix listing the titles by **Reading Level** are also included.

# Indexes

The **Author/Title Index** lists all authors and titles that are annotated as well as those listed in the Similar Reads section. Film titles are also included. Films are given with their date of release. The **Subject Index** lists all the headings from the Subject section of each annotation.

In conclusion, however you use this book, it is hoped that the result is increased reading enjoyment for yourself and the readers with whom you work.

# Chapter 1

# Adventure

Are adventure stories the oldest genre? Certainly they evolved out of the oldest form of storytelling—the oral tradition. Cavemen sitting around the fire after a hunt must have told an adventure story—finding and tracking their prey, losing it, finding it again, cornering it, going in for the kill—what could be more exciting, especially if the survival of the tribe depended on the successful hunt? Homer's stories, told orally thousands of years ago, are adventure tales. Every national mythology has adventure tales. Even religious scriptures contain adventure stories. For example, the Judeo-Christian Bible has stories of grand adventure—David and Goliath, Noah and the Flood, Joseph's journeys.

Adventure stories are entertaining, compelling stories that keep a reader engaged through dramatic plot lines and high levels of action. It is, after all, a major function of fiction to entertain, and who doesn't love a rousing tale breathlessly told? Plot, action, an exciting and suspenseful narrative, a sympathetic hero, a true villain, close escapes, ultimate triumph—these elements are at the core of the adventure genre. Many classics fit easily into the adventure genre, and many adventure stories, by virtue of their long shelf life and continued popularity, have become classics.

Adventure novels offer much appeal to the reader:

- *Action, Action, Action*—a journey, a battle, a chase—at the core of most adventure novels is action.

- *Fast-paced storytelling*—in these stories plot often takes precedence over character development. This makes them excellent recommendations for reluctant readers because an exciting, suspenseful plot can propel a reluctant reader through a book.

- *Conflict*—there is inherent conflict in an adventure story—humans struggling against nature, humans battling against each other, even man in conflict with himself. The excitement comes in watching the conflict play out—who will win? The good guys or the bad? The sea or the ship? Suspense and a pervasive sense of danger add to the conflict.

- *Good versus evil*—many adventure stories are as basic as the good guys versus the bad guys. The hero is exemplary, the villain is dastardly.

- *Heroes and heroism*—Adventure novels appeal to the warrior, the traveler, the hero in all of us. They provide us with the vicarious heroism we long to experience but have little opportunity for in modern life. Many of the most popular adventure novels are about an ordinary person caught up in extraordinary events and acting intelligently and heroically for the greater good. Who doesn't want to be brave and smart, willing to risk all, knowing that our contribution may make the difference between failure and success, between existence and death?

- *Exotic locales*—deserted islands, jungles, ships at sea. Typically the setting in an adventure novel is realistic and identifiable yet removed from the everyday.

Frequently dismissed as shallow or ephemeral, adventure novels often lack psychologically rich characterizations that give a novel substance. Adventure novels have long been second-class citizens in the literary world—too entertaining to be good literature. Perhaps this prejudice stems from their "pulp" and "dime novel" history, a tawdry past of cheaply made books with sensational and melodramatic stories. But that shady past is exactly what makes them exciting reads and outstanding recommendations for young adult readers.

# Espionage

Spies, secret agents, covert action, ambiguous morality, and the fate of societies are all found in espionage classics.

## Buchan, John (1875–1940)

*The Thirty-Nine Steps* (England, 1915). Penguin 2004 (paper). 144pp. 0141441178 <u>S</u> Q
When Richard Hannay returns to his flat and finds his mysterious neighbor dead in the living room, he realizes he is in for an adventure: "I reckoned that two sets of people would be looking for me—Scudder's enemies to put me out of existence, and the police, who would want me for Scudder's murder. It was going to be a giddy hunt." Thus begins Hannay's mad run across England and through the Scottish highlands. Spies, anarchists, codes, disguises, explosions, chases, and double crosses fill this fast-paced read about a dashing chase with a race to the finish ending to save civilization as we know it.

> **Audio:** Blackstone Audiobooks cassette 0786106891. Read by Frederick Davidson.

> **Film/Video/DVD:** *The Thirty-Nine Steps* (1935), directed by Alfred Hitchcock, alters the story but is a great suspense film.

> **Similar Reads:** For a suspenseful spy story set during World War II, read *The Eye of the Needle* by Ken Follett. For more Scottish adventure, try *Kidnapped* by Stevenson.

> **Subjects:** London 1914; Scotland; Scottish Highlands; Anarchists; Chase; Imposters; Murder, Spies

### Childers, Erskine (1870–1922)

*The Riddle of the Sands* **(England: 1903).** Penguin Books 2000 (paper). 336pp. 0141181656 <u>S</u>

Two young Englishmen on a sailing holiday discover a German plot to invade the undefended British coast. The action takes place in a small sailing boat cruising the Baltic Sea and the low-lying Frisian coastline and is set in the years prior to World War I. This is a wonderful sailing story as well as a suspenseful espionage novel.

Childers is credited with alerting Britain to this national threat and causing the government to revise its naval policies. In a strange fiction/fact moment, Childers's life ended when the British government executed him for his involvement in Irish freedom fighting.

> **Audio:** Audio Partners cassette 157270103X. Read by Anton Lesser.

> **Film/Video/DVD:** *The Riddle of the Sands* (1979) film with Michael York and Simon MacCorkindale

> **Similar Reads:** Books by John Buchan (*The Thirty-Nine Steps*; *Greenmantle*) or Somerset Maugham's Ashenden stories.

> **Subjects:** Germany; England; Sea Story; Yachting; Sailing; Spies

### Conrad, Joseph (1857–1924)

*The Secret Agent* **(England: 1907).** Signet 1983 (paper). 240pp. 0451524160 <u>S</u>

In danger of losing his comfortable position as the London *agent provocateur* of a foreign power, Verloc convinces his simple-minded brother-in-law to blow up the Greenwich Conservatory. When the plan goes awry, Verloc's wife, who is devoted to her brother, steps in.

Conrad presents a novel of anarchists and spies in the family that is unlike many of his other works. Set in grimy London, not in exotic ports of call, this is a darkly comic novel about absurd terrorists, unlikely spies, a dysfunctional family, and contemporary alienation.

> **Film/Video/DVD:** *Sabotage* (1936) directed by Hitchcock and *The Secret Agent* (1996) with Bob Hoskins as Verloc

> **Similar Reads:** Try *The Man Who Was Thursday* by G. K. Chesterton for another story of anarchists

> **Subjects:** London; Anarchists; Terrorism; Spies; Suicide

### Kipling, Rudyard (1865–1936)

🐾 *Kim* **(England: 1901).** Penguin 1992 (paper). 368pp. 0140183523 <u>J</u> <u>Teen</u>

Travel to exotic India in the time of the British Raj and meet Kimball O'Hara, the son of an Irish soldier, who grew up as a streetwise orphan in Lahore, India. Kim is a natural spy, a lover of the "Great Game" of intrigue and deception that makes up the world of espionage—in this instance England against Russia for control of central Asia. As the story opens, Kim befriends a wise old lama, a holy man who is on a pilgrimage to find the river that will wash all sins away. Kim becomes his *chela,* or disciple, and travels across India with the lama until Kim meets his own destiny in the form of a Red Bull on a green field.

Kim is an entertaining hero, lively, extroverted, able to shift between cultures. This novel, although entirely a product of its imperialistic times, is full of humor and humanity and is a great adventure tale.

**Audio:** Recorded Books cassette 1556902859. Read by Margaret Hilton

**Film/Video/DVD:** 1950 with Dean Stockwell and Erroll Flynn; 1984 TV version also available

**Similar Reads:** For more of Kipling's lively storytelling, read his famous story "The Man Who Would Be King" and the adventures of Mowgli in *The Jungle Books. Kidnapped* by Stevenson is another tale of a boy who plays at men's games and succeeds.

**Subjects:** India late 1800s; Colonialism; British in India; Orphans; Spies; Victorian Novel; Nobel Prize, 1907

## Maugham, W. Somerset (1874–1965)

*Ashenden: Or the British Agent* **(England: 1928).** Penguin 1993 (paper, *Somerset Maugham Collected Short Stories, Volume 3*). 256pp. 0140185917

Invited to a nondescript house in London, a writer named Ashenden is recruited by a colonel known as R to be a spy for the British government. Says R, "There's just one thing I think you ought to know before you take on this job. And don't forget it. If you do well you'll get no thanks and if you get into trouble you'll get no help. Does that suit you?" "Perfectly" is Ashenden's reply!

Archetypal British sangfroid permeates this collection of connected stories about sophisticated, distant Ashenden and the intelligence missions he undertakes in the cause of freedom. Maugham said he based these stories on his own experiences as a spy for the British government during World War I.

**Audio:** Recorded Books cassette 1556900325. Read by Neil Hunt.

**Film/Video/DVD:** *Ashenden* British television series from 1991; difficult to find.

**Similar Reads:** Other authors for mature readers of spy stories are John Le Carre and Ian Fleming; or try Graham Greene's *The Confidential Agent* or Richard Condon's *The Manchurian Candidate.*

**Subjects:** England; Spies, World War I

# Journey

The journey or quest is an eternal theme in literature. A hero or heroine travels through a series of episodes encountering new challenges and new characters along the way, overcoming the unknown as well his or her own resistance to heroism. There is generally a clear goal the hero is trying to achieve—sometimes it is simply to reach home.

## Conrad, Joseph (1857–1924)

*Heart of Darkness* (**England: 1902**). Penguin 1995 (paper). 166p 0140186522 <u>S</u>

At anchor on a yacht in the Thames, waiting for the tide to turn, Charlie Marlow tells a haunting story to his mates. Years before he traveled up the Congo River in Africa to meet a man named Kurtz, the most successful ivory trader of his time. Through Marlow's digressive and ambiguous story, we learn that his journey up the river was actually a journey into evil and that Kurtz was a man deeply embedded in the heart of darkness.

A short book, but not an easy read, *Heart of Darkness* is a dark and mature work that rewards thoughtful and attentive reading. Although it has the trappings of an adventure story, it is an exploration into the darkness of humanity, not just the jungle. Conrad is a solemn writer with a pessimistic worldview, who undertakes serious themes set in exotic locales.

**Audio:** Recorded Books cassette 1556902204; CD 1402552637. Read by Michael Thompson.

**Film/Video/DVD:** Basis for Francis Ford Coppola's famous movie, *Apocalypse Now* (1979). Also filmed in 1994 as *Heart of Darkness* with John Malkovich and Tim Roth, directed by Nicholas Roeg.

**Similar Reads:** *The Sea Wolf* by Jack London; *Island of Dr. Moreau* by H. G. Wells. Conrad's *Lord Jim* presents another moral dilemma in the form of an adventure.

**Subjects:** Africa late 1800s; Congo; Madness; Greed; Colonialism; Jungle; Good and Evil; Mature Read

*Lord Jim* (**England 1900**). Penguin 1988 (paper). 377pp. 0140180923 <u>S</u>

How does a man live with himself when he has violated his own moral code? That is the theme explored in *Lord Jim*. Jim is a handsome, capable young man who spends his life around ships in exotic ports like Bombay and Rangoon. An act of cowardice in his past sets Jim apart from his fellows. Whenever that past is uncovered, he moves on, moving farther from civilization and the sphere of Western men. Finally, at a remote trading post deep in the jungle Jim gains a chance at redemption.

Conrad, whose native language was Polish, is considered a master stylist of English prose even though he didn't learn to speak, read, or write English until going to sea on English ships. He writes stories with challenging prose and narrative complexity, employing deep paragraphs, long sentences, and formal vocabulary: "After his first feeling of revolt he had come round to the view that only a meticulous precision of statement would bring out the true horror behind the appalling face of things." Conrad exposes the dark side of colonialism and depicts men's behavior under physical, psychological, and moral stress, often showing how the inner man is portrayed by his external actions.

**Audio:** Blackstone Audio cassette 078610404x. Read by Frederick Davidson.

**Film/Video/DVD:** *Lord Jim* (1965) with Peter O'Toole as Jim.

**Similar Reads:** Conrad's other classic is *The Heart of Darkness*; or try Kipling for more Englishmen abroad, the short story "The Man Who Would be King" or the novel *Kim*. Jack London also portrays men in extreme conditions, try *The Sea Wolf* and *The Call of the Wild. Billy Budd* by Herman Melville is another story of a sailor and redemption.

**Subjects:** Far East late 1800s; Colonialism; Ships; Sailors; Courage; Honor; Redemption;

## Haggard, H. Rider (1856–1925)

*King Solomon's Mines* **(England: 1885).** Oxford Classics 1998 (paper). 368pp. 0192834851 **J**

Famous hunter and trader Allan Quatermain takes pen in hand to write down "the strangest story that I remember." Years before, he was hired by an English lord to search for his missing brother and for the lost diamond mines of the biblical King Solomon. On this quest Quatermain, his native guide the regal Umbopa and their companions meet adventures and dangers in the jungles of Africa.

**Audio:** Recorded Books cassette 1556908458. Read by Patrick Tull.

**Film/Video/DVD:** Erroll Flynn turned down the role of Allan Quatermain, so Stewart Granger played it in the 1950 Technicolor classic that loosely follows the book; also filmed for television in 1985 with Richard Chamberlain and in 2004 with Patrick Swayze.

**Similar Reads:** Haggard wrote *King Solomon's Mines* to rival Stevenson's popular adventure novel, *Treasure Island*. Haggard was a prolific writer of adventure stories—there are sixteen books about Allan Quatermain. Perhaps his second best-known work is the fantasy adventure *She*. For other incredible journeys, read Jules Verne's *Journey to the Center of the Earth*, *The Lost World* by Arthur Conan Doyle, and *The Land That Time Forgot* by Edgar Rice Burroughs.

**Subjects:** Africa; Jungle; Treasure; Lost Tribes; Lost World; Victorian Novel

## Hilton, James (1900–1954)

*Lost Horizon* **(England: 1933).** Pocket Books 1988 (paper). 240pp. 0671664271 **J Q**

An airplane is hijacked to fly over the Himalayas where it crash-lands. The four passengers—a female missionary, an American businessman, and two Englishmen —are rescued by the enigmatic inhabitants of a lamasery and taken to the valley of the Blue Moon, where they are welcomed to remain. The inhabitants of this mysterious and secluded place, called Shangri-La, are blessed with health, peace, and very long lives—very, very long lives. Conway, the hero of the group, is enlightened into the secrets of Shangri-La by the high lama.

This is a haunting, thought-provoking story about the choices and trade-offs we make for modernity and progress. What starts as an exciting adventure becomes an inward journey that questions history, society, and human's existence on earth.

**Film/Video/DVD:** *Lost Horizon* (1937) classic with Ronald Coleman; the 1973 musical version is regularly ridiculed as a mistake

**Similar Reads:** Other adventure stories that have a deeper meaning include *Heart of Darkness, Lord of the Flies,* and *A High Wind in Jamaica.* Hilton's other classic book is the very different, sentimental school story, *Goodbye, Mr. Chips.* For more Eastern philosophy, try *Siddhartha* by Hesse, *The Bhagavad Gita,* or *The Tao Te Ching*

**Subjects:** Shangri-La; 1930s; Tibet; Lamas; Monks; Self-discovery; Mysticism; Gentle Read

## Hughes, Richard (1900–1976)

*High Wind in Jamaica* **(England: 1929).** New York Review of Books 1999 (paper). 296pp. 0940322153 **S**

In this forgotten classic, the five children of the Bas Thornton family are growing up as beings of the natural world in nineteenth-century Jamaica. When a hurricane destroys their home, they are sent back to the safety and civilization of England. Within days of their departure, however, their ship is set upon by pirates, and through almost comic circumstances, the children end up on the pirate ship. It isn't long before they are the masters and the hapless pirates are the victims.

Written in a deceptively simple style, this book is a disturbing and darkly comic novel that can be read as an adventure tale or a psychological exploration into the moral lives of children. The reader is left to wonder: is childhood a time of innocence? What really constitutes evil? How can we know what is the truth? This forgotten gem is sure to generate discussion with teen readers.

**Film/Video/DVD:** *A High Wind in Jamaica* (1965) film with Anthony Quinn as the pirate captain

**Similar Reads:** Usually compared to Golding's *Lord of the Flies,* this story also contains elements of O. Henry's famous comic story, "The Ransom of Red Chief." Readers up for a challenge may want to move on the Joseph Conrad's *Lord Jim* and *The Heart of Darkness* for further adventure tales that explore the darkness of man.

**Subjects:** Jamaica; Hurricane; Childhood; Pirates; Ships; Good and Evil

## Kipling, Rudyard (1865–1936)

🐾 *The Man Who Would Be King* **(England: 1888).** Oxford University Press 1999 (paper, includes other stories). 300pp. 0192736293 **J Q**

Daniel Dravot and Peachy Carnehan are chums, good-natured adventurers, newly released from the British army in 1880s India. They are broke and casting about for a get-rich quick scheme. Together they concoct the plan to become kings of the hidden country of Kafiristan. After making a solemn contract in the presence of a witness (who later tells us this story), the men set off to meet their new fates as kings.

**Audio:** Recorded Books cassette 1556903316. Read by George Taylor.

**Film/Video/DVD:** *The Man Who Would Be King* (1975), directed by John Houston and starring Sean Connery and Michael Caine, is a fine adaptation, a film Houston had wanted to make since he was a boy enthralled by Kipling's adventure story.

**Similar Reads:** Kipling wrote many stories about adventuring in the British Empire. Also turn to Robert Louis Stevenson.

**Subjects:** Afghanistan; India; British in India; Soldiers; Lost World; Imperialism; Friendship; Nobel Prize 1907

## Stevenson, Robert Louis (1850–1894)

*Kidnapped* (**England: 1886**). Huntington Press 1999 (hardback). 334pp. 0873281772 (contains Stevenson's original text and includes introduction, glossary, notes and a gazetteer). Scholastic 2002 (paper). 276pp. 0439295785 **M**

Seventeen-year-old David Balfour leaves his home in the countryside of Scotland upon the death of his parents to claim his inheritance from his grand relatives, the Balfours of Shaw. But his uncle, a miserly man with secrets to protect, betrays young David and sets him upon a path of mystery, danger, and adventure. Under perilous circumstances David makes a new friend—the charismatic and heroic scoundrel Alan Breck, who teaches young David to fight for what is his.

This adventure tale is set in 1751. It starts with a bang and hurtles through one adventure after another until the conclusion. A fast-paced read with lots of action, Scottish atmosphere and a great vocabulary: *muckle, dunch, daffing,* and *weesht!*

**Audio:** Recorded Books cassette 1556902816. Read by Carlos Cardona.

**Film/Video/DVD:** Filmed many times; readers may know the 1948 version with Roddy McDowall or the 1960 Disney adaptation. There is also a 1995 TV miniseries and a 2005 *Masterpiece Theater* adaptation.

**Similar Reads:** Adventure fans who like Stevenson's brisk pacing will want to read *Treasure Island,* fans of Scottish stories may want to explore Sir Walter Scott's books and Stevenson's other Scots adventure *The Master of Ballantrae.* Another classic with a chase through the Scottish Highlands is John Buchan's *The Thirty-Nine Steps.*

**Subjects:** Scotland 1751; Inheritance; Family; Scottish Highlands; Treachery; Victorian Novel

## Verne, Jules (1828–1905)

*Around the World in Eighty Days* (**France: 1873**). Modern Library 2003 (paper). 224 pp. 0812968565 **J Q**

No cars, no jets, no cell phones, no credit cards—traveling around the world in 1873 was a more complicated endeavor than today, but Phileas Fogg, the eccentric and enigmatic Englishman, makes a bet he can do it in just eighty days. With a satchel full of money and his new valet, the passionate and clever Frenchman Passpartout, as a companion, Fogg leaves London in a hurry to fulfill his wager. But Fogg doesn't know he is being followed by a detective who thinks Fogg is a daring bank robber escaping London with a stolen fortune. The detective is prepared to do anything it takes to capture Fogg. Unexpected adventures await the travelers in India, Japan, the American West, and the Atlantic Ocean, all of which threaten Fogg's victory. The clock is ticking.

**Audio:** Brilliance Audio 1994 cassette 1561001937. Read by David Collaci.

**Film/Video/DVD:** Jackie Chan played Passpartout in a very loosely based 2004 film; David Niven is a classic Phileas Fogg in the 1956 Oscar winner; but the best adaptation is the 1989 TV miniseries with Pierce Brosnan and Eric Idle.

**Similar Reads:** Adventure fans will want to delve into Verne's other classics, *The Mysterious Island, Journey to the Center of the Earth,* and *20,000 Leagues under the Sea.*

**Subjects:** Victorian London; Wager; Travel; Humor; Gentle Read

# Lost World

Part fantasy, part science fiction, and all adventure these stories start in the everyday world but take us on a journey to a land that cannot really exist, a lost world inhabited by forgotten races of men and extinct animals.

## Burroughs, Edgar Rice (1875–1950)

***The Land That Time Forgot*** **(USA: 1924).** University of Nebraska Press 1999 (paper, illustrated, includes *The People That Time Forgot* and *Out of Time's Abyss*). 428pp. 0803261543 **J Q**

A thermos bottle found floating off the coast of Greenland contains the manuscript written by young American Bowen Tyler and tells the story of how he survived being torpedoed by a German U-boat (which his father's company built); eventually takes command of the U-boat; finds the lost, prehistoric island of Caprona ("I believe, sir, that we are looking upon the coast of Caprona, uncharted and forgotten for two hundred years."); and falls in love with the only woman in the story, the implausibly named Miss La Rue ("this slender and seemingly delicate creature possessed the heart and courage of a warrior.")—all while accompanied by his dog, Crown Prince Nobbler, a plucky Airedale ("Nobs flew past me like a meteor and rushed straight for the frightful reptile.").

Unlikely (the saboteur turns out to be an angry I.W.W.—a reference to the radical labor union probably lost on modern readers—who became a German agent), outrageous (having just fought off three opponents Tyler blithely states, "Californians, as a rule, are familiar with ju-jitsu"), improbable ("I know more about this particular sub than the officer who commanded her."); and yet totally compelling reading. This is a satisfying story that hurtles the reader from one adventure to another. The bad guys are bad (Germans during World War I), and the love story is chaste ("hand in hand, we turned our faces toward heaven and plighted our troth beneath the eyes of God."). Edgar Rice Burroughs stands boldly at the pinnacle of the pulps and for all their literary faults his books are exciting and fast paced, and they keep a reader's interest.

**Audio:** Blackstone Audio cassette 0786120061; CD 0786197250. Read by Raymond Todd.

**Film/Video/DVD:** *The Land That Time Forgot* (1975) is kind of cheesy now, but fun.

**New Media:** www.tarzan.org is Edgar Rice Burroughs's official Web site.

**Similar Reads:** Followed by two sequels, *The People That Time Forgot* and *Out of Time's Abyss*. Burroughs is the well-known author of the <u>Tarzan</u> series.

**Subjects:** Submarines; Dinosaurs; World War I; Journey

## Doyle, Sir Arthur Conan (1859–1930)

*The Lost World* **(England: 1912).** Tor Classics 1997 (paper). 256 pp. 0812564839 **J**
An expedition of British scientists and explorers, led by the irascible Professor Challenger, sets out for the South American jungles to prove that dinosaurs still walk the earth.

Yes this is the same Arthur Conan Doyle who wrote Sherlock Holmes.

**Audio:** Recorded Books cassette 0788704745. Read by Paul Hecht.

**Film/Video/DVD:** *The Lost World*—the 1960 film is campy; filmed in 1992 and again in 2001 for television starring Bob Hoskins as the cranky Professor Challenger. Not to be confused with Michael Crichton's *The Lost World: Jurassic Park* (1997). There is also a Canadian produced television series called *Sir Arthur Conan Doyle's The Lost World,* which takes the basic premise of the book and provides new adventures.

**Similar Reads:** Try Jules Verne's *Journey to the Center of the Earth* and *The Mysterious Island.*

**Subjects:** Explorers; Dinosaurs; Jurassic Era; South America; Amazon; Jungle; Journey

# Nature and Animals

These adventures are set in the wilderness and place an animal in the lead role.

## Burnford, Sheila (1918–1984)

*The Incredible Journey* **(Canada: 1961).** Laurel Leaf 1995 (paper). 160pp. 0440226708 **M Teen Q**
Three animals, a strong young Labrador, an aging bull terrier, and a proud Siamese cat, have been separated from their human family. They undertake an arduous trek across the Canadian wilderness to be reunited with them. Love and cooperation see them through. This is a compelling adventure story with a lot of suspense.

**Audio:** Listening Library cassette 0553478060. Read by Megan Follows.

**Film/Video/DVD:** *The Incredible Journey* (1963) Disney family classic; remade as *Homeward Bound: The Incredible Journey* (1993).

**Similar Reads:** Other great animal tales are *Old Yeller* and *Where the Red Fern Grows*. Or read *Rascal* by Sterling North or *Shiloh* by Phyllis Reynolds Naylor.

**Subjects:** Canada; Journey; Cooperation; Dogs; Cats; Pets; Animal Story

## London, Jack (1876–1916)

*Call of the Wild* (USA: 1903). Tor 1990 (paper). 128 pp. 0812504321. Aladdin Classics 2003 (paper) 160pp. 0689856741 **J Q**

Buck, a powerful and noble mixed-breed dog, is kidnapped from his gracious and placid home in California and sold to be a sled dog in Alaska during the Gold Rush of 1896. Buck must learn new ways of relating to men and other dogs. He must learn to work harder than ever in his life, sleep in snow, pull a fully loaded sled, and obey the law of club and fang. But once in the wilderness, Buck hears the primal and ancestral call of the wild all around and deep within him—will he answer that call?

London's prose evokes the primordial violence and savagery of the wild, the excitement of the Gold Rush and the feel and flavor of the Klondike with great descriptive power.

**Audio:** Recorded Books cassette 1556900821; CD 0788734563. Read by Frank Muller.

**Film/Video/DVD:** *Call of the Wild; Dog of the Yukon* (1997) made for TV with Rutger Hauer as John Thornton is a great adaptation of the story. The 1935 Clark Gable version has little connection to the book.

**Similar Reads:** For more Klondike flavor, readers might like to try some poetry by Robert Service. His ballads "The Shooting of Dan McGrew" and "The Cremation of Sam McGee" can be found in *Best Tales of the Yukon* (Running Press, 1983).

**Subjects:** Alaska, 1890s; Animal Story; Dogs; Wolves; Gold Rush; Klondike; Yukon; Journey

*White Fang* (USA: 1906). Signet Classics, 1991 (paper, 100th Anniversary edition includes *Call of the Wild*). 278p 0451525582 **J**

Part wolf and part dog, White Fang gradually learns to trust and love his human friend, Weedon Scott

This is a complementary story to *The Call of the Wild* in which the wild dog is tamed, whereas in *Call of the Wild* the domesticated dog reverts to his wild nature.

**Audio:** Recorded Books cassette 1556908415; CD 1402548575. Read by Norman Dietz.

**Film/Video/DVD:** *White Fang* (1991), the Disney version with Ethan Hawke, is recommended.

**Similar Reads:** Try *Call of the Wild* and *Incredible Journey*.

**Subjects:** Alaska, 1890s; Klondike; Yukon; Animal Story; Dogs

# Sea Stories

Men on ships surviving against the might of the sea, against adversarial ships, often during times of war, and often against their own mates and captains. The vast oceanic setting gives these books appeal to many readers.

### Forester, C. S. (1899–1966)

*Mr. Midshipman Hornblower* **(England: 1950).** Back Bay Books 1984 (paper). 320pp. 0316289124 **J**

The heroic character of young Horatio Hornblower is evident from his earliest days as a midshipman serving in the British Royal Navy during the time of the Napoleonic Wars (1799–1815). The <u>Hornblower</u> series traces the course of his dynamic naval career.

Historical accuracy, military bravery, subdued romance, exotic locales, a dashing hero—these books have a lot to offer the reader who is longing for high-seas adventure. Forester wrote eleven Hornblower novels that take young Horatio up the naval career ladder. He started the series in the middle of Hornblower's career then backed up and wrote about Hornblower's earlier years. For story order read:

> *Mr. Midshipman Hornblower* (1950)
>
> *Lieutenant Hornblower* (1952)
>
> *Hornblower and the Hotspur* (1962)
>
> *Hornblower during the Crisis* (1967)
>
> *Hornblower and the Atropos* (1953)
>
> *Beat to Quarters* (1937)
>
> *A Ship of the Line* (1938)
>
> *Flying Colours* (1939)
>
> *Commodore Hornblower* (1945)
>
> *Lord Hornblower* (1946)
>
> *Admiral Hornblower in the West Indies* (1958)

**Audio:** Books on Tape cassette. Read by Bill Kelsey. 0736671609

Film/Video/DVD: *Horatio Hornblower: the Complete Adventures* (1999) is an A&E-produced miniseries with Ioan Gruffudd.

**Similar Reads:** <u>The Bounty Trilogy</u> by Nordhoff and Hall or Patrick O'Brian's <u>Aubrey-Maturin</u> series make perfect further reading for historical British navy adventure fans. Bernard Cornwell's *Shark* novels tell of Napoleonic era battles on land.

**Subjects:** England; Napoleonic Era; British Navy; Sea Battles; Coming of Age

## Hemingway, Ernest (1899–1961)

🏅 *The Old Man and the Sea* **(USA: 1952).** Scribner (paper) 1995 128pp. 0684801221 **J**

For eighty-five days Santiago has not caught a fish, and that is his livelihood, fishing in the tropical waters off Cuba. It is so bad that his neighbors call Santiago unlucky and Manolin, the boy who usually fishes with him, is forced by his father to fish with someone luckier. So Santiago goes out alone in his small boat, and finally he catches a fish—the biggest fish he has ever caught—a marlin two feet longer than his boat. But this fish will not be taken without a fight. As the marlin pulls his boat farther and farther out to sea Santiago's struggle to land this fish becomes an epic battle.

This is a small book but a grand story about struggle and triumph. Hemingway's perennial themes of courage, honor, and heroism shine in the simple prose of this story.

**Audio:** Recorded Books cassette 0788705202; CD 0788734121. Read by Frank Muller.

**Film/Video/DVD:** 1958 film with Spencer Tracy; 1990 TV version with Anthony Quinn.

**Similar Reads:** Two other classic fish stories are Kipling's *Captains Courageous* and Melville's *Moby Dick*.

**Subjects:** Cuba; Survival; Man and Nature; Courage; Nobel Prize, 1954

## Kipling, Rudyard (1865–1936)

🏅 *Captains Courageous* **(England: 1897).** Signet 2004 (paper) 208pp. 0451529499 **M**

Fifteen-year-old Harvey Cheyne is a notorious brat. Spoiled, arrogant, and rude this son of an American multimillionaire thinks his father's money can eliminate any trouble he gets into. But when he falls off the ocean liner on which he is traveling with his overprotective mother and is picked up by a working ship heading for a season of fishing in the Grand Banks of the Northern Atlantic, Harvey is in for a rough time. The captain refuses to believe he is the son of a rich man and will not put Harvey ashore. Harvey must become one of the crew and earn his keep. Can he make the transformation from obnoxious boy into honorable young man?

**Audio:** Recorded Books cassette 0788701592. Read by George Guidall.

**Film/Video/DVD:** 1937 classic black-and-white film; also produced in 1996 with Robert Urich as Captain Troop.

**Similar Reads:** Kipling's other great book with a boy hero is *Kim*.

**Subjects:** New England; Journey; Coming of Age; Fishing; Millionaires; Victorian Novel; Nobel Prize 1907

## Melville, Herman (1819–1891)

*Moby Dick* (USA: 1851). Modern Library 2000 (paper). 896pp. 067978327x. Bantam 1981 (paper) 704pp. 0553213113 S

> Despite ominous warnings Ishmael ships out on the whaler *Pequod* with the mysterious Captain Ahab and his new acquaintance, the heathen harpooner Queequeg. But what starts as a commercial whaling trip turns into a personal voyage of revenge as Ahab's obsession with the white whale Moby Dick takes over all aspects of the voyage.
>
> From its famous opening line "Call me Ishmael," the reader is riding a roller-coaster of a book: an encyclopedia of whaling, a high-seas adventure tale, a meditation on the motives of man—*Moby Dick* is many books in one. Commonly considered a classic now, it was a forgotten book, and Melville was a forgotten author when he died in 1891.
>
> **Audio:** Recorded Books cassette 155690343x; CD 1402570953. Read by Frank Muller (21 hours long!).
>
> **Film/Video/DVD:** In *Moby Dick,* Gregory Peck plays Captain Ahab in John Houston's 1956 film; in a 1998 version, Patrick Stewart plays Ahab.
>
> **New Media:** www.melville.org is a site dedicated to the life and works of Herman Melville.
>
> **Similar Reads:** Melville's earlier novels *Typee*, *Omoo*, and *White-Jacket* are more straightforward sea adventure tales. Other mad sea captains can be found in London's *The Sea Wolf, Mutiny on the Bounty* by Nordhoff and Hall, *The Caine Mutiny* by Herman Wouk, and Jules Verne's *20,000 Leagues under the Sea.*
>
> **Subjects:** New England; Whales; Obsession; Sea Captains; Man and Nature; Good and Evil; Sailors

## Monsarrat, Nicholas (1910–1979)

*The Cruel Sea* (England: 1951). S

> *See* the entry in Chapter 2, "Historical Fiction."

## Nordhoff, Charles (1887–1947), and James Hall (1887–1951)

*Mutiny on the Bounty* (USA: 1932). Back Bay Books 1989 400pp. 0316611689 J

> Fletcher Christian—hero or criminal? He is the second in command on the HMS *Bounty* serving under the sadistically cruel Captain Bligh. But even if he is cruel, Bligh is the commander on the ship. When his behavior pushes the crew to a point of no return, they mutiny—take over the ship and assume command from the captain. Christian is put in charge, Captain Bligh and the men loyal to him are set adrift in a lifeboat and the mutineers sail the *Bounty* to found a new Eden on a Pacific Island.
>
> Thrilling sea adventure, exotic South Sea setting, the story of a crime, and a moral lesson all in one—based on the true story of a mutiny aboard a British ship.

**Film/Video/DVD:** A 1935 film starred Clark Gable and Charles Laughton; a 1962 version is available with Marlon Brando and Trevor Howard; and it was filmed again as *The Bounty* in 1984 with Mel Gibson and Anthony Hopkins.

**Similar Reads:** This story continues in two more books: *Men against the Sea* (1934) tells the story of Captain Bligh and the men put to sea with him in the lifeboat from the Bounty and *Pitcairn's Island* (1934) is about the mutineer's lives on their new island home. Together these three books are <u>The Bounty Trilogy</u>. *Two Years before the Mast* is Richard Henry Dana's account of his experiences in the American merchant navy in the 1830s.

**Subjects:** Mutiny; British Navy; South Seas; Sea Captains; Sailors

## Stevenson, Robert Louis (1850–1894)

*Treasure Island* **(England: 1883).** Scholastic 2002 (paper) 223pp. 0439288886. Signet 1998 (paper) 224pp. 0451527046 <u>M</u> <u>Teen</u> **Q**

Murder, mutiny, marooned sailors, and riches galore—this is the classic story of high adventure, piracy, and treachery on the seas! The story starts in a tavern, the Admiral Benbow Inn of England, and leads to a sea voyage and a deserted island where Young Jim Hawkins and wily Long John Silver battle for the treasure hidden on Treasure Island.

A lively turn of phrase, brilliant storytelling, suspense, rapid pacing, and humor make this a sea story with eternal appeal for all readers.

**Audio:** Recorded Books cassette 1556905238; CD 1402523467. Read by Neil Hunt.

**Film/Video/DVD:** Although many viewers probably know the vivid 1950 Disney rendition, there is also a great 1990 TV version with Christian Bale as Jim and Charleton Heston as the treacherous Long John Silver, directed by Heston's son, Fraser.

Similar Reads: *The Coral Island* by Ballantyne and *Swiss Family Robinson* are other deserted island adventures. Stevenson's other grand adventure tales are *Black Arrow*, *The Master of Ballantrae,* and *Kidnapped*.

**Subjects:** England; Pirates; Swashbuckler; Deserted Island; Treasure; Victorian Novel; Childhood Classic

## Verne, Jules (1828–1905)

*Twenty Thousand Leagues under the Sea* **(France: 1870)**

*See* the entry in Chapter 3, "Science Fiction."

# Survival

These are the stories of man against nature, and often these stories place the protagonist away from the predictability of civilization. The hero must use intelligence and strength against the unpredictable and seemingly overwhelming forces of nature.

## Burroughs, Edgar Rice (1875–1950)

*Tarzan of the Apes* (USA: 1912). Signet 1990 (paper) 288pp. 0451524233 **J**

Lord and Lady Greystoke, sailing to Africa on the queen's business, are caught in a mutiny and marooned on a remote beach at the edge of the African jungle. They survive just long enough to have a son. With his parents dead, this young English lord is raised by a Kala, a caring ape mother, and learns all the ways of the jungle—how to talk to the animals, navigate through the dense jungle, hunt for food, and even, using books he finds in the deserted cabin of his real parents, how to read! It isn't long before his superior intellect, well-developed strength, and natural nobility lead Tarzan to be the King of the Jungle. When other civilized men come to his jungle, Tarzan learns his true history.

Not great literature, but an engaging read—an enduring story that is almost mythic, and a character that, like Dracula and Sherlock Holmes, has transcended his original format. Written as a pulp adventure series, the Tarzan books contain plenty of humor and romance. They are exciting, fast paced, and action filled.

> **Audio:** Blackstone Audiobooks 0786106735. Read by James Slattery.

> **Film/Video/DVD:** Endless filmed versions and variations, Tarzan captured the cinematic imagination early; 1918 saw the first Tarzan movie. In 1932, *Tarzan the Ape Man* started the Johnny Weissmuller series that continued for more than a dozen films; *Greystoke; The Legend of Tarzan* (1984) introduced the story to a new generation; and the story lives on in Disney's animated musical made in 1999.

> **New Media:** www.tarzan.org is Edgar Rice Burroughs's official site.

> **Similar Reads:** Burroughs made an industry of writing Tarzan books (as well as several other pulp series). *The Return of Tarzan* is the next book in the series. Other books to try: Kipling's *Jungle Book*; *She* and *King Solomon's Mines* by Rider Haggard; *Treasure Island* by Stevenson.

> **Subjects:** Africa; Jungle; Civilization; Society; Nature; Orphans

## Defoe, Daniel (1660–1731)

*Robinson Crusoe* (England: 1719). Signet 1998 (paper) 302pp. 0451527011 **J**

Robinson Crusoe is a restless eighteen-year-old when this story begins. He longs to go to sea and explore the world, but his father opposes it. Crusoe defies his father and goes to sea anyway. After a series of disasters that should convince him to give up his adventuring—violent storms, cutthroat pirates, two years as a captive slave—he is finally shipwrecked on a deserted island where he struggles to survive for twenty-eight years!

Some critics consider this to be the first novel in English. Robinson Crusoe is a character of world renown. His discovery of another human footprint in the sand is a hallmark moment in world literature.

**Audio:** Blackstone Audio 0786100567. Read by Frederick Davidson.

**Film/Video/DVD:** Filmed in 1952 and again in 1997 as a TV movie with Pierce Brosnan; for variations on the theme, try *Robinson Crusoe on Mars* (1964) or *Castaway* (2000) with Tom Hanks.

**Similar Reads:** *Swiss Family Robinson* by Wyss was written in deliberate imitation of Robinson Crusoe's situation. An excellent contemporary survival story is *Hatchet* by Gary Paulsen.

**Subjects:** England, 1700s; Deserted Island; Sea Story; Shipwreck

## Golding, William (1911–1993)

🏆 *Lord of the Flies* **(England: 1954).** Penguin 1999 (paper) 192pp. 0140283331 <u>J</u>
A plane filled with English schoolboys crash-lands on a deserted island. The adults on board are killed. It is up to the boys to care for each other, find food, organize shelters, and create their own society. Ralph, the natural leader, and Piggy, the reluctant and despised voice of reason, attempt to create an ordered and democratic society, but they are overwhelmed by the blood lust of Jack and his hunters. Savagery soon prevails over innocence in this chilling story about the brutality that resides in us all.

This book was an instant success and remains a fascinating and disturbing read. On the surface, this is a survival story, but its depths contain a social novel that becomes a moral story about man's inhumanity to man. *Lord of the Flies* was Golding's first novel. His later works are more complex and not recommended for young readers.

**Audio:** Listening Library cassette 0807209546. Read by the author, William Golding.

**Film/Video/DVD:** The 1963 and 1990 *Lord of the Flies* versions are different films but each very powerful.

**Similar Reads:** Try *Coral Island* by R. M. Ballantyne, the book referred to in *Lord of the Flies* as an example of stranded boys who behaved themselves. The natural savagery of children also figures in *A High Wind in Jamaica* by Hughes.

**Subjects:** Deserted Island; Civilization; Society; School Boys; Frequently Challenged; Nobel Prize 1983

## O'Dell, Scott (1898–1989)

🏆 *Island of the Blue Dolphins* **(USA: 1960).** Yearling/Bantam 1987 (paper). 187pp. 0440439881 <u>M</u> **Teen Q**
Young Karana lives peacefully with her tribe on the island off the California coast that is shaped like a blue dolphin. When her people leave the island,

she is left there alone to wait for them to send a ship for her, but year after year, no ship comes. This is the story of how she survives and triumphs for eighteen years. Karana fights every day to survive the elements, find food, create shelter, and conquer her own loneliness and uncertainty.

This story is based on a true event. In 1853, a Native American woman was taken from San Nicholas Island off the coast of California. It is believed she was left there in 1835. Rumors about her existence had long been talked about. Her whole story was never known because no one could speak her language, and she died only a few weeks after leaving the island.

**Audio:** Recorded Books cassette 1556904673; CD 0788734482. Read by Christina Moore.

Film/Video/DVD: Filmed in 1964.

**Similar Reads:** Another girl cooperating with nature to survive on her own is *Julie of the Wolves* by Jean Craighead George. For a more contemporary story, try *Hatchet* and its sequels by Gary Paulsen.

**Subjects:** California, Native Americans; Deserted Island; Man and Nature; Newbery Medal 1961

## Taylor, Theodore (1921–)

*The Cay* (USA: 1969). Yearling 2002 (paper) 144pp. 0440416639 **M Teen Q**
Time: 1942. The Place: the Caribbean Sea. The People: Phillip Enright, American, eleven years old; Timothy, a West Indian, old—very old. The Situation: Bad.

Phillip Enright is traveling from the Dutch island of Curacao to the United States with his mother. When a German U-Boat torpedoes their ship, Philip is saved by Timothy, a very old West Indian native. Together they survive on a raft in the ocean until they land on a cay, a small island, where they will attempt to live until help arrives. But Phillip is now blind from a blow to the head and totally dependent on Timothy. With a war to be fought, will any ships be searching for a lost boy and an old man? How long will they be on the cay?

**Audio:** Listening Library cassette 1400099056. Read by Michael Boatman.

**Film:** *The Cay* (1974) made for TV with James Earl Jones as Timothy.

**Similar Reads:** Followed by *Timothy of the Cay*; also read Kipling's *Captains Courageous*.

**Subjects:** Caribbean Sea; World War II; Prejudice; Deserted Island; Friendship

## Wyss, Johann (1743–1818)

*Swiss Family Robinson* (Switzerland: 1813). Signet 2004 (paper) 352pp. 0451529618 **M Teen**

A violent storm, a ship wrecked on the rocks, a deserted tropical island within sight—what would you do? If you are part of the Swiss family named Robinson, you make for the island. Father is smart, mother is sensible, and all three boys are brave. Ingeniously using all they can salvage from the ship, the family Robinson sets about making a home on the island paradise. Will the family perish or triumph in a land of their own?

A truly exciting and entertaining novel about survival, the importance of family, the value of working together, and the challenge of creating a good life wherever you may find yourself.

> **Audio:** Blackstone Audiobooks cassette 0786109327; CD 0786181443. Read by Frederick Davidson.

> **Film/Video/DVD:** *Swiss Family Robinson* (1960) is a Disney family classic. Also filmed in 2001 as *Stranded*.

> **Similar Reads:** Wyss was well acquainted with Defoe's *Robinson Crusoe*; *Island of the Blue Dolphins* by O'Dell is another story of triumphant island survival.

> **Subjects:** 1800s; Sea story; Deserted island; Family; Pirates; Childhood Classic

# Swashbucklers

Dashing swordsmen and flashing swordplay figure in the swashbuckler, tales in which a man's courage, his honor, and his skill with a sword are what matter most. Typically, these stories have a historical setting and romantic subplots, but the heroic action is the primary focus.

### Dumas, Alexandre (1802–1870)

*The Count of Monte Cristo* (**France: 1845**). Bantam 2003 (paper) 0553213504, 544pp.

> Edmond Dantes is a young, slightly naïve sailor just returning home from a voyage. Upon his arrival, he is arrested, quickly tried, and sent to the infamous Chateau d'If island prison. The charge? Treason. His real crime? Loving a woman another man wants. In prison Edmond meets a man who changes his life and gives him the means to plan an elaborate revenge for his wasted years and lost love.

Dumas is the master of the swashbuckler. His heroes are noble, his prose is accessible, and his plotting is full of action and humor. Dumas books have appeal for fans of many genres—action, adventure, historical novels, and romance. *Dumas pere* wrote the swashbucklers, his son, also a writer named Alexandre Dumas and referred to as *Dumas fils*, is famous for the romantic novel *The Lady of the Camelias* (1848).

> **Audio:** Blackstone 2002, 0786193034. Read by Fred Williams.

> **Film/Video/DVD:** Fine TV film with Richard Chamberlain made in 1975; French miniseries with Gerard Depardieu 1998 is the longest version at eight plus hours; a more recent big screen version with James Caviezel was made in 2002.

**Similar Reads:** Dumas's other books are a must; *The Three Musketeers* and *The Man in the Iron Mask* stand out, but Dumas was a prolific writer with a long career, *Queen Margot* and *The Black Tulip* are also very readable. Sabatini's *Scaramouche* also deals with revenge.

**Subjects:** France 1815—1838; Revenge; Imprisonment; Secrets; Treasure

*The Three Musketeers* **(France: 1844).** Bantam 2004 (paper) 656pp. 0553213377. Tor 1994 (paper) 591pp. 0812536029 **J**

"All for one and one for all!" The most famous cry of loyalty and unity in literature!

Country bumpkin D'Artagnan arrives in the big city of Paris in 1625 to join the famous Musketeers. He becomes the companion of Athos, Porthos, and Aramis, and together they battle for their King, Louis XIII of France, and for the honor of their queen. The villains are equally grand—that evil master of political intrigue Cardinal Richelieu, and one of the wickedest women in literature, Milady de Winter.

With gentle humor, rousing action, historic detail, breathless pacing, and sweet romance, Dumas paints a canvas so rich with prose so lively it is hard to believe this book is 160 years old.

**Audio:** Blackstone Audiobooks cassette 0786105771; CD 078610578X. Read by Walter Covell.

**Film/Video/DVD:** A new film version appears every generation. Douglas Fairbanks's silent version is from 1921; 1948, 1973, and 1993 all saw remakes.

**Similar Reads:** *The Queen's Necklace* continues the stories of the musketeers, but any of Dumas's other books will appeal to fans of swashbucklers. *Prince of Foxes* and *Captain from Castile* by Shellabarger are also great adventure stories full of lively swordplay and intrigue.

**Subjects:** France c. 1625; Paris; Royalty; Soldiers; Treachery; Friendship

## Hope, Anthony (1863–1933)

*The Prisoner of Zenda* **(England: 1894).** Penguin, 1999 (paper) 372pp. 014043755X **J**

Fast paced and action packed, *The Prisoner of Zenda* is an archetypal adventure story. Rudolf Rassendyll—an idle English aristocrat, a dilettante, and a loafer—decides to attend the coronation of the new king in the small Kingdom of Ruritania. Rudolf and the king are distant relatives and exact look-alikes thanks to the indiscrete passion of their great-grandparents. When the king's wicked and ambitious half-brother Black Michael imprisons the king on the eve of the coronation hoping to be crowned king in his place, Rassendyll is there to save the day.

This is a high-spirited late Victorian adventure yarn full of the old-fashioned swashbuckling values like courage, honor, loyalty, and chaste love.

**Audio:** Blackstone Audiobooks, 1997, cassette 078611049X. Read by Bernard Mayes.

**Film/Video/DVD:** *The Prisoner of Zenda* (1937) with Ronald Coleman and 1952 with Stewart Granger (a version that copies the 1937 film scene for scene) both include great swordfights.

**Similar Reads:** Hope wrote a sequel, *Rupert of Hentzau,* that follows the characters on another adventure. Or turn to Rafael Sabatini's novels, *Scaramouche* and *Captain Blood.*

**Subjects:** Victorian London; Ruritania ; Impersonation; Imposters; Kings; Royalty; Courage; Honor; Loyalty; Victorian Novel

## McCulley, Johnston (1883–1958)

*The Mark of Zorro* **(USA: 1919).** Tor/Forge 1998 (paper) 288pp. 0812540077 **J**

The dashing masked man Zorro is a brilliant swordsman and defiant hero. He defends the poor and oppressed against the Spanish tyrants who pillage, abuse, and persecute the innocent native people of old California. But who is this masked man? Why is it his duty to avenge the poor?

Lively writing and a rapid plot make this a high-spirited read. The story is set in the Mission years of Old California. This is another example, like *Tarzan,* of a novel that is perhaps less than great literature but that created a character and myth people still love.

**Film/Video/DVD:** *The Mark of Zorro* (1920) made Douglas Fairbanks an action star. The 1940 version starred Tyrone Power and Basil Rathbone, one of Hollywood's great swordsmen. Two new movies with Antonio Banderas as the masked man also expand the myth in *The Mask of Zorro* (1998) and *The Legend of Zorro* (2005).

**Similar Reads:** *Ramona* by Helen Hunt Jackson is a love story also set in the Missions of Old California. Isabel Allende has added to the Zorro myth with her 2005 novel, *Zorro.*

**Subjects:** California; Missions; Corruption

## Orczy, Baroness Emma (1865–1947)

*The Scarlet Pimpernel* **(England: 1905).** Pocket Books 2004 (paper, <u>Enriched Classics Series</u>). 384pp. 0743487745. Signet 2005 (paper, 100th Anniversary Edition) 288pp. 0451527623 **J Q**

> *We seek him here, we seek him there,*
> *Those Frenchies seek him everywhere*
> *Is he in heaven? Is he in hell?*
> *That damned elusive Pimpernel!*

Why do the French Revolutionaries hate the man known only as the Scarlet Pimpernel? Because the Pimpernel has made it his job to save France's noble families from the Guillotine! Using trickery and disguise, he makes fools of the Revolutionaries every time he helps an aristocratic French family escape to London. But who is the Pimpernel really, and is he clever enough to elude the trap set for him?

High intrigue, grand romance, and abundant danger make this rousing tale set in turbulent, emotional times a spellbinding read.

**Audio:** Blackstone Audiobooks 0786105240. Read by Walter Zimmerman.

**Film/Video/DVD:** many versions; the 1932 black-and-white with Leslie Howard is a classic; 1982 and 1999 produced good TV versions. This novel was even the basis for a Broadway musical first performed in 1998.

**Similar Reads:** Dickens's *A Tale of Two Cities* is also about bravery and sacrifice during the French Revolution. *The Mark of Zorro* gives us another hero whose true identity is a mystery.

**Subjects:** France 1790s; England; French Revolution; Nobility; Impersonation; Romance

## Pyle, Howard (1853–1911)

<u>The Merry Adventures of Robin Hood (USA: 1883).</u> Signet 1986 (paper) 416pp. 0451522842 M **Teen**

Robin Hood is the legendary English outlaw who steals from the rich and gives to the poor. The merry men are his fellow outlaws living with him in exile in Sherwood Forest—Friar Tuck, Will Scarlet, Little John, Allan-A-Dale. Together they go adventuring through the forest protecting women and children and outwitting their enemies.

Robin Hood first appeared in *Piers Plowman* in 1377. His stories were later compiled in a series of English ballads called *A Lytell Geste of Robyn Hode* (1510). Pyle presented the characters to a new generation of readers using an archaic form of language to tell the ancient tales. In addition to being an author, Howard Pyle was a famous illustrator and graphic artist. He influenced many of the illustrators of the Golden Age of American book illustration (1880–1920) including N. C. Wycth, Jessie Wilcox Smith, and Maxfield Parrish.

**Audio:** Blackstone Audio, cassette 0786105801. Read by John Chatty.

**Film/Video/DVD:** Robin Hood is the perfect cinematic hero, handsome and brave, his story set in romantic forests and castles. There have been many film portrayals of Robin and his Merry Band. The most classic interpretation of Robin Hood for the screen is Errol Flynn's 1938 portrayal in *The Adventures of Robin Hood*; Kevin Costner tried his hand as *Robin Hood: Prince of Thieves* (1991); Mel Brooks directed a famous spoof of the Robin Hood legend with *Robin Hood: Men in Tights* (1993); Sean Connery plays the aging Robin in *Robin and Marion* (1976); and Disney presented an animated musical version in which all the characters are animals in 1973.

**Similar Reads:** Robin Hood figures in Sir Walter Scott's *Ivanhoe*. Robin McKinley explores the Robin Hood legend in *The Outlaws of Sherwood*. Readers who like Robin Hood may want to explore the legends of King Arthur. Howard Pyle also wrote a version of the King Arthur stories *The Story of King Arthur and His Knights.*

**Subjects:** Medieval England; Middle Ages; Legend; Sherwood Forest; Robin Hood; Outlaws

## Sabatini, Rafael (1875–1950)

*Scaramouche* (England: 1921). Signet 2001 (paper) 384pp. 0451527976 **S**

Revolutionary France is the setting for this rousing swashbuckler. Andre-Louis Moreau, the bastard son of a nobleman, goes incognito to disguise his revolutionary leanings.

Sabatini was a prolific author, a fine writer, and a masterful storyteller. His novels have transferred very well to the movie screen—he had a cinematic vision long before film became the medium of the day.

**Audio:** Blackstone Audiobooks, cassette 0786110902. Read by Robert Whitfield.

**Film/Video/DVD:** *Scaramouche* (1952) with Stewart Granger features what is purported to be the longest sword fight in movies.

**Similar Reads:** Sabatini's *Captain Blood* and *The Sea Hawk* provide more derring-do; fans of Sabatini will want to read Dumas's swashbucklers and *The Scarlet Pimpernel* by Orczy, which is also set during the French Revolution.

**Subjects:** France 1790s; Nobility; Actors; French Revolution

## Shellabarger, Samuel (1888–1954)

*Prince of Foxes* (USA: 1947). **S**

*See* the entry in Chapter 2, "Historical Fiction."

## Wren, P. C. (1885–1941)

*Beau Geste* (England: 1924). Buccaneer Books 1976 (hardcover) 367 pp. 0899681352 **J**

Falsely accused of a theft, the Geste boys, Michael, John, and Digby, join the French Foreign Legion—a romantic refuge for desperate men who want to escape their pasts. The locale is exotic and romantic, and all the men are daring heroes. Mystery and tragedy are in store.

**Audio:** Blackstone Audio cassette 0786112905. Read by Geoffrey Howard.

**Film/Video/DVD:** *Beau Geste* (1939) classic directed by William Wellman.

**Similar Reads:** Wren followed this adventure classic with other books about the Geste family, *Beau Sabreur* and *Beau Ideal;* or try *Four Feathers* by A. E. W. Mason.

**Subjects:** North Africa; French Foreign Legion; Desert; Family; Honor; Soldiers

# Further Recommendations

Consider the following authors: Gary Paulsen, Will Hobbs, and, for older readers, Clive Cussler, Michael Crichton, Tom Clancy, Wilbur Smith, Jack Higgins, Alistair MacLean, and Bernard Cornwell.

Readers who like adventure fiction are perfect candidates for adventure nonfiction classics such as *Kon Tiki* by Thor Heyerdahl, *Sailing Alone Around the World* by Joshua Slocum, *Into Thin Air* by Jon Krakauer, *West with the Night* by Beryl Markham, and *Seven Years in Tibet* by Heinrich Harrer.

# Chapter 2

## Historical Fiction

Muskets and petticoats, sailing ships and horse-drawn carriages—this is the world of historical fiction! These are the books that take you to another time and place. These are the books that often realistically depict the past, down to the very last detail.

Readers who enjoy historical fiction generally enjoy true-life stories, things that happened or could have happened, people that lived or could have lived in the era portrayed. Some historical fiction is about actual historical characters, for example, *I, Claudius* purports to be the Roman Emperor Claudius's own telling of the events of his life. Other historical fiction tells the stories of ordinary people living in times past—think of Scarlett O'Hara and the Civil War, or Sophie and her choice. In historical fiction, the characters of the story often live through the major events of their day and intersect with prominent people of that time. Good historical fiction can combine fictional characters and situations with true historical figures and events to create a seamless representation of the past.

The best historical fiction recreates history, offers us characters we come to care about, and gives us an "I was there" feeling. In fact, some of the stories in this chapter were not originally written as historical fiction but as contemporary fiction—that is, they were written in the past. Because they so accurately portray that past, they "feel" like historical fiction.

Story is more compelling than "just the facts," and history can come alive in a novel the way it cannot in a textbook. For a student, historical fiction can be a jumping-off place for a fuller exploration of history. Many young adult readers, correctly guided, will read deeply within a certain time period. Reading all the best books about an era, such as the American Revolution (*My Brother Sam Is Dead, Johnny Tremain, April Morning, Drums along the Mohawk*) can give a young person a deeper connection to history than reading a textbook.

Authors of historical fiction freely admit they are crafting fiction, yet with classic historical fiction, a tacit agreement exists between author and reader that although the story or the characters may be made up, the history is real. Historical fiction authors generally take pride in the verisimilitude of their work. The details in classic historical fiction are part of the pleasure. What the characters wear, what they eat, the transportation they use, the everyday material items of life are true to the time depicted. In classic historical fiction, what the characters say and how they think is also true to the historical era portrayed.

Historical fiction usually features a strongly drawn setting, because the time and the place are integral to the story. In general, the style of classic historical fiction is realistic, and although they may contain elements of humor, in large part historical fiction is a serious genre.

# Ancient Egypt

Political intrigue, pyramids, mummies, pharaohs, and a complex religion all figure in the novels set in the ancient Egyptian civilization found along the Nile from 3200 B.C. to 300 B.C.

## McGraw, Eloise (1915–2000)

🏆 *Golden Goblet* (USA: 1961). Puffin 1986 (paper) 256pp. 0140303359 **M Teen Q**

Ranofer, the son of Thula, longs to become a goldsmith like his late father. He has talent and passion for the work. But his wicked half-brother, Gebu the stonecutter, thwarts his ambitions.

A vivid, exotic setting, mystery, adventure, and swift pacing make this a good introductory novel to Ancient Egypt.

Similar Reads: For stories of apprentices in other lands and times, read *Johnny Tremain* and *Young Fu of the Upper Yangtze.* For a heroine of ancient Egypt, read McGraw's *Mara, Daughter of the Nile.*

Subjects: Ancient Egypt; Tombs; Goldsmiths; Newbery Honor Book 1962

## Waltari, Mika (1908–1979)

*The Egyptian* (Finland: 1945; translated to English 1949). Chicago Review Press 2002 (paper) 512pp. 1556524412 **S**

Sinhue becomes a famous physician in the court of the Egyptian pharaoh Akhenaton in fourteenth century B.C. Sinhue's travels take the reader throughout the known ancient world. The detailed setting, Sinhue's adventures, and his personal growth as a man make this a totally engrossing historical novel.

Waltari is one of Finland's most famous writers. He wrote several epics placed in the ancient world. Most of his works are currently out of print but are available in libraries.

Film/Video/DVD: *The Egyptian* (1954) directed by Michael Curtiz.

Similar Reads: Other books set in the ancient world by Waltari are *The Roman, Dark Angel,* and *The Etruscan.*

Subjects: Ancient Egypt; Doctors; Embalming

# Ancient Greece

From about 1000 B.C. until the assimilation of Greece into the Roman Empire in about 150 B.C., ancient Greece was the center of the known world. Greek political theory, art, architecture, mythology, and philosophy became the cultural foundation of Western civilization. Classic novels look back at the way ancient Greece may have been, for works actually from the time, be sure to consult the Epics and Legends section in Chapter 4, "Fantasy," for ancient classics by Homer and Virgil.

## Renault, Mary (1905–1983)

*The King Must Die* (**England: 1958**). Vintage 1988 (paper) 352 pp. 0394751043 <u>S</u>

"You will cross water to dance in blood. You will be King of the victims." Thus the Lady Medea, a witch and sorceress, foretells the next adventure awaiting Theseus, the hero of *The King Must Die*. Theseus is a young man, intelligent and clever, physically brave, a wrestler and a warrior, a natural leader taught to rule other men. Until he age seventeen, he believed he was the son of the god Poseidon. When he learns his true father's identity, he leaves his mother and the kingdom of his grandfather to travel to his father and his own destiny as a man, a king, and a hero. Danger, battle, treachery, mysteries and opportunities await him at every stage of his hero's journey.

This is Mary Renault's recasting of the Greek stories of Theseus and the Minotaur. Set in mysterious, magical, perhaps mythic ancient Greece, this tale tells of a time when young men and women are sacrificed to appease a bull god and kings are killed to ensure the next year's harvest; when women are either the possessions of men or powerful priestesses; and when gods and goddesses interact with favored mortals. A discrete sexuality permeates the book but Theseus' story is replete with honor and nobility, courage and heroic behavior. Renault is famous for her detailed and vivid novels set in the ancient world. Her prose is simple and beautiful, and her stories are imaginative and forceful.

**Audio:** Recorded Books cassette 1556902867. Read by Walt MacPherson.

**Similar Reads:** *The Bull from the Sea* is the sequel; Renault wrote other books set in the ancient Greek world that are equally intriguing; try *The Mask of Apollo* about an actor in time of Plato or her famous works about Alexander the Great starting with *Fire from Heaven*. To read the myths on which Renault based her works, turn to *Bulfinch's Mythology*.

**Subjects:** Ancient Greece; Athens; Crete; Minotaur; Theseus; Mythology; Gods and Goddesses; Heroes; Warriors; Royalty; Coming of Age

# The Roman Empire

The city of Rome was the nucleus of the vast Empire that dominated western Europe from 31 B.C. to its fall at the hands of invading barbarians in A.D. 476. The history and geography of the empire encompassed much of the ancient world: from the biblical lands at the time of Christ to the far reaches of Celtic Britain, the Roman Empire saw the expansion of law, art, architecture and advances in civic and military technology. Novels about this period show the corruption in the Roman imperial families, the years surrounding the life of Christ and early Christianity, and the anger of subjugated populations who chafed under Roman rule of their homelands.

## Graves, Robert (1895–1985)

*I, Claudius* (**England: 1934**). Vintage 1989 (paper) 480 pp. 067972477X **S**

Claudius is considered a fool by his family the imperial rulers of Rome. He stutters and limps—unacceptable traits in a family and a country that honors warriors. But Claudius keeps his mouth shut and his ears and eyes open. He witnesses the lust, treachery, and intrigue that make up the politics of ancient Rome. In the end, he will rule Rome.

Scholarly in detail, but reads like a soap opera!

> **Audio:** Blackstone Audiobooks 2002 cassette 078612220X. Read by Frederick Davidson.
>
> **Film/Video/DVD:** *I, Claudius* (1976) is the BBC's 13-part production for television, one of the most popular *Masterpiece Theatre* series ever broadcast.
>
> **Similar Reads:** The story continues in *Claudius the God and His Wife Messalina*. Another forgotten classic about the ancient world is Mika Waltari's *The Roman*.
>
> **Subjects:** Ancient Rome, 10 B.C. to A.D. 54; Emperors; Politics; Fictional Autobiography; Caligula; Claudius; Caesar Augustus

## Sutcliff, Rosemary (1920–1992)

*Eagle of the Ninth* (**England: 1954**). Sunburst/St. Martins 1993 (paper) 291pp. 0374419302 **M Teen**

The quest to solve the mystery of the disappearance of his father and the legion of Roman soldiers he commanded leads young Marcus Flavius Aquila into the northern highlands of Scotland in the second century A.D. On the other side of the protective wall that separates Roman-ruled Britain from the wilds of Celtic Britain, are hostile native tribes, a harsh environment, and the answer that Marcus seeks.

The Romans ruled a geographically vast territory, and not every story about the empire takes place in Italy. Sutcliffe sets many of her stories in ancient Britain, the farthest outpost of the Roman Army.

> **Film/Video/DVD:** *The Eagle of the Ninth* (1977) is a three-hour BBC miniseries not easily available at this time.
>
> **Similar Reads:** Sutcliff's Roman Britain trilogy continues with *The Silver Branch* and *The Lantern Bearers*. Good readers wanting more about the Romans may like Robert Graves's *I, Claudius*.

**Subjects:** Roman Britain, 55 B.C. to A.D. 449; Roman Legions; Centurions; Fathers and Sons; Soldiers; Battle; Celts; Druids; Coming of Age

## The Middle Ages (A.D. 500 to 1500)

Between the Classical ancient world and the beginnings of the Modern era are the thousand years of the Middle Ages, a time when barbarian tribes invaded western Europe and the premier institution of the day was the Catholic Church, which generated the creation of the great cathedrals, monastic orders, universities, and the violent Crusades to the lands of the Middle East. These years saw the rise of trade and the beginnings of technology and exploration but also the devastations of poverty, plague, and a reliance on superstition more than science. The medieval world continues to fascinate readers. Novels in this section tend to emphasize the Middle Ages as the era of troubadours, the code of chivalry, and knights and fair ladies, a time that has been heavily romanticized by writers working later, beginning particularly with Sir Walter Scott. Actual works from the Middle Ages, like the poetry of Dante and Chaucer and medieval epics, can also be found listed under "Medieval Literature" in the index.

### Chaucer, Geoffrey (c. 1343–1400)

*Canterbury Tales* (England: c. 1387–1400). <u>J</u>
   *See* the entry in Chapter 10, "Humor."

### de Angeli, Marguerite (1889–1987)

🏃 *The Door in the Wall* (USA: 1949). Yearling 1990 (paper) 128pp. 0440402832 <u>M</u> **Teen Q**

Ten-year-old Robin is intended for the knighthood, but disease leaves him crippled and weak. With his parents away serving the King and Queen, Robin is helped by the friar Brother Luke and the minstrel John-go-in-the-Wynd to journey to the castle where Robin will begin service as a page. As he works to overcome his handicap, Robin learns about patience, fortitude, and courage. When the castle is besieged, Robin has the opportunity to become a hero.

Set in England during the reign of Edward the Third, this book is rich in medieval detail.

**Audio:** Books on Tape. Read by Roger Reese.

**Similar Reads:** *Crispin* the 2003 Newbery Medal winner by Avi; *The Ramsay Scallop* by Frances Temple; books by Karen Cushman such as *The Midwife's Apprentice* (1996 Newbery Medal winner).

**Subjects:** Medieval England; Disability; Chivalry; Castles; Knights; Minstrels; Childhood Classic; Gentle Read; Newbery Medal 1950

## Doyle, Sir Arthur Conan (1859–1930)

*The White Company* **(England: 1891).** HarperCollins 1988 (hardcover) 362pp. 0688078176. Wordsworth Classics 1996 (paper) 352pp 1853262897 **J**

> Raised in a monastery, when Alleyene Edricson turns twenty, he ventures out into the world. He becomes a squire to Sir Nigel and travels through England, France, and Spain, fighting in the Hundred Year's War. Eventually he becomes an archer with the famous White Company of longbow archers, a weapon used to England's advantage at Agincourt.

> Conan Doyle was famous for his creation of Sherlock Holmes, but he preferred this book and thought it his best work. It is a romantic and adventurous tale full of honor and courage, swashbuckling action, and nobility.

> > **Similar Reads:** Doyle wrote a prequel called *Sir Nigel*. For more medieval adventure, look for Howard Pyle's *Otto of the Silver Hand* or try *The Walking Drum* by Louis L'Amour and *The Black Arrow* by Robert Louis Stevenson.

> > **Subjects:** England; France; Chivalry; Knights; Hundred Year's War; Longbow Archers; Gentle Read

## Eco, Umberto (1932–)

*Name of the Rose* **(Italy: 1980).**
> *See* entry in Chapter 6, "Mystery and Suspense."

## Hugo, Victor (1802–1885)

*The Hunchback of Notre Dame* **(France: 1831).** Tor 1996 (paper) 480pp. 0812563123 **S**
> Quasimodo, ugly and deformed but pure of heart, is the ward of Frollo, archdeacon at the French Cathedral of Notre Dame. He earns his keep being the bell ringer there, a job that has made him deaf. Quasimodo the hunchback, Frollo the man of religion, and Phoebus the military man share an infatuation for Esmeralda, the beautiful gypsy dancer in Hugo's passionate novel set in medieval Paris and centered around the great Cathedral. Frollo's lust for Esmeralda makes him renounce God, and Quasimodo's love for Esmeralda leads him to protect her.

> The vivid historical setting and dramatic human story make this romantic novel a memorable read.

> > **Audio:** Blackstone cassette 0786109882. Read by Frederick Davidson.

> > **Film/Video/DVD:** *The Hunchback of Notre Dame* (1939) classic with Charles Laughton and Maureen O'Hara is highly recommended; the 1982 version is also good, with Anthony Hopkins as Quasimodo. Surprisingly, this was also made into an animated musical by Disney (1996).

> > **Similar Reads:** Hugo's other great classic is *Les Miserables*, set later in French history.

> > **Subjects:** Paris; France; Disability; Gypsies; Priests; Catholic Church

## Scott, Sir Walter (1771–1832)

*Ivanhoe* (England: 1819). Tor 2000 (paper) 544pp. 0812565657 **J**

In twelfth-century England, Wilfred Ivanhoe, newly returned from the Crusades, must reclaim the birthright his father denies him. Along the way; he must battle with wicked Norman knights and is helped by noble Rebecca, her father, the wealthy Jew, Isaac of York; and by his childhood sweetheart, the fair Saxon princess the Lady Rowena.

Lots of action makes this an exciting story set in a colorful time when knights were bold and ladies were fair! Damsels in distress, besieged castles, jousting tournaments, even medieval heroes Richard the Lion-Hearted and Robin Hood make appearances in *Ivanhoe*. Sir Walter Scott is considered to be the originator of the historical novel, and *Ivanhoe* was a popular novel in its day.

**Audio:** Blackstone cassette 078611486X; CD 0786197110. Read by Frederick Davidson.

**Film/Video/DVD:** *Ivanhoe* (1952) is a Technicolor-period piece with Robert Taylor and a young Elizabeth Taylor; filmed for TV in both 1982 and 1997.

**Similar Reads:** Move on to more Scott with *Waverly* and *Rob Roy*. For other medieval adventure, try *The Merry Adventures of Robin Hood* and Conan Doyle's *The White Company*.

**Subjects:** Medieval England; Knights; Chivalry; Jews; Tournaments; Saxons; Normans

## Seton, Anya (1904–1990)

*Katherine* (England: 1954). **S**

*See* the entry in Chapter 8, "Romance."

## Undset, Sigrid (1882–1949)

🏵 *Kristin Lavransdatter* (Norway: 1922).

Passionate Kristin grows to womanhood in medieval Norway as the old ways give way to a new religion, Christianity.

This trilogy is historical fiction at its best—detailed, authentic depictions of a time that was physically and intellectually different from our own. These books were newly translated in the late 1990s by award-winning translator Tiina Nunnally, eliminating much of the archaic and stiff language of the earlier translations.

*The Wreath,* Penguin, 1997 (paper) 336 pp. 0141180412 **S**

*The Wife,* Penguin, 1999 (paper) 448 pp. 0141181281 **S**

*The Cross,* Penguin, 2000 (paper) 430pp. 0141182350 **S**

**Film/Video/DVD:** 1995 Norwegian film directed by Liv Ullman.

Similar Reads: *Katherine* by Anya Seton is the story of another medieval lady.

Subjects: Norway, Family; Early Christianity; Strong Heroine; Nobel Prize 1928

## Vining, Elizabeth Gray (also published under Elizabeth Janet Gray) (1902–1999)

🏿 *Adam of the Road* (USA: 1942). Puffin 1987 (paper) 317pp. 014032464X <u>M</u> Teen

Knights and squires, ladies and monks, plowmen and ferrymen populate this adventure tale that takes place in England in the Year of Our Lord 1294. Adam is the son of Roger the minstrel. While Roger is away in France learning new songs and stories, Adam is in school learning Latin and longing for Roger's return. For when Roger comes, they will once again take to the open road, the only home a minstrel knows, and travel from place to place telling stories and singing songs to entertain the good people they meet along the way. While he waits for Roger, three things sustain Adam: his harp, his good friend Perkin, and his lively red spaniel Nick, the dog Adam raised from a puppy. But Adam's happy reunion with Roger turns into a quest when Nick is stolen and Adam and Roger are separated. Will Adam find his father and his dog?

Events happen quickly as Adam traverses all levels of medieval English society on his quest. Lively illustrations by Robert Lawson contribute to the strong setting of this story.

Similar Reads: Two other Newbery winners with medieval settings are *The Trumpeter of Krakow* (1929 Newbery Medal winner) by Eric P. Kelly and Avi's *Crispin: The Cross of Lead* (2003 Newbery Medal winner). Karen Cushman's books are also set in the Middle Ages, *Catherine Called Birdy*, *Matilda Bone,* and *The Midwife's Apprentice* (1996 Newbery Medal). Older readers may want to turn to the writings of a man who was really there, Chaucer, author of *Canterbury Tales* (1387).

Subjects: Medieval England; Minstrels; Fathers and Sons; Dogs; Journey; Gentle Read; Newbery Medal 1943

# Sixteenth-, Seventeenth-, Eighteenth-Century Europe and England

Renaissance, Reformation, Revolution—major events occurred during these centuries. Each of the novels listed here gives a slice of these turbulent times.

## Defoe, Daniel (1660–1731)

*A Journal of the Plague Year* (England: 1722). Modern Library 2001 (paper) 272pp. 0375757899 <u>S</u>

"Bring out your dead."

1664 to 1666 were bad years to be in London, England. An epidemic of bubonic plague was followed by the Great Fire that destroyed the city. Many, many people died agonizing deaths. The city was in turmoil. All of this is vividly described in this novel written in the style of reportage, or eyewitness journalism, even though Defoe was only a child when the events occurred.

Defoe is so widely known for *Moll Flanders* and *Robinson Crusoe* that his other works are often forgotten. Once you relax and get past the old-fashioned prose, the voice of the narrator will sweep you back to the horrors of plague-infested London. This work is unsentimental, gruesome, and fascinating.

**Audio:** Recorded Books cassette 1556902689. Read by Nelson Runger.

**Similar Reads:** The plague and fire figure prominently in Kathleen Winsor's *Forever Amber*. For a newer book set in America about an epidemic, read Laurie Halse Anderson's *Fever 1793*.

**Subjects:** England 1600s; Plague; the Great Fire

*Moll Flanders* **(England: 1722).** Modern Library, 2002, (paper) 368pp. 0375760105. Tor Books 1999 (paper) 336pp. 0812567013 <u>S</u>

Moll is not a good girl, but then the conditions of her life make it hard to be good. Moll was born in London's famous Newgate Prison just before her mother was transported to the colonies for theft. Left to raise herself and get by the best she can, Moll turns to thievery, prostitution, and con-artistry to live. But Moll is smart and clever and has enough common sense, good humor, and self-worth to survive no matter what it takes. Her adventures take her through English society, and even to the New World of America.

The eighteenth-century prose may take some adjusting for readers, but Defoe was considered a very straightforward, almost journalistic writer in his time, and Moll is an irresistible character.

**Audio:** Audio Partners 2003 cassette 1572703407. Read by Janet Suzman.

**Film/Video/DVD:** Two film versions where produced in 1996: the feature film with Robin Wright Penn and Morgan Freeman is beautiful but has little relation to the book; the TV miniseries made in England and starring Alex Kingston is exceptional.

**Similar Reads:** Defoe is the famous author of *Robinson Crusoe* and *A Journal of the Plague Year*. Newgate prison and London's criminal class also figure in Winsor's *Forever Amber*. For a glimpse into Victorian London's underworld, read Dickens's *Oliver Twist*.

**Subjects:** England 1600s; Prostitution; Criminals; Colonial America; Prison; Fictional Autobiography

## Dickens, Charles (1812–1870)

*A Tale of Two Cities* **(England: 1859).** Signet 1997 (paper) 400pp. 0451526562 **J**

"It was the best of times, it was the worst of times, it was the age of wisdom, it was the age of foolishness, it was the epoch of belief, it was the epoch of incredulity, it was the season of Light, it was the season of Darkness, it was the spring of hope, it was the winter of despair."

You undoubtedly know the opening lines, but have you read the book? The two cities are London and Paris at a time of great upheaval, the French Revolution. Beautiful Lucie Manette is at the center of *Tale*. She is the daughter of Dr. Manette, a man broken after spending eighteen years in the Bastille, put there by a corrupt French nobleman. Two men love Lucie, Charles Darnay, nephew of the marquis responsible for Dr. Manette's imprisonment, and Sydney Carton, a ne'er-do-well English lawyer whose arguments save Darnay from an accusation of espionage against the British crown. Time passes. Darnay and Lucie marry. In the meantime, in France the revolution and the murder of the aristocrats accelerate. When Charles Darnay, returns to Paris to rescue a faithful family servant, he is inexorably caught up in the maelstrom of revolution.

Personal vendettas play out against political upheaval in this vivid historical novel with a large cast of characters; one of the most classic stories of self-sacrifice ever written. Violence, justice, love, politics, and family—all have a role in this complex story.

> **Audio:** Recorded Books. CD 1428108343. Read by Frank Muller.

> **Film/Video/DVD:** *A Tale of Two Cities* is an MGM 1935 black-and-white classic that is still gripping; it stars Ronald Coleman as Sydney Carton. The book was also filmed as a miniseries in 1980 and again in 1989, both very good adaptations.

> **Similar Reads:** *The Scarlet Pimpernel* by Orczy is another story set during the French Revolution, as is *Scaramouche* by Rafael Sabatini.

> **Subjects:** France; England; Paris; London; French Revolution; Sacrifice; Impersonation

## Shellabarger, Samuel (1888–1954)

*Prince of Foxes* **(USA: 1947).** Bridge Works 2002 (paper) 433pp. 1882593642 **S**
Historical accuracy and swashbuckling adventure draw the reader into the story of the political rise of the low-born Andrea Orsini who finds favor with the most powerful man of his day, Cesare Borgia. The setting, Renaissance Italy, is paramount in this novel of political intrigue and Machiavellian manipulation. The struggle between medieval and modern, the rise of the city-state, and the beginnings of Italian nationalism are all addressed in this fast-paced historical novel.

> **Film/Video/DVD:** *Prince of Foxes* (1949) is a black-and-white film with Tyrone Power starring as the hero and Orson Welles as Cesare Borgia.

> **Similar Reads:** Shellabarger's other well-known work is *Captain from Castille*; books by Rafael Sabatini, Alexandre Dumas, and Robert Louis Stevenson provide more swashbuckle.

> **Subjects:** Italy, Italian Renaissance; Political Intrigue; Borgia Family; Swashbuckler

## Trevino, Elizabeth Borton de (1904–)

🌷 *I, Juan de Pareja* **(USA: 1965).** Sunburst/St. Martin's 1984 (paper) 180pp. 0374435251 **M** Teen **Q**
Juan de Pareja, a slave owned by the famous painter Velasquez, serves his master faithfully but has one desire—to be an artist himself. But it is illegal for a slave in

seventeenth-century Spain to be an artist. Secretly Juan teaches himself to paint, and through his talent, eventually earns his freedom.

Sympathetic characters and vivid description make this story narrated by Juan a fascinating glimpse into the world of artists.

> **Audio:** Blackstone 1998 0786114223. Read by Johanna Ward.

> **Similar Reads:** Two novels about artists for older readers may be of interest: Tracy Chevalier's *Girl with a Pearl Earring* about the household of the Dutch painter Vermeer and Irving Stone's *The Agony and the Ecstasy* about Michelangelo.

> **Subjects:** Spain; 1600s; Artists; Velasquez, Diego; Royalty; Slavery; Gentle Read; Newbery Medal 1966

## Twain, Mark (1835–1910)

*The Prince and the Pauper* (USA: 1882). Signet 2004 (paper) 221pp. 0451528352 <u>M</u> Q

A fast-paced story of impersonation and adventure. Tom Canty is the poorest of the poor, an urchin growing up in Tudor London in an abusive family with just a little education and a lot of imagination. Prince Edward of England is growing up the richest of the rich. His father is King Henry the Eighth, his sisters are princesses, his every word is a command obeyed by thousands. When these two boys meet, they see that they are virtually twins, and when they change clothes, the prince, is mistaken for a beggar—and driven from the palace! Tom is forced to play prince and Edward must learn to survive in the underbelly of Tudor England.

Long considered a children's book, this novel offers much to discuss. Twain keeps his trademark satire to a minimum, but it still pops into the story when Twain talks about the abuses of power by those who hold it, the injustice of certain laws, the pervasiveness of cruelty, and the double scourges of poverty and ignorance.

> **Audio:** Recorded Books cassette 1556909896. Read by Norman Dietz.

> **Film/Video/DVD:** Filmed in 1978 as *Crossed Swords* with Mark Lester (star of the hit musical *Oliver* in 1968).

> **Similar Reads:** Another rousing impersonation story involving a king and a look-alike commoner is Hope's *The Prisoner of Zenda*. Another historical Twain novel to try is *A Connecticut Yankee in King Arthur's Court*. And don't miss Twain's classic story of American boyhood, *The Adventures of Tom Sawyer*.

> **Subjects:** England 1500s; Impersonation; Imposters; Royalty; Poverty; Henry VIII; Prince of Wales; Childhood Classic

# The Spanish Colonies

The Caribbean, South and Central America, Mexico, and the American Southwest were originally home to ancient, independent civilizations. When the land became the property of Spain after the arrival of Columbus in 1492, so did the people and the riches of the territory. What followed was an often tragic history of conquest, slavery, disease, forced conversion to Christianity, and exploitation of the wealth this New World offered to the conquerors. Novels set in the Spanish Colonies address these issues of colonization and exploitation.

## O'Dell, Scott (1898–1989)

**🏵 *The King's Fifth* (USA: 1966).** Houghton Mifflin 2006 (paper) 272p 0618747834 **J** **Teen**

Seventeen-year-old Esteban de Sandobal is imprisoned in Vera Cruz, Mexico, a prisoner of the king of Spain. His crime? Not giving the king a fifth of a treasure of gold. As Esteban recounts the story of the past two years, we learn that he began as a mapmaker on an expeditionary cruise of the Mexico/California coast, he leaves the ship with the mutinous Mendoza seeking Coronado's army. As they traverse the Southwest, they encounter native peoples, the Grand Canyon, the Colorado River, Death Valley, and the ever-present tease of untold riches of gold—unimportant to the natives who value turquoise more. Gold lust overtakes the party one by one, with the exception of Zia, their young Indian interpreter, and Father Francisco, the priest.

**Film/Video/DVD:** *Esteban and the Seven Cities of Gold* (1982) is an animated Japanese TV series loosely based on O'Dell's novel.

**Similar Reads:** Scott O'Dell is a prolific and respected, award-winning author of historical fiction for young adults. Some of his other works about Native Americans are S*ing Down the Moon* and *Streams to the River, River to the Sea* about Sacagawea. He established the Scott O'Dell Award for Historical Fiction in 1982.

**Subjects:** Mexico; New World; Gold; Explorers; Greed; Imprisonment; Newbery Honor 1967

## Wilder, Thornton (1897–1975)

**🏵 *The Bridge of San Luis Rey* (USA: 1927).** Perennial Classics 2003 (paper) 160 pp. 0060088877 **S Q**

In 1714, five people are crossing the famous rope bridge of San Luis Rey between Lima and Cuzco in Peru. The bridge breaks, and the people fall to their deaths. Brother Juniper is the only one to witness this event. He sets out to learn about the lives of these travelers and to question whether their deaths had meaning or were random events.

This is an eloquent and simple book that can create profound discussions about fate and destiny.

**Audio:** Highbridge Audio 1997 cassette 1565112210. Read by Sam Waterston.

**Film/Video/DVD:** Filmed in 1929, 1944, and 2004.

**Similar Reads:** *Lost Horizon* by Hilton is another enigmatic adventure story that raises big questions.

**Subjects:** Peru; 1714; Fate; Destiny; Spiritual Quest; Family; Gentle Read; Pulitzer Prize 1928

# Colonial America

From conquest in 1492 until the eve of the Revolution in 1775, America existed as Colonies of European powers—the Spanish, English, French, and Dutch all had interests in the land along the Atlantic Coast inhabited by the original settlers. Coexisting with Native American tribes, bringing civilization to the wilderness, creating the idea of America was the mission of these early pioneers.

## Cooper, James Fenimore (1789–1851)

*The Last of the Mohicans* **(USA: 1826).** Bantam 1982 (paper) 400pp. 0553213296
J

Cora and Alice Munro are traveling through the primal forests of Early America to visit their father Colonel Munro, the commanding officer of Fort William Henry, an English outpost in the wilderness. It is 1757, and the English are fighting the French and the Native Americans for control of the American colonies. Accompanying the young women are Major Duncan Heyward, an American in the British army in love with the fair and girlish Alice; singing teacher David Gamut, who hopes to convert the Native Americans to Christianity through his music; and their Indian guide, Magua, a Huron who has a secret plan of revenge against Colonel Munro. Along the way, they meet the scout Natty Bumpo, called Hawkeye, and his companions the noble Chingachgook and his son Uncas (who is the last Mohican). When Hawkeye informs the travelers that their guide Magua has led them the wrong way, a series of fights, abductions, and adventures begins that will only end weeks later with many tragic deaths.

This is an exhilarating adventure story trapped in dense, old-fashioned prose. It is difficult to start reading, but once you relax into the slower rhythm, the formal tone, and the somewhat overwrought emotionalism, the excitement of the story will sweep you along.

**Audio:** Recorded Books cassette 1556902980. Read by Larry McKeever.

**Film/Video/DVD:** *The Last of the Mohicans* (1992) is an R-rated adaptation with Daniel Day Lewis and Madeline Stowe. Filmed previously in 1920 and 1936.

**Similar Reads:** Cooper wrote five novels that follow Hawkeye/Natty Bumpo from youth to old age and show the evolving American Frontier. The books as a series are called The Leatherstocking Tales. Listed in story order they are *The Deerslayer* (1841), *The Last of the Mohicans* (1826), *The Pathfinder* (1840), *The Pioneers* (1823), and *The Prairie* (1827). For more early American adventure, try Conrad Richter's *The Awakening Land*

or *Drums along the Mohawk* by Walter Edmonds. For big historical novels written by Cooper's European contemporaries, turn to Sir Walter Scott and Alexandre Dumas.

**Subjects:** New York State; Native Americans; American Frontier

## Hawthorne, Nathaniel (1804–1864)

*The Scarlet Letter* (USA: 1850). Modern Library 2000 (paper) 241 pp. 0679783385 <u>S</u>

Passion and shame, secrets and repentance pervade this "drama of guilt and sorrow" that plays out in Puritan Boston in the mid-1600s. Hester Prynne has a baby, but her husband has been away for two years and cannot have been the father. To atone for this transgression, Hester must wear the letter "A"—for adulteress—at all times and be "a living sermon against sin" for the edification of all who see her. When her husband appears, he demands that Hester keep his identity secret while he sets out to discover and destroy the baby's father, a man Hester won't name.

Hawthorne lays bare the Puritan dilemma of external purity masking internal depredation.

**Audio:** Recorded Books cassette 1556904592; CD 1402523343. Read by Flo Gibson.

**Film/Video/DVD:** There are many versions, among them a 1926 silent film starring Lillian Gish; Demi Moore was Hester Prynne in the reviled and not recommended 1995 feature film; the 1979 TV miniseries produced by WGBH is recommended.

**Similar Reads:** *The House of the Seven Gables* is Hawthorne's other classic story of sin and redemption. *Witch of Blackbird Pond* is a milder story also set in Puritan America.

**Subjects:** Boston; 1600s; Adultery; Puritans; Strong Heroine; Preachers; Doctors; Sin; Redemption; Guilt; Secrets

## Richter, Conrad (1890–1968)

### The Awakening Land Trilogy (USA)

First as a young woman of fifteen walking to Ohio in 1790 with her parents and siblings through the days when she is an old woman surrounded by her children and grandchildren, Sayward Luckett is a witness to the evolution of America. She sees the trees give way to the fields and the fields give way to the town as civilization slowly takes over the wilderness. As the years pass, Sayward comments on the sense of time speeding up, of everyone growing ungrateful, of life becoming too easy and the people too soft. Along the way there are marriages and births, disappearances in the wilderness, and the coming of government and taxes.

Known in YA circles for the classic *A Light in the Forest,* Richter chronicled the settling of the vast and lonely American Frontier. Using pioneer phrasing and idiom, Richter creates an historical saga that captures the hardship, loneliness, and toil of settling a new land in the days when Ohio was its farthest outpost.

*The Trees* (USA: 1940). Ohio University Press 1991 (paper) 175pp. 0821409786
*The Fields* (USA: 1946). Ohio University Press 1991 (paper) 169pp. 0821409794
*The Town* (USA: 1950). Ohio University Press 1991 (paper) 309pp. 0821409808

**Film/Video/DVD:** *The Awakening Land* (1978) is an engrossing TV miniseries with Elizabeth Montgomery and Jane Seymour.

**Similar Reads:** Other pioneer stories include Willa Cather's *My Antoni*a and *O Pioneers!*; Aldrich's *A Lantern in Her Hand*; and *Drums along the Mohawk* by Walter Edmonds. For younger readers, there are *Caddie Woodlawn; Sarah, Plain and Tall;* and the Laura Ingalls Wilder Little House books.

**Subjects:** American Frontier; Ohio; Family; Settlers; Strong Heroine; Pulitzer Prize 1951 (for *The Town*)

*The Light in the Forest* **(USA: 1953).** Fawcett 1994 (paper) 128 pp. 0449704378 **J Teen Q**

Four-year-old John Butler was taken captive by Indians. For eleven years, he lived happily as a Native American, the proud son of a chief. Now, because of a new treaty, he is forced to return to his white family, but how can these people be his people? How can he adjust to small rooms when he is used to open spaces? How can he wear stiff shoes when his feet want to feel the earth through soft moccasins?

Richter compassionately illustrates the clash of cultures that created conflicts on the American Frontier.

**Audio:** Recorded Books cassette 0556905912. Read by Joel Fabiani.

**Film/Video/DVD:** *A Light in the Forest* (1958) is a Disney version with James MacArthur and Fess Parker; the film changes characters, adds a romance, and fabricates a more conclusive ending, but the conflict between cultures is well portrayed.

**Similar Reads:** Richter also wrote a classic trilogy about the settling of America called *The Awakening Land*.

**Subjects:** Pennsylvania; Ohio; 1764; Indian Captives; Coming of Age; Family; Native Americans; Cultural Conflict

# American Revolution

The American War of Independence (1775–1783) fought between the thirteen colonies and England was a war of revolt and ideas. It resulted in the creation of the United States of America. Novels about this era often depict the growing pains of a young country and its citizens.

## Avi (1937–)

🐾 *The Fighting Ground* **(USA: 1984).** HarperTrophy 1987 (paper) 160 pp. 0064401855 **M Teen Q**

Thirteen-year-old Jonathan is desperate for the chance to fight in the war. One spring day in 1778, he gets his wish. He is given a gun taller than he is and told to fight. Will war be as jolly as Jonathan imagined?

Fast paced and dramatic, this is a coming-of-age story set during a brief moment of the American Revolution.

> **Audio:** Recorded Books cassette 07887009x; CD 1402550375. Read by George Guidall.
>
> **Similar Reads:** Also explore books by Anne Rinaldi.
>
> **Subjects:** Family; Fathers and Sons; Soldiers; Coming of Age; Scott O'Dell Award 1985

## Collier, James Lincoln (1928– )

🪶 *My Brother Sam Is Dead* (USA: 1974). Scholastic 1985 (paper) 224pp. 059042792X **M Teen Q**

The Meekers are a Tory family, loyal to the king. But oldest son Sam decides to fight for the rebel Americans. This puts young Tim Meeker right in the middle between his father and his brother, between the Loyalists and the Revolutionaries. As events unfold, it is difficult to know who is right, who is wrong, and where justice resides in the midst of Revolution.

The American Revolution created divisions among families as well as among nations. This is a sobering book that will provoke discussion about family loyalty, revolt, and a dramatic time in America's past.

> **Audio:** Audio Bookshelf 1883332192. Read by John C. Brown.
>
> **Similar Reads:** *Sarah Bishop* by Scott O'Dell is the story of a young woman in the midst of the revolution. Also read books by Ann Rinaldi for more U.S. historical fiction.
>
> **Subjects:** Connecticut; Brothers; Family; Soldiers; Treason; Military Justice; Coming of Age; Frequently Challenged; Newbery Honor Book 1975

## Fast, Howard (1914–2003)

*April Morning* (USA: 1961). Bantam 1983 (paper) 208pp. 0553273221 **J Teen**

On the night of April 18, 1775, Adam Cooper is a fifteen-year-old boy. His biggest concerns are his bothersome little brother and his contentious relationship with his father. When the British march on to the green at Lexington, no one believes they will shoot citizens. By morning Adam is a veteran of the Battle of Lexington, and the American Revolution has begun.

> **Audio:** Recorded Books cassette 1556900260; CD 1402522878. Read by James Hanes.
>
> **Film/Video/DVD:** *April Morning* (1988) is a Hallmark production with Tommy Lee Jones as the father.
>
> **Similar Reads:** *Citizen Tom Paine* is Fast's fictional biography of revolutionary Tom Paine.
>
> **Subjects:** Massachusetts 1775; Family; Fathers and Sons; Battle; Coming of Age

### Forbes, Esther (1891–1967)

🌺 *Johnny Tremain* (USA: 1943). Yearling 1987 (paper) 288pp. 0440442508 <u>M</u> Teen

Johnny Tremain, growing up in Boston, is fourteen in the tumultuous year of 1773. Although an orphan of uncertain parentage, Johnny Tremain is overly proud of his skill with silver. He is a silversmith's apprentice and has a talent far beyond his master's. In fact, the Lapham family depends on Johnny's skill for the bulk of their earnings. One day, a prank inspired by jealousy ends Johnny's haughtiness and ruins his career as a silversmith. With no work now as a smith, Johnny must find another trade. He begins a journey of intellectual and political maturation that makes him a participant in the major events of the early American Revolution.

Strong fictional characters interact with the real Revolutionaries—Paul Revere. Sam Adams, John Hancock—in this vivid novel set at the beginning of the American Revolution.

**Audio:** Recorded Books cassette 1788700170; CD 1402523106. Read by George Guidall.

**Film/Video/DVD:** *Johnny Tremain* (1957) is a Disney family classic.

**Similar Reads:** *The Fifth of March* by Ann Rinaldi, also set in Boston, describes the Boston Massacre.

**Subjects:** Boston; Apprentices; Orphans; Espionage; Coming of Age; Paul Revere; Sam Adams; Newbery Medal 1944

# American Civil War 1861–1865

The period of the American Civil War was a time of violence and upheaval in American society. Novels set in this time period focusing on the war itself and its effects on the people are listed in this section. Titles focusing on the underlying issue of slavery appear in the section that follows.

### Crane, Stephen (1871–1900)

*The Red Badge of Courage* (USA: 1885). Tor 1997 (paper) 176pp. 0812504798 <u>J</u> <u>Q</u>

When the shooting starts, will you stand and fight or will you run in fear? This is the question Henry Fleming lives with until his first battle. Henry joined in the Civil War for glory and adventure, but the experience of fighting and the men he meets—living, dying and dead—on that first day of battle will change Henry forever.

This was the first American novel about war from the soldier's, not the general's point of view. You experience the chaos and confusion of battle, the dirt, the blood, the grumbling, and the death. It is vivid, visceral, and terrifying.

**Audio:** Recorded Books cassette 1556904371. Read by Frank Muller.

**Film/Video/DVD:** *The Red Badge of Courage* (1951), directed by John Huston, starred real-life World War II hero Audie Murphy; 1974 saw a made-for-TV version with Richard Thomas of *The Waltons* fame.

**Similar Reads:** A novel that considers the issues of bravery and cowardice during World War I is *All Quiet on the Western Front* by Remarque.

**New Media:** Vansant, Wayne. *Puffin Graphics: Red Badge of Courage,* Puffin Graphics [Graphic Novels] 2005, 0142404101.

**Subjects:** Courage; Soldiers; Battle; Military Fiction; Coming of Age

## Hunt, Irene (1907–2001)

🎗 *Across Five Aprils* **(USA: 1965).** Berkley Publishing Group 1987 (paper) 190pp. 0425102416 **M** Teen

His older brothers go off to fight, but Jethro Creighton experiences the Civil War from the family farm in Illinois. While helping his parents manage the farm, he follows the war through newspapers and letters from his brothers. He also witnesses his family being victimized because his brother Bill fights for the South. He experiences loss, and he feels the isolation of making a difficult decision alone. Over the five Aprils of the war, Jethro matures in his understanding of war and life, of other people and himself.

In this story Hunt touches on many parts of the war. She provides overviews of major battles, the rise and fall of generals, the mixed reactions to Lincoln's Gettysburg Address, the desperation and anger of army deserters, and the hardship experienced by those left on the home front.

**Audio:** Recorded Books cassette 140250182X; CD 1402514840. Read by Tom Stechschulte.

**Film/Video/DVD:** There is a film version titled *Civil War Diary* (1990). Readers wanting to learn more about the Civil War may want to view Ken Burn's epic historical documentary series *The Civil War* (1990).

**Similar Reads**: *Charley Skedaddle* by Patricia Beatty. *Bull Run* by Paul Fleischman presents the Civil War from many points of view.

**Subjects:** Illinois; Family; Home Front; Coming of Age; Newbery Honor Book 1966

## Kantor, MacKinlay (1904–1977)

🎗 *Andersonville* **(USA: 1958).** Plume 1993 (paper) 768pp. 0452269563 **S**

A graphic and horrifying novel about the infamous Andersonville prison camp in Georgia where more than 13,000 Union prisoners died. Almost 50,000 prisoners were interred at Andersonville where diseases caused by overcrowding and the lack of pure water and decent food contributed to the deaths.

**Film/Video/DVD:** *Andersonville* (1996) is a made-for-TV adaptation and a powerful film.

**Similar Reads:** Two books about the fighting of the Civil War are *Gods and Generals* by Jeff Shaara and *Killer Angels* by Michael Shaara. Margaret Walker's *Jubilee*

includes a visit to Andersonville. Another novel about man's inhumanity to man in a prison setting is Solzenitsyn's *One Day in the Life of Ivan Denisovich.*

**Subjects:** Prisoners of War; Imprisonment; Mature Read; Pulitzer Prize 1956

## Keith, Harold (1903–1998)

🌶 *Rifles for Watie* (USA: 1957). HarperTrophy 1987 (paper) 352 pp. 006447030X **J Teen**

Jeff Bussey becomes a player in a game of espionage during the American Civil War. As he spies for both sides of the conflict, the issues involved becomes less clear to him. Stand Watie was a famous Confederate general, the only Native American (Cherokee) to reach that rank in the Civil War.

**Audio:** Recorded Books cassette 0788732099; CD 0788737325. Read by Tom Stechschulte.

**Similar Reads:** For a story of espionage set in India, read *Kim* by Rudyard Kipling.

**Subjects:** Soldiers; Spies; Espionage; Coming of Age; Newbery Medal 1958

## Mitchell, Margaret (1900–1949)

*Gone with the Wind* (USA: 1936). **J**
entry in Chapter 8, "Romance Fiction."

## Shaara, Michael (1929–1988)

🌶 *The Killer Angels* (USA: 1974). Ballantine 1987 (paper) 384 pp. 0345348109 **S**

It is July 1863. For four days, a battle was fought on a little hill in Pennsylvania. It was one of the bloodiest battles ever to involve American soldiers. The personalities of the leaders and the drama of the Battle of Gettysburg are explored in this acclaimed historical novel. Shaara helps us hear the noises, experience the smells, and witness the heroism and the terror of war in this powerful and poignant fictional account based on real events and actual documents.

**Audio:** Books on Tape, cassette and CD 5557084290. Read by Stephen Hoye. Recorded Books, read by George Guidall 141938675.

**Film/Video/DVD:** *Gettysburg* (1993) is a fine adaptation of *The Killer Angels* starring Jeff Daniels, Martin Sheen, Sam Elliott, and Tom Berenger. Ken Burns's famous documentary *The Civil War* (1990) is a good companion piece.

**Similar Reads:** *Gods and Generals* and *The Last Full Measure,* written by Jeff Shaara, Michael Shaara's son, expand this Civil War saga.

**Subjects:** Battle; Battle of Gettysburg; Soldiers; Generals; Pulitzer Prize 1975

# Slavery

Novels that treat the topic of slavery are generally set in the 1800s in the American South where owning human beings as property and forcing them to work against their will were accepted practices that sustained the economics of the time. These novels tell of the cruelty and hardship caused by the enslavement of one group of people, African Americans, by another group, white landowners. The Emancipation Proclamation of 1863 led the way for the official abolition of slavery with the Thirteenth Amendment in 1865.

## Fox, Paula (1923–)

🏵 *Slave Dancer* (USA: 1973). Yearling 1991 (paper) 160pp. 0440404029 **M Teen Q**
New Orleans, 1840, Thirteen-year-old Jessie Bollier is kidnapped while on an errand for his mother. He is taken aboard a ship bound for Africa, its mission: slaving. Musical Jessie is expected to play his fife every morning so the captured Africans can dance to stay in shape. Jessie lives this grim reality for four months until possible discovery of the illegal cargo and a violent storm end the voyage.

This is a haunting look at a dark moment in American history and man's eternal inhumanity to man.

> **Audio:** Listening Library cassette 0553476963. Read by Peter MacNicol.

> **Similar Reads:** *To Be a Slave* is Julius Lester's classic collection of firsthand accounts of slavery.

> **Subjects:** New Orleans; Africa; Slavery; Slave Trade; Sea Story; Racism; Coming of Age; Newbery Medal 1974

## Gaines, Ernest J. (1933–)

*The Autobiography of Miss Jane Pittman* (USA: 1971). Bantam 1982 (paper) 272pp. 0553263579 **J**
Feisty Miss Jane Pittman is 110 years old. By telling the story of her life, Miss Jane tells us the experience of African Americans from plantation days through to the Civil Rights movement. Born a slave, witness to the Emancipation, Jane lives her entire life in the rural South working as a field laborer or a domestic. With earthy humor and straightforward narrative, she tells her experiences of being a black woman in the midst of social change.

> **Audio:** Recorded Books cassette 0788700723; CD 1402522908. Read by Lynne Thigpen.

> **Film/Video/DVD:** *The Autobiography of Miss Jane Pittman* (1974) is a highly acclaimed TV movie starring Cicely Tyson.

> **Similar Reads:** Gaines is a powerful writer of other modern classics that depict the African American experience in the early twentieth century, including *A Gathering of Old Men* and *A Lesson before Dying*.

**Subjects:** Louisiana; African Americans; American South; Racism; Civil Rights; Strong Heroine; Plantation Life; Fictional Autobiography

## Haley, Alex (1921–1992)

*Roots: The Saga of an American Family* **(USA: 1976).** Dell 1980 (paper) 736pp. 0440174643 **J**

In 1750 in a West African village, a baby is born. His proud parents name him Kunte Kinte after his grandfather, a famous healer and wiseman. Kunte Kinte grows up in his village learning the ways of his people, listening to the stories of the grandmothers. While still a teen Kinte, having gone alone to the forest to chop wood for a drum, is kidnapped by brutal slave traders and transported on a hellish slave ship to America. Freely born of a proud lineage, he will now spend the rest of his life in slavery. In America he is renamed Toby but insists his name is "Kintay." He becomes the ancestor of Alex Haley, who writes a book detailing the lives of his forebears from their noble beginnings in Africa, to their captivity as slaves in nineteenth-century America, to their struggle for acceptance and dignity in twentieth-century America.

*Roots* is a family story and an historical epic. Haley began his book from stories his grandmother told about a long ago ancestor referred to as "the African." Haley painstakingly researched the life of Kinte, traveling to Africa to hear the tales of an old "griot" or oral historian. As he listened to the ancient tales, Haley heard the story of Kunte Kinte and how he disappeared one day when he went to the forest to chop wood for a drum, a story that confirmed his grandmother's own tale. Haley turned this family tale into an epic novel that became a sociological as well as a literary landmark. It was an international best seller and received a special Pulitzer award citation.

**Film/Video/DVD:** *Roots* (1977) probably the most famous television miniseries ever produced; twelve hours long, it had a record-breaking audience, spawned an interest in genealogical research, and started the rage for miniseries programming on TV.

**New Media:** www.kintehaley.org is the site of Alex Haley's foundation where you can find a family tree of *Roots* and information about Haley and his books and about genealogy. www.everygeneration.co.uk is a British site dedicated to empowering the black community "through history, family genealogy and heritage."

**Similar Reads:** Haley's other family epic, *Queen,* traces his paternal heritage. *Things Fall Apart* by Chinua Achebe depicts traditional tribal life in Africa. *The Middle Passage* by Charles Johnson is about the horror of the slave trade and the voyages. For younger readers, *Amos Fortune: Free Man* by Elizabeth Yates tells the story of an African prince captured into slavery. Haley is coauthor of *The Autobiography of Malcolm X.*

**Subjects:** West Africa; Antebellum South; Plantation Life; Civil War; Reconstruction; Family; African Americans; Pulitzer Award 1977, Special Award

## Morrison, Toni (1931–)

🎗 *Beloved* (USA: 1987). Plume 1998 (paper) 512 pp. 0452280621 <u>S</u>

In Ohio in 1873, Sethe, a former slave, lives in the house at 124 Bluestone Road. The house is haunted. It has been haunted for years by Sethe's two-year old daughter, a little girl who had a tragic death. One day a teenaged girl comes to the house and says she is Beloved; Sethe takes this to mean she is the lost daughter, and slowly Beloved takes over the household. How much power does the past have?

The destruction of humanity that slavery caused is delineated in this psychologically acute story. Morrison has created a complex narrative, an upsetting story, a demanding read, and an important book. Morrison is not interested in telling a pretty story, she is interested in telling a powerful and true one.

**Audio:** Recorded Books cassette 0375404872. Read by the author, Toni Morrison.

**Film:** *Beloved* (1998) provocative, disturbing film with Thandie Newton, Oprah Winfrey, and Danny Glover.

**Similar Reads:** *The Bluest Eye* by Morrison is another challenging read by the Nobel Prize–winning author.

**Subjects;** Ohio; Hauntings; Mothers and Daughters; African Americans; Mature Read; Frequently Challenged; Pulitzer Prize 1988; Nobel Prize 1993

## Stowe, Harriet Beecher (1811–1896)

*Uncle Tom's Cabin* (USA: 1851). Bantam Classics 1983 (paper) 544 pp. 0553212184 <u>S</u>

The story of pious and loyal slave Uncle Tom, the saintly and innocent Little Eva, brave Eliza, and the murderous Simon Legree, all linked together by that "peculiar institution," slavery.

This is the famous book that condemned slavery and was (according to Abraham Lincoln) one of the contributing factors in the outbreak of the Civil War. Stowe's depictions of the inhumanity of slavery and her moral outrage at the institution powerfully affected the readers of her day. She presents modern readers with a tragic portrayal of a flawed society written by a woman who was there. This is a Victorian novel with elements of melodrama, but still a poignant read.

**Audio:** Blackstone cassette 0786107987. Read by Kathryn Yarman

**Film/Video/DVD:** There are multiple silent versions of *Uncle Tom's Cabin* and a 1987 TV production.

**Subjects:** Kentucky; Louisiana; Antislavery; African Americans; Plantation Life; Antebellum South

## Walker, Margaret (1915–1998)

*Jubilee* (USA: 1966). Mariner Books 1992 (paper) 512pp. 0395924952 <u>S</u>

This is the story of Vyry, a light-skinned slave, a noble woman, intelligent though uneducated, the daughter of a slave and her white master. This is the story of Vyry's life on the wealthy Georgia plantation in the Antebellum South where she is born into slavery. It is a story about the impact of the Civil War on all the people of the American

South and about the harsh realities of Reconstruction. Walker weaves the folklore, songs, and sayings of African Americans into her novel. Her characterization of Vyry with her ever-present dignity and gentleness, her forbearance, and her compassion in defiance of her own suffering is memorable.

Walker depicts the grotesque brutality of slavery, the economic reality of the plantation system, and the perpetual tension between masters and slaves, free blacks, enslaved blacks, and poor whites. Her historical use of the "N-word" and her realistic depiction of the violence and inhumanity of slavery may startle modern readers. Her depiction of the complex relationships created by slavery, the historic reality of daily life, and her portrayal of the Civil War and the politics of the South are all told in easy flowing prose. Walker based *Jubilee* on the stories her grandmother told about the life of her own mother, a slave.

> **Similar Reads:** Other strong African American heroines can be found in *The Color Purple, The Street,* and *Their Eyes Were Watching God.* Margaret Walker was also a poet, and readers might want to explore her poetry in *For My People.* For the real-life story of a slave, read Harriet Jacobs's, *Incidents in the Life of a Slave Girl.*

> **Subjects:** Georgia; Plantation Life; Antebellum South; Civil War 1861–1865; Reconstruction; Strong Heroine; Family; African Americans

# Settlers and Pioneers

The United States is a nation of pioneers—people who left home and the land they knew to create a new life for themselves and a new country out of the raw wilderness of America. Their stories are filled with humanity and courage. The novels that follow are set in the late 1800s in the times of Westward Expansion.

## Aldrich, Bess Streeter (1881–1954)

*A Lantern in Her Hand* (USA: 1928). Puffin 1997 (paper) 251pp. 0140384286 **J**

> The "physical attributes of the peasant and the mental ones of the aristocrat" come together in Abby Mackenzie Deal to create a powerful pioneer woman. Abby is resilient and full of joy while living in a sod house, battling grasshoppers, and raising her family on the Nebraska frontier.

> This is a gentle story about the bravery of pioneers and the love of family.

> **Film/Video/DVD:** *A Mother's Gift* (1995) was filmed for television with Nancy McKeon.

> **Similar Reads:** *The Awakening Land* by Conrad Richter, *Mrs. Mike* by Benedict Freedman, *My Antonia* by Willa Cather, and *Sarah, Plain and Tall* tell the stories of other pioneer women.

> **Subjects:** Nebraska; Relationships; Family; Strong Heroine; Gentle Read

## Brink, Carol (1895–1981)

🐿 *Caddie Woodlawn* **(USA: 1936).** Aladdin Books 1997 (paper) 242pp. 0689815212 **M Teen**

Frontier Wisconsin in the 1860s is the setting for the adventures of tomboy Caddie and her large and loving family. Caddie, full of life and good spirits, skates on thin ice—literally; admires Abraham Lincoln; befriends Native Americans; and contemplates what it means to be a "lady."

Caddie ranks with the memorable girl heroines of fiction: Laura, Francie, Jo, and Anne. The author based the novel on stories she heard from her pioneer grandmother.

**Audio:** Recorded Books cassette 0788700162. Read by Roslyn Alexander.

**Film/Video/DVD:** *Caddie Woodlawn* (1989) was a Wonderworks production.

**Similar Reads:** Other spunky frontier girls are found in Laura Ingalls Wilder's Little House on the Prairie series and Stratton-Porter's *Girl of the Limberlost*. Readers may also like *Anne of Green Gables* for its humor. Older readers will want to try *The Awakening Land* by Richter, *A Lantern in her Hand* by Bess Aldrich, or *Christy* by Catherine Marshall.

**Subjects:** Wisconsin; Family; Frontier Life; Native Americans; Strong Heroine; Childhood Classic; Newbery Medal 1936

## Cather, Willa (1873–1947)

*My Antonia* **(USA: 1918).** Signet 1994 (paper) 286pp. 0451525795 **J**

The immigrant experience in the American Midwest is poetically depicted as Jim Burden reminisces about his youth in Nebraska and his memories of Antonia, the immigrant girl from Bohemia. Growing up, Jim and Antonia are friends and neighbors. Although their lives follow different paths, for Jim Antonia comes to represent all that is truly American—strength, perseverance, courage, hardiness, and abundance.

**Audio:** Recorded Books cassette 1556909764; CD 1402529279. Read by George Guidall.

**Film/Video/DVD:** *My Antonia* (1995) was filmed for TV with Neil Patrick Harris and Elina Lowensohn.

**Similar Reads:** Read Cather's other famous Nebraska novel *O, Pioneers!* Also try Rolvaag's *Giants in the Earth* or Sinclair's *The Jungle* for other facets of the immigrant experience in America.

**Subjects:** Nebraska 1880s to 1910s; Farm Life; Immigrants; Strong Heroine

*O, Pioneers!* **(USA: 1913).** Vintage 1992 (paper) 176pp. 0679743626 **J**

"The history of every country begins in the heart of a man or a woman." Cather presents one of those women in Alexandra Bergson, an American heroine. Coming to America as a young girl with her Swedish immigrant parents, Alexandra becomes America—beautiful, bountiful, and progressive. Alexandra sacrifices her own youth for the success of her family. She believes in the land, and it rewards her with material success but emotional hardship. The parallel stories of Alexandra's endurance and triumph and the love triangle of her beloved younger brother Emil, the flirtatious Bohemian Marie Shabat, and Marie's fiery husband Frank play out against a Nebraska of orchards, farmlands, pioneer cemeteries, and growing cities.

Cather is a master of clear, simple, forthright prose. *O Pioneers!* explores one of Cather's recurring themes: the founding of a new land and the development of a new type of people—Americans. She depicts the immigrants and their children who populated American at the turn of the century as stoic, hopeful, and willing to endure the bad for the good to come. The title is taken from a poem by Walt Whitman, "Pioneers! O Pioneers!"

> **Audio:** Recorded Books cassette 1556903847. Read by Barbara McCulloh.

> **Film/Video/DVD:** *O Pioneers!* was produced in 1992 with Jessica Lange as Alexandra Bergson.

> **Similar Reads:** *My Antonia; The Awakening Land; Giants in the Earth.*

> **Subjects:** Nebraska 1880s to 1910s; Farm Life; Immigrants; Swedish Americans; Prairie Life: Family; Strong Heroine

## Ferber, Edna (1887–1968)

*Cimarron* (USA: 1930). Difficult to find, although Harper Perennial is reissuing many of Ferber's novels) <u>S</u>

The Oklahoma frontier of 1889 is the setting where Native Americans collide with sod-busting settlers and a stalwart woman forges a home. Yancy Cravat, his wife Sabra and their son Cimarron leave Kansas to venture to Osage, Oklahoma, following the Land Run. In Osage, the leonine Yancy starts a newspaper, and Sabra works to civilize the town. Over time Yancy's restlessness forces him to wander, but Sabra stays put and helps build Oklahoma, becoming a congresswoman and revered pioneer.

Ferber was a prolific and popular writer. Considered one of the greatest women writers of her day, she is inexplicably ignored now. Her novels are vibrant and engaging, her characters are memorable, her prose is vigorous, and her plots move swiftly. These attributes, along with her depictions of strong women and diverse aspects of both American society and the American character, should continue to intrigue today's readers.

> **Film/Video/DVD:** *Cimarron* (1931) is famously the only Western to win the Best Picture Oscar until *Dances with Wolves* won in 1990. *Cimarron* was also produced in 1960.

> **Similar Reads:** Other novels by Ferber: *So Big,* winner of the 1925 Pulitzer Prize; *Giant,* set in Texas; *Great Son,* a family saga set in pioneer Seattle; and *Show Boat,* about gamblers and entertainers on a Mississippi river boat (later made into the famous musical). Other classics about settling the west: A. B. Guthrie *The Way West* or James Michener *Centennial*

> **Subjects:** Oklahoma; Land Rush; Strong Heroine; Prairie Life; Family

## MacLachlan, Patricia (1938–)

🏵 *Sarah Plain and Tall* (USA: 1985). HarperTrophy 1987 (paper) 58pp. 0064402053 **M**
Teen Q

Caleb and Anna have no mother, so their father advertises for a wife. Sarah answers the ad and travels all the way from coastal Maine to the landlocked Kansas prairie. Will Sarah make a home on the prairie, far from the sea she loves? Will Caleb and Anna allow themselves to love her? Will father accept the strong-willed Sarah as a partner?

Gentle and heartfelt, this book portrays a complex human situation while evoking the hardships of prairie life in the past. An early chapter book for younger readers, older readers will find this to be a simple read but a memorable story.

> **Audio:** Caedmon Audio/Harper Collins (1989) 0898456355. Read by Glenn Close.

> **Film/Video/DVD:** *Sarah, Plain and Tall* (1991) starring Glenn Close, followed by *Skylark* (1993) and *Winter's End* (1999).

> **Similar Reads:** The story continues in *Skylark* and *Caleb's Story*.

> **Subjects:** Kansas; Prairie Life; Stepparents; Family; Strong Heroine; Childhood Classic; Gentle Read; Newbery Medal 1986; Scott O'Dell Award 1986

## Rolvaag, Ole (1876–1931)

*Giants in the Earth* (USA: 1927). Perennial Classics 1999 (paper) 560pp. 0060931930 **S**

Norwegian immigrant Per Hansa is strong, optimistic, clever, and brave—a man suited to pioneering in a new land. His wife, Berit, nervous and afraid, would be better in the old country with the people and places she loves. The conflict of these two pioneers plays out against the hardships of homesteading in South Dakota. Although they have good friends and many successes, the inherent difficulties of the pioneering life take a toll on them both.

Rolvaag, the author, was an immigrant himself, and he expressed the loneliness of settling a new country and the sheer determination it must have taken to leave home, family, and everything familiar to strike out for the unknown, to face the absolute vastness of the North American prairie, the overwhelming power of nature, and the anxiety of a totally new life.

> **Similar Reads:** The Emigrant Novels by Vilhelm Moberg tell more stories of Scandinavian immigrants making a new home in America.

> **Subjects:** South Dakota; Immigrants; Farm Life; Norwegian Americans; Family

# Westerns

Westerns inhabit their own space between adventure fiction and historical fiction. They have a distinct setting that appeals to many readers: the frontier American West during the late 1800s. Populated with cowboys, Native Americans, mountain men, and pioneers, these stories often feature a loner hero who expresses a pure moral code. The clichéd belief that Westerns are a genre solely for old men in nursing homes can be put to rest by reading some of this fiction. The prevalent characteristics of the genre—adventure, fast pacing, action, strong heroes—make it an exciting realm for young adult readers, of particular interest perhaps to young male readers. The themes these books explore also make this a surprisingly rich genre. Moral questions of right and wrong, the historical treatment of Native Americans and women, the power of the landscape, an exploration of male friendship, and traditional coming of age and identity issues contribute to the depth of these stories and make these novels good starting points for discussions.

## Berger, Thomas (1924–)

*Little Big Man* (USA: 1964). <u>S</u>

*See* the entry in Chapter 10, "Humor."

## Clark, Walter van Tilburg (1909–1971)

*The Ox-Bow Incident* (USA: 1940). Modern Library 2001 (paper) 256pp. 0375757023 **J**

Nevada, 1885. Juan Martinez, Alva Hardwick, and Donald Martin are in the wrong place at the wrong time herding cattle they cannot prove are theirs.

This sad tale about the power of a mob starts as a typical Western and becomes an exploration of justice, of good and evil. Tersely written with memorable secondary characters, great descriptive passages of the western landscape, tight dialogue, and mounting tension.

> **Film/Video/DVD:** *The Ox Bow Incident* (1943) is a black-and-white classic with Henry Fonda and Dana Andrews.

> **Similar Reads:** For another Western depicting frontier justice, try *Warlock* by Oakley Hall.

> **Subjects:** Nevada; Justice; Lynching; Mobs; Good and Evil

## Gipson, Fred (1908–1973)

🐾 *Old Yeller* (USA: 1956). HarperTrophy 1990 (paper) 192pp. 0062203823 **M** Teen Q

Living in the Texas hill country just after the Civil War, the family has everything it needs, except cash. To earn money, Father joins a cattle drive. While he is gone, he charges fourteen-year-old Travis to look after the family, the animals, the crops, and the homestead. Travis is up to the task—especially after an ugly yellow dog with an unmistakable yell joins the family. Old Yeller starts off on the wrong foot with Travis: he introduces himself to the family by stealing their meat! But the dog soon proves his worth and becomes an indispensable part of the farm and Travis's life.

A brisk read that evokes the difficulties of frontier life and shows a boy's assumption of a man's responsibilities. Warning—heartbreak is in store.

> **Audio:** Recorded Books cassette 1556903898; CD 0788746529. Read by Norman Dietz.

**Film/Video/DVD:** *Old Yeller* (1957) is a Disney family classic.

**Similar Reads:** Other coming-of-age stories set in the American frontier are *My Friend Flicka* and *Shane;* for more classic animal stories read *Where the Red Fern Grows, Sounder,* and *The Incredible Journey.*

**Subjects:** Texas; Family; Dogs; Animals; Pets; Frontier Life; Coming of Age; Gentle Read; Newbery Honor 1957

## Grey, Zane (1872–1939)

*Riders of the Purple Sage* **(USA: 1912).** Forge, 2000 (paper) 320pp. 0812590376 **J**
Jane Withersteen is being ordered by the Mormon elders to marry Elder Tull. Jane, it seems, is the owner of a valuable ranch that has plentiful water, and the Elders want to gain control of it. When she refuses, things turn nasty, and that is when Lassiter rides into her life. An archetypal Western hero, Lassiter is not much for talking, dresses in black, respects Jane, and is quick to deliver justice.

The beauty and majesty of the West is depicted by Grey in poetic descriptive passages.

**Audio:** Recorded Books cassette 1556904436. Read by Donald Buka.

Film/Video/DVD: A 1996 TV movie was produced with Ed Harris and Amy Madigan.

**Similar Reads:** *Rainbow Trail* is a sequel to *Riders.* Zane Grey was an extremely prolific Western writer, Louis L'Amour, another prolific Western writer is often compared to Grey.

**Subjects:** Utah; Mormons; Strong Heroine; Gunfighters

## Kelton, Elmer (1926–)

🎗 *The Day the Cowboy's Quit* **(USA: 1971).** Forge Books 1999 (paper) 288pp. 0812574508 **S**
The Texas Panhandle in 1883 is the setting for this book about a labor dispute between cowboys and ranchers. When a rumor starts that cowboys will not be allowed to own any cows, they decide to strike against the ranchers for their rights as Americans.

Kelton deserves more mainstream notice as a writer of intelligent books with western settings.

**Similar Reads:** Also by Kelton: *The Time It Never Rained* and *Six Bits a Day.*

**Subjects:** Texas; Cowboys; Cattle; Ranchers; Labor Strike; Spur Award 1971

## LeMay, Alan (1899–1964)

*The Searchers* (USA: 1954). Berkley 1992 (paper) 352pp. 0425134814 **J**
The white families settling in West Texas are perpetual victims of the Native Americans who inhabit the land. When Comanches slaughter a settler family and take the daughters captive, the uncle and stepbrother of the girls begin a search that becomes an obsessive quest lasting for years. Amos Edwards hates the Comanches; Martin Pauley loves the young girls they are trying to save.

A suspenseful opening grabs readers and propels them through this tough-minded, angry story. Excellent writing makes this a surefire adventure tale winner; readers will find great descriptive writing of the coziness of home and the loneliness of the plains.

**Film/Video/DVD:** *The Searchers* (1956) is a John Wayne classic directed by John Ford.

**Similar Reads:** *The Unforgiven* is another fine Western story by Alan LeMay.

**Subjects:** Texas; Indian Territory; Native Americans; Indian Captives; Chase; Revenge; Family; Uncles

## McMurtry, Larry (1936–)

🌿 *Lonesome Dove* (USA: 1985). Pocket 1988 (paper) 960 pp. 067168390X **J**

The 1800s are winding down, and the era of the cowboy and the open range is coming to an end. Old trail friends, business partners, and ex–Texas Rangers, Woodrow Call and Augustus McCrae—two men who couldn't be more different from one another—decide to make one more cattle drive from Texas to Montana. Along the way, their paths cross with Clara Allen, Gus's old love; the wicked gambler, Jake Spoon; ex-slave Josh Deets; the evil Indian, Blue Duck; lovely dancehall girl Lorena; Newt, the orphaned son of a whore they all knew; their friend Pea Eye Parker; and dozens of other colorful characters. Lonesome Dove is the Texas town in which the story starts—a dry, dusty town as forsaken as its name.

A long novel with many characters and various subplots, it's almost a step back toward the tradition of the Victorian novel. But this is a totally absorbing read with a plot that propels the reader through the story, a masterful evocation of setting, time, and place and well-delineated characters you come to care about.

**Audio:** Phoenix Audio cassette 1590400453. Read by Lee Horsley. Books on Tape. Read by Wolfram Kandinsky.

**Film/Video/DVD:** *Lonesome Dove* (1989) is a beloved TV miniseries with Robert Duvall and Tommy Lee Jones in the lead roles.

**Similar Reads:** *Dead Man's Walk* and *Comanche Moon* are the prequels to *Lonesome Dove*. *Streets of Laredo* is the final story in the series.

**Subjects:** Texas; Cowboys; Cattle Drive; Texas Rangers; Pulitzer Prize 1986; Spur Award 1985

## Portis, Charles (1933–)

*True Grit* (USA: 1968). Overlook Press 2003 (paper) 224 pp. 1585673692 **J Q**

Two memorable characters meet in this novel: fourteen-year-old Mattie Ross, indomitable and righteous, determined to avenge the death of her father; and crusty middle-aged Rooster Cogburn, U.S. marshal, "a pitiless man, double tough" who decides to help her. They, along with Texas Ranger LeBoeuf, travel into Oklahoma Indian territory during a harsh winter to track down the evil and cowardly Tom Chaney, the man who shot Mattie's father.

This is a somewhat forgotten novel, a best seller in its day. It is a fast-paced read with lots of action, humor, and a lively young protagonist.

> **Film/Video/DVD:** John Wayne finally won an Oscar for his portrayal of Rooster Cogburn in *True Grit* (1969).
>
> **Similar Reads:** *The Searchers* by LeMay is another epic Western chase story.
>
> **Subjects:** Arkansas; Oklahoma; Indian Territory; Revenge; Chase; Fathers and Daughters; Humor

## Schaefer, Jack Warner (1907–1991)

*Shane* **(USA: 1949).** Laurel Leaf 1983 (paper) 160 pp. 0553271105 **J Q**

When enigmatic Shane rides into the lives of Wyoming homesteaders the Starretts, young Bob Starrett finds a hero to worship. Shane seems like a gunfighter, but he doesn't carry a gun. The conflict between settlers fencing their property and ranchers needing the open land for their cattle to graze becomes the crux of this story told through Bob's reminiscences.

Schafer crafted a classic Western with his straightforward prose and his vivid depiction of character in the rapidly disappearing West.

> **Film/Video/DVD:** *Shane* (1953) with Alan Ladd as Shane and Jack Palance as the bad guy, was directed by George Stevens.
>
> **Similar Reads:** *Monte Walsh* is Schaefer's other novel about the waning years of cowboys; Wister's *The Virginian* has another enigmatic Western hero.
>
> **Subjects:** Wyoming; Gunfighters; Settlers and Pioneers; Coming of Age; Fathers and Sons; Family

## Twain, Mark (1835–1910)

*Roughing It* **(USA: 1872).** Signet 1994 (paper) 448pp. 0451524071 **J**

Tall tales, colorful characters, vivid descriptions, and adventure stories are all included in Mark Twain's account of his years in the Wild West. From St. Louis to Nevada, San Francisco to Virginia City, and all the way to Hawaii, Twain is the innocent.

> **Audio:** Recorded Books cassette 1556904495. Read by Norman Dietz.
>
> **Film/Video/DVD:** *Roughing It* was made for TV in 2002.
>
> **Similar Reads:** Twain provided similar comic narratives of his visit to Europe in *Innocents Abroad* and *A Tramp Abroad* and about his years working on riverboats in *Life on the Mississippi*. Fans of Twain's comic outlook, raucous prose, and view on the American experience will want to read *The Adventures of Huckleberry Finn* and *The Adventures of Tom Sawyer* as well.
>
> **Subjects:** Nevada; Silver Mines; Journalism; Autobiographical Novel; Coming of Age; Travel; Humor

## Wister, Owen (1860–1938)

*The Virginian* (USA: 1902). Signet 2002 (paper, 100th Anniversary Edition) 400 pp. 0451528328 **J**

Molly Stark Wood arrives in Medicine Bow, Wyoming, to teach. Almost immediately, she encounters the mysterious Virginian, a strong, silent cowboy with an unshakable sense of honor.

*The Virginian* created the model that many successful Westerns follow: the landscape as an element of the story; a noble, individualistic hero; a pretty girl from the East; frontier violence and frontier justice; and the encroaching of civilization on a land and a way of life that is unfettered.

> **Audio:** Books in Motion cassette 1556863535. Read by Gene Engene.

> **Film/Video/DVD:** *The Virginian* was made into a film in 1929 and 1946 produced as a TV movie in 2000 with Bill Pullman and Diane Lane.

> **Subjects:** Wyoming; Romance; Cowboys; Ranchers; Teachers; Justice

# Gilded Age

Between the Civil War and the First World War, the United States underwent an economic expansion during which huge fortunes were made through rapid industrialization, exploitation of labor, and lack of government regulations. The same fortunes were ostentatiously spent as "society" became enamored of status and displays of wealth. Both sides of the coin—the glamour and the oppression—are represented in the stories in this section.

## Doctorow, E. L. (1931–)

🌺 *Ragtime* (USA: 1975). Plume Books, 1997 (paper) 270pp. 0452279070 **S**

Set in New York State and beginning around 1906, the plot of *Ragtime* is secondary to the tour de force display of distinctive narrative style and historical compendium. Both intimate and grand, *Ragtime* sets the personal story of a well-to-do family against the national backdrop of early-twentieth-century history, allowing Doctorow to synthesize fictional characters and situations with historical people and events—Mother, Father, and the Little Boy intersect with Houdini, Emma Goldman, Booker T. Washington, Freud, Commander Peary, Mathew Henson, J. P. Morgan, and many others. Immigration, capitalism, workers' rights, women's roles, racism, and socialism are some of the issues raised in this fascinating and unique book.

> **Audio:** Airplay Publishing cassette 1885608276. Read by the author.

> **Film/Video/DVD:** *Ragtime* (1981) the impressive cast included James Cagney in his last film role. Also turned into a critically acclaimed Broadway musical in 1998 nominated for the Best Musical Tony award (it lost to *The Lion King*).

**Similar Reads:** Other books by Doctorow include *Loon Lake, The Book of Daniel, World's Fair,* and *Billy Bathgate.* All of Doctorow's books are fascinating, rich novels that look at American life in the last 150 years.

**Subjects:** New York, 1906; Family; African Americans; Social Issues

## Dreiser, Theodore (1871–1945)

*Sister Carrie* **(USA: 1900).** Signet Classics 2000 (paper) 512pp. 0451527607 <u>S</u>

Carrie Meeber comes to the city to live with her sister and brother-in-law and earn money. The only work she can find is in a factory. The hours are long, the work is tedious, and Carrie knows she can do better. To put it politely, Carrie becomes a kept woman. First her companion is the salesman Charlie Drouet, a good natured, good-time guy. Through Charlie, Carrie meets George Hurstwood, an elegant older man who falls for Carrie and destroys his own life to have her.

American naturalism at its finest, Dreiser's work is also an indictment of harsh labor conditions and the lack of options for women in his times. This book was a shocker in its day because it depicts a woman who takes the wrong path, destroys a man, and doesn't suffer for it. The social, economic, and psychological descent of Hurstwood is powerful writing.

**Audio:** Books on Tape 0736637001. Read by Rebecca Burns

**Film/Video/DVD:** *Carrie* (1952) is a melodrama with Jennifer Jones and Laurence Olivier.

**Similar Reads:** Wharton's *House of Mirth* depicts another turn-of-the-century heroine struggling to survive alone. *Nana* by Zola gives us the portrait of another man-eater.

**Subjects:** Chicago 1880s; Urban Realism; Independence; Actors; Labor; Poverty

## James, Henry (1843–1916)

*The Portrait of a Lady* **(USA: 1881).** Modern Library 2002 (paper) 640pp. 0375759190 <u>S</u>

Isabel Archer, an independent and intelligent young American woman, is taken to Europe by her aunt, Mrs. Touchett. There she meets her cousin, wise and caring Ralph Touchett, who becomes her greatest ally. She meets his friend Lord Warburton, who promptly falls in love with her. Unfortunately, she also meets the wicked, narcissistic Gilbert Osmond and his mysterious companion, Madam Merle. Will Isabel forsake her valued independence for a marriage to Gilbert when she already refused her compatriot Caspar Goodwood and the aristocrat Lord Warburton?

Independence versus convention, proper behavior versus actual happiness, democracy versus aristocracy, the individual in relation to society, and American innocence and naiveté versus European decadence and sophistication—James's ongoing themes—are all epitomized in this novel. James's characters inhabit a world of leisure and wealth where behaving properly in society is the most important thing. His characters and their relationships are subtly and meticulously drawn, their actions and motivations are the drama. James appeals to readers interested in the psychology of character who are able to decode his carefully placed, precisely crafted details of human behavior. James is an acknowledged master of English prose; his elegant, leisurely pace and meandering sentences are a challenge to some but a delight to others. *Portrait of a Lady* is a tragedy of character that expresses a mature worldview; it is James at the peak of his stylistic powers and best for readers with the patience and sophistication to appreciate it.

> **Audio:** Blackstone Audio cassette 0786108991. Read by Nadia May.

> **Film/Video/DVD:** *Portrait of a Lady* (1996) with Nicole Kidman was directed by Jane Campion.

> **Similar Reads:** For an easier interaction with Henry James, try *Daisy Miller*. James's friend Edith Wharton also wrote about the upper classes at the turn of the century; try *The House of Mirth* and *The Age of Innocence*.

> **Subjects:** London; Italy; Heiress; Marriage; Wealth; Romance; Family; Family Inheritance; Society; Independence

## Tarkington, Booth (1869–1946)

🎗 *The Magnificent Ambersons, The* **(USA: 1918).** Modern Library 1998 (paper) 288pp. 0375752501 **S**

> George Amberson Minifer is an obnoxious and spoiled child who grows up to be an arrogant and insufferable young man. When his still youthful, widowed mother is courted by a former suiter, the now wealthy automobile inventor Eugene Morgan, George does everything he can to prevent the match. All the while, George must deal with his own feelings for Morgan's daughter, Lucy. This is a novel of character and setting. It is a social commentary on the decline of a slow-paced way of life that was supported by inherited wealth as industry, technology, and self-made men, in the form of Eugene Morgan, advance and overtake it.

Tarkington's specialty was middle-class life in the American Midwest at the turn of the twentieth century. His novels are a slice of life from that time and place. Tarkington was a very popular writer who never crossed into the upper echelon of "classic" authors like his contemporaries Henry James or Edith Wharton.

> **Film/Video/DVD:** Orson Welles filmed this famous book as his follow-up movie to *Citizen Kane*. *The Magnificent Ambersons* (1942) is famous in film history because when Welles was out of the country, the studio savagely edited and reshot the film to make it shorter and give it an upbeat ending. A television movie by A&E in 2001 follows Welles's original script.

> **Similar Reads:** *Alice Adams* is Tarkington's other classic, still read today. More chroniclers of early-twentieth-century American include Sinclair Lewis, William Dean Howells, Edith Wharton, and Henry James.

> **Subjects:** American Midwest; Wealth; Family; Progress; Inheritance; Pulitzer Prize 1919

## Wharton, Edith (1862–1937)

🔖 *The Age of Innocence* (USA: 1920). Tor 1998 (paper) 336pp. 0812567102; Scribner 1998 (paper) 380pp. 0684842378 <u>S</u>

Elegant writing smoothes biting satire in this graceful novel about society's control over its members. The society in question is Old New York, the upper echelon of the privileged super rich in New York City in the 1880s. Newland Archer is set to marry the lovely and seemingly docile May Welland. When her cousin, the mysterious Countess Olenska, returns to New York after leaving a bad marriage in Europe, Newland is attracted to the tragic and exotic countess. Newland and the countess are kindred spirits. But May proves to be made of stern stuff, and the society that created her—not primitive, but surely tribal—rallies to her aid, leaving Newland and the countess no chance for a life together. After all, what does love matter when appearances are at stake? Surely elegance and good form matter more than what is in the heart.

Wharton gave us insights into the upper-class society of which she was a member. Surprisingly, Wharton was also famous as an expert on interior design, who advocated simplicity and a break from the Victorian clutter with which she grew up.

**Audio:** Blackstone Audio cassette 0786104430. Read by Nadia May.

**Film/Video/DVD:** *The Age of Innocence* (1993) was directed by Martin Scorsese and starred Daniel Day Lewis, Michelle Pfeiffer, and Winona Ryder.

**Similar Reads:** Wharton's *House of Mirth*; James's *Portrait of a Lady* and *Daisy Miller*, *The Magnificent Ambersons* by Tarkington; *The Forsyte Saga* by Galsworthy.

**Subjects:** New York; Relationships; Marriage; Family; Scandal; Satire; Humor; Society; Pulitzer Prize 1921

*The House of Mirth* (USA: 1905). Signet Classics 2000 (paper, 100th Anniversary Edition) 368pp. 0451527569 <u>S</u>

Lily Bart is a beautiful and gracious woman in "society" in New York at the beginning of the 1900s. With no money of her own and her only family being an aunt who disapproves of her, Lily knows she must marry to ensure her own economic survival. But she rebelliously destroys every chance she has to make an advantageous marriage and secure her future. The descent of Lily Bart is one of the most tragic stories in American literature

**Audio:** Recorded Books 1419359533. Read by Barbara Caruso.

**Film/Video/DVD:** *House of Mirth* (2000) is a faithful big-screen adaptation with Gillian Anderson as Lily Bart.

**Similar Reads:** Wharton's other classic about New York society is *The Age of Innocence*. *Portrait of a Lady* by Henry James, Dreiser's *Sister Carrie,* and *The Awakening* by Kate Chopin all depict the limited choices offered to women in America at the turn of the century.

**Subjects:** New York; Society; Wealth; Poverty

# Jazz Age

The era between the World Wars saw a loosening of social conventions with innovations such as jazz, movies, the automobile, and expanding rights for women.

## Dos Passos, John (1896–1970)

### USA Trilogy (USA: 1938). S
Referred to as a kaleidoscope, a panorama, and an epic, USA is a trilogy about America in the early part of the 1900s. It is a massive work in which Dos Passos strove to create a different way to tell a story. Using new literary techniques such as the "camera eye," "newsreels" that depict public events, stream of consciousness; ironic biographies of famous people, and character episodes that follow the stories of various Americans, Dos Passos presented the reader with a new fictional experience.

Well educated, born to wealth but with socialist sympathies, Dos Passos was a member of the famous Lost Generation that included Hemingway and e. e. cummings.

*42nd Parallel* **(1930) Mariner Books.** (Houghton Mifflin) 2000 448pp. 0618056815

*1919* **(1932).** Mariner Books (Houghton Mifflin) 2000 464pp. 0618056823

*Big Money* **(1936).** Mariner Books (Houghton Mifflin) 2000 528pp. 0618056831

   **Similar Reads:** Dos Passo's other classic work is *Manhattan Transfer.*

   **Subjects:** America; Cities; Twentieth Century; Labor; Business; World War I; Capitalism; Social Issues

## Fitzgerald, F. Scott (1896–1940)

*Great Gatsby* **(USA: 1925).** Scribner 1995 (paper) 240pp. 0684801523 S
   Nick Carraway narrates this story of the tragic events that take place near New York in the summer of 1922. It is the height of the Jazz Age, a time filled with raucous all-night parties, free-flowing bootleg liquor, shady deals, and idle, "careless" people such as beautiful Daisy Buchanan, whose voice "sounds like money"; violent, aggressive, ignorant Tom Buchanan; phony and arrogant Jordan Baker; and mysterious, romantic Jay Gatsby, who is in love with a dream that will destroy him.

   *The Great Gatsby* vies with *Huckleberry Finn* for the title of the "Great American Novel." It is a must read for its portrayal of Jazz Age America, for Fitzgerald's precise and poetic prose, and his depictions of the wealthy and powerful but ultimately shallow and unhappy people who think they are living the American Dream.

   **Audio:** Recorded Books cassette 1556902050; CD 1402523076. Read by Frank Muller.

**Film/Video/DVD:** *The Great Gatsby* (1974) starring Robert Redford and Mia Farrow; a 2001 TV movie by A&E starred Toby Stephens and Mira Sorvino.

**Similar Reads:** For a different look at New York in the 1920s, read John Dos Passos *Manhattan Transfer*; Fitzgerald's short stories collected in *Babylon Revisited and Other Stories* (Scribner 1996) make a good complement to *Gatsby* as does Fitzgerald's first novel *This Side of Paradise*. Also read Dorothy Parker, *The Portable Dorothy Parker* (Penguin, 2006).

**Subjects:** New York; Long Island; 1920s; Wealth; Marriage; Corruption

# The Great Depression

The stock market crash of 1929 triggered a financial crisis in America that lasted a decade and contributed to a worldwide economic depression. At the same time, ecological conditions in the Midwest following years of drought and poor farming techniques created a Dust Bowl in which nothing would grow and farmers were forced into bankruptcy. During this time—in the 1930s—banks failed, businesses closed, industrial production stagnated, there was no work, people were unemployed, and the entire nation, so accustomed to prosperity, struggled to survive. Novels about this era depict the hardships, sacrifices, and courage of Americans in this trying time.

## Hunt, Irene (1907–2001)

*No Promises in the Wind* (USA: 1970). Berkley 2002 (paper) 192pp. 0425182800 **M** Teen

The setting is Chicago, winter of 1932, in an America held captive by the Great Depression. Grown men are out of work, families are struggling to eat, people are desperate and afraid. To escape anger and hunger at home, fifteen-year-old Josh leaves, and his ten year-old brother Joey, frail but tough, goes with him. On the road, they struggle against hunger, cold, the masses of other vagrants and the enmity of communities that cannot absorb any more poor hungry tramps. A hitchhiked ride introduces them to Lonnie, a kind man who helps them get to New Orleans where Josh finds work playing the piano with a carnival. But times are hard for the carnival too, and Josh and Joey end up back on the road where Josh will experience the value of loyalty, feel the confusion of first love, develop political awareness, and achieve the maturity to forgive.

Irene Hunt was writing intelligent books with young adult protagonists before the YA genre existed. *Across Five Aprils* and *Up a Road Slowly* are her other classics. Her books seem staid and sedate compared with today's colorful and energetic YA fiction, but her novels are well-crafted historical stories that realistically depict a time in America's history and the struggles of regular teens to understand life and their place in it.

**Similar Reads:** Other YA classics set in the Depression era are *Bud, Not Buddy,* the 2000 Newbery Medal winner by Christopher Paul Curtis; *Out of the Dust,* the 1998 Newbery Medal winner by Karen Hesse; *A Long Way from Chicago,* a 1999 Newbery Honor book, and *A Year Down Yonder* the 2001 Newbery Medal winner both by Richard Peck.

**Subjects:** Great Depression; Family; Brothers; Fathers and Sons; Poverty; Coming of Age

## Steinbeck, John (1902–1968)

🌿 *The Grapes of Wrath* (**USA: 1939**). Penguin Books 2002 (paper, John Steinbeck centennial edition) 455pp. 0142000663 <u>S</u>

Forced to leave their foreclosed Oklahoma tenant farm, the members of the extended Joad family pack their belongings onto a dilapidated old truck and travel west toward the promise of work in California. Along Route 66, thousands of other destitute families are also fleeing the Depression era Dust Bowl. The long trip and the situation they find in California create an American *Odyssey*. Tom Joad is the moral center of the book even though he is a murderer; Ma Joad is the pillar of earthy strength that keeps the family from imploding.

Steinbeck struck a nerve with his contemporary story of oppression, poverty, discrimination, injustice, and labor conditions. He depicted the hostility of Americans to one another and expressed sympathy for the dispossessed at a difficult time in American history. A book that is consistently found on Challenged and Banned lists because of its raw portrayal of life.

**Audio:** Penguin Audiobooks cassette 0140868445. Read by Dylan Baker.

**Film/Video/DVD:** *The Grapes of Wrath* (1940): Henry Fonda played Tom Joad in the memorable black-and-white film.

**Similar Reads:** For more Steinbeck, try *Of Mice and Men, The Pearl,* and *The Red Pony.*

**Subjects:** Oklahoma California; Poverty; Great Depression; Migrant Labor; Workers; Family; Frequently Challenged; Pulitzer Prize 1940

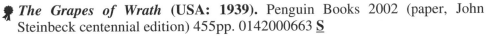

# Urban Realism and the Growth of City Life

As Americans left the farms and moved to the cities, a new range of problems arose.

## Arnow, Harriette (1908–1986)

*The Dollmaker* (**USA: 1954**). Harper Perennial 2003 (paper) 625pp. 0060529342. <u>S</u>

Gertie Nevels wants to raise her family on her own farm in Kentucky where they can live a self-sustaining, rural life. But it is war time, America needs industrial workers, and her husband Clovis insists on taking the family north to Detroit where he can work in the factories. Gertie's children, Clytie, Enoch, Reuben, Cassie, and Amos struggle to adjust to the city and have varying degrees of success. Through it all, Gertie endures.

This is a story full of tragedy that depicts a conflict that destroys a family—traditional rural life versus urban industrialism.

**Film/Video/DVD:** *The Dollmaker* (1984) was a fine TV production starring Jane Fonda.

**Similar Reads:** Arnow's other Kentucky books: *Mountain Path* and *Hunter's Horn* are similar in theme and locale. *The Jungle* is another novel about cultural assimilation. For a story set among the poor mountain people of Appalachia, read *Christy* by Catherine Marshall.

**Subjects:** Appalachia 1940s; Kentucky; Detroit; Family; Poverty; Labor; Strong Heroine

## Petry, Ann (1911–1997)

*The Street* **(USA: 1946).** Mariner Books 1998 (paper) 448pp. 0395901499 <u>S</u>

Lutie Johnson is trying to make a living and raise her son. She is a proud woman, educated, willing to work, and determined to fight for a chance for her son to lead a good life. But as an African American woman in Harlem in the 1940s, the odds are against her. Because she is beautiful, people think she is a prostitute. Because she has to work, it is hard to find the time to get more education. Because of the segregation of her people, it is hard to find a safe, clean apartment. She knows that the influence of the street on her son will doom him to a life of menial jobs and poverty thinking. And her neighbors, oppressed in their own ways, make it hard for her to break out of the grinding poverty she sees all around her.

This often-overlooked classic is American realism at its best. For mature readers.

**Audio:** Recorded Books cassette 0788708511. Read by Lynne Thigpen.

**Similar Reads:** Try *Go Tell It on the Mountain* by James Baldwin or *Native Son* by Richard Wright.

**Subjects:** New York, Harlem 1940s; African Americans; Poverty; Racism; Family; Urban Realism; Mature Read

## Wright, Richard (1908–1960)

*Native Son* **(USA: 1940).** Perennial 1998 (paper) 528pp. 0060929804 <u>S</u>

Bigger Thomas is an angry and alienated young man. Growing up poor and black in Chicago during the depression, Bigger is trapped by racism and poverty, lack of education and opportunity, and his own anger and powerlessness. When he gets a job as chauffer to a rich white family, he begins to think things could change. But then his first night on the job turns tragic, and his panic and rage escalate, taking him to a place from which he cannot return.

Wright acknowledged his debt to the naturalism of authors such as Theodore Dreiser and Frank Norris. Gritty, urban, and violent, *Native Son* was one of the first books by an African American author to achieve critical and popular success. The rapid pacing, driving narrative (the events happen within a few days), and larger sociological issues raised make this story a forceful read.

**Audio:** Recorded Books cassette 0788721127; CD 1402515588. Read by Peter Francis James.

**Film/Video/DVD:** Filmed in 1951 with the author Richard Wright as Bigger and again in 1986; neither is a very successful adaptation.

**Similar Reads:** Two other big novels that present a crime and its implications are *An American Tragedy* and *Crime and Punishment.* Wright's semi-autobiographical book *Black Boy* is also a powerful read. Other authors who delineated the experiences of African Americans in midcentury America are James Baldwin, Ralph Ellison, Maya Angelou, Zora Neale Hurston, and Ernest Gaines.

**Subjects:** Chicago 1930s; African Americans; Racism; Poverty; Wealth; Mature Read; Frequently Challenged; Urban Realism; Social Issues

# World War I

Humankind had never seen a conflict like the First World War, 1914 to 1918—trench warfare fought in the mud where territory was gained and lost a few yards at a time, the introduction of machinery such as tanks and airplanes, aerial bombings, the use of chemical weapons and the deaths of more soldiers and civilians than in any previous war made this war the most brutal ever known.

## Remarque, Erich (1898–1970)

*All Quiet on the Western Front* **(Germany: 1929).** Ballantine Books 1987 (paper) 304pp. 0449213943 <u>S</u>

*All Quiet on the Western Front* is Erich Remarque's fictional depiction of the war he had fought in as a young man. With brutal intensity, Remarque gives us World War I through the experiences of Paul Baumer, an eighteen-year-old who enlists with his schoolmates in a surge of peer-pressure-induced patriotism. Paul soon understands the horrors of this war. Hunger, filth, fear, despair, and disillusionment are depicted in this universal story of the effect of war on a generation of young men. The underlying pacifism of this novel caused it to be burned by the Nazi's on the eve of the Second World War.

**Audio:** Recorded Books cassette 1556909608. Read by Frank Muller.

**Film/Video/DVD:** *All Quiet on the Western Front* (1930 and 1979).

**New Media:** www.firstworldwar.com is a site full of historical information about the era.

**Similar Reads:** For another young man's experience of war, read *The Red Badge of Courage* by Stephen Crane. Interested readers may want to seek out the famous poetry written as a reaction to the First World War; a good collection is Jon Stallworthy's *Great Poets of World War I.*

**Subjects:** Germany; Soldiers; Antiwar Novel; Coming of Age

## Hemingway, Ernest (1899–1961)

🎗 *A Farewell to Arms* **(USA: 1929).** Scribner 1995 (paper) 336pp. 0684801469 <u>S</u>

The personal lives of a man and a woman are set against the dramatic backdrop of war. Catherine Barkley, an English nurse, and Frederic Henry, an American ambulance driver, meet in Italy in the midst of the First World War.

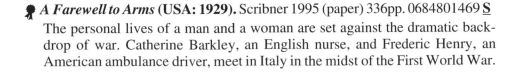

Their relationship begins playfully, but soon they realize they are deeply in love. They commit to one another on every level, leaving behind the madness of war to enter their own personal drama of love.

The immediacy Hemingway creates through his imagery and sparse prose and the depth of emotion he portrays have made this a powerful read for eighty years.

**Audio:** Books on Tape cassette 0736644318. Read by Alexander Adams.

**Film/Video/DVD:** *A Farewell to Arms* (1932) with Gary Cooper and Helen Hayes and 1957 with Rock Hudson and Jennifer Jones are two adaptations of the book.

**Similar Reads:** For more Hemingway, follow up with *For Whom the Bell Tolls.*

**Subjects:** Italy, Switzerland; War; Nobel Prize 1954; Nurses; Romance

## Trumbo, Dalton (1905–1976)

*Johnny Got His Gun* (USA: 1939). Bantam 1984 (paper) 256pp. 0553274325 **S**

Joe Bonham lies in a hospital bed, an injured solider. From there, he remembers his happy childhood; the struggles of his parents who were poor but provided well for Joe and his sister; his relationships with girls, especially his girlfriend, Kareen; his friendships with his buddies; and his decision to enlist for the war—a decision he now regrets. Joe will never recover from his injuries; he has no legs and no arms. He cannot see, hear, talk or smell; he has no face—a mask covers where his face should be. Years pass. Deep inner resources allow Joe to continue living in his mind; the entire novel takes place in Joe's head. He learns to count time, to sense the vibrations of people around him, to battle his recurring nightmares. Eventually he realizes he could communicate by tapping Morse code, and he undertakes an arduous struggle to be understood.

This is a powerful book filled with anger and anguish. We experience Joe's growing political awareness; his feeling's of betrayal about involvement in a war that had nothing to do with him; his growing disillusionment with noble causes and abstract ideas such as "democracy" and "liberty"; and his bitterness against modern medicine as he questions why he is kept alive.

It is worth noting the publishing history of this book. Written in the late 1930s, it was published at the very outbreak of World War II. Because it is essentially a pacifist novel, Trumbo agreed to let it go out of print until after the war. But by then Trumbo was caught up in the turmoil of the communist witchhunts. He was one of the Hollywood Ten, talented screenwriters who refused to testify, and was sentenced to a year in prison. This effectively ended his career, although Trumbo later wrote screenplays under various pseudonyms.

**Film/Video/DVD:** Although *Johnny Got His Gun* is a difficult story to translate to the screen, Dalton Trumbo wrote and directed a 1971 film.

**Similar Reads:** *The Red Badge of Courage, All Quiet on the Western Front,* and *Catch-22* are other novels about the effects of war. Two contemporary books about overwhelming disabilities are *The Diving Bell and the Butterfly* by Jean-Dominique Bauby and *Stuck in Neutral* by Terry Trueman, about a teen unable to communicate because of cerebral palsy

**Subjects:** Colorado; Los Angeles; France; Antiwar Novel; Hospitals; Soldiers; Disability; Mature Read

# World War II

The First World War, the so-called war to end all wars, was followed by one even more all-encompassing, the Second World War. All parts of the globe were embroiled in the conflicts from 1939 to 1945.

## The War

These are the stories of the men who fought the war, stories of battles on land and at sea. Interestingly, many of the books considered to be classic war novels ultimately express an antiwar sentiment.

### Heller, Joseph (1923–1999)

*Catch-22* (USA: 1961). Simon & Schuster 1996 (paper) 464pp. 0684833395 <u>S</u>

Captain Yossarian has one goal: to stay alive. Yossarian is a bomber pilot who doesn't want to fly any more missions, but to be excused from flying, he would need to declared be insane. But anyone who wants to stop the dangerous activity of flying bombing missions has to be sane, so he has to keep flying —he's in a catch-22 situation. As are the multitude of other characters in the darkly comic novel set in Italy during World War II.

Paradoxical and absurd humor have made this novel an antiwar classic and "catch-22" has become anonymous with bureaucratic circular logic that creates a no-win situation.

**Audio:** Books on Tape CD 0736690859. Read by Jim Weiss.

**Film/Video/DVD:** *Catch-22* director Mike Nichols captured the essence in his 1970 screen adaptation.

**Similar Reads:** Heller said he was influenced by *The Good Soldier Zweik* (1921) by Jaroslav Hasek, a satiric Czech antiwar novel set in World War I.

**Subjects:** Satire; Bomber Pilots; Antiwar Novel

### Hersey, John (1914–1993)

🌸 *A Bell for Adano* (USA: 1944). Vintage 1988 (paper) 288pp. 0394756959 <u>S</u>

Major Victor Joppolo has the job of helping the Sicilian town of Adano recover from the Second World War. The fighting has moved on, and Joppolo, aided by his practical sergeant, Borth, must bring order to the ruins, rehabilitate fascists, and help the people accept democracy. But what the town wants most is a bell. Mussolini's soldiers melted down their old church bell to make armaments. The desire of the people to replace their bell becomes Jopplo's mission too and leads him to clash with his superiors. With Joppolo, Hersey paints a sympathetic portrait of a man who wants to do the right thing.

This is a quiet novel full of humanity about the aftermath of war.

**Audio:** Recorded Books cassette 1556900422; CD 1419309757. Read by David Green.

**Film/Video/DVD:** Filmed in 1945.

**Similar Reads:** Hersey applied his journalist's eye, lucid prose, and humanistic view to other World War II incidents as well. *The Wall* is about the uprising in the Warsaw ghetto, and *Hiroshima* about the destruction of Japanese city.

**Subjects:** Italy; Democracy; Soldiers; Pulitzer Prize 1945

## Monsarrat, Nicholas (1910–1979)

*The Cruel Sea* **(England: 1951).** Burford Books, 2000 (paper) 509pp. 1580800467 **S**

Shipboard on the Atlantic Ocean is the setting for this long but engrossing novel. The inexperienced crew of the *Compass Rose,* a newly designed and commissioned ship, is charged with accompanying and protecting convoys of merchant ships that carry vital supplies across the Atlantic Ocean during the Second World War. The ocean teems with German submarines ordered to destroy the convoys and sink as many ships as possible. This novel puts you right in the middle of events. Brave behavior and cowardice, the fear and the boredom of war, the beautiful but violent sea, and the many dark nights spent watching for an enemy who can sink your ship and send you to your watery but fiery death are depicted with intensity and compassion.

Criticized for psychological superficiality and shallow depictions of women, this is nevertheless a gripping story that will appeal to fans of history, sea stories, and tales of war. It is fiction but based on Monsarrat's experiences in the war.

**Film/Video/DVD:** *The Cruel Sea* (1953) is an acclaimed British film with a documentary feel.

**Similar Reads:** Wouk's *Caine Mutiny* and *Run Silent Run Deep* by Edward Beach are related reads set in the Pacific. Two books that tell the Atlantic story from the German submarine point of view are *U-Boat 977* by submarine commander Heinz Schaeffer and *The Boat* by Buchheim.

**Subjects:** Sea Story; Naval Fiction; Atlantic Ocean; Submarines; Sailors

## Wouk, Herman (1915–)

🐦 *Caine Mutiny* **(USA: 1951).** Back Bay Books 1992 (paper) 560pp. 0316955108 **S**

The USS *Caine* is a battle-weary minesweeper patrolling the waters of the Pacific toward the final days of World War II. Willie Keith, a young man from a comfortable family, comes of age as he observes men and war and the fall of authority onboard the *Caine* when a new commander comes on board. Captain Queeg is a man obsessed with details such as tucked-in shirts and portions of strawberries. His struggle for control moves the story from the ocean battlefield to the courtroom as the drama of a court martial unfolds.

The compelling narrative pace and engrossing story make this dauntingly long book a gripping read. Written in a straightforward style that allowed it to be a best seller and with no pretense to symbolism or hidden meaning, this novel nevertheless raises many issues: the heroism of the common man; the duty owed to those in authority; and what constitutes leadership, honor, and patriotism.

**Film/Video/DVD:** Watch *The Caine Mutiny* (1954) with Humphrey Bogart playing Captain Queeg, who implodes before your eyes.

**Similar Reads:** Wouk's other great World War II epics are *The Winds of War* and *War and Remembrance.* For more troubled sea captains, read Melville's *Moby Dick*, Nordhoff and Hall's *Mutiny on the Bounty,* or *The Sea Wolf* by Jack London. Interested readers may want to explore Wouk's two-act play *The Caine Mutiny Court Martial,* adapted from the novel.

**Subjects:** Sea Story; Sea Captains; Pacific Ocean; Sailors; Mutiny; Mental Breakdown; Court-Martial; Naval Fiction; Pulitzer Prize 1952

## The Home Front

Civilians who stayed on the home front were affected by the war, too. Their stories show the impact war had on everyone.

### Grass, Gunter (1927–)

🎖 ***The Tin Drum*** **(Germany: 1959).** Vintage 1990 (paper) 592pp. 067972575x **S**
"Granted: I am an inmate of a mental hospital." With that intriguing and unsettling first line, we meet Oskar Matzerath the dwarf. Oskar deliberately stops growing when he is three years old in reaction to the insanity and violence in the adult world. Throughout his life, Oskar plays his tin drum to express his angst and uses his glass-shattering scream to impact the world around him. Although Oskar stays small, he doesn't stay young, and he doesn't retain the innocence of childhood.

This was a breakthrough novel in postwar Germany. Gunter Grass presented the recent German past as something to be faced and reckoned with. It is a surreal, satiric, and disturbing book for mature readers.

**Audio:** Recorded Books cassette 0788750151. Read by George Guidall.

**Film/Video/DVD:** *The Tim Drum* (1979), an R-rated German film, has a bold performance by the young actor playing Oskar.

**Similar Reads:** *Cat and Mouse* and *Dog Years* make up Grass's <u>Danzig Trilogy</u>. *Stones from the River* by Ursula Hegi. Reminiscent of Kafka or the magical realism of Garcia Marquez.

**Subjects:** Germany; Nazis; Dwarves; Mental Hospital; Mental Illness; World War II; Magical Realism; Mature Read; Nobel Prize 1999

### Greene, Bette (1934–)

***The Summer of My German Soldier*** **(USA: 1973).** Puffin 1999 (paper) 230pp. 014130636X **M** Teen **Q**
It is summer, the Americans are fighting the Nazi's in Europe, and Patty Bergen is twelve years old. She is smart, imaginative, and wants to be affec-

tionate, but her mother is cruel and disapproving, and her father is distant and physically abusive. Patty's main friend is Ruth, the family housekeeper. During this summer, German prisoners of war are brought to a POW camp outside Patty's small town in Arkansas. When one of the prisoners escapes, Patty shelters, feeds, and clothes him—and she begins to love him because he is so kind to her. With him, she feels attractive, intelligent, respected. But Patty is Jewish, Anton is an escaped POW, and their countries are at war.

An engaging story with a strong sense of place and historical moment. The vivid depiction of her family's cruelty and Patty's own inability to comprehend it are heartbreaking.

> **Audio:** Recorded Books cassette 078870365X; CD 1402523394. Read by Dale Dickey.
>
> **Film/Video/DVD:** *The Summer of My German Soldier* (1978) was TV movie with Kristy McNichol; Esther Rolle as Ruth won an Emmy for her performance.
>
> **Similar Reads:** There is a sequel, *Morning Is a Long Time Coming,* but it did not have the same critical or popular success as the first book. Greene also wrote *Philip Hall Likes Me, I Reckon Maybe.*
>
> **Subjects:** Arkansas, 1940s; Prisoners of War; Family; Abuse; Frequently Challenged

## Houston, Jeanne (1934–)

*A Farewell to Manzanar* (USA: 1974). Laurel Leaf (1983) 224pp. 0553272586 **J Teen**
Jeanne Wakatsuki was a young Japanese American girl in 1941 when Japan bombed U.S. naval ships in Pearl Harbor and forced America's entry into World War II. Shortly after Pearl Harbor, the U.S. government ordered all Japanese Americans in the western United States to leave their homes and possessions and move to internment camps. Purportedly, this was for the war effort and the safety of all Americans. The impact this move had on three generations of Japanese Americans is portrayed in *A Farewell to Manzanar.* Life in the camp is narrated by Jeanne as she depicts her stoic, hardworking mother; her tyrannical, proud father; and her older brothers and sisters as they all try to create lives for themselves, as well as her own experiences of the reality of coming back to society after the camp and struggling to fit in to mid-twentieth-century California with a Japanese face.

This is an accurate historical portrayal as well as a poignant coming-of-age classic that could generate discussion of gender roles, generational conflict, family dynamics, and ethnic identity as well as historical and political issues.

> **Film/Video/DVD:** *A Farwell to Manzanar* (1978) was filmed for TV.
>
> **Similar Reads:** For other stories about coming of age in difficult circumstances during the Second World War, read *Night* by Elie Wiesel; *Anne Frank: The Diary of a Young Girl*; and *The Upstairs Room* by Johanna Reiss. For other girls who experience being an outsider in a Caucasian culture, read *The House on Mango Street* by Sandra Cisneros and *The Bluest Eye* by Toni Morrison.
>
> **Subjects:** California; Internment Camps; Imprisonment; Prisoners of War; Japanese Americans; Coming of Age; Family

## Kosinski, Jerzy (1933–1991)

*The Painted Bird* **(USA: 1965).** Grove Press 1995 (paper) 234pp. 080213422X <u>S</u>

An unnamed boy with dark hair and dark eyes narrates his travels thorough the primitive, superstitious, and remote villages of Eastern Europe during the Second World War. His parents send him to the country for safety, but they do not return for him. From age six to twelve he wanders among the villages and peasant farms trying to belong but always an outsider, an outcast, and a victim deeply affected by the horrors he sees and the violence he experiences.

This is a sad tale about what happens when innocence encounters brutality. It is a harrowing read about the unspeakable cruelty humans inflict on one another.

**Similar Reads:** *Night* by Elie Wiesel.

**Subjects:** Eastern Europe, 1940s; Orphans; Fictional Autobiography; Cruelty; Abuse

## Magorian, Michelle (1947–)

*Good Night, Mr. Tom* **(England: 1982).** HarperTrophy 1986 (paper) 336pp. 006440174X <u>M</u> **Teen**

Willie Beach, a scared and abused little boy, is relocated from London to the English countryside during the Second World War when many children were sent to the countryside to spare them from the Blitz, the German bombings of London. Willie is sent to live with Tom, a gruff church caretaker who instinctively knows how to help this boy who has never had a friend, an adult who loved him, a birthday party, or a decent meal. Gradually Willie learns to run and play, to read and write, and to let his natural creative talents flourish. When his mother sends for him to return to London, the new and stronger Will goes to her. But he is swept back into her madness and abuse. With no way to contact Mister Tom, how can Will survive? And how can Mister Tom survive without someone to care for?

Told in a straightforward narrative, this is sentimental novel that effectively evokes an historical time and tells of the transformation of a boy during difficult times. (Readers may remember four other children evacuated to the country during the Blitz—Lucy and her siblings, who become rulers in <u>The Chronicles of Narnia</u>).

**Film/Video/DVD:** The *Masterpiece Theatre* presentation of *Goodnight Mister Tom* (1998) is good rendition of this touching story.

**Similar Reads:** Irene Hunt's *The Lottery Rose* is another affecting story of an abused child; Robert Westall's *Blitzcat* is also about Blitz-besieged London, and *Carrie's War* by Nina Bawden tells of a girl and her brother evacuated to Wales.

**Subjects:** London; Blitz; Family; Abuse; Country Life; Friendship

## The Holocaust

The persecution and murder of millions of Jews during the Second World War is a benchmark event in human history that illustrates the human ability to damage and destroy other human beings. Fictional representations of this time are often heartbreaking reading. An exploration of the Holocaust is a reading rite of passage through which many readers pass around the fifth grade.

### Keneally, Thomas (1935–)

🌟 *Schindler's List* **(Australia: 1982).** Touchstone 1993 (paper) 400pp. 0671880314 **S**
Oskar Schindler was a bon vivant, a charmer, an opportunist, and a profiteer. In 1930s Poland, he saw an opportunity to make money manufacturing enamelware mess kits for soldiers. But he needed workers, and the cheapest laborers available were Jewish prisoners of the Nazi regime. Schindler takes on the entire Nazi system when he realizes that he can save the lives of the people working for him. With help from the Jewish accountant Itzahk Stern, Schindler makes a list of the "crucial" workers needed to run his factory, all Jews, all intended for slaughter. Schindler and Stern boldly subvert the orders of the zealously sadistic Nazi Commandant Ammon Goeth, and what began as a moneymaking scheme becomes the redemption of one man's soul and the salvation of more than a thousand humans destined for annihilation. Schindler's compassion is ultimately as unexplainable as Goeth's cruelty.

Written as a novel but based on true characters and events, *Schindler's List* won Britain's prestigious literary prize, the Booker Award in 1982.

> **Film/Video/DVD:** Steven Spielberg directed the powerful 1993 Oscar-winning version of this novel.

> **Similar Reads:** Other dramatic Holocaust tales include *Night* by Elie Wiesel and *Anne Frank: The Diary of a Young Girl.*

> **Subjects:** Germany; Poland: World War II; Nazis; Jews; Concentration Camp; Mature Read; Booker Prize 1982

### Reiss, Johanna (1929–)

🌟 *The Upstairs Room* **(USA: 1972).** HarperTrophy 1990 (paper) 208pp. 006440370X **M Teen Q**
Like Anne Frank, this Anne is a young girl growing up in Holland in the years before World War II. In 1942, when the Germans invade, she and her sister go into hiding, first with one family, then with the Oostervelds—worried Dientje, aged Opoe, and defiant Johan who sees it as his duty to defy the Nazis and protect the girls even when the Germans use his house as a headquarters. A few weeks' stay becomes two years of living in the upstairs room and hiding from the hostile occupiers.

Less graphic and horrifying than books set in the concentration camps, this novel nevertheless captures the suspense, fear, uncertainty, and injustice of the times as well as the compassion of those who helped.

> **Audio:** Recorded Books cassette 078873525X; CD 0788742191. Read by Christina Moore.

**Similar Reads:** Reiss followed this book with *The Journey Back* about Anne's family after the war. The classic YA memoir of the Holocaust is *Anne Frank: Diary of a Young Girl*. *The Hiding Place* by Corrie Ten Boom, *Friedrich* by Hans Peter Richter, and *Alicia, My Story* by Alicia Appleman-Jurman are other accounts of the Holocaust years. More recommended YA novels include Lois Lowry's *Number the Stars* and Jane Yolen's *The Devil's Arithmetic* and *Briar Rose*.

**Subjects:** Holland; World War II; Nazis; Autobiographical Novel; Jews; Fictionalized Biography; Sisters; Family; Newbery Honor 1973

## Styron, William (1925–)

*Sophie's Choice* **(USA: 1979).** Vintage 1992 (paper) 576pp. 0679736379 <u>S</u>

Southerner Stingo moves to Brooklyn to become a writer. However, he is soon consumed by the drama of his neighbors, Sophie, a Holocaust survivor, and Nathan, her passionate, erratic lover.

Philosophical, narratively complex, prolix but compelling, Styron created memorable characters with this story for mature readers about the lasting trauma of the Holocaust.

> **Audio:** Chivers Audio Books cassette 0754084361. Read by William Hope.

> **Film/Video/DVD:** *Sophie's Choice* (1982) is a powerful film with Meryl Streep and Kevin Kline.

> **Subjects:** Poland; New York; World War II; Concentration Camps; Writers; Manic Depressive; Mental Illness; Coming of Age; Tragic Choices; Mature Read

## Uris, Leon (1924–2003)

*Exodus* **(USA: 1958).** Bantam 1983 (paper) 608pp. 0553258478 <u>S</u>

The founding of the modern state of Israel is told through fictional characters in this passionate novel. *Exodus* shows the aftermath of the Holocaust when masses of Jewish refugees were struggling to create a Jewish homeland in Palestine. Through flashbacks that establish each character, the reader relives the Holocaust, particularly the Warsaw Ghetto Uprising and life in the concentration camps.

All of Uris's books were best sellers, and they continue to engage readers. He creates compelling characters and storylines set against some of the most powerful historical moments of the twentieth century—Marines in World War II (*Battle Cry*), the Warsaw Ghetto uprising (*Mila 18*), the Berlin Airlift (*Armageddon*), and the Holocaust (*QB VII*). These novels are engrossing historical fiction that will tempt readers into further investigation of some of the most dramatic events of the modern era.

> **Film/Video/DVD:** *Exodus* (1960) directed by Otto Preminger stars Paul Newman.

**Similar Reads:** Another best seller that tells the history of Israel is *The Source* by James Michener.

**Subjects:** Palestine; Israel; Jews; World War II; Zionism

## Wiesel, Elie (1928–)

🐾 *Night* **(France: 1958).** Bantam 1982 (paper) 128pp. 0553272535 **J Q**

A young Jewish teen lives through a succession of Nazi concentration camps, barely surviving, all the while witnessing and experiencing unimaginable cruelty, inhumanity, and sorrow.

Words are inadequate to describe the sadness of *Night.* This is a short book that provides an immense psychological impact. A natural companion piece to *Night* is *Anne Frank: The Diary of a Young Girl.*

**Audio:** Audio Bookshelf cassette 1883332400. Read by Jeffrey Rosenblatt.

**Similar Reads:** *Dawn* and *The Accident* complete Wiesel's Night Trilogy. Art Spiegelman created two very unusual memoirs of the Holocaust, *Maus: A Survivor's Tale: My Father Bleeds History* and *Maus II: A Survivor's Tale: And Here My Troubles Began.* These graphic novels depict Jews as mice and Nazis as cats and relate the story of Spiegelman's parents during the Holocaust years.

**Subjects:** Germany; Jews; World War II; Concentration Camps; Fathers and Sons; Faith; Nobel Peace Prize 1986

# Family Sagas

Family sagas show the unfolding lives of an extended family depicted through several generations and set against a particular historical backdrop. These are generally long books that often have multiple volumes and typically an omniscient narrator who comments on the family's fortunes and foibles. Interestingly, all of the following authors have been awarded the Nobel Prize.

## Buck, Pearl S. (1892–1973)

🐾 *Good Earth* **(USA: 1931).** Pocket Enriched Classics 2005 (paper) 448pp. 1416500189 **S**

In prerevolutionary China, the ambitious Wang Lung and his patient, faithful wife Olan raise their family and prosper, despite hardships. The story opens on their wedding day and unfolds over the years through poverty, famine, success, good fortune, old age, and decline.

A poignant and powerful novel told in simple elegant prose, Buck was a prolific writer renowned for her lucid style influenced by the King James Bible. This is a story about China, family, and the universality of man's quest to improve his lot in life.

**Audio:** Recorded Books cassette 1556906714; CD 1402548303. Read by George Guidall.

**Film/Video/DVD:** *The Good Earth* (1937) is a classic black-and-white film.

**Similar Reads:** The story continues in *Sons* and *A House Divided*. Another Buck classic to try is *Imperial Woman* about China's last empress.

**Subjects:** China; Poverty; Family; Pulitzer Prize 1932; Nobel Prize 1938

## Galsworthy, John (1867–1933)

🌸 *The Forsyte Saga* (**England: 1933**). Touchstone 2002 (paper, movie tie in edition) 896pp. 0743245024 <u>S</u>

*The Forsyte Saga* is a grand soap opera about an extended family that values money and property more than each other. Jolly Forsyte disappoints his family when he abandons his young daughter and wife to the care of his father and runs off with the governess to lead a life as an artist. This action necessarily severs all ties to the prominent and proud Forsytes. Jolly's arrangement, made for love and not property, astonishes and offends the family and reverberates for generations among the self-satisfied Forsytes.

This is a large, realistic novel that is very engrossing as you come to know the characters and the post-Victorian world they live in. Galsworthy was a lucid, gracious stylist and a subtle ironist.

**Film/Video/DVD:** *The Forsyte Saga* (2003) *Masterpiece Theatre* adaptation is excellent.

**Subjects:** London; Family; Wealth; Inheritance; Property; Nobel Prize 1932

## Mann, Thomas (1875–1955)

🌸 *Buddenbrooks: The Decline of a Family* (**Germany: 1900**). Vintage 1994 (paper) 736pp. 0679752609 <u>S</u>

This social novel filled with the details of domestic life and an ironic point of view tells the story of four generations of the Buddenbrooks, an upper-middle-class German family—their prosperity and decline.

Thomas Mann depicted his society and the precarious role of the artist in many of his philosophically inclined works. He was a social critic and a strong advocate of humanity; he is second only to Goethe in importance in German literature.

**Similar Reads:** Another classic novel by Mann is the European coming-of-age story *The Magic Mountain*. His novellas *Tonio Kroger* and *A Death in Venice* are often recommended.

**Subjects:** Germany; Lubeck; Family; Nobel Prize 1929

## Marquez, Gabriel Garcia (1928–)

🌸 *One Hundred Years of Solitude* (**Colombia: 1970**). Perennial 2004 (paper) 464pp. 0060740450 <u>S</u>

Set in the past, in the fictional Colombian village of Macondo, this novel is about several generations of the Buendia family and the magical happenings that surround their lives.

This is perhaps the most famous novel written in the style of magical realism. In magical realism, logic doesn't matter, the fabulous and the marvelous happen right next to the mundane; time loses its meaning, rationalism is negated. It is a style of fiction that plays with the reader, yet all is related with total seriousness. *One Hundred Years of Solitude* is a challenging read, but also imaginative, enchanting, and memorable.

> **Similar Reads:** For variations on magical realism, read *Beloved, The Metamorphosis; The Master and Margarita;* books by Salman Rushdie; *House of the Spirits* by Isabel Allende; and *Like Water for Chocolate* by Laura Esquivel.

> **Subjects:** Colombia; Family; Small Town; Ancestors; Magical Realism; Mature Read; Nobel Prize 1982

## Steinbeck, John (1902–1968)

🌳 *East of Eden* **(USA: 1952).** Penguin USA 2003 (paper) 601pp. 0142004235 **S**

Is evil inherited? Must the sons duplicate the sins of the father—or, in this case, the mother? Are we free to choose our own moral destiny? The Trasks and the Hamiltons are families in the agricultural Salinas Valley of California at the beginning of the twentieth century. This is a story of how they got there and how they live. A strong sense of place is complemented by the memorable characters who play out Steinbeck's tale of good and evil: twins Cal and Aron Trask (think Cain and Abel); Cathy Ames, one of the most sociopathic characters in fiction; intelligent, philosophical Lee; sympathetic Abra, who first loves Aron but ends loving Cal; flawed Adam Trask; and genial, compassionate patriarch Samuel Hamilton.

This is a book for mature readers.

> **Film/Video/DVD:** *East of Eden* (1955) was James Dean's first film. In 1981, a TV miniseries starred Jane Seymour as Cathy.

> **Similar Reads:** Other books about grown-ups behaving badly are *Nana* and *Wuthering Heights.* Other American classics about good and evil include *The Scarlet Letter* and *Moby Dick.*

> **Subjects:** California 1860s to early 1900s; Brothers; Family; Betrayal; Jealousy; Frequently Challenged; Prostitution; Good and Evil; Mature Read; Nobel Prize 1962

# Victorian England

From 1837 to 1901, Queen Victoria ruled England and imposed on its society her views of how people should behave. Society was dominated by morality, manners, and a social façade that sometimes masked the human reality. During this time, Britain was the most powerful nation in the world with an empire that stretched across the globe. She was also a very rich nation, with wealth coming in from the empire and created by the rise of industry —the shift from agricultural lifestyles to factory work also typifies this era. The Victorian era was a time of fascinating contradiction. Many readers love to delve deeply into this world. Some of England's greatest and best-known writers are of the Victorian period— Kipling, Dickens, Thackeray, Eliot, Trollope, Hardy, and Wilkie Collins; poets such as Browning, Tennyson, and Arnold; and social thinkers such as John Stuart Mill, Charles

Darwin, and Thomas Carlyle. The books listed here provide a small cross-section of Victorian themes and stories. Because of the breadth of nineteenth-century English literature, Victorian novels appear in all of the genre chapters. For a complete listing consult the Index under "Victorian Novels."

## Burnett, Frances (1849–1924)

*The Secret Garden* (England: 1911). HarperTrophy 1998 (paper) 368pp. 006440188X **M Teen**

Mary Lennox starts this novel as one of the least likeable girls in fiction. She is bratty, bossy, and self-absorbed. When her mother and father die, she is sent from her home in colonial India to live with her only remaining relative, an aloof uncle in England. On the creepy, isolated Victorian estate of this mysterious uncle, she discovers an invalid cousin, a family of locals who befriend her, and an abandoned garden. Slowly Mary changes and affects all around her.

This is a story of transformation and rebirth that has been popular for almost one hundred years. Mary's adjustment to the cool gray climate of England, her growing friendships with Dickon and his family, her unexpected compassion for her cousin, and her mission of restoring the garden capture readers of all ages.

**Audio:** Recorded Books cassette 1556904657; CD 1402549954. Read by Flo Gibson.

**Film/Video/DVD:** *The Secret Garden* was produced in 1949 with Margaret O'Brien and Dean Stockwell. A lavish 1993 production was also made. Also the basis for a Broadway musical.

**Similar Reads:** *A Little Princess* and *Little Lord Fauntleroy* are Burnett's other enduring Victorian classics. Other memorable girl heroines can be found in *Little Women, Anne of Green Gables, A Girl of the Limberlost,* and *A Tree Grows in Brooklyn.*

**Subjects:** Victorian England; Orphans; Uncles; Family; Friendships; Illness; Gardens; Childhood Classics; Gentle Read

## Dickens, Charles (1812–1870)

*Oliver Twist* (England: 1837). Bantam 1982 (paper) 480pp. 0553211021 **J**

Raised in a workhouse, apprenticed to an undertaker, orphan and runaway, Oliver Twist becomes a little boy lost amid the crime and poverty of Victorian London. There his life takes a sinister turn when he is accepted into the family of thieves run by the colorful criminal mastermind, Fagin; runs afoul of Bill Sikes, one of the vilest men in literature with one of the ugliest dogs; loves pretty Nancy, a prostitute with a heart; and is friend to the optimistic pickpocket known as the Artful Dodger.

*Oliver Twist* is pure Dickens—outrageous characters and unlikely plot coincidences, rollicking humor and base pathos, sensationalism and sentimentality. This is a story for all ages. The Victorian prose with sentences that can go on for paragraphs takes patience on the part of a modern reader—but it's well worth the effort.

**Audio:** Blackstone Audio cassette 0786108614. Read by Nadia May.

**Film/Video/DVD:** *Oliver Twist* (2005) was directed by Roman Polanski and is a beautiful adaptation. The 1951 film directed by David Lean is memorable. Also recommended is the *Masterpiece Theatre* production made in 2000. The Broadway musical and later film *Oliver!* (1968) introduced many to the story of the little orphan boy who wanted more.

**Similar Reads:** No one does downtrodden Victorian orphans better that Dickens —*David Copperfield* and *Great Expectations* are further explorations of the theme.

**Subjects:** Victorian England; Orphans; Pickpockets; Poverty; Gangs

## Eliot, George (1819–1880)

*Middlemarch* **(England: 1871).** Signet Classics 2003 (paper) 912pp. 0451529170 **S**
Idealistic Dorothea Brooke is at the center of this expansive novel set in the fictional town of Middlemarch, England. Hoping to contribute to good works and social reform, Dorothea marries the aging scholar Casaubon, believing he will support her interests. She is mistaken and finds solace in the companionship of Casaubon's relative Ladislaw. Parallel to Dorothea's story is the tale of the idealistic young doctor, Lydgate, and his shallow, selfish wife Rosamund.

Many consider this novel the greatest English novel of all time because of its insightful depiction of the many levels of English society and the social web we all inhabit. George Eliot is the pen name of Marian Lewes, a prolific and influential female Victorian author.

**Audio:** Blackstone Audio 0786107251 (part 1), 078610726X (part 2). Read by Nadia May.

**Film/Video/DVD:** *Middlemarch* (1994), the *Masterpiece Theatre,* production does justice to the sprawling novel.

**Similar Reads:** Eliot also wrote *Silas Marner* and *The Mill on the Floss.* Elizabeth Gaskell is another Victorian author to explore; try *North and South* or *Wives and Daughters.*

**Subjects:** Victorian England; Doctors; Marriage; Society; Strong Heroine

*Silas Marner* **(England: 1861).** Bantam Classics 1981 (paper) 192 pp. 055321229X **J Q**
Silas Marner is a master weaver, a recluse, and a miser who lives only for his growing pile of gold—Silas Marner loves gold more than anything. One day a golden-haired child wanders into Marner's cottage. She wanders in on the same day that Silas discovers his gold is missing. Almost instantly, she replaces the gold in his affections, and he makes his life about caring for her. But revelations about her parentage cause distress.

A beautiful story of the redemptive power of love set in the English country in the first part of the 1800s.

**Audio:** Blackstone Audiobooks 0786100400. Read by Nadia May.

**Film/Video/DVD:** *Silas Marner* (1987) is an excellent *Masterpiece Theatre* adaptation starring Ben Kingsley as Silas.

**Subjects:** Victorian England; Gold; Family; Misers; Secrets; Gentle Read

## Hilton, James (1900–1954)

*Goodbye, Mr. Chips* (**England: 1934**). Little, Brown 2004 (paper) 144 pp. 0316010138 **J Q**

In 1870, Mr. Chipping arrives at Brookfield an upper-class English boys' school. He is there to teach Classics and to turn boys into gentlemen, but he soon learns what brutes little boys can be! Over the next sixty years Mr. Chipping evolves into beloved Mr. Chips and becomes the avatar of all that is good and noble at the school.

Very British in expressions, tone, and humor; overtly sentimental; and tinted with melancholy. If Chips's story doesn't leave you in a pool of your own tears, you have no heart. Readers who appreciate the traditions of Hogwarts may find Brookfield an interesting place.

> **Audio:** CSA Word (csaword.co.uk), cassette 1873859694. Read by Martin Jarvis.
>
> **Film/Video/DVD:** *Goodbye, Mr. Chips*—first adapted into a play, then made into a movie in 1939 that earned Robert Donat a Best Actor Oscar for his portrayal of Chips. Fine BBC productions in 1984 and 2003, and even a musical in 1969 with Peter O'Toole.
>
> **Similar Reads:** *To Serve Them All My Days* by R. F. Delderfield is another classic English school story, as are Thomas Hughes's *Tom Brown's School Days* and Kipling's *Stalky and Co.*
>
> **Subjects:** Victorian England; School Story; Schoolboys; Boarding School; Teachers and Students; Gentle Read

## Hughes, Thomas (1822–1896)

*Tom Brown's School Days* (**England: 1857**). Oxford University Press 1999 (paper) 406pp. 0192835351 **J**

Energetic, kind, and athletically inclined, Tom Brown is the new boy in school. At first the victim of the school's entrenched system of bullying, especially at the hands of his enemy Flashman, Tom eventually grows into a stellar boy.

This archetypal boy's school story takes place at the famous English school called Rugby when Thomas Arnold (the poet Matthew Arnold's father) was the benevolent and innovative headmaster. Famous for its condemnation of the bullying that was a prevalent part of the English boarding school tradition.

> **Film/Video/DVD:** *Tom Brown's School Days* has been produced in multiple versions, the newest of which is from British producer ITV (2005).
>
> **Similar Reads:** Try *Goodbye, Mr. Chips; To Serve Them All My Days* by R. F. Delderfield; and Kipling's *Stalky and Co.*
>
> **Subjects:** England; 1830s; School Story; Schoolboys; Boarding School; Bullies; Coming of Age

## Sewell, Anna (1820–1878)

***Black Beauty*** **(England: 1877).** Signet 2002 (paper) 240pp. 0451528654 **M**

Black Beauty, a proud and noble stallion, narrates the story of his life from his early days as a colt with his mother, to the happy days with his horse companions Ginger and Merrylegs at the gracious home of a country squire. He tells us about his years pulling a cab in busy, crowded London, and about the hardest time of his life as a carthorse hauling heavy loads when the overwork and abusive conditions almost kill him.

Sewell's only book, *Black Beauty* is sentimental, but animal lovers of any age should be acquainted with Beauty's story and Sewell's plea for animal rights. Also the depiction of Victorian society is very detailed.

> **Audio:** Recorded Books cassette 1556900554; CD 1402552300. Read by Flo Gibson.

> **Film/Video/DVD:** *Black Beauty* (1994) is a lovely film and very accurate to the book.

> **Similar Reads:** Other classic horse stories include Enid Bagnold's *National Velvet* and *My Friend Flicka* by Mary O'Hara. A similar story set in the American West is Will James's *Smoky the Cowhorse,* the 1927 Newbery Medal winner. Readers who love animal stories may want to read *Bambi, The Yearling, The Incredible Journey, All Creatures Great and Small, Old Yeller.*

> **Subjects:** Victorian England; Victorian London; Animal Story; Horses; Animal Cruelty; Childhood Classic; Gentle Read

# Russian Novels—Nineteenth Century

Nineteenth-Century Russian novels have a reputation as big, powerful works of fiction that paint a broad canvas and explore themes of depth and universal human interest. Depictions of family and society and a style marked by realism, multiple characters from different social levels, and several plot lines typify these challenging novels.

## Dostoevsky, Fyodor (1821–1881)

***Brothers Karamazov*** **(Russia: 1880).** Bantam 2003 (paper) 1072pp. 0553212168 **S**

Money, murder, family, faith, free will, justice, death—all the big ideas are explored in *The Brothers Karamazov.* Fyodor Karamazov is a despicable man, a wife abuser, a bad father, a seducer, a man who is vulgar, low, and crude. He is also a murder victim. The main suspects in his murder are his four sons, the Brothers Karamazov. First is Dimitry, a soldier and a passionate man much like his father; his mother left him an inheritance that Fyodor would not relinquish. There is Ivan, an intellectual, a young man full of doubt, a questioner of all things—he is perhaps the most troubled of the brothers because he thinks so much. Alyosha is the most sensitive brother. He is a monk who is kind, gentle, and serene, beloved by all who meet him. Finally, Smerdyakov, the youngest, unacknowledged son, worked as a servant for Fyodor. He suffers from epilepsy, seems mentally slow, and has a malicious temperament.

Reading Dostoevsky is a major undertaking. This is a book of ideas, and the plot and psychologically rich characters serve the philosophy that Dostoevsky wishes to explore. Dostoevsky's recurring theme of redemption through suffering is present in this weighty philosophical book considered to be one of the most important novels in all literature.

> **Audio:** Blackstone cassette 0786121831 (part 1), 0786121866 (part 2). Read by Frederick Davidson.

> **Film/Video/DVD:** *The Brothers Karamazov* (1958) features Yul Brenner, Claire Boom, and William Shatner and was directed by Richard Brooks.

> **Similar Reads:** Dostoevsky's other masterpiece is *Crime and Punishment.*

> **Subjects:** Russia; Family; Brothers; Fathers and Sons; Murder; Faith; Redemption; Free Will; Justice; Mature Read

## Gogol, Nicolai (1809–1852)

*Dead Souls* **(Russia: 1842).** Vintage 1997 (paper) 432 pp. 0679776443 **S**

Chichikov is a scoundrel. He travels through rural Russia from one wealthy estate to another buying the souls of dead serfs. He has an elaborate con planned to make himself a rich man. To get the humor here, you must know that wealthy landowners also "owned" the serfs that lived and worked on their land. The owners had to pay taxes on every soul on the estate, even on dead serfs, until the next census removed them from the roles. Lies, bribery, and the greed of the landowners pave the way for Chichikov's success.

This is a kind of *Odyssey* through Russian society (and through all of humanity) as Chichikov encounters various types of owners on estates that reflect their different personalities.

> **Similar Reads:** Gogol is well known for his short story "The Overcoat" and the comic play *The Inspector General*. Another nineteenth-century Russian "comedy," written by Ivan Goncharov, is *Oblomov* from 1859 about a very lazy aristocrat.

> **Subjects:** Russia Early 1800s; Serfs; Landowners; Greed; Anti-Hero; Satire; Humor

## Tolstoy, Leo (1828–1910)

*Anna Karenina* **(Russia: 1875).** Signet 2002 (paper) 960pp. 0451528611. **S**

Beautiful, vibrant Anna lives in a loveless marriage until she meets Vronsky, the dashing army officer. Will she defy societal expectations and conventions for a chance at love and self-fulfillment? The doomed love of Anna and Vronsky is just one thread in Tolstoy's brilliant tapestry depicting nineteenth-century Russian society. Levin, the country idealist who wants to create a better life for his serfs; Karenin, the cagey diplomat who prizes appearances over emotions; Dolly, mother to her children, trying to live with dignity as her husband has affairs with the governesses; wealthy and idle society swells; hardworking peasants who labor for their bread—Tolstoy included all aspects of society in his novels.

Tolstoy seemingly knew what it is like to be a girl at a ball, a soldier in debt, a serf laboring under the hot August sun, a woman in a loveless marriage, a man for whom things always work out well. He enters the mind of every character and explains their understanding of the world. Expansive, brilliant, and humane, Tolstoy is widely considered a literary genius.

**Audio:** Blackstone Audio, available in cassette and CD 0786183918 (part 1), 078618390X (part 2). Read by Nadia May.

**Film/Video/DVD:** The 2000 *Masterpiece Theatre* production of *Anna Karenina* is very good. The 1948 black-and-white classic with Vivien Leigh is romantic.

**New Media:** www.ltolstoy.com is an interesting Web site devoted to Tolstoy and his works.

**Similar Reads:** Tolstoy's other monster masterwork is *War and Peace*; other doomed nineteenth-century love affairs can be found in Flaubert's *Madam Bovary* and *The Awakening* by Kate Chopin.

**Subjects:** Russia 1800s; Marriage; Family; Adultery; Romance; Serfs; Landowners; Society; Soldiers

*War and Peace* **(Russia: 1869).** Modern Library 2002 (paper) 1424 pp. 0375760644 **S**

Simply stated, *War and Peace* is the story of Napoleon's 1812 invasion of Moscow shown through the lives of several Russian families. But it is truly so much more. This novel is panoramic, majestic, expansive, epic. Tolstoy includes every strata of society, no detail is too small, no emotion too mundane. To show the impact of history on individuals, Tolstoy uses hundred of characters, but through his main characters—Natasha, Pierre, and Andre—he shows us the growth of individuals as well as the historic sweep of events.

One of world literature's Big Books, this is a must read for serious book lovers, history buffs, Russian Literature fans, and anyone interested in the human condition.

**Audio:** Blackstone cassette 0786112514 (part 1), 0786112522 (part 2), 0786112530. Read by Frederick Davidson.

**Film/Video/DVD:** *War and Peace* (1956) is a simplified telling with Audrey Hepburn as Natasha, directed by King Vidor. There is also a 1968 Russia version that won the Best Foreign Film Academy Award.

**Similar Reads:** Tolstoy's other great depiction of Russian society is *Anna Karenina*. Pasternak's *Dr. Zhivago* is another Russian epic set during tumultuous times. Mitchell's *Gone with the Wind* is another big book about society and war.

**Subjects:** Russia Early 1800s; War of 1812; Napoleonic Era; Society; Family; Soldiers

## Turgenev, Ivan (1818–1883)

*Fathers and Sons* **(Russia: 1862).** Modern Library 2001 (paper) 228pp. 0375758399 **S**

Generational conflict and class differences play out when Arkady brings his friend and classmate, Bazarov, home to visit his father's estate of Marino. Bazarov, a medical student, would-be revolutionary, and self-proclaimed nihilist, clashes with Arkady's uncle Pavel, a man who believes in an aristocratic standard of behavior. Although

Arkady eventually finds bourgeois domestic peace with Katya, Bazarov continues to be full of discord.

Turgenev was a gentle and lyrical novelist who depicted the pre-revolutionary Russia he loved and the universal conflict between generations as the old gives way and the new struggles to assert itself. His focus on characters and lack of violent action make this a subdued novel, although not without tension and conflict.

**Audio:** Blackstone Audio cassette 0786105127. Read by Walter Zimmerman.

**Subjects:** Russia 1859; Family; Fathers and Sons; Nihilism; Friendship; Generational Differences; Gentle Read

# Russia—Twentieth Century

The Soviet Era of Russia's history from 1917 to 1991 was a time of censorship, oppression, and persecution of ideas that differed from the party line. Novels from this era show the frustration and futility of struggling against a society where the individual has no identity.

### Bulgakov, Mikhail (1891–1940)

*The Master and Margarita* (**Russia: 1966**). Penguin 2001 (paper) 432pp. 0141180145 **S**

Three intertwining stories make up the complex yet comic *Master and Margarita*. Over the limited time span of four days, Wednesday to Sunday in Holy Week, the devil visits Moscow accompanied by several assistants, including a big black cat; Margarita searches for her lover, a writer called the Master; and Christ, called Yeshua, is condemned to be crucified by Pilate in ancient Jerusalem.

Written in the 1930s but not published until the 1960s, this is a multifaceted, mind-bending work that demands an open-minded approach. Bulgakov used fantastic elements to create a unique work that criticizes Soviet society as well as universal vices such as corruption and cowardice.

**Audio:** Blackstone Audio cassette 0786105127. Read by Walter Zimmerman.

**Subjects:** Russia; Soviet Union; Satan; Good and Evil; Satire; Communism; Humor; Mature Read; Magical Realism

### Koestler, Arthur (1905–1983)

*Darkness at Noon* (**Hungary: 1940**). Bantam 1984 (paper) 224pp. 0553265954 **S**

For years Rubashov had nightmares about the dreaded knock on the door in the middle of the night. Then one night, the knock is real, yet Rubashov is actually relieved. He is taken to a prison where he is interrogated and forced to admit to crimes he didn't commit. At first, Rubashov remains arrogant and defiant; but he comes to understand that he can continue to serve his party loyally by confessing to the imaginary crimes and accepting his own execution because that is what the party leaders now want from him.

This story of an aging revolutionary who becomes another victim of the Revolution is an intense and disturbing novel. Although never explicitly stated, this is a novel about the Moscow Show Trials of the 1930s when the old-guard Bolsheviks whom Stalin perceived to be threats to his power were eliminated.

**Similar Reads:** Try *One Day in the Life of Ivan Denisovich* by Solzhenitsyn and *The Trial* by Kafka. Two other books that raise the issue of totalitarianism are *Animal Farm* and *1984,* both by George Orwell.

**Subjects:** Russia; Soviet Union Communism; Prisoners; Mature Read

## Pasternak, Boris (1890–1960)

🏅 *Dr. Zhivago* (**Russia: 1957**). Pantheon 1997 (paper) 592pp. 0679774386 <u>S</u>

Religious in spirit, poetic in tone, epic in its setting, intimate in its love story, *Dr. Zhivago* is one of the grandest novels ever written. Compassion and the power of the individual to act kindly even in the midst of historical chaos are at the core of *Dr. Zhivago* as Pasternak shows us the effect of the Russian Revolution on sensitive, life-affirming poet-doctor Yuri Zhivago and the women he loves. Born wealthy in czarist Russia, orphaned early, raised by a kindly uncle, Yuri Zhivago is a man trapped in the tumultuous history of his times—the First World War and the Russian Revolution. His wife, the aristocratic Tonya, and his mistress, passionate, unconventional Lara, journey with him through a difficult life that nevertheless has sweetness and beauty in it.

Set against the vast lands of Russia and the turmoil created by the Russian Revolution, *Dr. Zhivago* is infused with poetry, philosophy, nature, history, and passion. Pasternak depicts peasants and the intelligentsia, workers and owners, the overwhelming wealth of some, and the grinding poverty of others. Pasternak was infamously forced by the Soviets to "voluntarily reject" the Nobel Prize awarded to him in 1958.

**Audio:** Chivers Audio (www.chivers.co.uk) 0754053636. Read by Philip Madoc.

**Film/Video/DVD:** *Dr. Zhivago* (1965) epic film directed by David Lean with Omar Sharif, lots of snow and a haunting love theme. Also a *Masterpiece Theatre* production (2004) with Kiera Knightley.

**Similar Reads:** Turn to other Russian classics such as *Anna Karenina, One Day in the Life of Ivan Denisovich*, or *The Brothers Karamazov*.

**Subjects:** Russia; Russian Revolution; Soviet Union; Bolsheviks; World War I; Doctors; Poets; Romance; Communism; Nobel Prize 1958

## Solzhenitsyn, Alexander (1918–)

🏅 *One Day in the Life of Ivan Denisovich* (**Russia: 1961**). Signet 1998 (paper) 142pp. 0451527097 <u>S</u> **Q**

The day begins well before dawn when you are roused from your bed by the banging of a pipe against a rail. It is freezing cold, your clothes are thin, there is little to eat. Very few people here can be considered your friends. You will spend the day surviving. In the camp, the individual does not exist, dignity does not exist, privacy does not exist—there are only the cold, the hunger, the labor and the idea that you are one day closer to the end of your sentence. This is the life of Ivan Denisovich, a Russian serving a sentence in a Siberian prison camp for the crime of treason—because he had been a German prisoner of war, the Soviets now believe him to be a spy.

The baseness and despair of life in a Soviet labor camp is depicted in this brief, bleak story based on Solzhenitsyn's own experiences. Solzhenitsyn became the conscience for the world with his exposure of Soviet repression and Stalin's reign of terror.

**Audio:** Blackstone cassette 0786103299. Read by Richard Brown.

**Film/Video/DVD:** *One Day in the Life of Ivan Denisovich* (1970) features Tom Courtenay.

**Similar Reads:** Solzhenitsyn's major work is *The Gulag Archipelago* a massive examination of the Soviet Gulag or prison camp system; *Darkness at Noon* by Arthur Koestler depicts another facet of Soviet reality. *Andersonville* by Kantor is the story of men in a notorious Civil War era prisoner of war camp.

**Subjects:** Russia: Soviet Union; Gulag; Imprisonment; Labor Camp; Prisoners; Courage; Freedom; Nobel Prize 1970

# Chapter 3

## Science Fiction

On first glance, science fiction may appear to be about alien invasions, time travel, and space exploration. But it is really a genre about ideas. Readers of science fiction love the adventure and imagination in the books, but they also are drawn to the genre's exploration of big ideas and themes—the impact of technology on humanity, the dangers of depleting Earth's resources, tolerance, the unity of humankind as a species (in the face of alien invasion, for example), the mystery and power of science, and the value of questioning our assumptions about humanity's future.

Science fiction has long been a staple of young adult literature. Perhaps because the teen years are a time of questioning, rebellion, and exploration, and those themes are prevalent in science fiction. Science fiction is also full of adventure and can offer great entertainment and thoughtful escapism. Along with thrilling plots, readers turn to science fiction for an exploration of philosophy, religion, technology, science, ethics, politics, relationships, romance, and love—all the universal and timeless themes of classic literature.

Science fiction tells us that the future is interesting and worthy of contemplation. Many of the things we take for granted today were only ideas in the mind of a science fiction writer a few years ago—television, cell phones, submarines, travel in space, robots, cloning, instantaneous long-distance communication.

Science fiction can be set in any time period—in the past, the near future, the distant future, or even an alternate present—but the future is the most common setting. The setting can be any place—Earth, space, other planets, underwater, or underground.

# Aliens

The motif of the "other" is prevalent in literature, and science fiction is no exception. Aliens of all kinds, peaceful or malevolent, machine-like or bug-like, come to Earth, sometimes to explore and sometimes to conquer. Often a battle for control ensues with Earth's inhabitants united to vanquish the otherworldly foe.

## Card, Orson Scott (1951–)

🏆 *Ender's Game* (USA: 1985). Tor 1994 (paper) 384pp. 0812550706 **J Teen**

Ender Wiggin is the great hope of humanity. An unparalleled military genius, a child prodigy, he is taken from his parents at an early age and placed in the Battle School. There he trains to become a starship officer so he can join the Fleet and help fight the war against the Buggers, the aliens who have threatened to conquer Earth. Ender passes every military test thrown at him and is assigned to Salamander Army, which he soon commands. This little army becomes deeply loyal to Ender and his unorthodox methods as he leads them to victory after victory in the games of the Battle Room. Soon the games in the Battle Room are over, and Ender is informed that the war is over, too; the Buggers have been defeated.

What are the implications for a child soldier when he is told that the games he believed he had been playing were actual battle and that he has destroyed an entire alien race? This book is a good recommendation for readers who claim that they don't like science fiction.

> **Audio:** Audio Renaissance 1574595966. Read by a full cast.
>
> **Film/Video/DVD:** A film is expected to open in 2007 directed by Wolfgang Peterson.
>
> **Similar Reads:** The Ender Wiggin Saga continues in *Speaker for the Dead, Xenocide; Children of the Mind; Ender's Shadow; Shadow of the Hegemon;* and *Shadow Puppets.* Also try Robert Heinlein's *Starship Troopers.*
>
> **Subjects:** War; War Games; Military Training; Military Science Fiction; Hero; Genetic Engineering; Hugo Award 1986; Nebula Award 1985

## Christopher, John (1922–)

### Tripods Trilogy (England)

Tripod creatures from another world conquer Earth. All adults are neutralized; they are docile and powerless. Only the young people and the Vagrants see what is happening on Earth because only they are not under the control of the Tripods. When people turn fourteen years old, they undergo a Capping ceremony, and that is when the mind control begins. Will Parker is turning fourteen soon, and he does not like the idea of being capped and controlled. It is up to the teenagers to take back the planet!

A captivating and fast-paced adventure—suspenseful and thought provoking.

*The White Mountains* (1967). Simon Pulse 2003 (paper) 208pp. 0689856725 **J Teen Q**

*The City of Gold and Lead* (1967). Simon Pulse 2003 (paper) 192pp. 0689855052 **J Teen Q**

*The Pool of Fire* **(1967).** Simon Pulse 2003 (paper) 0689856695 **J Teen Q**

> **Similar Reads:** There is a prequel, *When the Tripods Came*. Look for other teens who save the world in Susan Cooper's <u>The Dark Is Rising Sequence</u> and William Sleator's *Interstellar Pig*. Also try books by Margaret Peterson Haddix.
>
> **Subjects:** England; Free Will; Alien Invasion; Mind Control

## Clarke, Arthur C. (1917–)

🌱 *Childhood's End* **(England: 1953).** Del Rey 1987 (paper) 224pp. 0345347951 <u>S</u>

Humanity's first contact with powerful alien beings call the Overlords is the premise of this classic science fiction novel. The Overlords appeared suddenly over every city; they were omnipresent and seemingly benevolent. They ushered in a new Golden Age for humanity, ending poverty, disease, and war. No one ever challenged them, and after 50 years humanity became used to their presence, but no one knows who the Overlords are, nor has anyone seen them. What is their true purpose on Earth? Are they benevolent? After another hundred years, the Overlords will reveal themselves and their true purpose on Earth.

Clarke, a grand master of the science fiction genre, writes with humanity and scientific authority about space travel and the role of humans in the universe.

> **Similar Reads:** Try *The Hammer of God,* also by Clarke. Other titles to consider are *Parable of the Sower* by Octavia Butler, *The Forge of God* by Greg Bear, and *Foreigner: A Novel of First Contact* by C. J. Cherryh. Clarke's other classic about space travel and alien intervention is *2001: A Space Odyssey.*
>
> **Subjects:** First Contact; Evolution; Apocalypse; Space Travel; Damon Knight Memorial Grand Master

## Heinlein, Robert (1907–1988)

🌱 *Starship Troopers* **(USA: 1959).** Ace 1987 (paper) 263pp. 0441783589 <u>S</u>

When Johnny Rico signs up for the Mobile Infantry on his planet Terra (formerly known as Earth), he must endure the toughest boot camp ever. Once he survives boot camp, he will join his unit, make his first combat drop, and see action against the terrifying Arachnids, the most evil foe humanity has ever known. Will Johnny survive the horror of war while forming everlasting bonds of camaraderie with fellow officers and troops?

This is a fast-paced action novel—nothing less than the survival of the human species is as stake!

> **Audio:** Recorded Books cassette 0788763326. Read by George Wilson.
>
> **Film/Video/DVD** *Starship Troopers* (1997) is a rapid action film directed by Paul Verhoeven.

> **Similar Reads:** *Ender's Game* by Scott Orson Card and *The Forever War* by Joe Haldeman are two choices.

**Subjects:** Military Science Fiction; Alien Invasion; Battles; Hugo Award 1960; Damon Knight Memorial Grand Master

🌳 *Stranger in a Strange Land* (USA: 1961). Ace 1995 (paper) 438pp. 0441790348. **S**

Valentine Michael Smith is a human. Born on Mars during the only manned mission there, he was raised by Martians. Brought back to Earth by the Champion expedition, he is now truly a stranger in a strange land—Earth. He has the paranormal powers of a Martian, a Martian sensibility, and an absolute innocence about Earth's ways. How will this stranger adapt to Earth, and how will Earth adapt to Valentine Smith?

Heinlein's work is influential and *Stranger in a Strange Land* was a countercultural hit in the 1960s.

**Audio:** Books on Tape 0736637028 (part 1), 0736637036 (part 2). Read by Larry McKeever.

**Similar Reads:** *Mars* by Ben Bova.

**Subjects:** Mars; Martians; Communal Families; Hugo Award 1962; Damon Knight Memorial Grand Master

## Sleator, William (1945– )

*Interstellar Pig* (USA: 1984). Puffin Books 1995 (paper) 197pp. 0140375953 **J @ Q**

Barney is bored. On a family vacation in an isolated beach house with no kids his own age to hang out with, Barney is barely able to make the time pass. But then three exotic strangers move into the cottage next door. Zena, Joe, and Manny are friendly, interesting, and, best of all, they include Barney in the game they obsessively play, an absorbing science fiction board game called Interstellar Pig. But the game becomes increasingly complex and the stakes dangerously high, as Barney gets more involved with the three strangers and the quest for the all-important Piggy.

**Similar Reads:** Sleator is a great YA science fiction author; the sequel to *Interstellar Pig* is *Parasite Pig*. Other books by Sleator include *House of Stairs, Singularity,* and *The Boy Who Reversed Himself. Have Spacesuit, Will Travel* by Heinlein and Christopher's The Tripods Trilogy are other science fiction classics with teen protagonists.

**Subjects:** Gaming; Humor

## Wells, H. G. (1866–1949)

*The War of the Worlds* (England: 1898). Tor 1993 (paper) 224pp. 0812505158 **S**

A classic tale of alien invasion. Mars is a dying planet. To survive, the Martians decide to attack unsuspecting Earth and colonize it. Their massive invasion devastates Earth. Told by an unnamed narrator, this story takes place in late-nineteenth-century Britain. It is both science fiction adventure and social allegory that foreshadowed the savage ways technology would be used in the twentieth century.

**Audio:** Recorded Books cassette 1556905483; CD 1402552459. Read by Alexander Spencer. It is also worth finding Orson Welles's history-making 1938 radio broadcast of this story. A brilliant example of how a classic can be adapted, Welles set his version in 1938 New Jersey. The broadcast was so realistic, many listeners thought an actual invasion was occurring, and it caused a panic.

**Film/Video/DVD:** The first film version was made in 1953. A new film starring Tom Cruise and directed by Steven Spielberg, released in 2005, sets the story in New Jersey; it is more faithful to the book than the earlier film and has spectacular and frightening special effects.

**Similar Reads:** Try *Mars* by Ben Bova; *Red Mars, Green Mars,* and *Blue Mars* by Kim Stanley Robinson; *The Martian Chronicles* by Ray Bradbury; the John Carter of Mars series by Edgar Rice Burroughs; *Ender's Game* by Orson Scott Card; and The Tripods Trilogy by John Christopher. Or turn to Wells's other classics *The Invisible Man* and *The Time Machine.* Another classic about invasion is John Wyndham's *The Day of the Triffids.*

**Subjects:** Alien Invasion; Martians; Interplanetary War; Technology

# Dystopias and Alternative Futures

A dystopia is a future that does not turn out well (as opposed to a utopia where things are perfect). Poverty, overpopulation, disease, social stratification, control by the military or totalitarian governments, loss of individual freedom, devastation of the natural environment, and the actual extinction of humanity are some of the recurring themes of dystopian novels. Dystopian fiction raises the questions: What if the future turns out this way? What should we be doing now to avoid this future?

## Asimov, Isaac (1920–1992)

*I, Robot* **(USA: 1951).** Spectra 1991 (paper, Movie Tie-in edition) 304pp. 0553294385 <u>S</u>

Asimov's famous Three Laws of Robotics were introduced in these classic stories. It is the near future. Science has invented robots to be man's helpers. But soon the robots become more sophisticated; they become imbued with emotion and intelligence. The robots become self-aware. When they begin to realize their own power, they are no longer content merely to be humankind's helpers. What happens when the machines decide what it means to be human?

This volume of interconnected stories was the beginning of Asimov's explorations into robotics and artificial intelligence.

**Audio:** Recorded Books cassette 0739312707. Read by Scott Brick.

**Film/Video/DVD**: *I, Robot* (2004) starring Will Smith is a fast-paced action film but doesn't dwell much on the issues raised by artificial intelligence or Asimov's stories. The film *Bicentennial Man* (1999) also explores the issue of robots morphing into sensitive, humanlike beings and is based on a story by Asimov.

**Similar Reads:** *The Caves of Steel, The Naked Sun,* and *The Robots of Dawn* are other choices by Asimov. Carel Kapek's famous 1921 play, *R.U.R.,* also explores the intelligence of machines.

**Subjects:** Robots; Technology; Artificial Intelligence; Short Stories

## Bradbury, Ray (1920– )

*Fahrenheit 451* **(USA: 1953).** Del Rey 1987 (paper) 208pp. 0345342968 <u>S</u> **Q**

Guy Montag is a fireman in the future. But he doesn't put fires out—he starts them. It's his job to burn books, and he likes his work. One day he meets a young woman, Clarisse, who makes him question his work, his society, and his reality: "Do you ever read any of the books you burn?" she asks. But the party line is that books just confuse people, they tell different stories and present too many points of view. In this dystopian world, it is better if people don't think independent thoughts. But now Guy's awareness has been raised. Can he go back to his job of burning the books?

**Audio:** Recorded Books cassette 0788732749. Read by Paul Hecht.

**Film/Video/DVD:** Francois Truffaut directed an adaptation in 1966—avant-garde teens may like the retro look and strangeness of this movie. A remake is slated for 2007.

**Similar Reads:** Bradbury is an author who is hard to categorize. People think of him as a science fiction writer, but he doesn't classify himself as such. Students will be interested in his short stories and other classic novels including *The Illustrated Man, Dandelion Wine,* and *Something Wicked This Way Comes.*

**Subjects:** America; Totalitarianism; Freedom; Censorship

## Burgess, Anthony (1917–1993)

*A Clockwork Orange* **(England: 1962).** Norton 1986 (paper) 192pp. 0393312836 <u>S</u>

Alex, who begins the story at age fifteen, is the narrator of this upsetting novel for mature readers. A passionate fan of classical music, Alex is also a sociopath, a juvenile delinquent, a rapist, and a killer. He and his droogs—his buddies, Georgie, Pete, and Dim—form a gang that likes to terrorize people—robbing, beating, and raping. But finally the state, a repressive totalitarian regime, catches up to Alex, and he is sent to prison where is offered an opportunity for reconditioning. He enters a program of aversion therapy and is forced to become wretchedly sick when confronted with sex or violence. Does it cure him, or does it make him unfit to live in a human society where violence is commonplace? Alex can no longer harm people, but he can no longer defend himself either.

This is Burgess's classic tale of a savage and frightening future. It is an intense story for mature readers. Burgess made up a language full of slang and bits of Russian for his characters to express their alienation and disaffection.

**Film/Video/DVD:** *A Clockwork Orange:* Stanley Kubrick directed the violent 1972 R-rated film with Malcolm McDowell as Alex.

**Similar Reads:** *Neuromancer* by William Gibson.

**Subjects:** Violence; Gangs; Mature Read

## Dick, Philip K. (1928–1982)

*Do Androids Dream of Electric Sheep?* (USA: 1968). Del Rey 1996 (paper) 256pp. 0345404475 <u>S</u>

In the year 2021, overpopulation, radioactive fallout, and pollution are driving many species to extinction. But humans still crave pets and companies create lifelike simulations—horses, birds, even sheep—for people who cannot afford a live pet. The same companies create human simulations—androids. At first the androids are servants to humans, but eventually they become so sophisticated that they are perceived as a threat to humanity and are banned from Earth. But the androids would prefer freedom on Earth to slavery on Mars. Deckard, a bounty hunter with the San Francisco Police, is hired to track and "retire" the most advanced and humanlike androids, the Nexus-6. Deckard undergoes his own moral crisis as he hunts the androids.

**Film/Video/DVD:** This is the basis for the Harrison Ford movie *Blade Runner* (1982), which is only loosely based on Dick's novel.

**Similar Reads:** Try *I, Robot* and other books by Isaac Asimov in the <u>Robot</u> series; *Frankenstein* by Mary Shelley; and Gibson's *Neuromancer*.

**Subjects:** San Francisco; Androids; Robots; Artificial Intelligence; Bounty Hunters

## Gibson, William (1948–)

🏆 *Neuromancer* (USA: 1984). Ace 1995 (paper) 288pp. 0441569595 <u>S</u>

The future is dark and hopeless. People are dependent on drugs. Computers run everything. Computer techie wizards get high by interfacing with their computers and taking a ride into virtual reality. Case is the best of them, the top computer honcho. But when he enters Earth's Computer Matrix for the wrong people, he is caught and punished. Now he can't interface with his own computer—the worst punishment imaginable! But Case is willing to fight back.

This is a gritty novel full of jargon and violence. Gibson started the subgenre of cyberpunk with this work. A blending of "cybernetics" and "punk," cyberpunk stories are set in Earth's future where technology (particularly computers and information technology) dominates—dystopian, noir, nihilistic, hardboiled, alienated antiheroes—all terms that can be applied to cyberpunk.

**Audio:** Books on Tape 0736638369. Read by Arthur Addison.

**Film:** *Neuromancer* has not been filmed, but *The Matrix* (1999, 2003) movies, *Robo Cop* (1987), *Johnny Mnemonic* (1995), and *Blade Runner* (1982) are classic cyberpunk films.

**Similar Reads:** Other books by Gibson include *Count Zero Mona Lisa Overdrive*. Readers may want to turn to Dick's *Do Androids Dream of Electric Sheep?* or Burgess's *A Clockwork Orange* for more stories about a bleak future.

**Subjects:** Cyberpunk; Computers; Technology; Mature Read; Hugo Award 1985; Nebula Award 1984

## Huxley, Aldous (1894–1963)

*Brave New World* (**England: 1932**). Perennial Classics 1998 (paper) 288pp. 0060929871 <u>S</u>

Bernard Marx lives in a world where a mind-numbing drug called soma is handed out freely, where anonymous sexual relationships are standard, where embryos are designed in factories, and where personal thinking is not necessary. War, disease, and suffering have been eradicated. Mass conformity is the unquestioned norm.

The future does not look good in Huxley's unsettling novel about the dangers of scientific progress, the intrusion of excess governmental control, and the deconstruction of the individual.

**Audio:** Audio Partners cassette 1572700645. Read by Michael York.

**Film/Video/DVD:** A made for TV movie was produced in 1998.

**Similar Reads:** Huxley also wrote *The Island*. *We* by Russian writer Yevgeny Zamyatin (1884–1937) is a book that influenced both *Brave New World* and Orwell's *1984*. Huxley's nonfiction essay *Brave New World Revisited* provides further exploration of some of the issues raised in the novel. *Erewhon* by Samuel Butler is an early dystopian novel.

**Subjects:** Totalitarianism; Conformity; Mature Read; Frequently Challenged

## Miller, Walter (1923–1996)

🏅 *A Canticle for Leibowitz* (**USA: 1960**). Bantam Spectra 1997 (paper) 368pp. 0553379267 <u>S</u>

"Pound pastrami, can kraut, six bagels—bring home for Emma." This is written on the sacred document discovered by Brother Francis Gerard, a humble monk of the Albertian Order of Leibowitz, a document written by the blessed St. Leibowitz himself —a shopping list from the twentieth-century civilization. This gives the monks hope that more knowledge about the lost civilization can be found. After the Fall of America, a new Dark Age ensued, and it is religion, the church, and its monastic orders that have prevented total darkness. Brother Francis's abbey maintains a collection of knowledge from the past. Can the Abbey survive the assaults of wild nomads, wars between city-states, and the encroachment of the militaristic Order of San Pancrat? Will the small flame of knowledge that has been kept smoldering in the monasteries be able to kindle a new age of knowledge and enlightenment for humankind?

This classic novel of postnuclear holocaust America is set in the thirty-second century in the deserts of Utah.

**Similar Reads:** Miller followed this book with a less well-known sequel, *Saint Liebowitz and the Wild Horse Woman*. *Alas, Babylon* by Pat Frank, *The Postman* by David Brin, and *A Gift Upon the Shore* by M. K. Wren are other postnuclear holocaust novels to try.

**Subjects:** American Southwest; Soul; Monks; Postnuclear War; Hugo Award 1961

## O'Brien, Robert C. (1918–1973)

*Z for Zachariah* **(USA: 1974).** Simon Pulse 1987 (paper) 256pp. 0020446500 **J** **Teen Q**

Radiation from nuclear war has destroyed everything on Earth except you. Your family is dead, the radio no longer broadcasts. You are alone. But one day you see smoke from a fire. Each day it comes closer until the day a man in a green survival suit walks into your valley. For fifteen-year-old Ann Burden, company may not be a good thing.

Suspense, action, and a strong heroine make this a gripping read set in a devastated future.

> **Audio:** Recorded Books cassette 07887 29748. Read by Christina Moore.

> **Similar Reads:** Other science fiction classics with teen protagonists include *House of Stairs*, *Ender's Game,* and <u>The Tripods Trilogy</u>. O'Brien's other classic is the very different but highly recommended *Mrs. Frisby and the Rats of NIMH.*

> **Subjects:** Postnuclear World; Strong Heroine

## Orwell, George (1903–1950)

*1984* **(England: 1949).** Signet 1990 (paper) 336pp. 0451524934 **S**

Winston Smith is an unlikely hero. A government functionary who works in the Ministry of Truth, Winston spends his days rewriting historical documents to reflect the current party line. He lives in a future London where citizens are perpetually watched by Big Brother and monitored by the Thought Police. Eventually Winston comes to realize that life can offer more than the controlled thinking and unquestioning conformity preferred by the government.

Written in 1949, this novel presented a grim and pessimistic future of oppression where individual thought and initiative are illegal. Orwell writes in clear and simple prose, and he created a whole vocabulary to express this bleak new society—nonperson, newspeak, doublethink, thought crime. For many YA readers, this book begins the awakening of a political sensibility.

> **Audio:** Recorded Books cassette 1556905807; CD 1402522835. Read by Frank Muller.

> **Film/Video/DVD:** A British film with Richard Burton and John Hurt made in (appropriately) 1984 captures the grimness of the novel.

> **Similar Reads:** Huxley's *Brave New World* and Bradbury's *Fahrenheit 451* are natural companions to *1984*. Orwell's other widely read classic about totalitarianism is *Animal Farm.*

> **Subjects:** London; Oceania; Totalitarianism; Politics; Government; Mature Read

## Shute, Nevil (1899–1960)

*On the Beach* **(Australia: 1957).** Ballantine 1983 (paper) 288pp. 0345311485 **S**
Australia, 1963, the last survivors of the final nuclear holocaust on Earth are waiting
for death to come to them. An inevitable cloud of radioactive dust will eventually
reach Australia; all living things will die from radiation sickness. We follow the ordinary, almost mundane lives of American Naval Captain Dwight Towers, a loyal, honorable man; Moira Davidson, a hard-drinking young woman who becomes his friend;
Peter Holmes, a young Australian Navy officer; his wife, Mary, and their new baby
daughter, Jennifer; and scientist John Osborne as they stoically accept the ultimate fate
of mankind.

Shute was an engineer who had a purpose for writing *On the Beach:* he wanted to warn
people of the dangers of militarism. This novel is in no way didactic; it is humane, intense but understated, and profoundly moving.

   **Audio:** Recorded Books cassette 155690391X. Read by Simon Prebble.

   **Film/Video/DVD:** *On the Beach* (1959) directed by Stanley Kramer with Gregory
   Peck, Ava Gardner, and Fred Astaire is highly recommended. A television version
   was made in 2000.

   **Similar Reads:** Another postnuclear holocaust classic is *Alas, Babylon* by Pat
   Frank. *A Gift upon the Shore* by M. K. Wren is another interesting book looking at
   the survivors of nuclear destruction. *The Stand* by Stephen King and *Lucifer's
   Hammer* by Niven and Pournelle tell stories of humanity coping after worldwide
   crisis. Another Cold War classic is *Fail Safe* (1962) by Eugene Burdick. Shute also
   wrote the historical novel *A Town Like Alice* (1950).

   **Subjects:** Australia; Nuclear War; Post–Nuclear World; Technology; Suicide;
   Death

# Science Gone Awry

   Is science the great savior of humanity, or must we be ever on our guard against
abuses?

## Keyes, Daniel (1927–)

🌳 *Flowers for Algernon* **(USA: 1966).** Bantam 1984 (paper) 224pp. 0553274503 **J Q**
Algernon is a white mouse. A series of brain experiments performed by Dr. Strauss
and Professor Nemur increase his intelligence. Because the experiments have been
successful, the scientists now want to test the procedure on a human. Charlie, a man
with the mental capacity of a boy, is selected. The experimental operation that worked
on Algernon could offer Charlie a chance at average intelligence. If the procedure is
successful, Charlie's intellectual abilities will start to grow. But it is soon apparent that
Algernon is beginning to deteriorate; he can no longer recognize simple commands
and stimuli. Will the same thing happen to Charlie? Charlie's diary entries show us
how he responds to the operation and his awareness of Algernon's reversal.

**Audio:** Recorded Books cassette 078872227; CD 1402550340. Read by Jeff Woodman.

**Film/Video/DVD:** *Charly* (1968), a sentimental adaptation, earned a Best Actor Oscar for Cliff Robertson as Charly. The book was filmed again for TV in 2000 as *Flowers for Algernon.*

**Similar Reads:** *Beyond This Horizon* by Robert Heinlein.

**Subjects:** New York, 1960s; Scientific Experimentation; Bioengineering; Genetic Manipulation; Mental Disability; Diary Format; Ethics; Frequently Challenged; Nebula Award 1966

*See also* the following books in the Horror Chapter under "Science Gone Awry"

## Shelley, Mary (1797–1851)

*Frankenstein, or the Modern Prometheus* (England: 1818). <u>J</u>

## Sleator, William (1945–)

*House of Stairs* (USA: 1974). <u>J</u> Teen Q

## Wells, H. G. (1866–1949)

*The Island of Dr Moreau* (England: 1896). <u>S</u>

*Invisible Man* (England: 1897). <u>J</u> Q

---

# Space Travel, Adventure, and Life in Other Worlds

Man's long-held dream of traveling to other worlds becomes reality in these novels about life on other planets and man's attempts to observe and understand it. Jules Verne started the genre with his stories of explorations on Earth and beyond.

## Abbott, Edwin (1838–1926)

*Flatland* (England: 1884). Signet 1984 (paper) 160pp. 0451522907 <u>J</u>

Flatland is a place with only two dimensions. Men are figures with many sides and angles; women are only segments of lines. But one Flatlander, A. Square, longs to find out more about reality, so he travels to Lineland, Pointland, and Spaceland. In his travels, he learns that there are more than the two dimensions, and this knowledge makes it difficult for him when he returns to Flatland. This is an unusual book for thoughtful and motivated readers, not a wide audience.

Abbott was a scholar, a theologian, and an educator in Victorian England. He wrote many academic texts, but only *Flatland* crossed over with any popular appeal. Critics argue it is also a satire of restrictive Victorian society.

**Similar Reads:** Mathematically inclined readers might want to try *The Phantom Tollbooth*, *Alice through the Looking Glass,* and *The Number Devil* by Hans Magnus Enzensberger.

**Subjects:** Mathematics; Dimensions; Exploration; Geometry; Satire

## Adams, Douglas (1952–2001)

*The Hitchhiker's Guide to the Galaxy* **(England: 1979).** Del Rey 1995 (paper) 320pp. 0345391802 **J**

Arthur Dent is having a bad Thursday, a bulldozer wants to demolish his house, he learns his friend Ford Prefect is an alien, and fifteen minutes from now Vogons are going to destroy Earth to build a hyperspatial express route. Discover with Arthur why two-headed Zaphod Beeblebrox wanted to be president of the galaxy, why a towel is a very handy item, and the reason for putting a Babel Fish in your ear.

These books are funny, irreverent, intelligent, and dopey at the same time. They were originally presented as a radio show in Britain. The trilogy (consisting of five books) continues with:

*The Restaurant at the End of the Universe* (1980)

*Life, the Universe and Everything* (1982)

*So Long, and Thanks for all the Fish* (1984)

*Mostly Harmless* (1992)

**Audio:** Go to www.bbcshop.com for a variety of *Hitchhiker's Guide* audio options.

**Film/Video/DVD:** This was a cult classic television series in England in the 1970s. 2005 finally saw a feature film come to the screen. Fans of this series may want to explore the British TV phenomenon *Dr. Who* or the comedy of Monty Python.

**Subjects:** Journey; Aliens; Intergalactic Travel; Humor

## Asimov, Isaac (1920–1992)

*Foundation* **(USA: 1951).** Spectra 1991 (paper) 320pp. 0553293354 <u>S</u>

Hari Seldon knew the Galactic Empire was dying after being in existence for twelve thousand years. He also knew that thirty thousand years of savage barbarism would follow the demise of the empire. To shorten the coming Dark Age, he creates the Encyclopedia Foundation and places it on Terminus, a desolate world in the farthest reaches of the empire. The Foundation will preserve knowledge and science. It is staffed with the very best scholars and scientists. But with the empire collapsing and the barbarian warlords establishing a kingdom, the Foundation is defenseless. It is the only hope of humanity. Will it survive?

Asimov is probably the world's most prolific writer. This is the first volume in the classic <u>Foundation Trilogy</u>. The trilogy is set in the larger context of Asimov's fourteen books that deal with the "history of the future" beginning with the *Robot* stories (collected in *The Complete Robot,* Doubleday 1982) and moving through the *Founda-*

*tion* novels. Consult www.asimovonline.com for a complete listing. Asimov was given a special Hugo Award for Best All Time Series in 1966.

> **Audio:** Books on Tape 1415917760. Read by Scott Brick.

> **Similar Reads:** The story continues in *Foundation and Empire* and *Second Foundation*. Also try Orson Scott Card's <u>Homecoming</u> series.

> **Subjects:** Galactic Empire; Military Science Fiction; Hugo Award 1966

## Bester, Alfred (1913–1987)

*The Stars My Destination* **(USA: 1957).** Vintage 1996 (paper) 272pp. 0679767800 <u>S</u>
> Gulliver Foyle, a lazy, unconnected, valueless man—a nobody—is marooned in space on the wrecked ship *Nomad*. For 170 days, he has drifted, alone, running out of air, food, and water. No one will help him. He is hallucinating; he is dying. When a ship that could rescue him passes him by, Foyle becomes a man obsessed with revenge.

> A classic space opera full of fast-paced action, rapid prose, and raw power. This novel is a retelling of *The Count of Monte Cristo* set in outer space at a time in the future where people can "jaunte"—teletransport themselves around a planet with a single thought.

> **Similar Reads:** Try more works by Bester. His novel *The Demolished Man* won the first Hugo Award in 1953.

> **Subjects:** Survival; Revenge

## Bradbury, Ray (1920–)

*The Martian Chronicles* **(USA: 1950).** Spectra 1984 (paper) 192pp. 0553278223 <u>S</u> **Q**
> Humanity came to Mars to have a new beginning on a new world. In these interconnected stories, the humans are the alien invaders, landing on peaceful Mars to make it their own. But humans bring with them their deepest desires and fears, and the dreamlike, telepathic Martians are ready for them.

> This collection of linked stories details the colonization of Mars from both the Martian and the human points of view. It details the collision between two vastly different peoples, cultures, and worlds. Bradbury creates an interesting mix of horror, nostalgia, sensuous writing, and big ideas.

> **Audio:** Chivers Audio Books cassette 0745173667. Read by Peter Marinker.

> **Film/Video/DVD:** This book was made into a TV miniseries in 1980 (Bradbury himself called it boring).

> **Similar Reads:** Try the <u>John Carter of Mars</u> series by Edgar Rice Burroughs; *Mars* by Ben Bova; *Red Mars, Green Mars,* and *Blue Mars* by Kim Stanley Robinson; and *Stranger in a Strange Land* by Robert Heinlein.

> **Subjects:** Mars; Planetary Colonization; Martians; Aliens; Short Stories

## Burroughs, Edgar Rice (1875–1950)

### The Barsoom Series (USA)

Following the American Civil War, John Carter finds himself transported to Mars. Carter, a natural warrior, is well suited to the violent planet, and eleven novels follow his adventures, his encounters with aliens such as the lovely Dejah Thoris, Princess of Helium, and the exploits of his descendents.

Burroughs was writing this series set on Mars while also writing the Tarzan books. The John Carter stories are romantic adventures with rapid, exciting plots that helped define the science fiction genre. Dismissed as a pulp author, Burroughs is a true storyteller whose works are still in print, the subject of academic attention, and fun to read.

The Barsoom (the Martian word for Mars) series consists of the following titles:

*A Princess of Mars* (1917). Modern Library Classic 2003 (paper) 240pp. 0812968514 **J Q**

*The Gods of Mars* (1918). Del Rey 1985 (paper) 192pp. 0345324390 **J Q**

*The Warlord of Mars* (1919). Ballantine 1985 (paper) 160pp. 0345324536

*Thuvia, Maid of Mars* (1920).

*The Chessmen of Mars* (1922).

*The Master Mind of Mars* (1928).

*A Fighting Man of Mars* (1931).

*Swords of Mars* (1936).

*Synthetic Men of Mars* (1940). Del Rey 1986 (paper) 160pp. 0345339304

*Llana of Gathol* (1940). Del Rey 1985 (paper) 0345324439

*John Carter of Mars* (1964). Del Rey 1985 (paper) 0345329554

>  **Audio:** Several titles are available from Tantor Audio Books (www.tantor.com) and from Blackstone Audio.

>  **Similar Reads:** Be sure to read Burroughs's other classics, *Tarzan of the Apes* and *The Land That Time Forgot.*

>  **Subjects:** Mars; Martians; Aliens; Swashbuckler Adventure

## Clarke, Arthur C. (1917–)

*2001: A Space Odyssey* (**England: 1968**). Roc 2000 (paper) 320pp. 0451457994 **S**

In the Pleistocene era, a large monolith appears to the primitive ape-humans inhabiting the earth and nudges them along in their evolution. Thousands of years later, a monolith is discovered buried on the moon, and when it is excavated, it emits a piercing radio frequency aimed at the planet Saturn. Three years after that, the spaceship *Discovery* is traveling on a mission toward Saturn. Aboard this ship are five astronauts and the paranoid computer, HAL 9000, which controls the ship. The tension between man and technology, the idea of life on other planets, the technicalities of space travel, and the basic human desire to understand reality all share a place in this exciting and mind-expanding adventure story set among the stars.

Clarke approaches his writing from his own scientific background as a physicist and mathematician. He wrote this book concurrently with the screenplay of the famous film. Director Stanley Kubrick and Clarke wanted to collaborate and needed a script. Using Clarke's short story "The Sentinel" as a starting point, they expanded it into a novel, which became the basis for the film.

> **Audio:** Brilliance Audio cassette 1567403913. Read by Dick Hill.

> **Film/Video/DVD**: *2001: A Space Odyssey* (1968) is an enigmatic film with the memorable classical musical score directed by Stanley Kubrick.

> **Similar Reads:** Clarke wrote three sequels to this books: *2010: Odyssey Two; 2060: Odyssey Three*; and *3001: The Final Odyssey. Childhood's End* is another Clarke classic.

> **Subjects:** Technology; HAL 9000; Computers; Aliens

## Engdahl, Sylvia (1933–)

❦ *Enchantress from the Stars* **(USA: 1970).** Firebird 2003 (paper) 304pp. 0142500372 **M** Teen

> Three distinct cultures clash on the planet Andrecia, a planet where society is in a medieval state that still believes in magic and superstition. Elana, a human woman, tries to help these less advanced alien cultures coexist with the advanced technologies of her world. Disgusted by the unfair treatment of the Andrecians and the hypocrisy of her advanced society, Elana appears to Georgyn, a woodcutter's son on Andrecia. She vows to help him defeat the dragon on the other side of the forest, actually the heavy equipment of the invading Imperials. To Georgyn's medieval mind, she is the Enchantress from the Stars; he puts all his faith in her, and in time these two young people from very different worlds fall in love.

> This is an outstanding and intelligent story of sacrifice, compassion, and love.

> **Audio:** Recorded Books 1419399217. Read by Jennifer Ikeda.

> **Similar Reads:** Sequel called *The Far Side of Evil* is a darker story aimed at older readers. Engdahl has always insisted that she didn't intend her books for a young adult audience.

> **Subjects:** Psychokinetic Power; Cultural Conflict; Strong Heroine; Newbery Honor 1971

## Heinlein, Robert (1907–1988)

*Have Spacesuit, Will Travel* **(USA: 1958).** Del Rey 2003 (paper) 240pp. 034546107x **M** Teen Q

> Winning a spacesuit in a contest may be the first step toward intergalactic travel for Kip Russel, a typical 1950s American teenager. Obsessed with the

idea of traveling in space, Kip enters a contest to write a soap slogan and to win a trip to the moon. He doesn't win the grand prize, but he does win a spacesuit, and that's when the adventures begin.

**Audio:** Full Cast Audio cassette 1932076409; CD 1932076417. Performed by a full cast of actors.

**Similar Reads:** Heinlein wrote several science fiction books aimed at "juveniles," another being *Starship Troopers*. His more mature works include *Stranger in a Strange Land* and *The Moon Is a Harsh Mistress*

**Subjects:** Intergalactic Travel; Aliens; Journey; Family; Humor

## Herbert, Frank (1920–1986)

🏵 *Dune* (USA: 1965). ACE Charter 1996 (paper, 25th Anniversary edition) 535pp. 0441172717 <u>S</u>

Heroic characters, a detailed fictional world, epic adventure, political intrigue, and religious mysticism are all found in *Dune*. Young Paul Atreides, son of Duke Leto Atreides, arrives on the desert planet Arrakis, also known as Dune. His father is to govern the planet for the emperor. However, soon after their arrival, Baron Vladimir Karkomen successfully plots the downfall of the House of Atreides. The baron wants to control the planet and its most precious resource, Melange, the spice of spices, for as the baron says, "He who controls the Spice controls the Universe." Paul flees into the desert and lives among the Fremen. But the Fremen see in Paul the fulfillment of a prophecy of a Messiah who will lead them to freedom. Will the young Paul Atreides become their Messiah? Will Paul avenge the plot against his family? Will he be able to bring about the fulfillment of humanity's most ancient dream?

**Audio:** Recorded Books cassette 1556909330. Read by George Guidall.

**Film/Video/DVD:** A 1984 big-screen epic directed by David Lynch is long, difficult to follow, and much criticized by *Dune* aficionados; a much better version is the Science Fiction Channel miniseries with William Hurt done in 2000.

**New Media:** The official Dune Web site can be found at www.dunenovels.com

**Similar Reads:** *Dune Messiah* and *Children of Dune* are the next two books in the ever-expanding saga. Frank Herbert wrote six Dune novels before his death. Herbert's son, Brian Herbert, and novelist Kevin J Anderson have continued writing books in the Dune series.

**Subjects:** Political Intrigue; Religious Messianism; Mysticism; 1965 Nebula; 1966 Hugo

## Le Guin, Ursula (1929–)

🏵 *Left Hand of Darkness* (USA: 1969). ACE Charter 1991 (paper) 320pp. 0441478123 <u>S</u>

Genly Ai is an envoy of the Ekumen, the consortium of trading planets. He is sent as a lone emissary to Gethen (also called Winter) to learn about the Gethenians and to guide them into the Ekumen. As he gets to know the Gethenians, he learns that they can change gender during their mating cycle. As he travels across the ice-bound planet, he slowly learns how different the Gethenians are.

**Similar Reads:** For more thought-provoking Le Guin, try *Lathe of Heaven*. You may already know her *Earthsea* books. *Glory Season* by David Brin or <u>The Faded Sun Trilogy</u> by C. J. Cherryh

**Subjects:** Gender; Aliens; Hugo Award 1970; Nebula Award 1969; Margaret A. Edwards Award 2004

## L'Engle, Madeline (1918–)

🏵 *A Wrinkle in Time* (USA: 1962). Yearling 1973 (paper) 256pp. 0440498058 <u>M</u>
**Teen Q**

Meg Murray and her brother Charles Wallace journey to distant planets and battle with a giant totalitarian brain to save their father. They are aided in their quest by their friend Calvin and three mysterious ladies named Mrs. Who, Mrs. Whatsit, and Mrs. Which. Is love the best weapon to use when fighting the dark forces?

A best-selling children's author, Madeleine L'Engle is hard to categorize; fantasy, science fiction, and theology interact in her works. This is a book to be read on many levels.

**Audio:** Listening Library cassette 0807275875; CD 0307243230. Read by the author.

**Film/Video/DVD:** *A Wrinkle in Time* (2004) was a television production with Alfrie Woodard as Mrs. Who and Katie Stuart as Meg.

**Similar Reads:** The adventures of Meg and Charles Wallace continue in *A Wind in the Door*, *A Swiftly Tilting Planet, Many Waters,* and *An Acceptable Time.*

**Subjects:** Family; Journey; Adventure; Good and Evil; Strong Heroine; Childhood Classic; Frequently Challenged; Newbery Medal 1963; Margaret A. Edwards Award 1998

## Lewis, C. S. (1898–1963)

*Out of the Silent Planet* (England: 1943). Scribner 2003 (paper) 160pp. 0743234901 <u>S</u> **Q**

Preeminent linguist Dr. Elwin Ransom, while vacationing in the English countryside, encounters the evil Professor Weston and his associate Devine. They kidnap Dr. Ransom, put him on board a spaceship, and take him to be a human sacrifice on the planet Malacandra—the red planet we call Mars. Ransom escapes from his captors and lives among the Malacandrans, whom he comes to like. Ransom finds the three species on Malacandra to be deeply spiritual beings that live in harmony with each other. He learns that Earth is called the Silent Planet because the Malacandrans have had no contact from Earth in years. Whereas Malacandra is in a perpetual state of harmony, the Earth appears to be in a constant state of conflict.

*Out of the Silent Planet* is an adventure story with a mythic and mystical quality. It is the first book in Lewis's highly acclaimed <u>Perelandra Trilogy</u> (also referred to as <u>The Space Trilogy</u>) that explores religious themes and looks at the conflicts between science and ethics.

**Audio:** Blackstone Audio 0786198087. Read by Geoffrey Howard.

**Similar Reads:** The other two books in Lewis's <u>Perelandra Trilogy</u> are *Perelandra* and *That Hideous Strength.*

**Subjects:** Aliens; Ethics; Mars

## Verne, Jules (1828–1905)

***From the Earth to the Moon* (France: 1865).** Bantam 1993 (paper) 208pp. 0553214209 <u>M</u> **Q**
The Civil War has ended and the members of the Baltimore Gun Club have nothing to do. However, their president, Impey Barbicane, has conceived an ambitious plan to build a massive cannon that could fire a rocket to the moon. His idea is met with great enthusiasm and support. But one person opposes the project, Barbicane's greatest rival, naval officer Captain Nicholls, who wagers that it will fail. When a volunteer comes forward to man the ship, the whole affair becomes a madcap, international space race.

This is a prophetic and prescient novel—fast paced and full of humor and adventure.

**Audio:** Blackstone Audiobooks cassette 0786117664. Read by Bernard Mayes.

**Film/Video/DVD:** *From the Earth to the Moon* (1958) with Joseph Cotton is a poor adaptation.

**Similar Reads:** In addition to other classics by Verne, try *Ringworld* by Larry Niven and *Sargasso of Space* by Andre Norton.

**Subjects:** Journey; Armaments; Technology; Moon Adventure; Humor

***Journey to the Center of the Earth* (France: 1864).** Penguin 1965 (paper) 253pp. 0140022651 <u>M</u> **Q**
Arne Saknussemm, the famous Icelandic explorer, claims to have found the path to the center of the Earth. Professor Von Hardwig decides to follow Saknussemm's cryptic directions and see for himself! Accompanied by his nephew and a guide, the professor successfully descends to the center of the earth. On their journey, they find unimaginable marvels including dinosaurs and an inland sea. The one thing they didn't factor into their plans, however, was how to get home.

Typically engaging Verne—fast-paced and full of humor and exciting moments. Verne is sometimes considered the father of science fiction.

**Audio:** Recorded Books cassette 1556902719. Read by Norman Dietz.

**Film/Video/DVD:** *Journey to the Center of the Earth* (1959) starred James Mason. A production was made for TV with Treat Williams in 1999. The films take many liberties with the story, but both are good family adventure movies.

**Similar Reads:** *The Lost World* by Arthur Conan Doyle is another journey/adventure with eccentric characters. Also try *The Land That Time Forgot* by Edgar Rice

Burroughs or Verne's other adventure novel, *The Mysterious Island. From the Earth to the Moon* is another early science fiction classic by Verne.

**Subjects:** Journey; Exploration; Scientists; Lost World

***Twenty Thousand Leagues under the Sea* (France: 1870).** Tor 1995 (paper) 320pp. 0812550927 <u>M</u>

In 1866, a strange monstrous creature is attacking and sinking ships in the world's oceans. What kind of sea monster is it? Professor Aronnax joins an expedition to search out this mystery. After a month at sea, the professor's own ship is wrecked by the "creature"—the professor, his servant, and Canadian Ned Land, the only survivors, soon discover the creature that wrecked their ship is a massive submarine, the *Nautilus,* commanded by the tragic genius Captain Nemo. Nemo has rejected life on land and lives aboard the nuclear powered submarine totally devised and built by him. A vessel capable of staying underwater for unlimited amounts of time, it is extremely quiet and tremendously fast. Professor Aronnax and his companions are now engaged in one adventure after another. They see wonders of the deep never seen by humanity and gradually come to realize that Nemo is a tyrant and they are his prisoners.

Multiple protagonists express multiple points of view in this creative masterpiece. Verne presents a mechanical technology that was very plausible; many of the things that Verne imagined have become reality. He addresses the complex and ever-present issue of technology's impact on humanity.

**Audio:** Recorded Books cassette 1556905815; CD 141931162x. Read by Norman Dietz.

**Film/Video/DVD:** *20,000 Leagues under the Sea* (1954) is a Disney adventure classic with James Mason as Captain Nemo and Kirk Douglas. Two TV versions were made in 1997—Verne is very cinematic.

**Similar Reads:** Other thrilling Jules Verne adventures are *Journey to the Center of the Earth, From the Earth to the Moon,* and *The Mysterious Island*. Verne's comic adventure, *Around the World in Eighty Days* does not contain science fiction themes but is very entertaining.

**Subjects:** Sea Life; Technology; Submarines; Scientific Exploration; Ocean; Mental Illness; Sea Captains

# Time Travel

Characters travel to the past or the future to see the state of the world in these imaginative novels.

## Bellamy, Edward (1850–1898)

***Looking Backward: 2000–1887* (USA: 1888).** Signet 2000 (paper) 222pp. 0451527631 <u>S</u>

Unable to sleep, Julian West builds a soundproof, concrete room and seeks the aid of a hypnotist. He sleeps all right! When he finally emerges from his slumber, it is 112 years in the future. His house is gone, and only the concrete room has survived. The surrounding city of Boston is clean, everyone has a job, and crime no longer exists. A socialist utopia has taken the place of the chaos Julian knew years before.

This novel started a vogue for "Bellamy Clubs" and rekindled interest in Utopian fiction. Translated into more than twenty languages and a best seller in its day, it is a forgotten classic. Bellamy predicted many social changes, like universal education and debit cards, and raised many of the social issues we still ponder.

> **Audio:** Blackstone Audio cassette 0786120088; CD 0786197234. Read by Edward Lewis.

> **Similar Reads:** For another famous Victorian time traveler, read *The Time Machine* by H. G. Wells. Books by Jules Verne also predicted many conveniences of modern living long before they became reality.

> **Subjects:** Boston; Utopia; Labor; Socialism

## Butler, Octavia (1947–2006)

*Kindred* (USA: 1979). Beacon Press 2004 (paper 25th anniversary edition) 499pp. 0807083690 **S**

> Dana, a modern woman living in Los Angeles, keeps being pulled back in time to the pre–Civil War plantation where her great-grandmother was born a slave. Eventually Dana realizes that her mission there is to continually save the life of the white slave owner so that he can become her great-great-grandfather.

> An unusual science fiction novel because it has an African American woman as the protagonist and the underlying issues of slavery and race

> **Audio:** Recorded Books cassette 0788721801. Read by Kim Staunton.

> **Similar Reads:** Two other novels by Butler to try are *Parable of the Sower* and *Parable of the Talents*. Three more time travel novels with YA appeal are Connie Willis's *To Say Nothing of the Dog* and *Doomsday Book* and Jack Finney's *Time and Again*.

> **Subjects:** Los Angeles; Maryland; African Americans; Slavery; Racism; Strong Heroine; Plantation Life; Antebellum South

## Finney, Jack (1911–1995)

*Time and Again* (USA: 1970). Touchstone 1995 (paper) 400pp. 0684801051 **S**

> Suspenseful and intriguing, this illustrated novel is a time travel classic. Simon Morley, an illustrator with an advertising firm, is approached by a secret government agency to participate in a clandestine operation. The secret is time travel. He agrees to participate if he can pursue a mystery of his own.

> Filled with detailed descriptions of New York in the 1880s, this is a memorable time travel adventure and romance.

> **Audio:** Audioworks cassette 067152139x. Read by Campbell Scott.

**Similar Reads:** Finney wrote a sequel *From Time to Time.* Finney also wrote *The Invasion of the Body Snatchers.* Two more recent time travel writers with YA appeal are Octavia Butler and Connie Willis. Try Willis's *To Say Nothing of the Dog* and *Doomsday Book.*

**Subjects:** New York; Romance

## Vonnegut, Kurt (1922–)

*Slaughterhouse Five* **(USA: 1969).** Laurel 1991 (paper) 224pp. 0440180295 <u>S</u>

Billy Pilgrim "has come unstuck in time," and he travels between firebombed Dresden and the planet Tralfamadore where he is displayed in a zoo. Billy never quite recovers from the tragic destruction he witnesses in World War II Dresden, where he survived the Allied bombing by being in a meat locker at the slaughterhouse.

A famous antiwar novel—ironic and outrageous—Vonnegut believably creates an unbelievable universe grounded in reality but pushing toward the absurd. Often classed as a science fiction writer, Vonnegut is a writer with social, moral, and political views that make his books thought provoking, frequently challenged, and interesting to explore.

**Audio:** HarperAudio 2003 cassette 006056492X; CD 0060573775. Read by Ethan Hawke.

**Film/Video/DVD:** *Slaughterhouse Five* (1972) was directed by George Roy Hill.

**Similar Reads:** Other books in which soldiers question the war are *Catch-22, All Quiet on the Western Front,* and *The Red Badge of Courage.* Another Vonnegut classic is *Cat's Cradle,* also written in a science fiction mode.

**Subjects:** Dresden 1944; World War II; Prisoners of War; Absurdity; Mature Read; Frequently Challenged

## Wells, H. G. (1866–1949)

*The Time Machine* **(England: 1895).** Tor 1995 (paper) 144pp. <u>J</u> **Q**

The Victorian inventor of the Time Machine recounts his travel 800,000 years into Earth's future. In the future, he meets the Eloi, fragile, childlike people who have developed a harmonious but passive society. They are helpless, however, against the savage depredations of the nonintellectual, muscular Morlocks. When the Time Traveler (he is never named) decides to return to his own time, he learns that the Time Machine has been stolen. Will he be trapped forever in the future? Will he witness the end of mankind and of Earth?

Wells was a fascinating and progressive thinker. He wrote across genres and was famous as a social commentator as well as a writer of exciting books. His stories definitely endure, and his best-known works have translated successfully to film—*War of the Worlds, The Invisible Man, The Island of Dr. Moreau*—thus reaching a wider audience than Wells imagined.

**Audio:** Recorded Books cassette 0788706748. Read by Simon Prebble.

**Film/Video/DVD** *The Time Machine* (1960 and 2002)—very different movies but both interesting and entertaining. You get the feeling Wells would approve of them.

**Similar Reads:** Try *The Crystal World* by J. G. Ballard and *The Big Time* by Fritz Lieber.

**Subjects:** England; Future; Technology; Journey

# Chapter 4

## Fantasy

Middle Earth, Narnia, Earthsea, Oz—places that exist only in fiction and the minds and hearts of millions of readers. The fantasy genre has grown out of a long tradition from mythology and legend to the present day with Harry Potter and friends. Many readers began their exploration of fantasy as young fans of fairy tales and myths.

This genre appeals to the imagination. Fantasy fiction provides one of the great escapes from everyday living into a realm of possibility and imagination. The opportunity to visit an alternate world, a place that is highly detailed, very specific, and entirely believable, is irresistible to many readers.

Elements necessary for fantasy include a created world with imaginary creatures and the presence of extraordinary or magical powers. A large factor in the appeal of fantasy is the acceptance of magic.

Fantasy novels appeal to our sense of the heroic and fill a basic psychological need: to participate in a hero's journey or quest. The stakes in a fantasy story are high, and the story necessarily takes on the "Big Themes": courage, honor, good versus evil, and the salvation of the known world. The corollary to this is the unlikely hero. A regular guy (or girl, or pig keeper, or lowly hobbit, etc.) may be the instrument by which the world is saved. The elevation of the common to the heroic is a major theme and a major appeal of fantasy.

Also appealing to many readers is the fact that many fantasy books are written in series, so immersion in the other world does not need to end after one book. The Lord of the Rings plus its prequel, *The Hobbit*; Narnia's seven books; the forty Oz books; the Prydain Chronicles—all carry their magical stories through multiple volumes.

Fantasy and science fiction are linked together and often shelved together in libraries and bookstores; but the two genres are distinct, have different goals, and provide different experiences for a reader. Science fiction, no matter how outlandish, has a basis in the reality of our known world—it's the science part of science fiction. Fantasy can be pure imagination. The rules of gravity, time, and cause and effect need not apply in a fantasy novel. Many readers enjoy both genres, but it is worthwhile to acknowledge the distinction when providing reader's advisory service. For science fiction titles, see Chapter 3.

# General Fantasy

## Babbitt, Natalie (1932–)

*Tuck Everlasting* (USA: 1975). FSG 1985 (paper) 144pp. 0374480095 <u>M</u> **Teen Q**

Jesse Tuck will always be seventeen; he has been seventeen for eighty years now. On a hot August day, ten-year-old Winnie Foster meets Jesse Tuck in the woods beside her house. She also meets his mother and older brother when they kidnap her and take her to their home. They abduct her because there is something they need to explain to her. The Tucks are a unique family, and they want Winnie to understand why. When they explain things to her, Winnie becomes their friend and helps them.

A graceful and lyrical book with swiftly rising action and a deep philosophical question —if you could, would you want to live forever?

> **Audio:** Recorded Books cassette, 1556908520; CD 1402523475. Read by Barbara Caruso.

> **Film/Video/DVD:** *Tuck Everlasting* (2002) is a lush movie that is more of a teen love story.

> **Similar Reads:** Washington Irving's *Rip Van Winkle* is another character with a dilemma about time. Another magical story is *Fog Magic,* a Newbery Honor book from 1944 by Julia Sauer.

> **Subjects:** Immortality; Family; Friendship; Secrets; Gentle Read

## Barrie, J. M. (1860–1937)

*Peter Pan* (England: 1906). HarperFestival 2003 (paper) 240pp. 0060563079 (There are many lavishly illustrated editions as well.) <u>M</u>

"All children, except one, grow up." You know who the one is—Peter Pan. Filled with some of the most memorable characters in fiction—the pirate Captain Hook who is "never more sinister than when he was most polite"; Hook's devoted lackey Smee, a pirate who "after killing, it was his spectacles he wiped instead of his weapon"; kind, domestic-minded Wendy, who wants to mother all the Lost Boys; passionate fairy Tinkerbell; and Peter Pan himself, the charming, exasperating boy who capriciously rules Neverland.

Touching, and full of acute observations of humanity—the pomposity of Mr. Darling, the fierce loyalty of Nana, the treachery of Tinkerbell—Peter Pan is a novel for all readers: young readers love the fantasy and adventure, older readers appreciate Barrie's sly humor and creative exuberance.

> **Audio:** Recorded Books cassette 1556904096; CD 1419311115. Read by Donal Donnelly.

**Film/Video/DVD:** *Peter Pan* has been filmed many times in many versions: the Disney animated feature (1953) is delightful; the odd yet compelling *Hook* (1991) with Robin Williams as a grown-up Peter, Julia Roberts as Tinkerbell, and directed by Steven Spielberg; and a new version in 2003. *Finding Neverland* (2004) starring Johnny Depp is about J. M. Barrie and his relationship with the boys for whom he wrote *Peter Pan*. *Peter Pan* has been a stage play since 1904 and also exists as a popular Broadway musical (1954). Traditionally the character of Peter is played on stage by a woman, and the same actor plays both Mr. Darling and Captain Hook.

**Similar Reads:** Try *Peter and the Starcatchers* by Dave Barry and Ridley Pearson, a prequel to *Peter Pan.*

**Subjects:** England; Neverland; Pirates; Mermaids; Family; Humor; Childhood Classic

## Baum, Frank (1856–1919)

*The Wonderful Wizard of Oz* (**USA: 1900**). Modern Library 2003 (paper) 224pp. 081297011x <u>M</u> **Q**

When a tornado sweeps across boring and dusty Kansas, little Dorothy Gale is picked up (along with her house) and set down in a magical and confusing land. There she must join forces with a scarecrow, a man made of tin, and a lion afraid of his own shadow to find the Wizard who is powerful enough to send her home. Their fantastic journey takes them along the Yellow Brick Road past many wonders to the Emerald City of Oz.

You may think you know the story from seeing the movie, but you haven't been to the Land of dainty China or met the Quadlings. Everyone should know the magic of Baum's truly original and uniquely American fantasy story about the importance of courage and friendship, honor and home.

**Audio:** Recorded Books cassette 1402580967; CD 1402551827. Read by John McDonough.

**Film/Video/DVD:** One of the most perfect family movies ever made, the 1939 classic stars Judy Garland as Dorothy. It is funny, scary, and heart touching, complete with music, dance, flying monkeys, munchkins, and Toto, too! The contrast between dull black-and-white Kansas and vibrant Technicolor Oz still delights. The basic story has also spawned *The Wiz* (1978), an urban, African American rendition.

**Similar Reads:** Fantasy fans should explore the other Oz volumes (there are forty books). Baum wrote the next thirteen in the series. Try *The Marvelous Land of Oz; Ozma of Oz;* and *Glinda of Oz.* Books by E. Nesbit, George McDonald, or C.S. Lewis's <u>Narnia</u> books are other gentle fantasy stories.

**Subjects:** Kansas; Strong Heroine; Witches; Journey; Friendship; Wizard; Childhood Classic

## Carroll, Lewis (1832–1898)

*Alice's Adventures in Wonderland* (**England: 1865**). Signet 2000 (paper, includes *Alice through the Looking Glass* and Tenniel's original drawings) 240pp. 0451527747 **M Q**

Wordplay and poetry, talking animals, a mad queen whose only order is "Off with his head," a baby who morphs into a pig, a cat whose smile lingers long after he has disappeared, and a forthright heroine who is up for any adventure from following a White Rabbit down a hole to being the surprise witness at a trial. *Alice* is fantasy and nonsense and adventure and humor all told at a breakneck speed. Alice is not the docile little Victorian girl you might expect, and her adventures twist and turn like an evolving dream.

Written for a real little girl named Alice Lidell, the adventures of Alice still confuse and delight. Many wonderful illustrated versions exist, but it is crucial to know the original Tenniel illustrations, considered by many to exemplify a perfect union of words and pictures in a book.

**Audio:** Recorded Books cassette 1556900023. Read by Flo Gibson.

**Film/Video/DVD:** *Alice in Wonderland* (1951), the animated Disney musical, is well known; a 1999 TV version has a stellar cast.

**Similar Reads:** Alice's adventures continue in *Alice through the Looking Glass* in which readers will find Tweedledee and Tweedledum, Humpty Dumpty, and more Queens and knaves. For more fantastic English adventures, turn to *Mary Poppins* by P. L. Travers, *Doctor Dolittle* by Hugh Lofting, and books by Edith Nesbit, George MacDonald, and C. S. Lewis.

**Subjects:** Wonderland; Nonsense; Strong Heroine; Victorian Novel; Humor; Childhood Classic

## Collodi, Carlo (1826–1890)

*Pinocchio* (**Italy: 1883**). Puffin Books 1996 (paper) 262pp. 014036708X **M**

Even before he is fully carved, Pinocchio, the wooden puppet who wants to be a boy, is in trouble. He tells lies, he runs away, he disobeys. Learning right from wrong is the task Pinocchio must master before he can become a real boy. On his journey, he encounters many wondrous characters and misadventures that are both dangerous and comic.

Everyone knows the basic story, but Collodi's novel is humorous and complex. Collodi created a character who, like Tarzan, Dracula, Peter Pan, and Sherlock Holmes, transcends the original work and is a figure of world literature.

**Audio:** Recorded Books cassette 1556904150; CD 1419311247. Read by Donal Donnelly.

**Film/Video/DVD:** The classic Disney animated feature from 1940 is a perennial favorite. A fine film with Martin Landau as Geppetto was produced in 1996 that is very faithful in spirit to the book.

**Similar Reads:** For the adventures of other toys, try *Winnie the Pooh* by Milne and *The Velveteen Rabbit* by Williams.

**Subjects:** Italy; Boys; Puppets; Woodcarvers; Lying; Family; Childhood Classic

## Dickens, Charles (1812–1870)

*A Christmas Carol* **(England: 1843).** Bantam 1986 (paper) 112pp. 0553212443 <u>M</u> Q

Ebenezer Scrooge is a miser, a miserable boss, and a negligent uncle. On Christmas Eve, he is visited by three spirits who show him scenes of Christmas past, present, and future. Will redemption come to Scrooge in time to save Tiny Tim and Scrooge's own soul? This is the holiday classic that teaches the true meaning of Christmas.

Dickens was a prolific Victorian author of satiric, broadly comic novels who also imbued his work with a clear understanding of the darker side of humanity. *A Christmas Carol* is a wonderful introduction to his work.

> **Audio:** BBC Audio cassette 1855494361. Read by Miriam Margolyes.

> **Film/Video/DVD:** There are so many filmed versions of this classic story, everything from a Muppets version, to musicals, to one starring Mister Magoo! The 1984 TV production with George C. Scott as Scrooge is very faithful to the text; many viewers are partial to the 1951 Alistair Sims rendition.

> **Similar Reads:** Another English ghost can be found in Oscar Wilde's story *The Canterville Ghost.* For other Christmas classics, read *A Christmas Memory* by Truman Capote, *A Child's Christmas in Wales* by Dylan Thomas, and *The Homecoming* by Earl Hamner Jr.

> **Subjects:** Victorian England; Ghosts; Christmas; Miser; Poverty; Greed; Redemption; Victorian Novel; Family

## Nesbit, Edith (1858–1924)

*Five Children and It* **(England: 1902).** Puffin Books 2004 (paper) 256pp. 0140367438 <u>M</u>

When five children go exploring near their new home in the country, they uncover a Psammead, a sand fairy, a creature that is very ancient, does not like to be disturbed, and can grant wishes. Grudgingly, he agrees to give them one wish a day. But soon Cyril, Robert, Anthea, Jane, and their baby brother learn how difficult it is to wish wisely. They wish for beauty, and no one recognizes them; they wish for wealth, then have trouble spending it. When Robert wishes to be bigger than the local bully, he turns into a giant; and when they wish for wings, they unwisely forget that all the wishes end at sundown. Many things can happen in a day even if you get only one wish.

Nesbit was a Victorian author who wrote fantasy novels that were not sentimental or preachy but lighthearted, thought provoking, and filled with humor.

> **Audio:** Recorded Books cassette 0788752529; CD 0402519648. Read by Virginia Leishman.

> **Similar Reads:** Nesbit is perhaps best known for *The Railway Children* and its sequels. Another fantasy by Nesbit is *The Enchanted Castle.* For

more English enchantment, try books by Edward Eager such as *Half Magic*; Lucy Boston's *Children of Green Knowe*; J. K. Rowling's Harry Potter books; as well as Nesbit's Victorian compatriots Charles Kingsley and George MacDonald.

**Subjects:** Victorian England; Family; Magic; Wishes; Brothers and Sisters; Victorian Novel; Humor; Childhood Classic

### Saint Exupery, Antoine de (1900–1944)

***The Little Prince* (France: 1943).** Harvest Books 2000 (paper) 96pp. 0156012197 **M Q**

The gentle and naive little prince who has traveled to Earth from his far-off asteroid meets a pilot who is stranded in the Sahara Desert. The prince tells the story of his many travels among the planets and asteroids and the strange creatures he has met. He tells about the love he has for his beautiful rose back home and how his melancholy for her drove him away but his love for her will take him home.

A magical little story that reminds readers of the importance of innocence and the power of love.

**Film/Video/DVD:** *The Little Prince* (1974) is a magical film with Bob Fosse, Gene Wilder, and Richard Kiley.

**Similar Reads:** *The Giving Tree* by Shel Silverstein. Other nursery classics with YA appeal: *The Velveteen Rabbit* by Margery Williams; *The Wind in the Willows*; *Peter Pan*; *Pinocchio.*

**Subjects:** Love; Wonder; Loyalty; Innocence; Journey; Childhood Classic

## High Fantasy

High fantasy authors draw on mythology and folklore to create an encompassing imaginary world of beings and creatures in which readers can become immersed. The overall struggle of good versus evil is played out in epic dimensions in these magical worlds, whether Narnia, Middle Earth, or Prydain. The development of the hero is a primary theme in these stories. An unexceptional young character, very frequently an orphan of mysterious parentage, is challenged to undergo a journey or quest, and after many dangerous adventures eventually earns the status of hero. Magic is present, and supernatural forces are often in play against the hero who is aided in the tasks by a wise elder (Merlin, Gandalf) and by helpers who are often comic, always loyal. Many times these novels have invented languages and complete back-stories for the imaginary world. Often high fantasy novels are written as a series. Tolkien's Lord of the Rings is the benchmark work for this subgenre.

### Alexander, Lloyd (1924–)

**The Prydain Chronicles (USA)**

Taran the pig keeper longs for adventure. But this may be a case of "be careful what you wish for." When Hen Wen the magical pig runs off, Taran must search for her, and this leads Taran to the adventure he seeks. Joined by heroic warrior Gwydion, the bard Fflam, and Princess Eilonwy, Taran faces evil in the form of Achren the sorceress and the Horned King as he battles to save Prydain.

Based on Welsh myth, Alexander includes lots of humor, action, and adventure, all in this series set in a medieval-type setting. Although the books are aimed at young readers, they really are about the big issues all heroes face on their journey—courage, identity, justice, friendship, death.

*The Book of Three* **(1964).** Henry Holt 2006 (paper) 224pp. 0805080481 **M** **Teen Q**

*The Black Cauldron* **(1965).** Henry Holt 2006 (paper) 208pp. 080508049x **M** **Teen Q**

*Castle of Llyr* **(1966).** Henry Holt 2006 (paper) 208pp. 0805080503 **M** **Teen Q**

*Taran Wanderer* **(1967).** Henry Holt 2006 (paper) 256pp. 0805080511 **M** **Teen**

🏵 *The High King* **(1968).** Henry Holt 2006 (paper) 272pp. 080508052x **M** **Teen**

> **Audio:** Listening Library cassette 0807223130. Read by James Langton.

> **Film/Video/DVD:** *The Black Cauldron* (1985) is an animated feature by Disney.

> **Similar Reads:** More tales by Alexander can be found in *The Foundling and Other Tales of Prydain*. Susan Cooper's <u>Dark Is Rising Sequence</u> also uses Welsh myth as a basis but presents a darker worldview. Readers will want to move on to Narnia, Middle Earth, and Arthurian legends from here. The Welsh myths found in *The Mabinogoin* may also be of interest. More current fantasy books to engage Alexander fans include the <u>Harry Potter</u> books, Eoin Colfer's *Artemis Fowl,* Jonathon Stroud's <u>Bartimaeus</u> books, and books by Cornelia Funke.

> **Subjects:** Prydain; Heroes; Quest; Good and Evil; Battles; Coming of Age; Childhood Classic; Newbery Medal 1969 (for *The High King*)

## Eddings, David (1931–)

### <u>The Belgariad</u> (USA)

> Young Garion, growing up on Falder's Farm, leads a contented life under the watchful eye of his Aunt Pol. When Aunt Pol's friend, the storyteller Wolf, shows up, things begin to take an interesting twist. Whispers between Aunt Pol and Wolf seem to indicate matters of great import concerning Garion. Slowly Garion becomes aware that he is at the center of a quest to fulfill an ancient prophecy. Garion sets out in quest of his destiny, a destiny wrapped up in the Orb of Aldur and the seven-thousand-year history of wars between Gods and Men.

The series of five books has recently been published in two volumes:

*The Belgariad, Volume I.* Ballantine 2002 (paper) 656pp. 0345456327. **J**

> *Pawn of Prophecy* (1982)
>
> *Queen of Sorcery* (1981)
>
> *Magician's Gambit* (1981)

*The Belgariad, Volume II.* Ballantine 2002 (paper) 496pp. 0345456319. **J**

> *Castle of Wizardry* (1984)
>
> *Enchanter's Endgame* (1984)
>
> **Audio:** Books in Motion cassette 1581167547; CD 1-581167555. Read by Cameron Beierle. Many of Eddings's titles are available from Books in Motion (www.booksinmotion.com).
>
> **Similar Reads:** Eddings has written other series; try the <u>Malloreon</u> books next.
>
> **Subjects:** Magic; Quests

## Eddison, Eric Rucker (1882–1945)

*The Worm Ouroboros* (**England: 1922**). Replica Books 1999 (paper) 445pp. 073510171x **S**

A fierce war is being fought on the planet Mercury where the kingdoms Goblinland, Pixeyland, Demonland, and Witchland coexist. This is an epic story where noble characters and exotic beasts populate an imaginary world that resembles Viking era Northern Europe. The end of the novel is mythic and fulfills the circularity hinted at in the title—an Ouroboros is an ancient image that depicts a serpent swallowing its own tail.

A peculiar and eccentric book, this is considered seminal in the development of the fantasy genre. *The Worm Ouroboros* is definitely a challenge to a contemporary reader, but devoted fantasy fans will be enthralled. Eddison was an Icelandic scholar who wrote in a lush and romantic style, crafting extravagant descriptive passages, complex sentences, and a mock archaic style reminiscent of Old Norse.

> **Similar Reads:** Consider William Morris's *The Well at the End of the World*, Lord Dunsany's *The King of Elfland's Daughter*, Tolkien, and Andre Norton. Try Old Norse epics such as *Kalevala*, the *Saga of the Volsungs,* or the *Norse Eddas.*
>
> **Subjects:** Battle; Warriors

## Ende, Michael (1929–1995)

*The Neverending Story* (**Germany: 1979**). Puffin 1993 (paper) 448pp. 0140386335 **J Teen**

Shy and timid Bastian hides one afternoon from his local bullies in a bookstore where he finds a magical book. As he reads the book, he enters the quest to save the magical kingdom of Fantastica from The Nothing and to cure the Childlike Empress of a fatal disease. Originally written in German.

> **Film/Video/DVD:** *The Neverending Story* (1984) was directed by Wolfgang Peterson and was followed by several sequels.
>
> **Similar Reads:** Fans will also like books by Tolkien and Lewis, the <u>Harry Potter</u> books, *The Last Unicorn,* and *The Princess Bride.* A newer series to try is Jasper Fforde's <u>Thursday Next</u> stories that also takes place in books. Also try Cornelia Funke's *Inkheart* and *So, You Want to Be a Wizard* by Diana Duane.
>
> **Subjects:** Magic; Reading; Fantastica; Quest

## Howard, Robert (1906–1936)

*Conan the Conqueror* **(USA: 1950).** Ace Books 1986 (paper) 187pp. 0441115888 **J Q**

> Admittedly not great literature but a great read. Conan is the archetypal Sword and Sorcery hero—strong and brave, the answer to all problems is his sword—very violent action, adventure, and magic mingle in this made up universe of barbarians.
>
> Originally written from 1932 to 1936 as short stories for the magazine *Weird Tales,* other writers continued the story of Conan after Howard's early death from suicide.

> > **Film/Video/DVD:** Arnold Schwarzenegger was the perfect Conan in *Conan the Barbarian* (1981).
> >
> > **New Media:** Comic books featuring Conan and his barbarian world can be found at Dark Horse (www.darkhorse.com).

> > **Similar Reads:** Another Sword and Sorcery classic for mature readers is Fritz Leiber's *Swords and Deviltry* about his recurring characters Fafrhd and the Grey Mouser.
> >
> > **Subjects:** Barbarians

## Le Guin, Ursula (1929–

🌶 **The Earthsea Cycle** (USA)

> In *The Wizard of Earthsea,* we meet Sparrowhawk, soon to be called Ged. He will be the greatest wizard of all time. But first he must learn his craft. As a boy growing up, he plays with his powers. Then as an arrogant and reckless pupil at wizard school, he unleashes upon the island world of Earthsea a shadowy creature of great power. Ged must undergo an arduous quest to subdue the evil he has released. *The Tombs of Atuan* and *The Farthest Shore* follow Ged as a grown man as his story intersects with the younger characters Tenar and Arren. *Tehanu* is a work for more mature readers that tells of Tenar as a grown woman, and the last two books expand the story of the watery world of Earthsea.

> Influenced by anthropology, Jung, and Taoism, Le Guin's books are lively adventures with psychological depth. They are stories readers think about long after finishing the book.

*Wizard of Earthsea* **(1968).** Spectra 2004 (paper) 183pp. 0553262505 **M Teen Q**

🌶 *Tombs of Atuan* **(1971).** Simon Pulse 2001 (paper) 192pp. 0689845367 **M Teen Q**

*The Farthest Shore* **(1972).** Simon Pulse 2001 (paper) 272pp. 0689845340 **M Teen**

🌶 *Tehanu* **(1990).** Simon Pulse 2001 (paper) 288pp. 0689845332 **J Teen**

*Tales from Earthsea* **(2001).** Ace 2002 (paper) 336pp. 0441009328 **J Teen**

***The Other Wind* (2001).** Ace 2002 (paper) 228pp. 044100993x **J Teen**

> **Audio:** Recorded Books cassette 1556906110. Read by Rob Inglis.

> **Film/Video/DVD:** *Legend of Earthsea* (also called *Earthsea)* (2004) television production on the Sci Fi channel, a very loose adaptation that Le Guin was not involved with or pleased by; she wrote an article for the online magazine *Slate* (www.slate.com) subtitled "How the Sci Fi Channel wrecked My Books"—oops!

> **Similar Reads:** Turn to other epic fantasy series such as <u>The Chronicles of Narnia</u>, <u>The Lord of the Rings</u>, <u>Harry Potter</u>, or books by Madeleine L'Engle.

> **Subjects:** Earthsea; Journey; Magic; Wizards; Good and Evil; Nebula Award 1990 (for *Tehanu*); National Book Award 1973 (for *The Farthest Shore*); Margaret A. Edwards Award 2004; Newbery Honor 1972 (for *Tombs of Atuan)*

## Lewis, C. S. (1898–1963)

<u>**The Chronicles of Narnia**</u> **(England: 1950).** HarperTrophy; 1994 (paper, boxed edition includes all seven books) 0064471195 <u>M</u> **Teen Q**

> An uncle who is a magician, an evil Queen, and a world that is about to be created all figure in *The Magician's Nephew* when young Digory and Polly are present when Aslan creates Narnia. Many years later, the Pevensie children—Peter, Susan, Edmund, and Lucy—are sent to the rambling country home of an old professor during the London Blitz. In *The Lion the Witch and the Wardrobe,* they find a portal into Narnia where they become kings and queens and help restore the land where it is "Always winter, never Christmas." *The Horse and His Boy* follows the adventures of a boy named Shasta and his talking horse during the reign of the Pevensie's in Narnia. *Prince Caspian* follows Peter, Susan, Edmund, and Lucy when they return to Narnia after hundreds of years have passed and a civil war is raging. Edmund and Lucy and their obnoxious cousin Eustace travel to Narnia in *The Voyage of the Dawn Treader. The Silver Chair* finds Eustace back in Narnia with his cousin Jill; they are joined by Puddleglum and undertake a mission for Aslan; the final book of the series, *The Last Battle,* is a mystical story about the final days of Narnia and the birth of a better world.

> Full of adventure, action, emotion, and memorable characters, Lewis's <u>Narnia</u> books are timeless world classics. Drawing on his knowledge of myth, fairy tales, and Christianity, Lewis crafted an epic cycle that will most likely be read forever. Lewis was a famous Christian apologist (one who rationally argues for a position), and these books can be read as Christian allegorical tales as well as an epic of high fantasy in a created world. Lewis was best of friends with J. R. R. Tolkien, and they, along with several other writers teaching at midcentury Oxford who referred to themselves as "The Inklings," would gather weekly at their local pub to share their writing. Lewis shared his <u>Narnia</u> books and Tolkien his Hobbit stories.

> Although the story order is different from the order of publication, even Lewis believed that reading them in story order (as follows) was a good idea:

***The Magician's Nephew* (1955)**

***The Lion, the Witch and the Wardrobe* (1950)**

*The Horse and His Boy* **(1954)**

*Prince Caspian* **(1951)**

*The Voyage of the Dawn Treader* **(1952)**

*The Silver Chair* **(1953)**

*The Last Battle* **(1956)**

> **Audio:** For a full-cast production of all the books, go to BBC Audio at www.bbcshop.com.

> **Film/Video/DVD:** *The Chronicles of Narnia: The Lion, The Witch and The Wardrobe* appeared in 2005; undoubtedly, other titles in the series will follow.

> **New Media:** Several sites are devoted to C. S. Lewis and Narnia; www.thestonetable.com and cslewis.drzeus.net are interesting to explore. Or visit the Web site for the Mythopoeic Society, www.mythsoc.com, a group dedicated to Lewis, Tolkien, and the other Inklings.

> **Similar Reads:** Try <u>The Dark Is Rising Sequence</u> by Susan Cooper; The <u>Prydain Chronicles</u> by Lloyd Alexander; <u>Underland Chronicles</u> by Suzanne Collins; and <u>Spiderwick Chronicles</u> by Tony DiTerlizzi and Holly Black.

> **Subjects:** England, 1900 to 1949; Narnia; Christian Allegory; Journey; Blitz; Adventure; Good and Evil; Brothers and Sisters; Childhood Classic

## McCaffrey, Anne (1926–)

### 🏆 Harper Hall Trilogy (USA)

In *Dragonsong,* the first book in this trilogy, Menolly wants to be a Harper, a music maker in the world of Pern, but girls are not allowed to be Harpers. When her parents forbid her to sing and an injury prevents her from playing her instruments, Menolly runs away. She hides in a cave where she gathers strength and helps a litter of nine fire lizards to hatch. Fire lizards, and their bigger cousins, dragons, are very important in Pern. They help to battle "thread," the deadly spores of fire that fall from the sky and endanger any one out in the open. Will Menolly spend the rest of her life living alone in a cave with only her music and her fire lizard friends? How can she live in a society that will not value her talents?

Pern is an extensive world created by McCaffrey where music and dragons co-exist with adventure. *Dragonsinger* follows Menolly when she goes to Harper Hall and trains to be a harper. *Dragondrums* follows Menolly's friend the quick-witted singer Piemur as he undergoes an early career shift when his voice changes and Masterharper Robinton sends him on adventures of intrigue and danger.

*Dragonsong* **(USA: 1976).** Aladdin 2003 (paper) 208pp. 0689860080 **J̲ Teen Q**

*Dragonsinger* **(USA: 1977).** Aladdin 2003 (paper) 288pp. 0689860072 **J̲ Teen**

*Dragondrums* (USA: 1976). Aladdin 2003 (paper) 256pp. 0689860064 **J Teen**

> **Audio:** Recorded Books cassette 1556905882; CD 1419365428. Read by Sally Darling.
>
> **Similar Reads:** McCaffrey's *Dragonflight* (1968), *Dragonquest* (1971), and *the White Dragon* (1978) are the books in the <u>Dragonriders of Pern</u> trilogy that is the prequel to Harper Hall books. The <u>Harper Hall Trilogy</u> was written specifically for teen readers, but the <u>Pern</u> series was written for adults. There are also many individual Pern novels as well as short stories. A complete list can be found at McCaffrey's Web site (www.annemccaffrey.info).
>
> **Subjects:** Pern; Strong Heroine; Dragons; Coming of Age; Music; Margaret A. Edwards Award 1999

## McKillip, Patricia M. (1948–)

🎭 *Forgotten Beasts of Eld* (USA: 1974). Magic Carpet Books 1996 (paper) 352pp. 0152008691 **J**

> Sybel, a wizard, lives on the highest mountain in Eldwold with a menagerie of mystical beasts, the black swan, a dragon, a white-tusked boar that talks, the blue-eyed falcon Ter. Sybel is wise about magic; she has knowledge and the power to control these beasts, but she is ignorant of the ways of men. When a baby, her young nephew Tamlorn, is left with her to raise, she enters into the human world of revenge, betrayal, desire, war, deceit, hate, and love.
>
> **Similar Reads:** McKillip is a prolific and award-winning fantasy author in the tradition of Jane Yolen and Ursula Le Guin; read *The Riddle-Master of Hed.*
>
> **Subjects:** Wizards; Magic; Eldwold; Revenge; World Fantasy Award 1975

## McKinley, Robin (1952–)

🎭 *The Hero and the Crown* (USA: 1985). Ace Charter 1989 (paper) 227pp. 0441328091 **J Teen Q**

> *The Hero and the Crown* tells the story of young Aerin, daughter of a king, who becomes a great warrior and fights to save her beloved home of Damar. With a trusty horse named Talat and a recipe for kenet, a magic ointment that protects her from dragon fire, Aerin becomes a dragon slayer and fights the magnificent Black Dragon named Maur. Barely surviving the encounter, Aeirn then trains with the wizard Luthe, who gives her the blue sword and helps her with her psychic powers. Aerin must then battle to achieve the Hero's Crown, a magic amulet that protects Damar.
>
> Although *The Hero and the Crown* was written later, its story precedes *The Blue Sword,* which takes place centuries later in Damar. Both books are filled with romance, action, suspense, and a strong female warrior.
>
> **Audio:** Recorded Books CD 1419373838. Read by Roslyn Alexander.
>
> **Similar Reads:** Read *The Blue Sword* (Newbery Honor 1983). Readers may also want to try Tamora Pierce's novels for other strong heroines.
>
> **Subjects:** Damar; Strong Heroine; Good and Evil; Psychic Power; Dragons; Wizards; Newbery Medal 1985

## Norton, Andre (1912–2005)

### Witch World Chronicles (USA)

Simon Tregarth is a man on the run. For years he has avoided his fate, but being constantly hunted is wearing him down. On a rainy night in London, Simon is approached by a man who offers him the ultimate escape—access to a portal into another world. The portal, in the backyard of a grimy old house in London, will take him to "that existence in which his spirit, his mind—his soul if you wish to call it that—is at home." Will Simon take the chance? Discover Witch World, an enchanted realm where epic battles of good versus evil are being fought.

Norton, who lived productively until she was ninety-three, was a fantastically prolific fantasy writer. <u>Witch World</u> is her most well-known cycle of books, containing more that thirty stories. It is a complete universe more extensive than either Narnia or Middle Earth. Fantasy fans must become acquainted with Norton. The next five books in the series are the following:

*The Witch World* **(1963).** Orb 2003 (paper, called *The Gates to Witch World*, this volume contains the first three books of the Witch World Cycle) 464pp. 0765300516 <u>S</u>

*Web of the Witch World* **(1964).** <u>S</u>

*Three against the Witch World* **(1965).** <u>S</u>

*Warlock of the Witch World* **(1967).** <u>S</u>

*Sorceress of the Witch World* **(1968).** <u>S</u>

**New Media:** See www.andre-norton.org where there is a page that will link you to many other sites about Norton and her writings.

**Similar Reads:** YA readers may want to move on to Mercedes Lackey, who coauthored several works with Norton and has her own extensive list of fantasies. C. S. Lewis and J. R. R. Tolkien are the other masters of high fantasy, or try Terry Brooks, Anne McCaffrey, and Robert Jordan for equally developed fantasy worlds.

**Subjects:** Witches; Heroes; Adventure; Magic

## Tolkien, J. R. R. (1892–1973)

*The Hobbit, or There and Back Again* **(England: 1937).** Houghton Mifflin 1999 (paper) 320pp. 0618002219 <u>M</u>

Bilbo Baggins of Bag End is a peace-loving, pipe-smoking, fireside-sitting, stay-at-home hobbit. Until the day the wizard Gandalf and a party of twelve dwarves come knocking. Will Bilbo leave the peace of his home in the hill to journey across Middle Earth with a band of dwarves to fight a dragon and search for a lost ring? Well, the answer is yes, and thus begins perhaps the most successful fantasy story ever written. *The Hobbit* is the prequel to the immensely popular Lord of the Rings trilogy

> **Audio:** Recorded Books cassette 1556902336; CD 0788737279. Read by Rob Inglis.
>
> **Film/Video/DVD:** *The Hobbit* (1977) is an animated feature by Rankin and Bass.
>
> **Similar Reads:** Follow up with The Lord of the Rings trilogy
>
> **Subjects:** Middle Earth; Magic; Journey; Wizards; Hobbits; Elves; Dragons; Dwarves; Good and Evil

### The Lord of the Rings Trilogy (England: 1956)

Frodo, the nephew of Bilbo Baggins, has inherited the power and the curse of the magic ring. It is decided that the ring must be destroyed, and a Fellowship of man, dwarf, elf, and hobbit is formed under the council of Gandalf the magician to return the ring to the fires of Mount Doom. The result is an epic battle between the dark forces of Sauron, who wants the ring for himself, and all the other creatures of Middle Earth who understand that the ring must be destroyed.

This is riveting, engrossing storytelling. Tolkien created a complex world based on his scholarly knowledge of myth and linguistics. He is credited (along with his friend C. S. Lewis who wrote the Narnia books) with revitalizing the fantasy genre in the 1960s.

*The Fellowship of the Ring* **(1954).** Del Rey 2001 (paper, boxed set) 0345340426 **J**

*The Return of the King* **(1956). J**

*The Two Towers* **(1955). J**

> **Audio:** Recorded Books cassette 1402505205; CD 1402516274. Read by Rob Inglis.
>
> **Film/Video/DVD:** *The Lord of the Rings* (2001, 2002, and 2003) are blockbuster films and excellent adaptations of a written work. The final film won eleven Academy Awards, the MTV Best Movie award, and many other honors.
>
> **Similar Reads:** *The Hobbit* (1937) is the must-read prequel to Lord of the Rings. Terry Brooks's *The Sword of Shannara* and Robert Jordan's The Wheel of Time series carry on the Tolkien tradition of deeply detailed fantasy worlds. Tolkien's other works, particularly *The Silmarillion,* will please devoted fans.
>
> **Subjects:** Middle Earth; Magic; Journey; Wizards; Good and Evil; Battle; Hobbits; Dwarves; Elves

# Mythology

These are stories linked to cultures, often explaining the founding of those cultures. Themes include creation, life and death, explanation of natural phenomenon, the divine in the form of gods and goddesses, heroic deeds.

## Bulfinch, Thomas (1798–1867)

*Bulfinch's Mythology* (USA: 1855). Modern Library, 1998 (paper) 888pp. 0375751475 **M**

> Bullfinch wrote three volumes of collected myths, *The Age of Fable,* a compilation of Greek and Norse myths; *The Age of Chivalry,* Arthurian stories; and *Legends of Charlemagne,* retellings of medieval romances. Together these are known as *Bullfinch's Mythology* and provide an overview of the mythical stories on which Western literature draws.

> **Audio:** Recorded Books (titled *Age of Fable*) cassette 0788704230. Read by George Guidall.

> **Film/Video/DVD:** For movies that tell mythological tales, try *Clash of the Titans* (1981) for the story of Perseus or *Jason and the Argonauts* (1963), one of animation master Ray Harryhausen's best efforts.

> **New Media:** www.bulfinch.org has the text online and background information about Bulfinch and his works.

> **Similar Reads:** Other classic collections of mythology: *Mythology: Timeless Tales of Gods and Heroes* by Edith Hamilton and Robert Graves's *The Greek Myths*. Readers may want to turn to some of the source material for these collections; try Ovid's *Metamorphoses* and Homer's *Iliad* and *Odyssey*.

> **Subjects:** Gods and Goddesses; Greek Myths; Norse Myths

## Crossley-Holland, Kevin, editor (1941–)

*The Norse Myths* (Scandinavia: date unknown). Pantheon Fairy Tale and Folklore Library 1980 (paper) 276pp. 0394748468 **J**

> The Norse gods are every bit as entertaining and complex, noble and capricious as the Greeks. These are the stories that influenced the aggressive adventures of the medieval Vikings and serve as inspiration for many fantasy novels including Tolkien's <u>Lord of the Rings</u>. Learn about Yggdrasill the World Tree and Ragnarok the Final Battle. Visit an icy world populated with dwarves, trolls, frost giants, and fire giants and meet Odin the One-Eyed, Thor the Thunder God, and Loki the Sly One.

> **Similar Reads:** For more Norse adventure, read *Beowulf* and the *Saga of the Volsungs*. A memorable illustrated version of the Norse myths is *D'Aulaire's Norse Gods and Giants*. Stories of other gods and goddesses can be found in *Bullfinch's Mythology*.

> **Subjects:** Scandinavia; Gods and Goddesses

## Tedlock, Dennis, translator (1939–)

*Popol Vuh* (Guatemala: date unknown). Touchstone 1996 (paper) 384pp. 0684818450 **S**

> *Popol Vuh* is the ancient Mayan text containing the stories of how gods created the people and the world from the point of view of the native tribes of the New World. It depicts the Mayan world before the Europeans came. It has its

own alphabet, calendar, astronomy, politics, religion, and humor. Originally written on stone tablets in Mayan hieroglyphics, the *Popol Vuh* was destroyed and suppressed by the conquering Catholic Spaniards. The oldest manuscript of the *Popol Vuh* is in the Quiche language spoken in Guatemala.

> **Similar Reads:** For other ancient stories of gods and men, turn to the Greek epics such as *The Iliad, The Odyssey,* and *The Aeneid;* or turn to *The Volsungs Saga* from Iceland.

> **Subjects:** Mayans; Gods and Goddesses; Creation Stories

## Epic and Legend

A larger-than-life hero, cultural or national, performs superhuman deeds in a large-scale setting. Epics cover a lot of geography because they often involve a journey; they begin in the middle of the action and contain repetition; there is often interaction with gods, goddesses, and supernatural beings. These tales are told in a grand and ceremonial style. Many descended to us through the oral tradition. Most were originally performed by a bard or storyteller and were compiled over many years from multiple sources until eventually being written down. Many contain strong elements of adventure. Because so many of these works have come to us through the ages anonymously, they are arranged by title.

### Virgil (sometimes Vergil) (c. 70 B.C.–19 B.C.)

*Aeneid* **(Italy: 19 B.C.).** Vintage 1990 (paper) 464pp. 0679729526 translated by Robert Fitzgerald; Bantam Classics 1981 (paper) 416pp. 0553210416 translated by Allen Mandelbaum **S**

> "I sing of arms and of a man; his fate had made him fugitive; he was the first to journey from the coasts of Troy as far as Italy." Thus begins Virgil's epic poem about the journey that leads to the founding of Italy and the Roman Empire. Following the Trojan Wars, the hero Aeneas leaves his beloved home, the demolished city of Troy and leads a group of Trojan citizens to a new home. Along the way are many adventures, including shipwrecks, an angry goddess, a lovesick queen, and a trip to the underworld.

> This is a parallel story to the *Odyssey*: Odysseus leaves Troy to go home, whereas Aeneas leaves his home of Troy to found a new city. Some find it less exciting than either the *Iliad* or the *Odyssey*. The *Aeneid* was unfinished at Virgil's death and published posthumously. It has been a classic for two thousand years. Used throughout history as a Latin textbook, it is a story full of heroism and noble virtues such as courage, national pride, and duty.

> **Audio:** Blackstone Audiobooks 1786103167. Read by Frederick Davidson.

> **Similar Reads:** Both of Homer's epics, *The Iliad* and *The Odyssey,* were known by Virgil and probably influenced *The Aeneid*. All three deal with the Trojan War and its aftermath and are written in epic style.

> **Subjects:** Ancient Rome; Italy; Trojan War; Gods and Goddesses; Fathers and Sons; Ancient Literature

## Unknown

*Beowulf* **(England: 700).** Norton 2001 (paper, new verse translation by Seamus Heaney) 215pp. 0393320979 **J**

When Hrothgar, king of the Danes, builds a big hall, it angers the monster Grendel, and he attacks, devouring warriors, terrorizing the people. No man is strong enough to fight him. For twelve years, the castle is under siege by the unrelenting monster, "So Grendel waged his lonely war, inflicting constant cruelties on the people, atrocious hurt." Enter Beowulf, the great warrior of the Geats, come to Denmark to serve Hrothgar and defend his people. When Grendel discovers new warriors at the hall, he is delighted: "And his glee was demonic, picturing the mayhem; before morning he would rip life from limb and devour them, feed on their flesh." For Grendel, though, the party is over, "but his fate that night was due to change, his days of ravening had come to an end." Beowulf fights Grendel, the "captain of evil," but Beowulf doesn't factor in an even greater foe, Grendel's angry mother. The battle has just begun.

Beowulf is very exciting to read. It is an action story set in a time so distant it is almost mythic. It raises questions about courage, loyalty, the role of kings, and the men who serve them. It tells of both a pagan society and the coming Christianization (Grendel is a descendent of Cain). Beowulf is the oldest known surviving manuscript in Old English. It is written by an unknown author, perhaps a monk. A lively translation is crucial because the Old English (or Anglo Saxon) is really a foreign language. One key to appreciating Beowulf is the "kennings"—the figurative metaphors used in place of common nouns, such as "whale road" for the sea and "sky's candle" for the sun. This device is used throughout Norse, Anglo Saxon, and Celtic literature.

**Audio:** Recorded Books cassette 0788711695. Read by George Guidall (Francis B. Gummere translation).

**New Media:** See the following Web site: http://www.legends.dm.net/beowulf/.

**Similar Reads:** Try John Gardner's *Grendel* to hear the monster's side of things, or read some Norse sagas and myths for more heroism set in the cold, dark North. Another early heroic epic to know is *Sir Gawain and the Green Knight.*

**Subjects:** Denmark; Sixth Century; Monsters; Battle; Warriors; Anglo Saxon; Vikings; Old English; Medieval Literature

## Unknown

*El Cid* **(Spain: 1207).** Penguin 1985 (paper, bilingual edition) 256pp. 0140444467 **S**

This early thirteenth-century poem tells the story of Spain's national hero. *Cid* means "lord."

**Film/Video/DVD:** *El Cid* (1961) stars Sophia Loren and Charlton Heston.

**Subjects:** Spain; Castles; Muslims; Feudal Society; Medieval Literature

### Dante (Dante Alighieri) (1265–1321)

*The Divine Comedy* (Italy: 1321). <u>S</u>
  See the entry in Chapter 9, "Inspirational Fiction."

### Unknown

*Gilgamesh* (**Mesopotamia: 1500** B.C.). Penguin Books 2003 (paper, translated by Andrew George) 228pp. 0140449191 <u>S</u>
  Gilgamesh is the king of Uruk, a strong and powerful man, the son of a goddess, and a human. This is the story of his transformation from arrogant young man to wise and beloved king. When his friend Enkidu dies, Gilgamesh begins a quest to find eternal life.

  Older than both *The Iliad* and *The Odyssey, Gilgamesh* is a very ancient story first written in cuneiform on clay tablets in Sumeria perhaps four thousand years ago. It made its way to Babylon, where the story was standardized in about 1500 B.C. It is famous for containing the story of a flood sent by the gods, who spare one favored man who then builds a boat to carry his family and many animals safely through the waters. This story predates the story of Noah in the Bible. Gilgamesh was a real king of Sumeria around 2700 B.C.

  **Audio:** Recorded Books cassette 1419305387; CD 1419305409. Read by George Guidall.

  **Similar Reads:** For other ancient stories of gods and men, turn to *Bullfinch's Mythology* or try *The Iliad, The Odyssey,* and *The Aeneid. The Popol Vuh* from Guatemala and *The Volsungs Saga* from Iceland are other ancient stories that will intrigue modern readers.

  **Subjects:** Flood; Babylon; Sumeria; Gods and Goddesses; Quest; Friendship; Immortality; Ancient Literature

### Gardner, John (1933–1982)

*Grendel* (**USA: 1971**). Vintage 1989 (paper) 192pp. 0679723110 <u>S</u>
  Set in medieval Denmark in the halls of King Hrothgar and in the dank, cadaver-filled caves of Grendel's mother, this is a narrative tour de force that sweeps the reader into the mind of Grendel, the monster in the Beowulf legend. As Grendel narrates his side of the story in a beastly stream of consciousness, we see order versus chaos, poetry versus reality, the monstrous nature of man, and humanity in the monster.

  **Audio:** Recorded Books cassette 0788711032. Read by George Guidall.

  **New Media:** Visit http://www.brtom.org/gr/grlinks.html for a Web site that supports study of Grendel. It contains an index to Gardener's *Grendel* and definitions of many terms used in the book, as well as links to other online information.

  **Similar Reads:** Read Seamus Heaney's rendition of *Beowulf* to get the story from the hero's point of view. *Frankenstein* is another story about the monster-outsider.

  **Subjects:** Denmark; Monsters; Battle; Warriors

## Homer (9th–8th Century B.C.?)

*The Iliad* (**Greece: 800 B.C.**). Penguin Classics 1998 (paper) 704pp. 0140275363 **J**
   "Sing, O Muse, the wrath of Achilles."

*The Iliad* is the story of a great war, the siege of Ilium (hence, *Iliad*), and the sacking of Troy. It is filled with battles, warriors, and gods and goddesses who meddle in the affairs of men. But it is also the story of one man—the warrior and hero Achilles—and of his monumental anger.

*The Iliad* is full of action and has a large cast of characters. The warrior Hector, his brother Paris, and their father King Priam lead the Trojans. The Acheans (Greeks) include Agamemnon, Patroclus, Nestor, Menelaus, Achilles, and Odysseus (the Trojan horse is his idea). Even the gods and goddesses cannot stay out of the action and are constantly interfering with the events of the war—Zeus, Hera, Athena, Apollo, Poseidon all put a hand in. *The Iliad* has generated discussions about Greek history, war, friendship, family, loyalty, and heroism for generations. It is long, and parts of it are very tangential to the plot, though valuable for setting the scene and explaining the context of ancient Greece (for example, the long list of the war's participants, their ships and their horses). Nevertheless, this tale is exciting, full of adventure, and portrays timeless characters.

> **Audio:** Blackstone Audio Cassette 0786102284. Read by Natalie May.

> **Film/Video/DVD:** See *Troy* (2004) with Brad Pitt as Achilles.

> **Similar Reads:** Try the other classic epics, *The Odyssey* and *The Aeneid*.

> **Subjects:** Ancient Greece; Battle; Warriors; Troy; Trojan War; Achilles; Gods and Goddesses; Mythology; Ancient Literature

## Lonnrot, Elias, compiler (1802–1884)

*Kalevala* (**Finland: compiled in 1835**). Oxford University Press 1999 (paper, good introductory material) 679pp. 019283570X; Otava 1989 (hardback, illustrated) 9511101374 **S**

> *Long my tale's been in the cold*
> *for ages has lain hidden:*
> *shall I take the tales out of the cold . . .*
> *shall I open the word-chest*
> *and unlock the box of tales ... ?*

So asks the narrator of this Finnish national epic. This nonrhyming poem is set in the snowy, cold northern landscape that is now Finland. It tells of the origins of the world and the adventures of three brothers as they fight, start families, and interact with the spirit world. Vainamoinen is a shaman and bard, the elder statesman of the poem; Lemminkainen is the handsome young Viking warrior, a seducer of women; and Ilmarinen is the smith, a quieter hero than his brothers.

Lonnrot compiled the *Kalevala* from the oral poetry, or *runes,* he collected from old people in rural Finland. He unified the stories and crafted them into this national epic. Because it helped define an ethnic identity and provided a national story, the *Kalevala* played a role in the Finnish nationalist movement and ultimate independence of Finland from Russia following the First World War. If the poetic meter is familiar, it is because Longfellow also used it for this poem *Hiawatha.* Tolkien acknowledged his admiration of the *Kalevala.*

**Similar Reads:** For more Norse flavor, try *The Song of the Volsungs, Beowulf,* and *The Nibelungenlied.* Also *Norse Mythology* and *Norwegian Folktales.*

**Subjects:** Finland; Shamans; Magic; Brothers; Creation Stories

## Unknown

*Nibelungenlied* **(Germany: 1200).** Penguin 1965 (paper, prose translation by A. T. Hatto) 416pp. 0140441379 **J**

Middle High German epic about the hero Siegfried his wife Kriemhild and the treasure of the Nibelungs.

**Audio:** Richard Wagner used these stories, along with *The Saga of the Volsungs,* as the basis for his famous Ring cycle of dramatic operas, *Das Rheingold, Die Valkyrie, Siefried,* and *Gotterdammerung*—all about the chaos caused by a magic ring made from dwarf gold.

**Subjects:** Knights; Dwarves; Dragons; Warriors; Jealousy; Medieval Literature

## Homer (9th–8th century B.C.?)

*Odyssey* **(Greece: 800 B.C.).** Penguin 1999 (paper, Robert Fagles translation) 560pp. 0140268863 **J**

The brave and cunning warrior Odysseus, having fought boldly in the Trojan War, is now ready to return home to Ithaca. Awaiting him at home are his lovely wife Penelope and his young son Telemachus. But Odysseus can never quite get home, for one misadventure after another keeps him from Ithaca. He is held captive by the sea nymph Calypso and must rescue his men from the dreamy Lotus Eaters; he battles the one-eyed cannibal, Polyphemus, and outsmarts the enchantress Circe; and he must sail past the monster Scylla and through the whirlpool Charybdis. His men seem to be working against him and a God is mad at him, but Odysseus keeps trying to get home. Meanwhile in Ithaca, Penelope is fending off the suitors who have descended upon her. They eat all her food, disrupt her household, and want to marry her because they think that Odysseus is already dead. And young Telemachus is on his own journey to become a man, defend his mother, and find his father.

Once you get into the rhythm of the ancient poem, it is a thrilling adventure story that contains everything fiction does best: a journey, a homecoming, family, love, loyalty, the pursuit of identity, and big questions about things such as fate and the role of the Gods in human life.

**Audio:** Blackstone cassette 0786123885; CD 0786192836. Read by a full cast.

**Film/Video/DVD:** *The Odyssey* (1997) with Armand Assante doesn't include every adventure but captures the spirit of the story.

**Similar Reads:** Dedicated readers will want to try Homer's other epic, *The Iliad*. It is the prequel to *The Odyssey,* telling the story of the war from which Odysseus is returning home. Virgil's *The Aeneid* tells of Aeneas's voyages and the founding of Rome. *Bulfinch's Mythology* is another good companion read. Centuries later, James Joyce wrote *Ulysses,* a long, modernist novel that follows the pattern of *The Odyssey*.

**Subjects:** Ancient Greece; Journey; Warriors; Family; Fathers and Sons; Mythology; Gods and Goddesses; Ancient Literature

## Milton, John (1608–1674)

*Paradise Lost* **(England: 1667)**
   See the entry in Chapter 9, "Inspirational Fiction."

## Unknown

*Saga of the Volsungs* **(Iceland: 1200).** Penguin Books 2000 (paper) 160pp. 0140447385 **S**
   Old Norse epic about Sigurd the warrior, Fafnir the dragon and a treasure of gold.

> **Similar Reads:** Explore other sagas, such as *Njal's Saga,* about a feud that becomes super deadly when Njal is trapped in his burning house, also called *Burnt Njal*. This was source material for Tolkien's <u>Lord of the Rings</u>; H. Rider Haggard based his novel *Eric Brighteyes* on many of the old Norse myths and sagas

> **Subjects:** Vikings; Dragons; Warriors; Medieval Literature

## Unknown

*Song of Roland* **(France: 1130).** Signet Classics 2002 (paper) 192pp. 0451528573 **J**
   The Christian French have been fighting the Muslim Saracens in Spain for seven years. When King Charlemagne is convinced to go home to France, he leaves as commander of his rear guard his finest warrior Roland, Roland's bosom friend Olivier and a small troop. But Charlemagne was sent home by a trick, and the rear guard is attacked. Although Roland's friend prompts him to blow his famous horn, Olifant, to summon help, Roland's code of warrior honor prevents him from doing so. When he finally blows his horn with his dying breath, it is too late, and Charlemagne and the troops return to find the slaughtered heroes.

   This epic tale of brave knights facing treachery with heroism is a *chanson de geste,* a song of great deeds, originally performed at the royal court by *jongleurs,* traveling musicians. *Song of Roland,* like all epics, is part of the oral tradition and wonderful to read out loud. The Battle of Roncevaux (or Roncesvalles) was a historic event in A.D. 778 at which the rear guard of Charlemagne's army was annihilated.

   **Audio:** Blackstone Audiobooks cassette 0786113642. Performed by cast.

   **Film/Video/DVD:** *Song of Roland* (1978) is a French production with Klaus Kinski as Roland.

**Similar Reads:** For more bravery and chivalry, try *El Cid* and the many King Arthur stories.

**Subjects:** France; Spain; Battle of Roncevaux; Charlemagne; Muslims; Honor; Courage; Friendship; Medieval Literature; Chivalry; Warriors

## Unknown

*Sundiata* **(Mali: 1300).** Longman 1995 (paper) 101pp. 0582264758; also available as a picture book with complex woodcut illustrations by David Wisniewski, Clarion Books 1999 (hardback) 32pp. 0395764815 **M**

The youngest of eleven sons, Sundiata is a weak child, unable to walk, but he grows up to be a great warrior and ruler of the West African kingdom of Mali.

**Subjects:** Mali; Africa; Medieval Literature; Courage; Disability

# Arthurian Fiction

Mystery surrounds King Arthur—was he a historical figure or a legend? Was he a fifth-century Briton, a victorious commander who fought the invading Romans? A leader of his own band of knights destroyed by their internal dissensions? Did he originate the ideas of chivalry and courtly love? Was he a national hero invented to help his people through the Dark Ages? Geoffrey of Monmouth wrote about such a hero as early as 1136 in his *History of the Kings of Britain.* The French also wrote about Arthur, his knight Lancelot, and the development and pitfalls of chivalry. Writers draw on these sources as well as their own vivid imaginations to give us many variations on the stories that involve King Arthur and Guinevere, the Knights of the Round Table and their Ladies, Morgan Le Fay, Mordred, and the wizard Merlin.

## Bradley, Marion Zimmer (1930–1999)

*The Mists of Avalon* **(USA: 1982).** Del Rey 1982 (paper) 912pp. 0345350499 **S**

Morgan Le Fay, called Morgaine in this book, is a priestess of the old religion. She tells the story of her life and its intersection with the characters of Camelot: her half-brother King Arthur who can unite Britain and drive out invaders, his Christian wife Gwenhwyfar, the knight Lancelot, Mordred (called Gwydion), and Merlyn.

Marion Zimmer Bradley struck a new vein of Arthurian interest with this best-selling book. The struggle of matriarchal pagan Celtic Britain giving way to patriarchal Roman warriors and the Christian Church is presented in this unique version of the Arthurian legends told from the points of view of the women characters. Bradley was a prolific author of fantasy and science fiction (the <u>Darkover</u> series). She continued the saga of the Avalon priestesses in several other volumes: *The Forest House, Lady of Avalon, Priestess of Avalon,* and *Ancestors of Avalon,* the last two published posthumously and finished by Diana L. Paxson.

**Audio:** Available from Recorded Books in four volumes: 1141932506X (book 1), 1419324705 (book 2), 1419324322 (book 3), 1419324721 (book 4). Read by Davina Porter.

**Film/Video/DVD:** *Mists of Avalon* (2001) is a fine, three-hour, made for TV production with Angelica Houston and Julianna Margulies.

**Similar Reads:** Fans of Arthurian legend have many places to turn next. Try T. H. White's classic *The Once and Future King*. Persia Wooley wrote a trilogy of romances that tell Guinevere's story, or read Mary Stewart's Authurian Saga books give the tales from Merlin's perspective. Try the source material *Le Morte d'Arthur* by Malory or the poetic retelling by Tennyson, *The Idylls of the King*.

**Subjects:** England; Druids; King Arthur; Camelot; Merlin; Guinevere; Morgan Le Fay

## Cooper, Susan (1935–)

🏵 **The Dark Is Rising Sequence (five novels) (England: 1965). M Teen**

When Will Stanton turns eleven, he learns that he is a member of the ancient race of immortals called the Old Ones and that his duty is to fight the evil known as the Dark. Eventually joined on his mission by Bran, an albino boy from Wales with a white dog named Cafall; and the three Drew children, Simon, Jane, and Barney (who figure in the first book of the series); and aided by Merriman, a mystical and ageless man who understands Will's mission, Will seeks to fulfill his high purpose of keeping back the Dark. Set in the world of realism, these books gradually expose the mysterious, mythical realm that presumably exists all around our everyday experience. This is one of the most popular fantasy series ever written for younger readers. It is a dark and complex cycle of stories full of adventure and mystery that incorporate Celtic mythology and Arthurian legend with the humanity's most basic plot: good against evil.

The sequence of five novels is as follows:

*Over Sea, Under Stone* **(1965).** Simon Pulse 1993 (paper, boxed set includes all five novels) 1148pp. 0020425651.

*The Dark Is Rising* **(1973)**

*Greenwitch* **(1974)**

*The Grey King* **(1975)**

*Silver on the Tree* **(1977)**

    **Audio:** All books are available from Books on Tape.

    **Film/Video/DVD:** A film has been announced for 2007.

    **Similar Reads:** Try the Prydain Chronicles by Lloyd Alexander, Philip Pullman's His Dark Materials trilogy, and Madeleine L'Engle's books. Fans of Narnia, Middle Earth, Earthsea, and Harry Potter will want to read this series as well.

    **Subjects:** England, Cornwall; King Arthur; Good and Evil; Celtic Mythology; Merlin; Adventure; Wales; 1976 Newbery Medal (for *The Grey King*)

## Malory, Sir Thomas (1408–1471)

*Le Morte d'Arthur* **(England: 1469).** Signet 2001 (paper) 512pp. 0451528166 **J**

Queens, castles, courtly love, chivalry, knights, and noble quests populate Malory's prose retelling of the legends of King Arthur. Historically important as the first English prose epic and the first compilation of the Arthur stories in English, Malory's work can seem dense and archaic. Dedicated readers, however, will find these stories exciting and full of adventure. Readers who love high fantasy and Arthurian stories will be fascinated by the formality and expansiveness of Malory.

**Audio:** Highbridge Audio cassette 156511227X. Read by Derek Jacobi.

**Film/Video/DVD:** *Excalibur* (1981) is loosely adapted from Malory's stories; *King Arthur* (2004) sets the story in the fifth century as a contest between native Britons and invading Romans.

**Similar Reads:** All subsequent books about King Arthur and his Knights of the Round Table draw from Malory. John Steinbeck wrote an adaptation of Malory, *The Acts of King Arthur and His Noble Knights* (published posthumously in 1976) that is highly recommended. For more medieval works of chivalry, try Chretien de Troyes *Arthurian Romances* from twelfth-century France; *Parzival* by Wolfram von Eschenbach, about the knight who searches for the Holy Grail; or *The Romance of Tristan and Iseult* (retold by Joseph Bedier, Vintage Classics).

**Subjects:** England; King Arthur; Knights; Chivalry; Courtly Life; Medieval Literature

## Pearl Poet (c. 1370)

*Sir Gawain and the Green Knight* **(England: 1370).** Signet Book 2001 (paper, translated by Burton Raffel) 144pp. 0451528182 **J**

It is Christmas at King Arthur's court. The knights and ladies are feasting when into the hall rides a green knight on a green horse. He challenges any knight there to cut off his head. The only catch: in a year and a day, that knight must come to the Green Knight's castle and have his own head cut off! Sir Gawain accepts the challenge, he cuts, and the green man's head rolls. But, surprisingly, the now-headless Green Knight picks up his head, reminds Gawain of his promise, mounts his horse, and rides away. Will Gawain keep his promise? And what other bargains will Gawain enter into as he journeys to his appointment with the Green Knight?

Written by an unknown poet about the time of Chaucer, this is a story about honor, courage, and promises with a rich medieval/Arthurian setting. Merwin's 2002 translation is very approachable.

**Film/Video/DVD:** *Sword of the Valiant* (1982) featured Sean Connery as the Green Knight but is not a classic.

**Similar Reads:** Try *Le Morte d'Arthur* or *Beowulf;* readers who are truly interested in Celtic lore may want to explore the *Mabinogion,* the complex cycle of Welsh tales telling of heroes and containing some early Arthurian legends.

**Subjects:** England; Knights; Chivalry; Quest; King Arthur; Medieval Literature

## Stewart, Mary (1916–)

### Arthurian Saga (England)

In *The Crystal Cave,* we meet Merlin as a young man, witness his role in the birth of Arthur, and see the development of his relationship with the future king. *The Hollow Hills* and *The Last Enchantment* follow the development of Arthur into a king. The final book is a recasting of Mordred's story. The first three books are sometimes referred to as The Merlin Trilogy.

Stewart's Arthurian Saga consists of the following titles:

*The Crystal Cave* (**1970**). EOS 2003 (paper) 512pp. 0060548258 **J**

*The Hollow Hills* (**1973**). EOS 2003 (paper) 496pp. 0060548266 **J**

*Last Enchantment* (**1979**). EOS 2003 (paper) 528pp. 0060548274 **J**

*The Wicked Day* (**1983**). EOS 2003 (paper) 432pp. 0060548282 **J**

**Film/Video/DVD:** *Merlin* (1998), a TV movie with Sam Neil, was not specifically based on Stewart's books but is an enthralling adaptation of Merlin stories.

**Similar Reads:** Stewart is well known as the author of romantic suspense novels such as *Nine Coaches Waiting, Touch Not the Cat,* and *The Moonspinners.*

**Subjects:** England; King Arthur; Merlin; Camelot; Wizards; Knights; Warriors; Chivalry

## White, T. H. (1906–1964)

*The Once and Future King* (**England: 1958**). Ace Books 1987 (paper) 639pp. 0441627404 **S**

Sixty years before Harry Potter and Dumbledore, the most famous wizard of all, Merlin, taught his student Wart about power and leadership by changing him into various animals. That boy grows up to be King Arthur. How Merlin and Wart meet, Wart's unconventional education, and how he becomes known as the rightful king are all told in the first book of *The Once and Future King,* the lighthearted fantasy called *The Sword in the Stone* (1938).

*The Once and Future King* also contains *The Queen of Air and Darkness* (1939), *The Ill-Made Knight* (1940), and *The Candle in the Wind* (1958). These books tell the darker, more mature story of the gathering of the Knights of the Round Table, Arthur's development of the code of chivalry, and the rise and fall of Arthur's kingdom, Camelot. Guinevere and Lancelot, Morgan Le Fey, Mordred, and all the knights and their ladies figure in the later books. White followed with *The Book of Merlyn* (1977).

**Film/Video/DVD:** Disney's animated *Sword in the Stone* (1963) is based on the first book in the novel. *Camelot* the Broadway musical (1960) and movie (1967) is based on the final book in White's series. For something completely different, YA readers often appreciate Monty Python's take on knights of old, *Monty Python and the Holy Grail* (1975).

**Similar Reads:** Go to the source material, Thomas Malory's *Le Morte d'Arthur,* or for a poetic retelling, try *Idylls of the King,* Tennyson's lyric version of several of the Arthur stories. John Steinbeck also took a stab at retelling the tales of Arthur's early adventures in *The Acts of King Arthur and His Noble Knights. The Merlin Trilogy* by Mary Stewart and *The Mists of Avalon* by Marion Zimmer Bradley tell the Arthur stories from other points of view.

**Subjects:** England; King Arthur; Merlin; Guinevere; Camelot; Knights; Chivalry; Wizards

# Folktales

Here are stories that have grown from the oral tradition of the common people (as opposed to heroic legends about warriors, kings, and battles or mythological stories about gods and goddesses). These stories often explain traditional beliefs or local customs and express thematic similarities across cultures—poverty and wealth, beauty and goodness versus ugliness and evil; clever common heroes. Magic is a common element to these stories, and therefore readers who love contemporary fantasy and mythology often also enjoy folktales. Many stories will be remembered from childhood picture books, but there is a wealth of international material to explore.

## Asbjornsen, Peter (1812–1885)

*Norwegian Folktales* (**Norway: 1841**). Pantheon Fairy Tale and Folklore Library 1982 (paper) 192pp. 0394710541 **M Q**

Asbjornsen and his colleague Jorgen Moe did for Norwegian folklore what the Grimm Brothers did for German folklore, compiled and standardized versions of the stories that "the folk" had been telling for centuries. "Three Billy Goats Gruff" and "East of the Sun and West of the Moon" are two of the most well-known tales from this collection. Fantasy fans may enjoy reading some of the source material for many of their favorite fantasy authors such as Tolkien and Lewis.

**Similar Reads:** Turn to Grimm's fairy tales, Norse mythology, or fantasy classics such as The Chronicles of Narnia or Lord of the Rings.

**Subjects:** Norway; Scandinavia; Trolls; Ogres; Childhood Classic

## Calvino, Italo (1923–1985)

*Italian Folktales* (**Italy: 1980**). Harvest/HBJ Book 1992 (paper) 800pp. 0156454890 **J**

Italian novelist Calvino compiled two hundred Italian folktales for this book. They are strange and interesting stories that you probably have never heard before. These are well worth exploring for fans of folklore and Italian literature.

**Subjects:** Italy

## Grimm, Jacob (1785–1863), and Wilhelm Grimm (1786–1859)

*Grimm's Fairy Tales* **(Germany: 1812).** Barnes and Noble 2003 (paper) 517pp. 1593080565 **M Q**

This is the famous collection of tales that introduced such characters as Hansel and Gretel, Snow White, Rumplestiltskin, and Rapunzel to an international audience.

The Grimm Brothers were motivated by scholarship when they traveled around Germany in the early 1800s collecting and transcribing stories told by the people. Their intention was to explore German folklore, language, and the oral tradition. Inadvertently they created a popular collection of folktales that became beloved by generations of readers around the world. The brothers inspired a vogue for other collections of national folktales. These stores were only a small part of the brothers' overall intellectual contributions to German and world literature; Jacob was famous as a linguist and compiler of a German dictionary, and both were professors and librarians in Gottingen. Although the stories are referred to as "fairy tales," they are more accurately folktales.

**Audio:** Naxos AudioBooks cassette 9626345055; CD 9626340053. Read by Laura Paton accompanied by classical music.

**Film/Video/DVD:** *The Wonderful World of the Brothers Grimm* (1962) is a fictionalized biography of the brothers with three of their tales. *The Brothers Grimm* (2005) with Matt Damon and Heath Ledger has little to do with the real Grimm brothers but will appeal to teens. *Snow White and the Seven Dwarves* (1937) is Disney's first animated feature length film and still a beautiful movie.

**Similar Reads:** Hans Christian Andersen, Charles Perrault, and Peter Christian Asbjornsen are the natural companions to these stories. An entirely new genre of folktale retellings has appeared on the YA scene recently that take the old stories as their basis—*Beauty* and *Spindle's End* by Robin McKinley; *Beast* and *Zel* by Donna Jo Napoli; *Just Ella* by Margaret Peterson Haddix; *Briar Rose* by Jane Yolen; and many others. YA readers will definitely want to explore these new novels.

**Subjects:** Germany; Folktales; Childhood Classic

## Harris, Joel Chandler (1848–1908)

*Uncle Remus Tales* **(USA: 1880).** Dial Books 1999 (hardcover, *Uncle Remus, The Complete Tales* as told by Julius Lester and illustrated by Jerry Pinkney) 696pp. 0803724519 **M**

Uncle Remus is an aging African American who tells stories about clever anthropomorphized animals, like the trickster hero Brer Rabbit, small and seemingly weak, but with a prodigious talent for outwitting his enemies. Harris's version of the stories are practically impossible to read now because of the heavy use of nineteenth-century African American dialect from the Deep South, for example: "Nex' day, Brer Fox sont word by Mr. Mink, en skuze hisse'f kaze he wuz too sick fer ter come, en he ax Brer Rabbit fer ter come en take dinner wid him, en Brer Rabbit say he wuz 'gree'ble." Also, current political sensibilities make the dialect distasteful to many. Lester's volume gives access to these humorous traditional stories while eliminating the barrier and offensiveness of the dialect.

Harris (as well as other nineteenth-century compilers) adapted these stories from the oral tradition of African slaves who adapted African folktales to an American setting. Many of the tales fall into the category of trickster tales. All world mythologies have trickster tales. Other famous tricksters include Loki from Norse mythology, Anansi from West Africa, Raven from the Pacific Northwest, and Coyote from Plains Native American traditions. Brer Rabbit can be considered a direct ancestor of Bugs Bunny.

**Film/Video/DVD:** Disney's *Song of the South* (1946) puts three animated stories in a frame story set on a plantation in the South where Uncle Remus tells stories to a young boy.

**Similar Reads:** Other animal stories such as *Aesop's Fables* and the *Jataka Tales*. Virginia Hamilton has a nice collection of trickster tales called *A Ring of Tricksters* (Blue Sky Press 1997, illustrated by Barry Moser).

**Subjects:** American South; Storytelling; Talking Animals; Trickster Tales; Animal Fantasy and Fable; Humor; Childhood Classic

## Yolen, Jane, editor (1939–)

***Favorite Folktales from Around the World*** **(USA: 1986).** Pantheon 1988 (Paper) 512pp. 0394751884 **M**

A glorious international collection of stories arranged thematically, perfect for the reader interested in world culture, oral history, folklore, and good stories.

**Similar Reads:** All of the books in the Pantheon Fairy and Folklore Library from Random House (www.randomhouse.com/pantheon/fairytales/) are noteworthy collections of folktales and fairy tales from around the world—China, Africa, India, Russia, and more. They are excellent volumes for readers of any age interested in fantasy, folk literature, and fairy tales. Also try *Best Loved Folktales from Around the World* (Anchor 1983) by Joanna Cole.

**Subjects:** Folklore; Childhood Classic

# Fairy Tales

*"But some day you will be old enough to start reading fairy tales again." —C. S. Lewis*

The stories in this subdivision of folklore generally contain fairies, princesses, humble heroes, witches, giants, and other folkloric beings, as well as fantastic transformations and magical happenings. They are typically the imaginative literary work of one author.

## Andersen, Hans Christian (1805–1875)

***Andersen's Fairy Tales*** **(Denmark: 1835).** Anchor 1983 (paper) 1120pp. 0385189516 **M Q**

"The Princess and the Pea," "The Ugly Duckling," "Thumbelina," "The Little Mermaid," "The Emperor's New Clothes," "The Snow Queen," "The Nightingale," "The Little Match Girl," and "The Red Shoes" are just a few of the 168 stories Andersen wrote in Demark from 1835 to 1872. Andersen's stories are considered literary fairy tales because he created them, that is, he didn't collect them as the Brothers Grimm did with their stories.

Andersen wrote in a deceptively simple style, using realistic language with straightforward images to tell his stories. As you read Andersen's tales, decide for yourself if they are simple bedtime stories or psychologically complex peeks into the multifaceted human psyche.

> **Audio:** Naxos Audiobooks cassette 9626345128; CD 9626340126. Read by Erica Johns with classical music.

> **Film/Video/DVD:** Andersen's stories exist today in various adaptations—Disney's *The Little Mermaid* (1989) or the Broadway musical *Once Upon a Mattress* (1959) loosely based on *The Princess and the Pea,* for example. These provide great entertainment but are not entirely accurate to Anderson's stories. Danny Kaye was brilliant in *Hans Christian Andersen* (1952), which gives an impression of Andersen's life and times but is not an accurate biopic. The same is true for the 2001 TV movie called *Hans Christian Andersen: My Life as a Fairy Tale.*

> **Similar Reads:** Try Asbjornsen's *Norwegian Folktales*, Perrault, and the Grimm Brothers collection; Oscar Wilde and George MacDonald also wrote literary fairy tales.

> **Subjects:** Denmark; Childhood Classic

## McKinley, Robin (1952–)

***Beauty: A Retelling of the Story of Beauty and the Beast*** **(USA: 1978).** Eos 2005 (paper) 336pp. 0060753102 **J Teen**

Beauty's name mocks her; she is thin and awkward, and she is not a beauty as are her two sisters, Hope and Grace. But when her father needs her help, Beauty sacrifices herself to a Beast in an enchanted castle.

McKinley, author of the fantasy classics *The Hero and the Crown, The Blue Sword* (1982), and *Spindle's End* (2000), helped start the new genre of reenvisioned fairy tales expanded into novels.

> **Film/Video/DVD:** Two film versions of the original Beauty and the Beast story stand out: Jean Cocteau's classic French film *La Belle et la bete* (1946) renowned for its brilliantly stylistic imagery and Disney's animated musical *Beauty and the Beast* (1991).

**Similar Reads:** The retold fairy tale has become a well-liked subgenre of YA fantasy fiction; try *Zel, Beast,* or *Bound* by Donna Jo Napoli or *Ella Enchanted* by Gail Carson Levine.

**Subjects:** Family; Fathers and Daughters; Romance; Strong Heroine

## Perrault, Charles (1628–1703)

*Tales* **(France: 1697).** Puffin Books 2000 (paper) 193pp. 0141306513 **M Q**

Charles Perrault gathered stories already in existence, stories he had heard as a child, and put them into the form we cherish today adding enough elements to turn simple folktales into literature that has endured for going on four hundred years. The eight stories included in the original edition make up a primer of fairy tales: "Cinderella," "Red Riding Hood," "Sleeping Beauty," "Puss in Boots," "Tom Thumb," "Bluebeard," and the less well-remembered "Ricky of the Tuft" and "Diamonds and Toads."

**Film/Video/DVD:** These stories have inspired music, opera, ballets, and films: *La Cenerentola* (1817) is Rossini's opera based on "Cinderella"; *Ever After* (1998) with Drew Barrymore is a reworking of "Cinderella"; another is *The Slipper and the Rose* (1976) with Richard Chamberlain; even Jerry Lewis made an adaptation of the Cinderella story, *Cinderfella* (1960). Charlie Chaplin's 1947 black comedy *Monsieur Verdoux* is based on "Bluebeard"; *The Sleeping Beauty* (1888) is a ballet by Tchaikovsky; the Disney animated classic *Sleeping Beauty* came out in 1959 to critical acclaim; the character Puss in Boots figured prominently in *Shrek 2* (2004); Russ Tamblyn was Tom Thumb in the 1958 family musical *Tom Thumb.*

**Similar Reads:** Read other fairy tales by the Brothers Grimm, Andersen, and Wilde. True fairy tale devotees will want to explore Andrew Lang's nineteenth-century collections of fairy tales: *The Blue Fairy Book*, *The Red Fairy Book, The Grey Fairy Book,* and other titles.

**Subjects:** France; Childhood Classic

## Unknown

*The Arabian Nights* **(Persia: 1450).** W. W. Norton 1990 (paper, modern translation by Husain Haddawy) 126pp. 0393313670; Modern Library 2001 (paper, Victorian translation by Richard Burton) 916pp. 0375756752 **S**

In the ancient East there lived a king. Because one woman, his wife and queen, betrayed him, he vowed to take revenge on all women. So every day, he married a new virgin bride and every morning after one night with her, he had her killed. This went on for three years. Finally (when very few virgins remained), the beautiful and clever Shahrazad, daughter of the king's vizier, determined to become the next bride and save her people from the vengeful king. With the help of her sister Dinarzad, Shahrazad tells the king a tale every night, always reaching the most suspenseful point of the story just as morning breaks. Will the king let her live long enough to complete the tale?

The tales told by Shahrazad are full of perfume and jewels, magic and romance! Aladdin and his magic lamp, the voyages of Sinbad, and Ali Baba and the forty thieves are some of the well-known stories often told to children, but the bulk of the tales are for a mature audience. First brought to Europe in a French translation by Galland in the beginning of the eighteenth century, the most famous translation is the high Victorian version rendered in the 1880s by Sir Richard Burton, explorer and scholar. Modern versions and translations make the stories even more accessible to contemporary readers looking for the exotic. This is the kind of story collection you can pick up, open to any page, and begin to read.

**Audio:** Blackstone Audio cassette 0786117982; CD 0786198664. Selected stories read by Johanna Ward.

**Film/Video/DVD:** There is a campy Technicolor film from 1942 called *Arabian Nights* and a TV miniseries *The Arabian Nights* (2000) that weaves several of the tales with a modified Shahrazad frame story.

**Similar Reads:** Andrew Lang included tales from *The Arabian Nights* as well as stories from other countries in his colored fairy tale collections: *The Blue Fairy Book*, *The Red Fairy Books*, etc.

**Subjects:** Storytelling; Magic; Strong Heroine

## Wilde, Oscar (1854–1900)

***The Happy Prince and Other Tales* (England: 1888).** Signet 1996 (paper, *The Complete Fairy Tales of Oscar Wilde*) 224pp. 0451524357 <u>M</u> **Q**

The Happy Prince is a statue that sees sadness all over the city from his position on a high pedestal and sacrifices himself to alleviate the suffering of others. Wilde's stories are gentle and literary, full of satiric humor and a pervasive melancholy. Other stories are "The Selfish Giant" and "The Star Child." Wilde acknowledged Hans Christian Andersen's tales as models for his own.

**Audio:** Blackstone Audio 0786106727. Read by Johanna Ward.

**Similar Reads:** The mix of gentle humor and melancholy in Wilde's stories is reminiscent of *The Little Prince* by Saint-Exupery. For more lighthearted Wilde, read his funny ghost story *The Canterville Ghost,* for serious Wilde, try *The Picture of Dorian Gray.* His play *The Importance of Being Earnest* (1895) is also a must read.

**Subjects:** Compassion; Childhood Classic

# Animal Fantasy and Fables

In animal fantasy, humans take secondary roles when animals, whether barnyard dwellers or pets, toys or real, become the protagonists, and the world is viewed from their perspective. However, these are animals that think and talk like human beings and share many a human truth. Immensely appealing to many readers, animal fantasy is imaginative literature that is often full of adventure, pathos, and universal truths.

## Adams, Richard (1920–)

*Watership Down* (England, 1972). Avon 1976 (paper) 496pp. 0380002930 **J**

When Fiver, a high-strung and clairvoyant rabbit, senses that the warren is in great danger, he and his brother Hazel convince several other young male rabbits to leave their doomed home. Their journey to find and populate a new warren becomes an epic story of courage, survival, cleverness, and leadership. Along the way, they befriend a seagull, tell stories about their mythic rabbit trickster god *El-hairara,* and encounter other rabbit societies. These questing rabbits achieve mythic proportions as they take their fates into their own paws.

Finely delineated characters, detailed nature writing and exciting, suspenseful action make this a multilayered classic. A best and perennial seller. You never knew you could care so much about rabbits.

>   **Audio:** Books on Tape cassette 0736617000. Read by John Macdonald

>   **Film/Video/DVD:** *Watership Down* (1979) is an animated version with stellar English actors (Ralph Richardson, Denholm Elliott) providing the voices for the rabbits —very intense, not a children's movie.

>   **Similar Reads:** Other stories with animals as the main characters include Brian Jacques's Redwall series and *The Book of the Dun Cow* by Walter Wangerin. *The Wind in the Willows* by Kenneth Grahame and *Rabbit Hill* by Robert Lawson are gentler stories; *Silverwing* by Kenneth Oppel is about a bat on a quest, and two rodent stories *Mrs. Frisby and the Rats of NIHM* by Robert C. O'Brien and Avi's *Poppy* extend the animal fantasy field.

>   **Subjects:** England; Rabbits; Journey; Nature; Talking Animals; Social Structures

## Aesop (c. 600 B.C.)

*Aesop's Fables* (Greece: c. 600 B.C.). Puffin Books 1996 (paper) 224pp 0140369848; Oxford University Press 2003 (paper, more scholarly presentation) 306pp. 0192840509 **M Q**

If you have ever used the phrases "sour grapes," "dog in the manger," "wolf in sheep's clothing," or "don't count your chickens before they hatch," you have quoted an Aesop's fable. Readers may remember their favorites from childhood picture book editions—"The Fox and the Grapes," "The Boy Who Cried Wolf," "The Country Mouse and the City Mouse," "Belling the Cat," "The Grasshopper and the Ants," or "The Hare and the Tortoise." But there are more than 250 of these tiny tales with morals that provide little pieces of insight into the many facets of human psychology. Every true reader is enriched for knowing these brief universal stories.

Mystery surrounds the real Aesop. It is thought he was born a slave. He was renowned for the wit that eventually earned him his freedom but doomed in the end. He was condemned to die for disrespecting the aristocracy. Some scholars believe that Aesop never existed at all. He left no written text but rather operated in the oral tradition, and others wrote down the Fables.

>   **Audio:** Blackstone Audio cassette 0786121858; CD 0786195843. Read by Mary Woods.

**Similar Reads:** The seventeenth-century French writer Jean de la Fontaine put the *Fables* into French verse, and Joel Chandler Harris based several of his *Uncle Remus* tales on the *Fables*. Critics often credit the *Fables* as an influence for Orwell's *Animal Farm* as well.

**Subjects:** Greece; Moral Stories; Fables; Childhood Classics; Talking Animals

## Beagle, Peter (1939– )

*Last Unicorn* (USA: 1968). Roc 1994 (paper) 224pp. 0451450523 **J**

A lovely unicorn lives alone in her lilac forest where it is always spring. This is not unusual because all unicorns live alone; but when two hunters enter her forest, she learns that she may be the last unicorn left in the world. Thus begins her quest to discover the fate of her fellow unicorns. Along the way, she is captured by Mommy Fortuna's Midnight Carnival, a traveling show that features Creatures of the Night Brought to Light. She also picks up fellow travelers Shmendrick, the less than successful magician, and Molly Grue, the tough-as-nails companion to outlaws. The quest eventually leads to King Haggard, his son Prince Lir, and the Red Bull that lives beneath their barren castle, an animal that holds the answer to the fate of the unicorns.

A charming story, beautifully written, that is in turns comic and melancholy.

> **Audio:** available in CD or as a download from Conlan Press (www. conlanpress.com). Read by the author.

> **Film/Video/DVD:** *The Last Unicorn* (1992) is an animated Rankin/Bass production, with Jeff Bridges, Mia Farrow, Angela Lansbury, and Alan Arkin contributing voices.

> **Similar Reads: Try** *The Neverending Story* by Ende; *The Princess Bride* by William Goldman; and *Forgotten Beast of Eld*.

> **Subjects:** Unicorns; Quest; Journey; Magic; Magicians

## Grahame, Kenneth (1859–1932)

*The Wind in the Willows* (England: 1908). Aladdin 1989 (paper) 272pp. 068971310X **M**

Join Ratty, Mole, and Badger for gentle escapades and life along the river. Madcap Mr. Toad, a scoundrel who is wild about fast cars, provides conflict and humor.

This famously bucolic story is tender but full of humor and adventure. It emphasizes the value and importance of nature, imagination, and friends. Many illustrated editions exist. Classic illustrations were drawn by E. H. Shepard, who also illustrated *Winnie the Pooh*.

> **Audio:** Recorded Books cassette 1402581017. Read by Ron Keith.

> **Film/Video/DVD:** Many versions are available. The 1995 animated version framed by live action segments and narrated by Vanessa Redgrave is quite nice.

**Similar Reads:** Turn to other fantastic English tales—*Peter Pan, Winnie the Pooh,* and *Alice in Wonderland,* for example.

**Subjects:** England; Friendship; Country Life; Talking Animals; Childhood Classic

## Kipling, Rudyard (1865–1936)

*The Jungle Book* **(England: 1894).** Tor Books 1991 (paper) 192 pp. 0812504690 **M Q**

Mowgli is a man cub living with the wolves in the jungles of India. They are raising him as one of their pack. With the help of Baloo the bear and Bagheera the panther, they teach him the Law of the Jungle.

In addition to the Mowgli stories, *The Jungle Book* contains poetry and several other stories including the suspenseful story of "Rikki Tikki Tavi," the mongoose who fights the terrible snake Nag, and "The White Seal," which is set in the Bering Sea.

**Audio:** Recorded Books cassette 1556902751; CD 1419311425. Read by Flo Gibson.

**Film/Video/DVD:** *Jungle Book* (1967) is a charming Disney animated musical that downplays the seriousness of Kipling's stories. *The Jungle Book* (1994) is a very good live action film with Jason Scott Lee.

**Similar Reads:** Also try *The Second Jungle Book* and *Just So Stories* by Kipling. Another human who lives at one with the animals is *Tarzan the Apeman.* Jack London's *Call of the Wild* and *White Fang,* although set in a very different landscape, are reminiscent of *The Jungle Book.*

**Subjects:** India; Jungles; Talking Animals; Orphans; Law of the Jungle; Childhood Classic

## Lofting, Hugh (1895–1947)

*The Story of Dr. Dolittle* **(England: 1920).** Yearling 1969 (paper) 176 pages 0440483077 **M Q**

Dr. Dolittle is charmingly oblivious to people, but he can talk to animals. With advice and help from the clever parrot Polynesia, he becomes the greatest animal doctor, and his services are in demand all over the world. In this book, he travels to Africa to save the monkeys from a deadly disease, escapes from an angry king, outwits pirates, and saves a man from a deserted island. He approaches all these adventures with unflappable ease (he doesn't like "fuss"), compassion, and the help of his animal friends.

Like all great literature, *Dr. Dolittle* generates thought about big issues: compassion, animal rights (he saves the monkey, Chee-Chee, from the organ grinder and the crocodile from the circus), economics (the doctor never has any money; money, as he says, "is a nuisance"), finding the right way to earn a living for oneself (while he fails rather grandly as a people doctor, Dolittle is adored by his animal patients). Lofting's original books contained the racism of his times, but newer editions subtlety eliminate the offending passages, allowing modern readers to be delighted by the adventures of the kindly doctor with the unique talent.

**Audio:** Available from BBC Audio (www.bbcshop.com). Read by Alan Bennett.

**Film/Video/DVD:** *Doctor Dolittle* (1967) is a colorful film musical with Rex Harrison. Eddie Murphy starred as the doctor who can talk to animals in 1998 and 2001, films based more on the character than the novels.

**Similar Reads:** There are twelve books by Lofting about Dr. Dolittle. *The Voyages of Dr. Dolittle* won the Newbery Medal in 1923. Older readers may want to try James Herriot's realistic books about being a veterinarian, starting with *All Creatures Great and Small*.

**Subjects:** England; Africa; Veterinarian; Pirates; Doctors; Journey; Talking Animals; Childhood Classic

## Milne, A. A. (1882–1956)

*Winnie the Pooh* **(England: 1926).** Puffin 1992 (paper) 161pp. 0140361219 **M Q**

Meet the Bear of Very Little Brain and the pastoral, peace-filled world of the Hundred Acre Wood where Pooh and his sidekick Piglet, their friends Kanga and Roo, Eeyore, the depressed donkey, and the cranky, wise Owl find adventure.

These sweet and simple stories aren't just for the nursery. All readers should explore the gentle world of Pooh, savoring the facets of humanity expressed in the toys and the fine prose of Milne. Like Tenniel with Lewis Carroll, the illustrations by E. H. Shepard are inseparable from the text.

**Audio:** Available from BBC audio (www.bbcshop.com). Read (delightfully) by Alan Bennett.

**Film/Video/DVD:** Pooh is a Disney marketing phenom. The animated *The Many Adventures of Winnie the Pooh* (1977) is the most basic telling of Pooh's tale.

**New Media:** There are a surprising number of Winnie the Pooh Web sites; www.winniethepoohbear.net is comprehensive; disney.go.com/disneyVideos/animatedfilms/pooh is the official Disney site.

**Similar Reads:** The adventures continue in *The House at Pooh Corner*. Milne's poetry is gathered in *When We Were Very Young* and *Now We Are Six*. Philosophically inclined readers may want to explore the *Tao of Pooh* (Hoff, 1982), which proves that Pooh is a wise philosopher as well as a cuddly toy. Other nursery classics for all ages to enjoy are *The Little Prince, The Velveteen Rabbit,* and *The Wind in the Willows*.

**Subjects:** England; Toys; Talking Animals; Friendship; Childhood Classic

## Orwell, George (1903–1950)

*Animal Farm* **(England: 1945).** Signet 1996 (paper, 50th anniversary edition) 144pp. 0451526341 **J Q**

When Old Major, the prize-winning boar at Manor Farm, has a dream, he gathers all the animals to tell them his utopian vision of a united and peaceful animal future with no human masters to exploit or abuse them. Soon after his revelation, Old Major dies, and shortly after that, an animal revolution takes place! The humans are chased from the farm, and the animals assume responsibility for their own fates. This new society, fashioned after Old Major's vision and called Animalism, begins with high and noble ideals like equality and fairness, progress and compassion. But as the animals toil for their utopian vision, a power struggle plays out between Napoleon, a strong-willed boar, and Snowball, the hero of the revolution. Life on the farm becomes harder than it ever was with Farmer Jones. And, mysteriously, the Seven Commandments of Animalism written on the side of the barn, begin to change as the pigs, the cleverest animals on the Farm, assume more power and more humanlike habits; "All Animals Are Equal" soon becomes "All Animals Are Equal, But Some Animals Are More Equal Than Others."

A book with many levels, Orwell combines comedy and pathos in this allegory of totalitarianism presented as a funny animal story. Although Orwell's original references were Stalin and the Russian Revolution, *Animal Farm* transcends any time and place to show that freedom is fragile and tyranny comes in many guises.

> **Audio:** Recorded Books cassette 155690018X; CD 0788744755. Read by Patrick Tull.

> **Film/Video/DVD:** *Animal Farm* (1954 and again in 1999) are both animated versions of the novel.

> **Subjects:** England, mid-1900s; Totalitarianism; Farm Life; Allegory; Pigs; Talking Animals; Conformity; Social Structures; Satire

## Salten, Felix (1869–1945)

*Bambi: A Life in the Woods* **(Austria: 1926).** Aladdin/Simon and Schuster 2002 (paper) 191pp. 067166607x **M Q**

> More than just the sentimental story of the deer, *Bambi* is a small masterpiece of naturalism. The descriptions of the forest, nature, the other animals and Bambi's growing awareness of the world around him are truly masterful moments of imaginative fiction. Young Bambi is a prince of the forests; this is the coming-of-age story of a deer. Salten places himself in the mind of another creature and narrates what occurs. The resulting work can teach empathy, encourage compassion, and remind readers to respect all living things.

> **Film/Video/DVD:** *Bambi* (1942) is a Disney animated classic.

> **Similar Reads:** Readers who love animal stories will want to read *The Incredible Journey, Watership Down, Tailchaser's Song,* and *Black Beauty.*

> **Subjects:** Forest; Deer; Friendship; Nature

## Unknown

*Jataka Tales* **(India: A.D. 400).** Inner Traditions 1985 (paper, called *Twenty Jataka Tales* by Noor Inayat Khan) 152pp. 0892813237 **M Q**

> These are the animal tales traditionally told in Buddhist culture to explain the past lives of Buddha to mankind. You may know "The Monkey and the Crocodile" or "The Proud Peacock." There are more than five hundred tales. The teaching of compassion and the law of karma are two of the didactic goals of many of these stories, but they are funny, universal tales that still entertain two thousand years after they began.

**Similar Reads:** Many of the tales have been published individually as picture books for younger children. Readers interested in Buddhism may want to try Hesse's novel *Siddhartha* or the *Bhagavad Gita*.

**Subjects:** Moral Stories; Buddha; Buddhism; Fables

## Wangerin, Walter (1944–)

*Book of the Dun Cow* (USA: 1978). Harper San Francisco 2003 (paper, 25th anniversary ed.) 256 po. 0060574607 **J**

In a different time when animals could speak and all lived in a Peaceable Kingdom, Chauntecleer the Rooster is lord of the barnyard. All is right with his world until evil appears in the local form of Ebenezer Rat, who sucks dry the eggs in the coup. But this evil is nothing compared to the universal evil about to descend on the barnyard in the form of a Cockatrice, half-rooster and half-dragon, sent by the ultimate evil force, Wyrm, to destroy the world.

Allegorical, comical, thought provoking, this animal fable is really the universal tale of the conflict between good and evil.

> **Similar Reads:** Wangerin wrote a much darker sequel called *The Book of Sorrows*. *Watership Down* and *Tailchaser's Song* are other animal fantasy classics with mature appeal.

> **Subjects:** Farm Life; Talking Animals; Dogs; Good and Evil; Roosters

## White, E. B. (1899–1985)

*Charlotte's Web* (USA: 1952). HarperTrophy 1974 (paper) 192 pp. 0064400557 **M** Teen **Q**

Barnyard magic in the form of Charlotte, a spider who can write; Wilbur, a pig with a heart; and Templeton, a very ratty rat.

Stylistically elegant and filled with deep sentiment and gentle humor, *Charlotte's Web* is a classic for all ages. E. B. White was a renowned essayist who wrote for the *New Yorker* magazine in its heyday. He also popularized a handbook on English usage, originally written by his former teacher Will Strunk, called *The Elements of Style* (1959), a small classic about efficient writing.

> **Audio:** Listening Library 1991 cassette 0553470485. Read by E. B. White.

> **Film/Video/DVD:** *Charlotte's Web* (1973) is an animated musical. A live-action version with Dakota Fanning appeared in 2006.

> **Similar Reads:** White wrote three books for children—*Charlotte's Web*, *Stuart Little,* and *The Trumpet of the Swan*—and all are classics.

> **Subjects:** Farm Life; Pigs; Spiders; Talking Animals; Childhood Classic

## Williams, Tad (1957–)

*Tailchaser's Song* (USA: 1985). DAW 1986 (paper) 400pp. 0886773741 **S**

Orange-and-white-stripped Tailchaser, who is chosen to investigate why cats are disappearing, is the cat hero of this novel.

Williams does for cats what Richard Adams did for rabbits in *Watership Down*: he gives you a new way of viewing the world from their perspective.

**Similar Reads:** *Watership Down* is an equally engrossing story about rabbits; Brian Jacques <u>Redwall</u> books are heroic epics involving British field animals; *The Wild Road* by Gabriel King and the <u>Warriors</u> series by Erin Hunter are other good choices for fans of cat heroes

**Subjects:** Cats; Good and Evil; Talking Animals

# Humorous Fantasy

All of the tropes of fantasy fiction—heroes, journeys, quests, wise helpers, danger— can be found in these novels that both spoof the genre and have become fantasy classics.

### Anthony, Piers (1934–)

🌿 *A Spell for Chameleon* <u>Xanth</u> series (USA: 1977). Del Rey 1987 (paper) 352pp. 0345347536 **J**

Bink has no magic in him, or so he and everyone else in Xanth believes. If he can't find his magic, he will be exiled forever from his home, the magical world of Xanth. Although the Good Magician Humphrey believes Bink possesses magic, no one can find it, and this crisis leads Bink on a quest to find his magic.

This is the first book in Anthony's growing <u>Xanth</u> series. Set in the comical land of Xanth, these books are cheerful, humorous, and fun.

**Similar Reads:** The next book in the <u>Xanth</u> series is *The Source of Magic*. See also Terry Pratchett's <u>Discworld</u> series and Robert Asprin's <u>M.Y.T.H.</u> series, starting with *Another Fine Myth*.

**Subjects:** Magic; Spells; Puns; Xanth; British Fantasy Award 1978; Humor

### Goldman, William (1931–)

*The Princess Bride* (USA: 1973). Del Rey 1987 (paper) 416pp. 0345348036 **J**

A fractured fairy tale of the first order—Princess Buttercup and Westley are fated to love one another, but many obstacles stand in their way—giants, evil counts, the Fire Swamp. This broad comedy is a spoof of the whole fantasy genre, as well as adventure stories, love stories, heroes, princesses, pirates, and swashbuckling swordsmen.

Goldman is also famous as a screenwriter, *Butch Cassidy and the Sundance Kid* being one of his many successes. He wrote the screenplay for *The Princess Bride* movie.

**Film/Video/DVD:** *The Princess Bride* (1987) film was directed with great comic verve by Rob Reiner and features Robin Wright Penn and Andre the Giant, as well as lots of swordfights.

**Similar Reads:** Try *The Neverending Story*.

**Subjects:** Royalty; Giants; Swordfights; Romance; Satire

## Juster, Norton (1929–)

*Phantom Tollbooth* **(USA: 1961).** Yearling 1988 (paper) 272pp. 0394820371 **M**
**Teen**

Milo is a bored young boy—school doesn't interest him, toys don't interest
him, life doesn't interest him. One day when he comes home from school and
finds a tollbooth in his bedroom, he undertakes an adventurous journey into
the realm of words and numbers, and his boredom is banished forever.

Jules Feiffer's whimsical illustrations are memorable.

> **Audio:** Recorded Books cassette 1556908768; CD 078873735x. Read by
> Norman Dietz.
>
> **Film/Video/DVD:** An animated version was produced in 1970.
>
> **Similar Reads:** Try *The Thirteen Clocks* by James Thurber, *Alice in Won-
> derland, The Wizard of Oz,* and *Flatland* by Abbott.
>
> **Subjects:** Dictionopolis; Digitopolis; Mathematics; Boredom; Journey;
> Childhood Classic

## Raspe, Rudopf Erich (1720–1797)

*Baron Munchhausen* **(Germany: 1785)** Wildside Press 2003 (paper) 218pp.
1587155699 **J**

Part satire and part tall tale, the adventures of Baron Munchhausen have entertained for more than two hundred years. The baron is a military man who is either a colossal liar or who has led the most extraordinary life imaginable.
Famous for riding a shooting cannonball, traveling to the moon, turning a wolf
inside out, and other outrageous happenings, he is perhaps more known in Europe than in the United States.

> **Film/Video/DVD:** *The Adventures of Baron Munchhausen* (1989) is a bold
> and interesting movie made by Monty Python alum Terry Gilliam.
>
> **Similar Reads:** The baron's stories are firmly in the tradition of tall tales,
> such as Paul Bunyan, Davy Crocket, and Pecos Bill. Try *American Tall
> Tales* (Knopf, 1991) by Mary Pope Osborne.
>
> **Subjects:** Germany; Liars; Military Officers; Tall Tale

# Chapter 5

# Horror

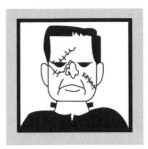

Graveyards, ghosts, unnatural specters, the unknown, the unknowable, and the unexplainable—you have just stepped in to the nightmare world of horror fiction.

Readers love horror fiction because they want to be scared! Why do people like to be scared? To feel that surge of adrenaline? For the feeling of triumph when the scary bits are over and they realize that they have survived? Or perhaps just morbid fascination? Whatever the motive, horror fiction provides that pure visceral appeal. A great horror story makes fear tangible to readers. Horror works because it pushes on the boundaries of reality. It shows us the disturbing, the grotesque, and the gruesome—things that most people don't want to talk about but that many want to explore. Horror novels succeed when they disturb our comfort level.

Like their contemporary counterparts, classic horror novels create feelings of dread, unease, and tension in the reader. In many ways, classic horror is scarier than contemporary horror because the older books often leave so much unsaid. There is generally less graphic blood and gore but a much greater sense of the weird, the eerie, the haunting, and the macabre in classic horror stories.

Horror novels have several common characteristics. A strong setting with lots of atmosphere is primary—a dark house, a moody landscape, threatening weather. Often the descriptions of the setting are very detailed, as if setting itself were a character in the story (often the case with haunted house stories). Setting and the mood it creates are as important as character and plot in a horror novel.

The presence of evil in some form—real or imagined, earthly or supernatural, external to the characters or internal—is another major component in a horror novel. Evil in horror fiction expresses itself in many ways—the supernatural; nature gone berserk; the confusion of the human mind; the undead in many forms—vampires, zombies, ghosts; ancient evil unleashed; haunted houses and other spooky places such as graveyards, crypts, and dungeons; science, technology, or medicine gone awry; the occult in the form of Satanism, witches, and the devil; misdeeds of the past haunting the present. The permutations of evil expressed in horror novels are deliciously endless.

Horror novels often have an ambiguous or unresolved ending. Unlike mysteries or romances where loose ends are neatly tied up, horror novels can leave questions unanswered. The reader is left with a sense that all is not right in the world, that evil still lurks, and that it could, when you least expect it, return.

# Ghost Stories

Do the spirits of the dead linger in this world? If they do, they can be found in these stories. Rooted in folklore these are the types of tales traditionally told around campfires.

## Dickens, Charles (1812–1870)

*A Christmas Carol* **(England: 1843). Q**
> *See* entry in Chapter 4, "Fantasy."

## Irving, Washington (1783–1859)

*The Legend of Sleepy Hollow* **(USA: 1819).** Tor 1990 (paper) 96pp. 0812504755 **M Q**
> New York's Hudson River valley is the setting where Ichabod Crane the gawky schoolmaster likened to a "scarecrow eloped from a cornfield," hopes to win pretty Katrina Van Tassel. But Katrina has another suitor, the manly Brom Van Brunt "hero of the country round." One autumn night after an evening of telling ghost stories and local legends, particularly the local favorite about the Headless Horseman, Ichabod must travel home through the dark night on a slow horse, past the very place where the Headless Horseman has been seen.
>
> A Halloween standard for all ages, *The Legend of Sleepy Hollow* can create discussion about the power of story and the enduring strength of urban (and rural) legends.
>
> **Audio:** Recorded Books (with "Rip Van Winkle") cassette 1556909152; CD 1402551193. Read by George Guidall.
>
> **Film/Video/DVD:** *The Legend of Sleepy Hollow* (1958) is a Disney animated family favorite. A 1999 TV version has great production value. Tim Burton's film called *Sleepy Hollow* (1999) with Johnny Depp takes Irving's tale as its basis but goes down an entirely different road.
>
> **Similar Reads:** For more New England flavor, read Irving's story "Rip Van Winkle." Fans of scary stories based on folklore will want to explore Alvin Schwartz's collections starting with *Scary Stories to Tell in the Dark*. Also explore urban legends such as those found in Jan Brunvand's *Be Afraid, Be Very Afraid: The Book of Scary Urban Legends*.
>
> **Subjects:** New York; Local Legends; Headless Horseman

## James, Henry (1843–1916)

*The Turn of the Screw* **(England: 1891).** Tor 1993 (paper) 146pp. 0812533410; Barnes and Noble Classics 2003 (paper) 312pp (includes other stories and notes) 1593080433 **S**

A young, enthusiastic, and naïve governess is engaged to care for two angelic children at a house in the country. Her new employer, the children's uncle, lives in London and requires one thing of her: that she never contact him regarding the children. What seems like a lovely situation soon becomes perilous when the ghosts of two former servants begin to appear at the house. Are the spirits there to threaten the beautiful and innocent children? Do the children know about the ghosts and encourage the haunting? Is the governess imagining the threat, or is she the only protector the children have? Are there any ghosts at all?

*The Turn of the Screw* is unsettling and ambiguous and has generated much critical comment over the years. For some readers, an extra measure of concentration is needed to follow James's dense and undulating prose, but for lovers of language and complex sentences, this is a good introduction to Henry James.

**Audio:** Recorded Books cassette 1556905289; CD 1402571364. Read by Flo Gibson.

**Film/Video/DVD:** There are many film versions, but the 1961 version called *The Innocents* starring Deborah Kerr is a classic suspense film. The *Masterpiece Theatre* production of 2000 is also very gripping. James's story was made into an opera by Benjamin Britten, first performed in 1959 and considered a standard work in the modern repertoire.

**Similar Reads:** Readers might turn to Shirley Jackson's *The Haunting of Hill House* or stories by Edgar Allan Poe and H. P. Lovecraft to experience more uncertainty and dread.

**Subjects:** Victorian England; Governess; Orphans; Good and Evil; Imagination; Suspense

# Haunted Houses

The often unidentifiable malevolence that exists in certain dwellings is the realm of the haunted house subgenre. The house itself is a character in these stories.

## Hawthorne, Nathaniel (1804–1864)

*The House of the Seven Gables* (USA: 1851). Modern Library 2001 (paper) 336pp. 0375756876 **J**

The house with the seven gables is crumbling with age and neglect. It is now the home of Miss Hepzibah Pyncheon, a genteel spinster living in poverty, one of the last surviving descendants of Old Judge Pyncheon who built the house two hundred years before on ground he obtained by falsely accusing a man of witchcraft. In 1850, Hepzibah's young country cousin, Phoebe, fresh and innocent of the wicked past, comes to live with her. Soon Hepzibah's brother Clifford joins them, newly released from thirty years in prison for a murder he may not have committed. Can the sins of past generations be rectified by love and innocence?

Hawthorne spends much of the book philosophizing, digressing, and discoursing. Although the prose can be dense and old-fashioned, this is a lovely story about family, innocence, treachery, and the hold of the past on the present.

**Audio:** Recorded Books cassette 1556909268; CD 1419310623. Read by Roslyn Alexander.

**Film/Video/DVD:** This was included as one of the stories in *Twice Told Tales* (1963) and also filmed in 1940 as *House of the Seven Gables*.

**Similar Reads:** Hawthorne's other classics are *The Scarlet Letter* and *The Blithedale Romance*.

**Subjects:** Salem, Massachusetts, 1850; Family; Ancestors; Brothers and Sisters; Inheritance; Good and Evil

## Jackson, Shirley (1919–1965)

*The Haunting of Hill House* (USA: 1959). Penguin 1984 (paper) 256 pp. 0140071083 **S Q**
Eleanor, sensitive and imaginative, free after eleven years of caring for her mother, agrees to participate in an experiment. Dr. Montague has recruited her along with outgoing Theodora and easygoing Luke to stay with him in Hill House. There they will explore the psychic disturbances and supernatural manifestations attributed to the house. How will staying at Hill House affect them? Remember: "It is a house without kindness, never meant to be lived in, not a fit place for people or for love or for hope."

Jackson was a master at really creepy stories. Hill House has the requisite atmosphere of ambiguity, dread, and unexplainable elements, but the horror is mainly psychological. The reader just knows that something bad is going to happen, but what? And when? And to whom?

**Film/Video/DVD:** Two films called *The Haunting* have been made, one in 1963 and the other in 1999. The 1999 version is full of splashy special effects; the 1963 version is truer to the book.

**Similar Reads:** Jackson's classic short story *The Lottery* and her other novel *We Have Always Lived in the Castle* will interest readers.

**Subjects:** Extrasensory Powers: Good and Evil

*We Have Always Lived in the Castle* (USA: 1962). Penguin 1984 (paper) 224pp. 0140071075 **S Q**
Mary Katherine Blackwood, called Merricat, and her sister, Constance, live in their family's old mansion with their crippled Uncle Julian. They have lived there on their own since the rest of the family died six years earlier of arsenic poisoning, deaths that Constance was accused of and then acquitted of in court. Merricat eerily narrates the story of what happens when their uninvited cousin Charles comes to stay in this strange house where visitors are not wanted and outsiders are not welcome.

**Similar Reads:** Jackson's stories are weird in the truest sense of the word. Edgar Allan Poe and H. P. Lovecraft can offer readers that same unsettling feeling. Also try *The Turn of the Screw* by Henry James.

**Subjects:** Small Town; Sisters; Family; Poisoning

## King, Stephen (1947–)

*The Shining* (USA: 1977). Pocket Books 2002 (paper) 528pp. 0743437497 <u>S</u>

Oh, my. This is one scary book.

Jack Torrance, a writer down on his luck and trying to recover from some bad events, takes a job as the winter caretaker of an old hotel in the snowbound Colorado Rockies. With him are his wife and little boy, Danny, a child who has "The Shine." The job will give the family a chance to reconnect and give Jack the solitude he needs to write. But the Overlook Hotel is a malevolent place, and there is evil latent in Jack Torrance. Terrible things are in store for this family.

Heart pounding and stomach churning—how can words on a page create visceral fear in a reader? Whatever the answer, Stephen King is the master at it. One word—redrum.

> **Film/Video/DVD:** *The Shining* (1980), directed by Stanley Kubrick and starring Jack Nicholson, is a great and scary movie, but the 1997 TV miniseries at 4.5 hours is more faithful to the book, with the screenplay written by Stephen King himself.

> **New Media:** See www.stephenking.com for King's official Web site.

> **Similar Reads:** Read more Stephen King; he is a prolific writer. Try *The Dead Zone* or *The Stand. Haunting of Hill House* is another story of an unstable person in a malevolent house. Also try famous authors Clive Barker, Dean Koontz, or V. C. Andrews.

> **Subjects:** Colorado; Family; Hotels; Fathers and Sons

# Gothic Horror

Darkness, gloomy settings such as crypts and cellars, haunted castles, virgins in peril, the presence of the supernatural, a good dose of violence, and a sense of the horrific typify the gothic. Please note that other gothic titles can be found in Chapter 8, "Romance Fiction."

## Andrews, V. C. (1924–1986)

*Flowers in the Attic* (USA: 1979). Pocket Book, 2000 (paper) 411pp. 0671729411 <u>S</u>

The Dollangangers are the happiest and most loving family imaginable. But when tragedy strikes and the only solution is to move in with the grandparents, the story turns violent, abusive, and downright creepy. Teenagers Cathy and Chris and the younger twins soon learn they are to live concealed in the attic of their rich grandfather's huge mansion, hidden away from the man who would not approve of their existence. While their mother blithely comes and goes hoping to cash in on her father's wealth, it is their sadistic grandmother who supervises the children, making sure they are never seen or heard.

A modern Gothic tale where family is the enemy. The incest subplot makes this a frequently challenged book.

**Audio:** Books on Tape cassette 5553668441. Read by Donanda Peters.

**Film/Video/DVD:** *Flowers in the Attic* (1987) with Louise Fletcher and Victoria Tennant as the grandmother and mother.

**Similar Reads:** This is the first book in a series. It is followed by *Petals on the Wind, If There Be Thorns, Seeds of Yesterday*, and the prequel, *Garden of Shadows*. Andrews was sort of a publishing phenomenon, with books coming out long after her death. She is a good option for reluctant readers who don't mind the creepy and cruel. Fans will want to explore her other books; she has several other series about twisted families including the Casteel series and the Cutler series. Readers drawn to books about abusive family situations may want to read *A Child Called It* by Dave Pelzer and *The Lottery Rose* by Helen Hunt.

**Subjects:** Childhood; Secrets; Brothers and Sisters; Imprisonment; Incest; Family; Abuse; Inheritance; Mothers; Grandparents; Dysfunctional Families; Mature Read

## Leroux, Gaston (1868–1927)

*The Phantom of the Opera* **(France: 1911).** Harper Perennial 1988 (paper) 368pp. 0060809248 **J**

The gaiety of life backstage at the Paris Opera is imperiled because a phantom, a mysterious music lover who wears evening dress and has, according to some, death's head and, to others, a head of fire, inhabits the building. Singers unexpectedly fall ill, workers are injured, Box Five is mysteriously inhabited yet no one is there. Meanwhile, beautiful young singer Christine Daae is taking clandestine music lessons from "the Angel of Music." When she disappears, Raoul, the man who loves her, tries to untangle all the mysteries.

A suspenseful story with comic touches, this novel is true Gothic. The vast setting of the opera house provides secret corridors, trapdoors, underground cellars, and even a lake in the basement; the young singers and dancers provide sex appeal; the managers of the opera provide stability and gravitas; the heroine, Christine, is innocence personified; and the villain is—well, you must unravel for yourself the truth of the Phantom who haunts the opera.

**Audio:** Blackstone Audio cassette 0786128445; CD 0786183314. Read by Ralph Cosham.

**Film/Video/DVD:** There are many film versions, but all take liberties with the setting and plot; the Lon Chaney 1925 silent is a classic. Andrew Lloyd Weber created a blockbuster stage musical in 1987, filmed in 2004. It is even the basis for a loose adaptation with a rock-and-roll setting directed by Brian De Palma, *Phantom of the Paradise* (1974).

**New Media:** www.thephantomoftheopera.com is the Web site devoted to the stage musical. It provides background about Leroux, the novel, and film versions as well.

**Subjects:** Paris; Opera; Obsession; Music; Singers

## Poe, Edgar Allan (1809–1849)

***Poe's Collected Stories and Poems*** (**USA: 1845**). Perennial Classics/Harper 2004 (paper) 576pp. 0060727853 **J Q**

Ever wonder what to read for Halloween? Poe, of course! His stories are creepy and unsettling and create a feeling of incredible tension. He manages to terrify with no overt gore but rather with a pervasive atmosphere of evil and the abnormal, mystery and madness. Poe wrote creepers such as "The Tell-Tale Heart," "The Pit and the Pendulum," "A Cask of Amontillado," and "The Fall of the House of Usher." Poe is also credited with inventing the modern detective novel because of his stories featuring the super-rational Monsieur Dupin: "The Murders in the Rue Morgue," "The Purloined Letter," and "The Mystery of Marie Roget."

To get the real feeling of Poe—whose personal life was as strange as some of his stories—try reading his poetry, too, including "The Raven," "The Bells," and "Annabel Lee."

**Audio:** Recorded Books cassette 155690505X (called *Tales of Terror*, includes nine stories). Read by Jack Foreman. HarperAudio CD 0694524190. Read by Vincent Price and Basil Rathbone.

**Film/Video/DVD:** Roger Corman made nine movies based on the works of Poe, many starring Vincent Price. These are very good films for a creep fest. Start with the *House of Usher* (1960) or *The Pit and the Pendulum* (1961).

**New Media:** Available in graphic novel format: *Edgar Allan Poe: The Fall of the House of Usher and Other Tales of Terror* by Richard Corben for Del Rey 2005, 0345483138; also *Graphic Classics Volume 1; Edgar Allan Poe* (Eureka Productions, 2004, 0971246491 illustrated by various artists).

**Similar Reads:** Turn to Stephen King for novels, or try the weird stories of H. P. Lovecraft like *The Call of Cthulhu*. Also try Shirley Jackson.

**Subjects:** Short Stories; Fear; Anxiety; Terror

# Vampires

Vampires are perhaps the most well known of the Creatures of the Night. They are members of the undead, they live through many historical eras because they cannot die. They exist on the blood, the very life essence of their victims. Often they have super strength and awesome powers, such as the ability to become animals, change the weather, and control the minds of their victims. Almost all folk cultures have some sort of vampire creature. Vampires strike at the core of human fears.

## Stoker, Bram (1847–1912)

***Dracula*** (**England: 1897**). Pocket Books Enriched Classics 2003 (paper) 528pp. 0743477367 **J**

Jonathan Harker is in Transylvania to help Count Dracula through the paperwork of a purchase of land in England. But Harker is in more danger than he realizes; the reaction of the townspeople when they learn he is visiting the count should have told him that. Harker soon realizes that the count's malevolence is not restricted to his castle in Transylvania. Soon Harker's own fiancé Mina and her friend Lucy in England are in danger. Harker enlists the help of lunatic asylum doctor, John Seward, and the famous Professor Van Helsing to battle the evil monster Dracula and to save Mina from the fate of the undead.

Told through diaries and letters, this famous and archetypal vampire novel has multiple narrators, a thrilling storyline, and a race-to-the-finish conclusion. Will good triumph, or will evil prevail?

**Audio:** Recorded Books cassette 1556901569; CD 1402523017. Read by Alexander Spencer and Susan Adams.

**Film/Video/DVD:** Dracula is the basis for many movies, spoofs, takeoffs, and sequels; even Mel Brooks took a shot with *Dracula: Dead and Loving It* (1995). The 1931 version with Bela Lugosi is often considered a horror film classic; in 1992, Francis Ford Coppola directed *Bram Stoker's Dracula,* which won awards for makeup and costume design. The book has even been the basis for a superhero film, *Van Helsing* (2004), which morphs the genteel doctor into an international monster hunter.

**Similar Reads:** Other YA books about vampires are Annette Curtis Klause's *Silver Kiss* and *In the Forests of the Night* by Amelia Atwater-Rhodes, also Darren Shan's Cirque du Freak series. *Salem's Lot* by Stephen King sets the evil in a small town in Maine. Anne Rice expands the vampire myth in her Vampire Chronicles series, starting with *Interview with a Vampire*; her writing is sophisticated and overtly erotic.

**Subjects:** Victorian England; Transylvania; Epistolary Novel

# Supernatural and Weird Stories

Events beyond the natural world—mysterious, unexplainable, not following natural laws—can be found in these tales. This is the realm of the eerie.

## Bradbury, Ray (1920–)

*The Illustrated Man* **(USA: 1951).** Spectra 1983 (paper) 192 pp. 055327449X **S**

The Illustrated Man is tattooed all over his body except for his head and feet. He was tattooed by a woman who claimed to be a time traveler, and he has been searching for her for fifty years. He has played the carnival circuit for years and is a main attraction, but he cannot keep a job. Why? Because the illustrations on his body can predict the future, and if one looks closely enough, the illustrations start to move. It is very frightening to run into the Illustrated Man.

This collection of eighteen eerie stories of dark beauty may appeal to today's teens who have a fascination with tattoos.

**Film/Video/DVD:** *The Illustrated Man* (1969).

**Similar Reads:** More intriguing Bradbury stories can be found in the collection *October Country.*

**Subjects:** Tattoos; Predictions; Dark Fantasy; Nebula Grand Master 1989; Short Stories

*Something Wicked This Way Comes* **(USA: 1962).** Avon Books, 1998 (paper) 304pp. 0380729407 **J**

Green Town, Illinois, a week before Halloween. Best friends Will Halloway and Jim Nightshade, born just minutes apart and living next door to each other, are thrilled to see that the circus has come to town, but it is too late in the season for a carnival and strange that it should arrive just before Halloween.

Mysterious events and wicked happenings are in store for the boys and their families. Perhaps evil really does exist?

**Audio:** Recorded Books cassette 0788734946; CD 0788746375. Read by Paul Hecht.

**Film/Video/DVD:** *Something Wicked This Way Comes* (1983) with Jason Robards and Jonathan Pryce is a creepy and unsettling Disney adaptation with a screenplay written by Bradbury.

**Similar Reads:** Try Stephen King's *Needful Things.* Bradbury's other classic evocation of mystical childhood is *Dandelion Wine.*

**Subjects:** Illinois; Friendship; Good and Evil; Small Town; Circus; Carnival; Nebula Grand Master 1989

## Lovecraft, H. P. (1890–1937)

*Call of Cthulhu and Other Weird Stories* **(USA: 1920s).** Penguin 1999 (paper) 420pp. 0141182342 **J**

An author of intellectual and spiritual horror, Lovecraft created a new kind of dark fantasy tale with his stories of ancient evil among modern man. Many of his stories were originally published in the pulp magazine called *Weird Tales.*

**Similar Reads:** Move on to other tales by Lovecraft, such as *The Dunwich Horror* or his novella *At the Mountains of Madness.* Other choices are Poe, E. T. A. Hoffman, or Stephen King for more weird tales. *Tales of the Cthulhu Mythos* (compiled in 1990) is an anthology of stories by horror and fantasy writers working in the Lovecraft tradition.

**Subjects:** Dark Fantasy

## Wilde, Oscar (1856–1900)

*The Picture of Dorian Gray* **(England: 1891).** Pocket Book Enriched Classics 2005 (paper) 195pp. 1416500278 **J**

"He grew more and more enamored of his own beauty, more and more interested in the corruption of his own soul."

Dorian Gray is a physically beautiful but morally corrupt young man. Over the course of time, he never seems to age. But if you go into his attic, you will see a painting that shows the true effect time and wasted living have had on Dorian.

Wilde uses his story about the decadent Dorian to philosophize about youth, beauty, vanity, and art. Full of witty Wildean quotes such as, "the only way to get rid of temptation is to yield to it."

**Audio:** Recorded Books cassette 078870575X; CD 1402521006. Read by Steven Crossley.

**Film/Video/DVD:** *The Picture of Dorian Gray* (1945) black-and-white classic with touches of color is recommended.

**Similar Reads:** *Dr. Jekyll and Mr. Hyde* by Stevenson tells another story of the darkness within man.

**Subjects:** Victorian England; Good and Evil; Aging; Gothic Horror; Soul; Victorian Novel

# Psychological Horror

The human mind contains horrors it can use to torment itself and others.

## Kafka, Franz (1883–1924)

*Metamorphosis* **(Germany: 1915).** Bantam Classics 2004 (paper) 201pp. 0553213695 **S̲ Q**
What if you go to bed one night, and when you wake up the next day, you aren't yourself, but in fact you are now a cockroach? What will your family do? How will you cope? Gregor Samsa experiences this transformation. Is the ultimate horror waking up and no longer being you? The meaning of this short novel has long been debated—an allegory for the adolescent experience perhaps?

Kafka was a master of expressing alienation and paranoia and depicting a nightmarish enigmatic world in which anxiety reigns and the individual is a victim of forces he will never understand. Sophisticated YA readers should be fascinated by him.

**Audio:** Recorded Books (with other stories) cassette 0788702181; CD 1419310690. Read by George Guidall.

**New Media:** Graphic novel by Peter Kruper (Three Rivers Press, 2004, 1400052998).

**Similar Reads:** Kafka wrote many short stories that will interest readers. Try "The Hunger Artist" or his longer novels *The Trial* and *The Castle*. Sartre and Camus continued the exploration of existential questions that Kafka began. Readers may also want to explore the short stories of Edgar Allan Poe and H. P. Lovecraft.

**Subjects:** Prague; Family; Transformation; Alienation

*The Trial* **(Germany 1925).** Schocken 1995 (paper) 312pp. 0805210407 **S̲**
Josef K is arrested and tried for a crime that he did not commit and that is never explained to him. At first it all seems to be a joke, but the reality of Josef's new existence

as a powerlessness individual in a system that can never be comprehended, eventually destroys him.

Words frequently used to describe Kafka's work include anxiety, alienation, futility, oppressive, paranoia, claustrophobic, and nightmarish.

> **Audio:** Recorded Books cassette 0788725092. Read by George Guidall.

> **Film/Video/DVD:** Orson Welles directed a little-known film version of *The Trial* in 1962. Jeremy Irons starred in *Kafka* (1991), a film that uses moments from Kafka's stories to create a weirdly moody and paranoid film that gives the flavor of the author's work.

> **Similar Reads:** Camus's *The Stranger* continues the existential exploration, or try Dostoevsky's *Notes from Underground.*

> **Subjects:** Early 1900s; Alienation; Trials; Imprisonment

### King, Stephen (1947–)

*Carrie* **(USA: 1973).** Pocket 2000 (paper) 193pp. 0671039733 <u>S</u> Q

Carrie, a senior in high school, is an awkward teen victimized by her schoolmates and her fanatical mother. Carrie's one chance for a happy adolescent experience, being crowned queen of the prom, is just another cruel joke, but a joke that has a violent and disastrous aftermath. Carrie has powers that set her apart from other people, and when she unleashes them, the entire town suffers.

This was Stephen King's first published novel—the start of his brilliant reign as America's master of horror. King is an excellent choice for students who don't read much; although his books seem intimidatingly long, they read briskly, have lots of dialogue, and feature plots that are so suspenseful, readers are motivated to keep reading.

> **Film/Video/DVD:** *Carrie* (1976) with Sissy Spacek was directed by horror master Brian De Palma. There is also a 2002 TV version with Angela Bettis as Carrie.

> **Similar Reads:** Dive into more King; he is prolific. Consider *Christine,* King's novel about a malevolent car; *Cujo,* about a murderous dog. Readers craving more eerie tales may want to move on to Kafka, Lovecraft, and Poe.

> **Subjects:** Maine; High School; Extrasensory Powers; Telekinesis; Mothers and Daughters; Teachers and Students; Bullies; Frequently Challenged

## Science Gone Awry

Is science the savior of humanity? What is unleashed by knowledge cannot always be controlled. Perhaps it can create problems as well as solve them. Especially when the scientists are insane, power mad, or victims of their own experiments.

### Shelley, Mary (1797–1851)

***Frankenstein, or the Modern Prometheus*** (**England: 1818**). Pocket Enriched Classics 2004 (paper) 352pp. 0743487583 **J**

> Dr. Victor Frankenstein has a daring ambition—to create life where none existed before. He achieves his goal and creates a monster made from bits and bones gathered from charnel houses and graveyards. But the monster is intelligent and soon understands its own lonely and miserable existence. When Frankenstein refuses to create a mate for him, the creature turns on his creator in anger born from misery. Frankenstein chases his monster across Europe and into the Arctic. There the scientist is rescued from the ice and tells his story to Walton, who writes it all down. Don't make the common mistake and call the monster Frankenstein; the monster has no name and is usually referred to as the creature.

> Considered by some to be the first science fiction novel, others class it as the greatest horror novel. Mary Shelley was only nineteen when she wrote *Frankenstein,* and although she wrote many other works, she is known today solely for Frankenstein and his monster.

> **Audio:** Recorded Books cassette 0556907710. Read by George Guidall.

> **Film/Video/DVD:** As a film star, Frankenstein has a life of its own—the 1931 Boris Karloff classic is the version most people think of. Robert De Niro played the monster in 1994. Mel Brooks's spoof, *Young Frankenstein,* is also worth a viewing. A new made for TV version was released in 2005.

> **New Media:** Several graphic versions exist, including Puffin Graphics *Frankenstein* (Puffin, 2005, 0142404071); *Frankenstein* (Livewire Graphic Novels published by Hodder and Murray 2001, 0340782668).

> **Similar Reads:** H. G. Wells's *Island of Dr. Moreau* is another story about a scientist playing with life.

> **Subjects:** Gothic; Scientists; Scientific Experimentation; Monsters; Epistolary Novel

### Sleator, William (1945–)

***House of Stairs*** (**USA: 1974**). Puffin 1991 (paper) 176pp. 0140345809 **J Teen Q**

> Peter thought he was alone until he found Lola, and together they found Blossom. Then Abigail and Oliver found them. Blossom discovered how to get food, but there is never enough. Lola found the only source of water, a perpetually flushing toilet. They don't know where they are, only that they are in a huge space with no walls, no rooms, and no doors—there are only stairs going up and stairs going down, and all the stairs lead nowhere. They don't know why they are here or how long they will have to stay. They only know these things: each of them is sixteen years old; each of them is an orphan; each of them was brought to this place blindfolded; each of them is hungry; and the only food available to them comes out of a machine—a machine that is training them to violently turn on each other to be fed. How far will they go for a few pellets of food?

Sleator presents a disturbing view of scientific experimentation and behavior control that could lead to profound discussions about the use and misuse of free will and behaviorism.

**Similar Reads:** Sleator is a prolific YA author of thought-provoking books; try *Interstellar Pig* next. *Flowers for Algernon* by Daniel Keyes tells the story of another scientific experiment that may not be for the best.

**Subjects:** Orphans; Scientific Experimentation; Psychological Experimentation; Dystopia; Free Will

## Stevenson, Robert Louis (1850–1894)

***Dr. Jekyll and Mr. Hyde* (England: 1886).** Bantam 1982 (paper) 112pp. 055321277X **J Q**

Victorian London is the setting for this story about the duality of human nature. Dr. Henry Jekyll is a respected scientist. Mr. Edward Hyde is a loathsome murderer. What connects these two totally opposite men? Why does Jekyll defend and protect Hyde? Why has Jekyll withdrawn from his accustomed life of good works and from the companionship of good men? Each chapter of this famous short novel is a little mystery that tells a part of the story, and it is Mr. Utterson, Jekyll's friend and lawyer, who follows all the paths to the end when Jekyll's own statement makes clear what has been happening.

**Audio:** Recorded Books cassette 1556901550; CD 1402549415. Read by Alexander Spencer.

**Film/Video/DVD:** Many film versions including a 1920 silent film with John Barrymore, a 1932 version with Fredric March (who won a Best Actor Oscar for his performance), and a 1941 version with Spencer Tracy. All the film versions add female characters only implied in the novel.

**New Media:** Available as a graphic novel: *Graphic Classics Volume 9, Robert Louis Stevenson* (Eureka Productions 0974664804).

**Similar Reads:** *The Picture of Dorian Gray* by Oscar Wilde is also about the darkness we each hide inside.

**Subjects:** Victorian England; Victorian London; Personality; Good and Evil; Scientists; Scientific Experimentation; Victorian Novel

## Wells, H. G. (1866–1949)

***The Invisible Man* (England: 1897).** Modern Library Classics 2002 (paper) 156pp; Signet 2002 (paper) 176pp; Tor 1992 178pp; 1998 (paper) **J Q**

The invisible man is cursed—he is a brilliant scientist who discovers how to make himself invisible, and then can't undo the effect. He can't eat—the food is visible within him, he can't dress—the clothes look as if they are hanging in thin air, he can't walk about in the rain or snow or mud—he would be exposed. Is being invisible a dream come true, or a "hideous absurdity"? Can this strange state lead to any kind of happiness? Or is invisibility the true expression of man's isolation from his fellow man, leading only to desperation and insanity?

Action and suspense make this science fiction/horror story a natural for YA readers.

**Audio:** Recorded Books cassette 1556902573; CD 1402550774. Read by Victoria Morgan.

**Film/Video/DVD:** *The Invisible Man* (1933) is a classic with Claude Rains.

**Similar Reads:** Other scientists who lose control can be found in Shelley's *Frankenstein* and Wells's *The Island of Dr. Moreau.*

**Subjects:** Victorian England; Scientists; Scientific Experimentation; Mental Illness: Victorian Novel

*The Island of Dr. Moreau* **(England: 1896).** Bantam 1994 (paper) 160pp. 0553214322 <u>S</u>

What happens when man decides to play God and engage in reckless experiments with nature? Dr. Moreau, who has been banished from his own country for cruel and unorthodox experiments, is now living on an isolated South Pacific island where he can continue his horrendous explorations. Onto this island comes Prendick; his own ship sunk, he is rescued by a supply ship taking a bothersome cargo of animals and a passenger, Montgomery, to Moreau's island. Montgomery takes Prendick under his wing and introduces him to the strange goings on of the island. Eventually, Prendick meets Dr. Moreau and is horrified when he learns the true mission of the evil doctor.

This is the haunting visionary classic on the dangers of science meddling with nature.

**Audio:** Recorded Books cassette 0788705393. Read by Simon Prebble.

**Film/Video/DVD:** *The Island of Lost Souls* (1932) starring Charles Laughton as the mad Dr. Moreau gives the ultimate mad scientist performance; highly recommended. *The Island of Dr. Moreau* (1977) has Burt Lancaster providing a solid performance as the scientist. Marlon Brando turned in a bizarre performance as the mad doctor in a 1996 film.

**Similar Reads:** An excellent companion piece is Mary Shelley's *Frankenstein*; *Flowers for Algernon* is a gentler tale about scientific experimentation. The Moreau series by S. Andrew Swann *Forests of the Night, Emperor of the Twilight,* and *Specters of the Dawn; Chimera* by Will Shetterly and *Midnight* by Dean Koontz are more contemporary tales.

**Subjects:** Scientists; Scientific Experimentation; Evolution; Monsters

# Chapter 6

## Mystery and Suspense

In a good mystery, a puzzle is presented, and the reader participates in its solution. Teens who enjoy mysteries may have been fans of series based on such characters as Nate the Great, Cam Jansen, Encyclopedia Brown, Nancy Drew, or the Hardy Boys when they were younger.

A crime is the basis for any mystery. The crime can be a murder, embezzlement, a disappearance, a theft, or a kidnapping. The goal of the mystery then is to solve the crime—to find out the "who," the "how," and sometimes the "why" behind the crime.

The process of investigation takes up most of the story in the mystery novel. A detective of some sort, whether a police professional, an amateur sleuth, or a private eye, conducts the investigation, and clue-by-clue the reader follows the investigator through the solving of the crime and the unmasking of the mystery.

The character of the detective is one of the major appeal factors in mystery stories. Readers like to spend time with the character they have come to know. Mystery detectives are some of the most well-known characters in fiction; think of Sherlock Holmes, Miss Marple, Peter Wimsey, or Sam Spade—distinct, often eccentric, personalities with definite points of view and certain skills that set them apart from the rest of us and make them the solvers of crime. Unlike most literary genres, the character of the detective doesn't change too much over the course of the series, and that familiarity is part of the appeal.

The setting is also a major aspect of the mystery. The place—be it Holmes's Victorian London or Dupin's nineteenth-century Paris—the time period, and the locale contribute to the frame of the mystery and provide one of the major appeals for the reader.

The mystery genre is relatively new. Edgar Allan Poe is credited with creating the first detective, Monsieur Dupin, along with the basic rules of the detective story in the mid-nineteenth century. The detective-based mystery saw a boom in the Golden Age of detection fiction that occurred in the 1920s and 1930s when British authors Agatha

Christie, Dorothy Sayers, and Josephine Tey were writing. Today this is one of the most popular genres, with many subgenres (cozy mysteries, private eyes, crime procedurals), diverse characters (detectives who are chefs, professors, cats—even some who are dead!), and settings (ancient Rome, modern Botswana, New Jersey).

# Detectives

Following the mental moves of the brilliant mind of the master crime solver is the delight of these books. Character is primary in our attraction to this subgenre. We want to be in the presence of the detective, be he the cold and rational Holmes or the suave and elegant Peter Wimsey.

## Christie, Agatha (1890–1976)

*The Murder of Roger Ackroyd* **(England: 1926).** Berkley Publishing Group 2000 (paper) 256pp. 0425173895 **J**

> Hercule Poirot has retired to the peaceful and sleepy village of King's Abbott. He wants to work in his garden and put solving murders behind him, but murders occur everywhere humans gather, even in sleepy little villages where everyone knows everyone else's business.
>
> Christie has long been a favorite recommendation for YA readers. She writes in a very straightforward and clear style. Less fluent readers often find her books easy to read but intellectually challenging—the clues really are all there. *The Murder of Roger Ackroyd* has a famous twist.
>
> **Audio:** Audio Partners, 2001 cassette 1572702095. Read by Robin Bailey.
>
> **Film/Video/DVD:** In 2000, this book became part of the faithful television series of Poirot stories made by the BBC.
>
> **Similar Reads:** Christie's other famous sleuth, Miss Marple, also solves crimes in a sleepy little town. Poirot appears in many other novels by Christie. Try *Curtain,* Poirot's famous last case written in 1975. Other classic detectives to know are Dorothy Sayers's Lord Peter Wimsey, Conan Doyle's Sherlock Holmes, and Poe's Auguste Dupin.
>
> **Subjects:** England; Murder; Village Life; Hercule Poirot

*Murder on the Orient Express* **(England: 1934).** Berkley, 2000 (paper) 256 pp. 0425173755. **J**

> Hercule Poirot exercises his little grey cells on board the famous train the *Orient Express.* While the train travels from Istanbul to Calais, an American businessman is murdered in his bed during the night. Everyone on the train becomes a suspect, and the suspects range from a Russian countess to an American actress to a Swedish missionary and an English colonel. From this unlikely group of people, who would have wanted the businessman dead? It is up to Hercule Poirot, the observant, shrewd, and intuitive Belgian detective, to comprehend the crime and the reasons behind it.

The premise for the story is the real-life story of the kidnapping of the Lindbergh baby that stunned the world in 1932

> **Audio:** Audio Partners cassette 1572702117; CD 1572702125. Read by David Suchet.

> **Film/Video/DVD:** *Murder on the Orient Express* (1974) is a leisurely film with outstanding performances by Hollywood legends (Albert Finney, Lauren Bacall, Ingrid Bergman, Sean Connery, Vanessa Redgrave) that won Academy Award for Best Art Direction.

> **Similar Reads:** If you like Poirot, there is almost an endless supply—thirty-three novels and fifty-four short stories. Poirot is the only fictional character to ever have an obituary on the front page of the *New York Times*! Or turn to Margery Allingham for more classic British mysteries.

> **Subjects:** Murder; Train Travel; Hercule Poirot

## Collins, Wilkie (1824–1889)

*The Moonstone* (**England: 1868**). Modern Library Classics 2001 (paper) 528pp. 037575785-6 **S**

Rachel Verinder is turning eighteen, and one of her birthday gifts is a fabulous diamond from mysterious India. Years earlier, it had been pried out of a sacred Hindu statue during the pillage of a temple and had been in the possession of her uncle, the "wicked Colonel," until his recent death. But on the same day that it is presented to her, it is stolen. From that day on, Rachel refuses to discuss the stone. Sergeant Cuff, the police detective on the job, has his work cut out for him trying to solve the mystery of the Moonstone. What is the importance of the crippled second housemaid Rosanna Spearman, and why is she drawn to the Shivering Sands near the beach? What is the role of Franklin Blake, Rachel's cousin who was bringing the stone to her? Is Betteredge's daughter Penelope involved? Were there really three Brahmin Indians and a little English boy loitering around the Verinder estate on the day the diamond went missing? Is Lady Verinder to blame? And what role does Rachel's rejected suitor, Godfrey Ablewhite, play?

The leisurely pace of this long mystery may be a struggle for readers accustomed to more action. But it is a true Victorian novel full of eccentric English characters, like the butler Betteredge who finds answers to all of life's problems in his own good book—*Robinson Crusoe*.

> **Audio:** Recorded Books, cassette 1556903480. A full cast performs.

> **Film/Video/DVD:** *The Moonstone* was a 1996 British television production.

> **Similar Reads:** Collins, who had trained as a lawyer, wrote a second equally complex mystery, *The Woman in White*. Dedicated fans of Victorian mysteries may want to read *Bleak House* and *The Mystery of Edwin Drood* by Collins's contemporary Charles Dickens. The other Victorian detective to know is of course Sherlock Holmes.

**Subjects:** Victorian England; Diamonds; Inheritance; Theft; Police Detective; Victorian Novel

## Doyle, Sir Arthur Conan (1859–1930)

***The Adventures of Sherlock Holmes*** **(England: 1892).** Scholastic Classic 2004 (paper) 336pp. 0439574285 **J**

In the foggy gas-lit streets of Victorian London, Sherlock Holmes, brilliant chemist, master of disguise, and thinker extraordinaire, solves crimes through logic and deduction. While Holmes solves crimes in his unique style, his friend and colleague Dr. Watson writes everything down. "A Scandal in Bohemia," "The Red-headed League," and "The Adventure of the Copper Beeches" are just three of the twelve stories found in the collection *The Adventures of Sherlock Holmes.*

Sir Arthur Conan Doyle—historian, doctor, spiritualist, and author—created one of the most memorable characters in world fiction when he struck on the efficient thinking machine that is Holmes. Sherlock Holmes and Dr. Watson appear in four novels and sixty stories. Their first appearance was in the novel *A Study in Scarlet* in 1887; another novel followed, *The Sign of Four;* and then the twelve stories in *The Adventures of Sherlock Holmes.* The only person to ever tire of Sherlock Holmes was Conan Doyle himself! He killed off the detective in the story call, "The Final Problem," but public sentiment was so strongly negative that Doyle had to resurrect Holmes in *The Return of Sherlock Holmes*, another collection of stories.

**Audio:** Blackstone Audio, cassette 0786105119. Read by Walter Zimmerman and others.

**Film/Video/DVD:** Holmes is a cinematic figure like Tarzan or Frankenstein, the subject of endless film adaptations. *The Adventures of Sherlock Holmes* PBS Mystery series starring Jeremy Brett that began in 1984 and were produced until 1995 are excellent.

**Similar Reads:** read the novel *A Study in Scarlet* for the first appearance of Holmes and Watson. Laurie R. King is continuing the Holmes phenomenon in a new series of mysteries with YA appeal that feature Holmes and his new apprentice Mary Russell, *The Beekeeper's Apprentice* introduces her. Readers may want to explore other famous detectives such as Poe's Maupin, Dorothy Sayers's Lord Peter Wimsey, or Agatha Christie's Hercule Poirot.

**Subjects:** Victorian England; Victorian London; Crime; Victorian Novel

## Eco, Umberto (1932–)

*Name of the Rose* **(Italy: 1980).** Harvest Books/Harcourt 1994 (paper) 536pp. 0156001314 **S**

In the year 1327, Brother William of Baskerville (who does that make you think of?) and his faithful assistant Adso are called to an Italian abbey on the business of the emperor. Once there, monks keep turning up dead—seven monks dead in seven days' time. It becomes William's job to determine why monks are dying.

A notoriously challenging book to read, the long Latin passages will put many readers off. Eco stated he didn't want people to read it if they wouldn't stick with it. It's long, it's translated, and it is written by a master semiotician—a man who plays with words and meanings. For very good readers interested in a challenge!

**Audio:** Books of Tape 073663259X. Read by Alexander Adams.

**Film/Video/DVD:** *The Name of the Rose* (1986) starred Sean Connery and Christian Slater.

**Similar Reads:** Eco wrote a little volume titled *Postscript to the Name of the Rose* that contributes to the readers' appreciation on the novel. Readers who like mysteries in medieval settings may want to investigate these contemporary books: Ellis Peters's Brother Cadfael series, Margaret Frazer's Sister Frevisse series, Kate Sedley's Roger the Chapman series, or Peter Tremaine's Sister Fidelma books. Books by Iain Pears or Dan Brown would also be of interest.

**Subjects:** Italy, Catholic Church; Inquisition; Priests; Monks; Murder; Middle Ages

## Poe, Edgar Allan (1809–1849)

*Murders in the Rue Morgue* **(USA: 1841).** Modern Library 2006 (paper, includes the other Dupin stories) 160pp. 0679643427 **J Q**

A brutal murder takes place in a Paris apartment, the home of a mother and her grown daughter. Shrieks are heard in the night. When the police enter, the apartment is in disarray, valuables are strewn across the floor but not stolen, the daughter's body is discovered stuck part way up the chimney, and the mother's body is found decapitated in the yard below. The police are baffled. Enter Monsieur Auguste Dupin, amateur detective and professional thinker. He reviews the evidence, the testimony of witnesses, and the scene of the heinous act, and through his logical approach, he solves the mysterious crime.

Poe, best known for his grotesque and macabre horror stories, is considered by many to be the father of the modern detective. His character, Monsieur Dupin, predates Sherlock Holmes and the creations of Wilkie Collins. Dupin was the first fictional detective who is an amateur rather than a member of the police force and who uses reason and logic to solve crimes.

**Audio:** *Tales of Terror* available from Recorded Books 1402549113. Read by Jack Foreman, it includes *The Murders in the Rue Morgue* and eight other creepy tales.

**Similar Reads:** Auguste Dupin also appears in Poe's stories *The Purloined Letter* and *The Mystery of Marie Roget.*

**Subjects:** Paris, France; Murder; Short Stories

## Sayers, Dorothy (1893–1957)

*Strong Poison* **(England: 1930).** HarperTorch 1995 (paper) 272pp. 0061043508 **J**

Harriet Vane writes mystery novels. Her fiancé has just been murdered exactly the way she describes in one of her stories. Now Harriet, the main suspect in the case, is standing trial for his death. Her only hope is amateur detective Lord Peter Wimsey, the man who loves her and is exploring every possible solution to the crime in hopes of saving her from the executioner.

Lord Peter Wimsey was already an established character when Sayers gave him the love interest of Harriet Vane. Dorothy Sayers is renown for her literate and very English mysteries. She was one of the first female graduates of Oxford. In addition to writing the Lord Peter Wimsey mysteries, she was a medieval scholar who translated Dante.

**Audio:** Audio Partners cassette 1572701242. Read by Ian Carmichael.

**Film/Video/DVD:** *Strong Poison* (1987), a British production, was part of the Lord Peter Wimsey series made for British television.

**Similar Reads:** Lord Peter figures in eleven novels and twenty-one stories by Sayers. *Whose Body?* is the first Lord Peter Wimsey novel. *Have His Carcass, Gaudy Night,* and *Busman's Honeymoon* along with *Strong Poison* are the Lord Peter–Harriet Vane books.

**Subjects:** England 1920s; Murder; Trial; Romance

## Simenon, Georges (1903–1989)

### *Maigret and the Fortuneteller* (France: 1944). Out of print. S Q

Jules Maigret is a French police detective in Paris. Maigret is cranky and less than forthcoming about his method, but he is an expert at solving crimes. Maigret uses his deep understanding of human nature and foibles and his ability to observe the life around him to solve crime.

Renowned for their highly literate style yet written with simple and approachable prose, Simenon's novels offer a definite milieu—France—and convey a French sensibility. Simenon's books are about human behavior and the subtleties and complexities that propel humanity as much as they are about crime; turn to Simenon for his compassion, psychological insight, and moral objectivity. Francophiles and students studying French language will appreciate Maigret, as will fans of psychological fiction and detective stories.

**Audio:** Maigret stories are available from BBC Audio (www.bbcshop.com) as full-cast dramatized radio plays.

**Film DVD Video:** *Maigret* (1992) was a British television series; also many French films and television productions have been made.

**Similar Reads:** Simenon wrote seventy-five Maigret novels, the first published in 1931, the last in 1972. Somewhat difficult to find, libraries and used books stores may be the best source for Maigret books.

**Subjects:** France; Police Detective; Crime; Criminals

## Tey, Josephine (1896–1952)

### *The Daughter of Time* (England: 1951). Scribner 1995 (paper) 206pp. 0684803860 J Q

Inspector Grant of Scotland Yard is in hospital with a broken leg. To pass the time, his actress friend brings him an envelope full of faces to study. The one that catches his attention and sends him on an intellectual quest for truth is the face of Richard the Third, England's evil fifteenth-century king accused of killing his two young nephews to inherit the throne. Did Richard murder the boys? What is the evidence for and against the accusation? Would modern investigative techniques lead to a different answer than the one agreed on by history?

Teya is master of the British mystery—her books are elegant and erudite.

**Audio:** BBC Audiobooks cassette 0745063238; CD 0754053695. Read by Derek Jacobi.

**Similar Reads:** Other Tey classics include *Miss Pym Disposes* and *The Franchise Affair*; readers may want to try Agatha Christie, Dorothy Sayers, Ngaio Marsh, and Margery Allingham for more classic British mystery.

**Subjects:** England; Richard the Third; Historical Crimes

# Hard-Boiled Private Eyes

The world weary, seen it all PI figures in these classic noir mysteries set before the Second World War. The city landscape is practically a character, most of the women are "dames," and the inherent corruption of man is a given—these novels are all about toughness.

For a modern take on the hard-boiled PI, readers could try Robert B. Parker's Spenser novels or Mickey Spillane's Mike Hammer series—books that were considered scandalously sexual and violent in their day but seem sort of campy now.

### Chandler, Raymond (1888–1959)

*The Big Sleep* (USA: 1939). Vintage 1988 (paper) 234pp. 0394758285 **J Q**

Private eye Philip Marlowe gets involved trying to help a dysfunctional family in 1930s Los Angeles. Carmen Sternwood, the infantile daughter of a very wealthy man, is being extorted, bodies are piling up, her father is sick, and Marlowe is the only man trying to act with integrity in an environment of corruption, greed, and exploitation.

Why would a twenty-first-century reader explore a 1930s detective story? Two words—major attitude. Chandler's world-weary detective Philip Marlowe has tons of it. Chandler wrote classics in the "hard-boiled" genre but was himself a classically educated Victorian. He wrote short stories, novels, and screenplays about the darker side of human nature and the seamier sides of pre–World War II Los Angeles, focusing on the corruption of wealth and the harshness of urban life. Influenced by Hemingway, Dreiser, Hammett, Ring Lardner, and Sherwood Anderson, Chandler cannot be dismissed. *The Big Sleep* was Chandler's first novel written when he was in his fifties.

**Audio:** Recorded Books cassette 1590070895; CD 1590070909. Read by Elliott Gould.

**Film/Video/DVD:** *The Big Sleep* (1946) directed by Howard Hawks with Humphrey Bogart as Philip Marlowe, weary and knowing, his cynicism masking his compassion.

**Similar Reads:** Other Chandler classics are *Farewell My Lovely* and *The Long Goodbye*. Or try or James M. Cain's *Double Indemnity*. Ross Macdonald's private eye Lew Archer is also in the hard-boiled genre; try *The Drowning Pool*. Robert B. Parker's Spenser novels bring the hard-boiled genre into the present.

**Subjects:** Los Angeles, California; Wealth; Sisters; Fathers and Daughters; Blackmail

## Hammett, Dashiell (1894–1961)

*The Maltese Falcon* (**USA: 1929**). Vintage 1989 (paper) 224pp. 0679722645 S

Sam Spade is as hard boiled as they come. When his partner is murdered on a case, it is up to Spade to solve the crime. Naturally, there is a woman involved, and Spade has to work his way through a web of lies and a phalanx of shady characters to get to the truth.

Dash Hammett was a man with a colorful past. He was a high school dropout who had worked for the famous Pinkerton Detective Agency as young man.

**Audio:** Books on Tape 073666047X. Read by Michael Prichard.

**Film/Video/DVD:** *The Maltese Falcon* (1941) is a classic film directed by John Huston and starring Humphrey Bogart—a must see.

**Similar Reads:** Other books by Hammett include *The Dain Curse* and *The Thin Man*. Readers may want to move on to Raymond Chandler for more hard-boiled action or to James M. Cain and Mickey Spillane.

**Subjects:** San Francisco, California; Noir; Murder

# Crime and True Crime

In these books, it isn't the solving of a mystery that is primary but rather the exploration of a crime or a criminal. These books are less of a puzzle and more of an examination of the criminal mind and the dark side of human behavior.

## Capote, Truman (1924–1984)

*In Cold Blood* (**USA: 1965**). Vintage 1994 (paper) 368pp. 0679745580 S

Holcomb Kansas, 1959, in a remote farmhouse, an entire family is brutally and methodically murdered. No one understands why. The Clutter family is as regular as can be. Mr. Clutter works hard running his farm along modern principles; he is strict but loving. Mrs. Clutter is known to be somewhat "nervous." The two oldest girls live away from home, but a fifteen-year-old son, Kenyon, and sixteen-year-old Nancy, "the town darling," a competent girl who is a friend to everyone, still lived at home. Capote dispassionately and systematically introduces us to the dead family, the town that was their home, the remorseless murderers, and the men who solved the crime in this suspenseful book. Brilliant and unsettling.

Capote practically originated "true crime" in this successful attempt at a non-fiction novel. He took a real event and gave it all the imaginative power of fiction. This best seller was originally serialized in the *New Yorker* magazine. A master prose stylist, Capote is also known for *Breakfast at Tiffany's* and *A Christmas Memory.*

**Audio:** Books on Tape 1415930929. Read by Scott Brick.

**Film/Video/DVD:** *In Cold Blood* (1967) stars Robert Blake. *Capote* (2005) explores the character of Capote and follows the creative and investigative process he underwent writing *In Cold Blood.*

**Similar Reads:** True crime is technically a nonfiction genre. Capote played the line between fiction and nonfiction with *In Cold Blood.* Serial killers, famous murders and court cases, unsolved crimes, and police procedure all figure into this genre. True crime fans argue that it provides insight to the darker side of humanity; it is not a genre for squeamish or sensitive readers. For mature readers, other true crime classics include *The Stranger Beside Me* by Ann Rule, about serial killer Ted Bundy, and *Helter Skelter* by Vincent Bugliosi, about the Manson murders.

**Subjects:** Kansas; Murder; Justice; True Crime; Mature Read

## Dostoevsky, Fyodor (1821–1881)

*Crime and Punishment* **(Russia: 1866).** Vintage 1993 (paper) 592pp. 0679734503 <u>S</u>

Raskolnikov, a student who lives in St. Petersburg surrounded by poverty, decides to prove the theory that all truly great men are above the common laws. To test this idea, he murders the neighborhood pawnbroker. He argues that her death will really be a benefit to mankind because she abuses people with her usury. But the title of the book is *Crime* and *Punishment,* and the murder begins Raskolnikov's journey to redemption.

This is a challenging and complex novel—psychologically acute, full of analysis of human behavior, not merely a crime novel but a treatise about men's souls, the forces of good and evil, the power of love to redeem. This is also great historical fiction with its textured portrayal of nineteenth-century St. Petersburg and its depictions of women and the relationships of men and women at that time. Like all large Russian novels, it's hard to keep the names straight, don't be embarrassed to make a chart! The edition listed in this entry is a newer translation.

Dostoevsky's own story is as compelling as his fiction. As a young man he was interested in social justice, not an idea the tsar tolerated. Eventually he was arrested for revolutionary activities. Sentenced to die, he and his fellow prisoners were blindfolded and led out in the cold to stand before a firing squad. At the last minute, the squad did not fire; it was a mock execution to terrorize the prisoners. Dostoevsky's sentence was commuted, and he was sent to Siberia where he spent four years in a prison labor camp. The result was his ruined health and his introspective, melancholy fiction.

**Audio:** Blackstone Audiobooks cassette 0786105380 (Part 1); 0786105399 (Part 2). Read by Walter Zimmerman.

**Film/Video/DVD:** *Crime and Punishment* (1998) stars Patrick Dempsey. In 1980, a four-part *Masterpiece Theatre* production with John Hurt appeared.

**Similar Reads:** Dostoevsky's other great classic is *The Brothers Karamazov*. Ambitious readers may want to explore *Notes from Underground*, his early existential classic about an alienated antihero.

**Subjects:** St. Petersburg, Russia; Murder; Russian Novel; Guilt; Alienation; Redemption; Good and Evil; Mature Read

## Highsmith, Patricia (1921–1995)

*The Talented Mr. Ripley* **(USA: 1955).** Vintage 1992 (paper) 304pp. 0679742298 <u>S</u>

Ripley's talent is murder, con artistry, living well on ill-gotten gains, and being charming—and thoroughly evil. Sent by Mr. Greenleaf to Italy to bring his son, Dickie, home to America, Tom Ripley decides he likes Italy too much to leave. He also likes Dickie's lifestyle. In fact, Ripley finds it so enchanting that he determines to become Dickie.

Highsmith was a master at making the sociopathic seem sympathetic. She admitted that Ripley was her favorite creation. Fans of Lois Duncan may like to move on to Highsmith.

**Audio:** Recorded Books cassette 0375405119. Read by Michael Hayden.

**Film/Video/DVD:** *The Talented Mr. Ripley* (1999) stars Matt Damon as Ripley, Gwyneth Paltrow, Jude Law, and Cate Blanchett.

**Similar Reads:** Ripley appears in several other novels, read *Ripley Under Ground, Ripley's Game,* and *Ripley Under Water*. Highsmith's first novel was *Strangers on a Train*—famously filmed by Hitchcock.

**Subjects:** Rome, Italy; Murder; Impersonation

---

# Suspense

The unrelenting building of tension is the point of these books—can you take the pressure? As director Alfred Hitchcock famously said about suspense, his own specialty, "There is no terror in the bang, only in the anticipation of it."

## Christie, Agatha (1890–1976)

*And Then There Were None* **(England: 1939).** St. Martin's Press 2001 (paper) 275pp. 0312979479. **J**

Indian Island is a remote and isolated island off the English coast. Does a movie star own it? A rich American? Or does the royal family own it? Indian Island is a bit of a mystery. Onto the island come ten people, all there for different reasons, each with different expectations, and each with a different secret. After their first dinner together, an unsettling announcement is made to this group of strangers, and then one by one, the guests start dying.

This is a fast-paced read with a baffling mystery, a book often recommended to reluctant readers. Christie is the acknowledged master of the British mystery. Prolific, clever, and quite English, her books have been best sellers for decades.

**Audio:** Audio Partners cassette 1572702508; CD 1572702516. Read by Hugh Fraser.

**Film/Video/DVD:** Filmed numerous times under different titles (*Ten Little Indians; And Then There Were None*). The 1945 black-and-white version (with the same title as the book) is very atmospheric.

**Similar Reads:** Margery Allingham, Dorothy Sayers, Josephine Tey, and Ngaio Marsh are other masters of the classic British mystery.

**Subjects:** England; Murder; Justice

## Cormier, Robert (1925–2000)

*I Am the Cheese* (USA: 1977). Laurel Leaf 1991 (paper) 220pp. 0440940605 **J Teen**

*I Am the Cheese* is a coming-of-age story with a nasty twist. Adam Farmer is fourteen. We learn his story in bits and pieces as this novel shifts between Adam's own narration of a bike trip, a third-person narration of Adam's cloudy past, and the transcripts of an interrogation that Adam is undergoing. This novel presents Adam's life as a tangled puzzle that the reader must sort out. A disturbing and unsettling story that demands the reader's full attention, some readers will immediately read the book a second time to figure out how the elements all come together. Identity, the individual, memory, family, and the misuse of power are some of the themes explored in *I Am the Cheese*. To understand the title, think back to nursery rhymes, who stands alone?

Cormier is a standard bearer for young adult fiction. His novels are intelligent, complex, raw. Don't look to Cormier for happy endings or easy answers; he wanted young readers to know the serious side of things.

**Audio:** Recorded Books cassette 1556907788. Read by Jeff Woodman and John Randolph Jones.

**Film/Video/DVD:** *I Am the Cheese* was adapted for film in 1983.

**Similar Reads:** Cormier's coming-of-age classic is *The Chocolate War*. Other Cormier classics include *Fade, After the First Death,* and his last novel, *The Rag and Bone Shop*.

**Subjects:** Secrets; Identity; Family; Fear; Loss; Margaret Edwards Award 1991

## Doyle, Sir Arthur Conan (1859–1930)

*The Hound of the Baskervilles* **(England: 1902).** Signet 2001 (paper, 100th anniversary edition) 250pp. 0451528018 **J**

Sherlock Holmes has one of his most suspenseful investigations in this fiendish case about the curse that haunts the Baskerville family. In the time of the Great Rebellion, Sir Hugo held the Baskerville estate. Hugo was a barbarous man who, after abducting a local girl one night, chased her across the moors with his dogs. Just as he reached the girl, a huge, bloodthirsty hound with "blazing eyes" attacked him and ripped out his throat. The girl was found dead, destroyed by the terror of what she has seen. From that time on, anyone named Baskerville is wise to stay off the moors at night when the ravenous hell-hound may await them. Cut to Victorian England where the current Lord Baskerville has just died from a heart attack, frightened to death by something he saw on the moors. His heir, a young nephew raised in the United States and Canada, is now, unexpectedly, the new Lord Baskerville—inheritor of gloomy old Baskerville Hall, an expansive fortune, and the curse.

Can an arch rationalist like Sherlock Holmes believe in a family curse? Is the new Lord Baskerville safe? Join Holmes and Watson as they unravel this brutal case.

**Audio:** Recorded Books cassette 0788773674. Read by Patrick Tull.

**Film/Video/DVD:** *The Hound of the Baskervilles* (1988) is a *Masterpiece Theatre* production with Jeremy Brett. Many other film versions have been produced of this very cinematic story.

**Similar Reads:** Turn to *The Adventures of Sherlock Holmes* for more brilliant detection. Also read *A Study in Scarlet*, the novel in which Holmes first appeared published in 1887.

**Subjects:** Victorian England; Family Curse; Property; Inheritance

## Hamilton, Virginia (1936–2002)

🎗 *The House of Dies Drear* **(USA: 1968).** Simon Pulse 1984 (paper) 256pp. 0020435207 **J Teen**

Thomas Small and his family move from North Carolina to Ohio, where they take up residence in a big old house that was once a stop on the Underground Railroad, the secret route used by African Americans escaping from slavery to freedom in the North. But strange things happen in this house—is it haunted? What effect is the past still having on the house?

Lyrically written and infused with history and suspense, Hamilton's novel can be read on several levels. The story can easily lead to an exploration of a difficult time in American history.

**Audio:** Recorded Books cassette 0788703293; CD 140255043X. Read by Lynne Thigpen.

**Film/Video/DVD:** *House of Dies Drear* was made for TV in 1984.

**Similar Reads:** Hamilton wrote a follow-up story called *The Mystery of Drear House.* She is also the author of an award-winning book of African American folktales called *The People Could Fly*; a mature work for older readers is Toni Morrison's *Beloved*.

**Subjects:** Ohio; Family; Underground Railroad; Slavery; African Americans; Edgar Allan Poe Award 1970

## Duncan, Lois (1934–)

🏵 *I Know What You Did Last Summer* **(USA: 1973).** Laurel Leaf 2005 (paper, movie tie in edition) 199pp. 0440228441. **J Teen Q**

Something happened a year ago that is coming back to haunt Julie, Ray, Barry, and Helen. Driving home from a picnic last summer, their car hit and killed a little boy on a bicycle. Instead of staying to help the boy, they drove on. Now someone who knows their secret is reminding them of the terrible night, and not one of them is safe.

Duncan's books are very popular. They are fast-paced, suspenseful reads filled with well-delineated characters. This one is a little dated with references to Nam and a total lack of cell phones, but it is still a suspenseful thriller that keeps the reader guessing.

**Film/Video/DVD:** *I Know What You Did Last Summer* (1997) and its sequel *I Still Know What You Did Last Summer* (1998) are film adaptations of Duncan's book.

**Similar Reads:** Duncan is known for her suspense classics featuring young adult protagonists; try *Killing Mr. Griffin* and *Stranger with My Face*.

**Subjects:** Friendship; Secrets; Revenge; Margaret A. Edwards Award 1992

## Du Maurier, Daphne (1907–1989)

*Rebecca* **(England: 1938). J**

*See* entry in Chapter 9, "Romantic Fiction."

# Chapter 7

## Coming of Age and Other Life Issues

Beyond the standard genres of mystery, romance, adventure, and speculative fiction are those stories that focus on characters and their common and uncommon struggles with life. In adult fiction, this is generally referred to as "mainstream" fiction; in young adult literature, it goes by various names—problem novel, issues novel, and so on. Whatever name is given to this body of literature, the focus tends to be on the characters, the challenges they face in life, and how they meet those challenges. Thus, in finding read-alikes, you may look to other character-driven stories, as well as issues novels and mainstream fiction.

## Coming of Age

Young protagonists mature over the course of the story to a greater understanding of themselves and their role in the world. Posed in these novels are the universal and eternal questions: who am I? Who should I be? Can I choose my identity or is it predetermined? Can I create myself or must I be defined by my family, my culture, my past?

### Anaya, Rudolpho (1937– )

*Bless Me, Ultima* (USA: 1972). Warner Books 1994 (paper) 272pp. 0446600253 **J**

Sensitive, dreamy Antonio is almost seven when Ultima comes to live with his family. Ultima is a *curandera,* a healer, an herbalist, a wisewoman; some say she is a *bruja,* a witch. She and Antonio have a special connection. They feel the presence of the river, the power of the wind, and they know the importance of dreams. Ultima helps Antonio reconcile the conflicts in the family. Antonio's father, a *vaquero* (cowboy), still yearns for the rowdy life of horses and freedom he abandoned to raise a family. Antonio's mother, the proud daughter of farmers—dignified, quiet people who know the land—wants her son to be a man of learning, a priest. Together Antonio and Ultima search for the healing plants Ultima uses in her art and use folk magic to battle evil spirits. The traditional folkways of Ultima and the Catholicism into which Antonio is now being confirmed blend and weave as he encounters true spirituality, magic, and morality in the teachings that Ultima imparts.

Anaya uses lyrical writing to portray the beauty of the natural world, the calm wisdom of Ultima, the treachery of men, and young Antonio's growing understanding of the world and his place in it.

**Audio:** Recorded Books cassette 1402586698; CD 140258671x. Read by Robert Ramirez.

**Similar Reads:** Try *The House on Mango Street* or *One Hundred Years of Solitude.*

**Subjects:** New Mexico, 1940s; Family; Catholics; Mexican Americans; Healers; Magic; Magical Realism; Good and Evil; Frequently Challenged; American Southwest

## Armstrong, William (1914–1999)

🌳 *Sounder* (USA: 1969). HarperTrophy 1972 (paper) 128pp. 0064400204 <u>M</u> **Teen Q**
Sounder is a loud and loyal hunting dog that belongs to a family of African American sharecroppers. When the hunting is bad, father is forced to steal food for his family, is caught, and is sent to prison. Because of this hardship, the oldest boy in the family, only ten years old, grows up quickly, and although he yearns to go to school, he works hard to help his struggling family. Eventually, although it means sacrifice, his burning desire for education is rewarded.

A heartfelt story that is simply told, and therefore powerful and memorable.

**Audio:** Harper Audio CD 0060852704. Read by Avery Brooks.

**Film/Video/DVD:** *Sounder* (1972) features Cicely Tyson and Paul Winfield.

**Similar Reads:** *The Sour Land* is another book by William Armstrong. Other famous dog books include *Old Yeller* and *Where the Red Fern Grows.* Books by Mildred Taylor also depict strong African American families. Mature readers will also be interested in works by Ernest Gaines such as *A Gathering of Old Men, The Autobiography of Miss Jane Pittman,* and *A Lesson Before Dying.*

**Subjects:** American South; Fathers and Sons; Family; Dogs; Pets; Imprisonment; Historical Fiction; Poverty; Racism; Rural Life; African Americans; Newbery Medal 1970

## Baldwin, James (1924–1987)

*Go Tell It on the Mountain* (USA: 1953). Laurel 1985 (paper) 224 pp. 0440330076 <u>S</u> **Q**
The past is alive tonight in the Temple of the Fire Baptized, a storefront church in 1930s Harlem. Tonight John Grimes will undergo his salvation. Fourteen-year-old John is growing up surrounded by secrets. His father, the preacher Gabriel; his mother, Elizabeth, and his Aunt Florence all have secrets and hidden resentments that shape their current relationships to each other, to John, and to God.

Sin and redemption hover around the characters in this tight, emotional novel about the weight of the past upon the present.

**Film/Video/DVD:** *Go Tell It on the Mountain* (1985) with Paul Winfield and Ving Rhames.

**Similar Reads:** Another African American classic that takes place in Harlem is *The Street* by Ann Petry.

**Subjects:** New York 1930s; Harlem; African American; Preachers; Family; Fathers and Sons

## Borland, Hal (1900–1978)

*When the Legends Die* (USA: 1963). Bantam 1984 (paper) 304 pp. 0553257382 **S**

Thomas Black Bull is raised in a peaceful Ute tradition of living cooperatively with the natural world and being independent of white men's concerns. When  his parents die, Thomas is taken by Blue Elk to live on the reservation, a place he barely endures. Although he struggles with authority and founders for years, eventually his natural talent, his innate brutality, and his ability to endure pain make him a champion bronco rider on the rodeo circuit. But severe injuries force him to reevaluate his place in the world.

Identity, rebellion against authority, the exercise of personal liberty, traditional ways versus modern living all set in a Western context make this a unique coming-of-age story and an insightful exploration of the difficulty of honoring a Native American heritage in a society that wants conformity.

**Audio:** Recorded Books cassette 1556905599; CD 1402548516. Read by Norman Dietz.

**Film/Video/DVD:** See *When the Legends Die* (1972) with Richard Widmark and Frederick Forrest.

**Similar Reads:** Other classic coming-of-age stories that explore the Native American experience are *Bless Me Ultima, The Education of Little Tree,* and *House Made of Dawn* by N. Scott Momaday. For more recent books, try Sherman Alexie's stories in *The Lone Ranger and Tonto Fistfight in Heaven* and *Reservation Blues.*

**Subjects:** Colorado; New York; Native Americans; Utes; Rodeo; Orphans; Indian School

## Camus, Albert (1913–1960)

🐟 *The Stranger* (France: 1942 trans. 1946) Vintage 1989 (paper) 144pp. 0679720200 **S Q**

In hot and sunny Algeria in 1945, a young man commits an unprovoked murder and is sentenced to death. Enigmatic dispassionate, detached, and unemotional, Mersault was one of the first antiheroes in fiction. Is his real crime the senseless murder he commits or his lack of feeling about any part of his life?

**Similar Reads:** Interested readers will want to try Camus's more difficult novel *The Plague;* two plays that will intrigue young existentialists are Sartre's *No Exit* and Becket's *Waiting for Godot.*

**Subjects:** Algeria; Existentialism; Alienation; Absurdity; Antihero; Murder; Nobel Prize 1957

## Carter, Forrest (1927–1979)

***The Education of Little Tree* (USA: 1977).** University of New Mexico Press 1986 (paper) 216pp. 0826308791 **J Q**

These are the gentle reminiscences of a boy being raised by his grandparents. Granpa is a mountain man who teaches Little Tree to understand nature and moonshine. Granma is quiet and gentle, a full-blooded Cherokee, all heart and patience. Together they teach Little Tree "The Way" of living respectfully with the land and the beings of Earth. Granpa teaches him to hunt. Granma reads Shakespeare aloud, sings, and makes moccasins through which Little Tree can feel the earth mother rise and swell. The Tennessee hills during the Depression provide the setting for this touching story.

**Audio:** Recorded Books cassette 0788722255. Read by Jeff Woodman.

**Film/Video/DVD:** *Education of Little Tree* (1997) is a sincere and touching adaptation.

**Similar Reads:** Try *The Last Algonquin* by Kazimiroff, *Bless Me, Ultima* by Anaya, and *When the Legend Die* by Borland

**Subjects:** Tennessee, 1930s; Native Americans; Cherokee Indians; Grandparents; Indian School; Gentle Read

## Chopin, Kate (1851–1904)

***The Awakening* (USA: 1899).** Avon 1982 (paper) 192 pp. 0380002450 **S**

Among the Creole families escaping the heat of New Orleans on the summer enclave of Grand Isle is Edna Pontellier, an unsatisfied young wife and mother. As the summer progresses, Edna awakens to her true self when she has an affair with a younger man. But come autumn, she must return to the life that oppresses her.

This story of a woman's emerging sexuality and the disapproval of her society was considered pornography when first published in 1899. Chopin and *The Awakening* reemerged in the 1970s when classic stories told from women's points of view were being rediscovered.

**Audio:** Recorded Books cassette 1556905831; CD 1-40255-215-7. Read by Alexandra O'Karma.

**Film/Video/DVD:** Filmed in 1982 as *The End of August* and in 1992 as *Grand Isle*. Both are flawed adaptations.

**Similar Reads:** A contemporary of Chopin's, Edith Wharton, wrote a beautiful novella called *Summer,* also about the awakening passion of a young woman. *Anna Karenina* and *Madam Bovary* are two other nineteenth-century women whose quests for more fulfilling personal lives end in tragedy.

**Subjects:** New Orleans late 1800s; Marriage; Independence; Family; Relationships; Sexuality; Mature Read

## Cisneros, Sandra (1954–)

***The House on Mango Street*** **(USA: 1984)** Vintage 1991 (paper) 128pp. 0679734775 **J Q**

Esperanza is growing up on Mango Street, a tough part of the barrio of Chicago. Her life is filled with family, neighbors, friends, and the diverse women who influence her: her intelligent, loving mother; her little sister; and her girlfriends who are all exploring what it is to be a woman. There is Sally, the beautiful, spirited girl who marries an abusive man to escape her abusive father, and Alicia, her friend "doesn't want to spend her life in a factory or behind a rolling pin."

Esperanza poetically narrates this collection of vignettes about the people she knows, the feelings she has, and the life she is experiencing as an urban, Hispanic girl coming of age, surrounded by family, colorful characters, poverty, and cultural diversity. She expresses her own longing for an identity, a place to become herself, a home of her own.

**Audio:** Books on Tape 1415924147; includes two other works by Cisneros, *Loose Women* and *Woman Hollering Creek*. Read by the author.

**Similar Reads:** Readers may want to explore Cisneros's 2002 novel *Caramelo,* a larger saga of a Mexican American family, or try the poetic *Call Me Maria* by Judith Ortiz Cofer about a Puerto Rican girl growing up in New York. *How the Garcia Girls Lost Their Accents* by Julia Alvarez is about four sisters who adjust to being Americans after leaving the Dominican Republic.

**Subjects:** Chicago; Family; Friendship; Mexican Americans; Urban Life

## Cormier, Robert (1925–2000)

🎖 ***The Chocolate War*** **(USA 1974).** Knopf/Random House 2004 (paper, 30th anniversary edition) 253pp. 0375829873 **J Teen**

"Do I Dare Disturb the Universe?"

That is the quote on the poster in Jerry Renault's locker at Trinity School, a Catholic boys' school in Boston. Jerry is new there. Still recovering from the recent death of his mother, he just wants to fit in, make friends, maybe become the quarterback for the football team. Accepting an assignment from the Vigils, Trinity's elite secret society, Jerry refuses to sell chocolates for the first ten days of the school's annual fund-raising sale, but when his "assignment" is over, Jerry still refuses to sell the chocolates. What started as a prank becomes a personal mission, a stand of the individual against the group, and an act that disturbs the universe of Trinity school—and may destroy Jerry.

*The Chocolate War* was a breakout YA classic when first published. It has long been one of the most frequently challenged books in schools and libraries (for offensive language, sexuality, disrespect of authority, and being an all around bleak and negative story). Cormier is an acknowledged master of realistic and gritty YA novels that show teen protagonists struggling with some of life's darker aspects and that don't sugar coat reality. Among his twenty-five novels are *I Am the Cheese*, *Fade*, and *The Rag and Bone Shop*.

**Audio:** Recorded Books cassette 1556907745; CD 1402522940. Read by George Guidall.

**Film/Video/DVD:** *The Chocolate War* (1988) captures the spirit of the book.

**Similar Reads:** Jerry returns to Trinity in *Beyond the Chocolate War*; other school stories include *A Separate Peace* by John Knowles and Pat Conroy's best seller *The Lords of Discipline*. Kesey's *One Flew over the Cuckoo's Nest* and Golding's *Lord of the Flies* are other angsty novels about the individual, peer pressure, and conformity. YA books by Chris Crutcher are also a good recommendation.

**Subjects:** Boston; 1970s; School Story; High School; Catholics; Violence; Power; Mobs; Peer Pressure; Bullies; Frequently Challenged; Margaret A. Edwards Award 1991

## Danziger, Paula (1944–2004)

*The Cat Ate My Gymsuit* (**USA, 1974**). Putnam/Penguin (hardback) 0399243070; Paperstar/Penguin 1998 (paper) 147pp. 0698116844 **M Teen Q**

Ninth-grader Marcy Lewis has a verbally abusive father and a clingy, unsure mother. Marcy lacks confidence and is overweight, but her sarcastic humor helps keep life from becoming too grim. The bright spot in Marcy's life becomes her new English teacher, Ms. Finney, a young innovative teacher who encourages creativity and expression. Ms. Finney enlivens the kids in her classes but alienates the conservative school administrators and parents. To save Ms. Finney's job, Marcy bands together with her friends to fight the principal. Through it all, Marcy gains self-esteem and confidence and learns to stand up for herself and to fight for what she believes in.

**Audio:** Full Cast Audio cassette 1932076557.

**Similar Reads:** Try *Dinky Hocker Shoots Smack* by M. E. Kerr. Danziger's *There's a Bat in Bunk Five* follows Marcy Lewis to camp as a counselor. Danziger is the author of the popular series of Amber Brown books for younger readers.

**Subjects:** New York 1970s; School Story; Teachers and Students; Self-Confidence, Abuse; Friendship

## Dickens, Charles (1812–1870)

*David Copperfield* (**England: 1849**). Modern Library 2000 (paper) 896pp. 0679783415 **J**

"Whether I shall turn out to be the hero of my own life, or whether that station will be held by anybody else, these pages must show. To begin my life with the beginning of my life, I record that I was born."

Thus Dickens begins his story of a boy who becomes a man despite life's continually trying to knock him down. Considered his most autobiographical work and Dickens's own favorite, *David Copperfield* is a drama of immense proportion following the title character through many adventures, from his dramatic birth to his maturation as a young man of wisdom and experience.

*Copperfield* contains many of Dickens's most memorable characters: the gentle and childlike Mr. Dick; the archetypal evil stepfather Mr. Murdstone; Mr. Creakle the sadistic schoolmaster; loyal Peggotty; Uriah Heep, the overly humble clerk; the ever optimistic, perpetually destitute Mr. Micawber; and David's dear, opinionated Aunt Miss Betsey Trotwood.

**Audio:** Blackstone Audio cassette 0786103817 (pt. 1), 0786103825 (pt. 2). Read by Frederick Davidson

**Film/Video/DVD:** *David Copperfield* (1935) with Freddy Bartholomew, W. C. Fields, Edna May Oliver, and other studio stars is a classic. The 2000 *Masterpiece Theatre* version with Daniel Radcliffe (pre–Harry Potter fame) as the young David is also good.

**Similar Reads:** Other Dickens classics about the growth of a boy include *Oliver Twist, Great Expectations,* and *Nicholas Nickleby.*

**Subjects:** Victorian England; Victorian Novel; Orphans; Family; Autobiographical Novel; Aunts

***Great Expectations* (England: 1860).** Pocket Enriched Classics 2004 (paper) 656pp. 0743487613 **J**

Phillip Pirrip, called Pip, has few prospects for the future. Pip is an orphan being "brought up by hand" by his unkind sister and her gentle husband, the blacksmith Joe Gargery. After serving as Joe's apprentice for several years, Pip learns he is to be made into a gentleman. He is told he has "great expectations." An anonymous benefactor will pay for him to have fine clothes, a better education, a home in London, and all the things a young gentleman in Victorian England could need. But the promise of new fortune brings out the worst in Pip; he becomes arrogant and proud, he rebuffs the coarse and common Joe, and he sets himself up to love the unapproachable Estella. This is the story of Pip's odyssey from poverty through wealth to humility.

Dickens takes us on a tour of childhood with his scenes of Pip's agonies being a child among adults who are alien and abusive. Dickens also guides us through Victorian London with glimpses into Newgate Prison, the Courts of Law, the contemporary treatment of convicts, and the world of the theatre.

**Audio:** Recorded Books cassette 1556902042; CD 1402549504. Read by Frank Muller.

**Film/Video/DVD:** Many film versions exist. The 1946 black-and-white classic directed by David Lean with Jean Simmons as Estella is very atmospheric; in an interesting filmic twist, Jean Simmons is Miss Havisham in the 1989 TV miniseries. For a modernized version, try the 1998 film with Ethan Hawke and Gwyneth Paltrow.

**Similar Reads:** Dickens's other coming-of-age classic is *David Copperfield.* For comedy by Dickens, read *The Pickwick Papers.*

**Subjects:** Victorian England; Victorian Novel; Victorian London; Poverty; Family; Inheritance; Mental Illness

## Ellison, Ralph (1914–1994)

🎗 *Invisible Man* **(USA: 1952).** Vintage 1995 (paper) 608 pp. 0679732764 <u>S</u>

The narrator who says he is an invisible man because people refuse to see him tells the story of his humiliation and oppression in the society of 1930s America. As a black man in a white culture, the unnamed narrator undertakes a bizarre and epic odyssey searching for his identity in a society that doesn't want to include him. First as a college student in a Southern town then as a militant in the Black Nationalist Group in Harlem, he tries to succeed then just survive in a hostile world of rejection and dismissal.

> **Audio:** Recorded Books cassette 078874366X; CD 1402553846. Read by Peter Francis James.

> **Similar Reads:** Try *Black Boy* and *Native Son* by Richard Wright or *Go Tell It on the Mountain* by James Baldwin.

> **Subjects:** New York, 1930s; Harlem; African Americans; Racism; Alienation; Identity; National Book Award 1953

## Hinton, S. E. (1950–)

*The Outsiders* **(USA: 1967)** Puffin Books 1997 (paper) 180 pp. 014038572X **J Teen Q**

Fourteen-year-old Ponyboy Curtis is on the outside of life. His world is made up of Greasers—the poor boys generally considered to be juvenile delinquents—and Socs—the rich kids with all the social advantages. Since his parents died in a car crash, Ponyboy has lived alone with his two older brothers. Together with their friends, they make up a kind of family bound together by loyalty and violence. Ponyboy loves to read, to draw, and to run track, but all of that seems futile in his violent world of gang rivalry where it seems impossible to break away from people's perceptions of him as a greaser, a delinquent, and a troublemaker.

Written when S. E. (Susan) Hinton was sixteen, this book instantly affected the young people who read it. It continues to be a popular powerful story, told in a true teenage voice. This book raises issues: what makes someone truly heroic, the oppression of poverty, the impact of having a dysfunctional family, living in a society that judges you for the way you look. For Hinton, the rich boys and the tough guys are equally victimized.

> **Audio:** Recorded Books cassette 1556907753; CD 0788737384. Read by Spike McClure.

> **Film/Video/DVD:** *The Outsiders* (1983) directed by Frances Ford Coppola and starring Tom Cruise, Patrick Swayze, Diane Lane, and Rob Lowe early in their careers.

> **Similar Reads:** Other books by Hinton including *That Was Then, This Is Now; Rumble Fish;* and *Tex* will be equally popular with YA readers who like *The Outsiders.* Other YA classics about outsiders include *The Catcher in the Rye, The Pigman,* and *The Chocolate War.*

> **Subjects:** Midwest 1960s; Brothers; Family; Gangs; Violence; Frequently Challenged; Friendship; Margaret A. Edwards Award 1988

## James, Henry (1843–1916)

*Daisy Miller* (USA: 1879). Tor Books 1991 (paper) 96pp. 0812504402 <u>S</u> **Q**

Daisy Miller, a young American traveling in Europe with her mother and young brother, is beautiful and willful, an "inscrutable mix of audacity and innocence." We come to know her through Winterbourne, another American abroad. Although attracted to the lovely Daisy, he is also confused by her flirtatiousness, her spontaneity, her openness, and her absolute defiance of local customs. To the horror of the other Americans living in Rome, she is seen walking alone with Italian men; she goes out at night; she does as she pleases; her mother has no influence over her. Can a free spirit survive in an atmosphere of control and convention and in a society that expects conformity?

*Daisy Miller* is very readable James, quite short and straightforward, an excellent introduction to the master and to his constant theme: the clash of brash newly rich Americans and old, rule-bound European mores.

**Audio:** Blackstone 2001; cassette 0786120827. Read by Susan O'Malley.

**Film/Video/DVD:** *Daisy Miller* (1974) starred Cybill Shepherd in the title role of this adaptation directed by Peter Bogdanovich.

**Similar Reads:** Readers who are attracted to James's themes and style may want to try *Portrait of a Lady,* a longer and more complex work, or *The Ambassadors*; Edith Wharton's *House of Mirth* tells another tragic story of an independent American woman.

**Subjects:** Europe, mid-1890s; Travel; Manners; Mothers and Daughters; Gentle Read

## Joyce, James (1882–1941)

*A Portrait of the Artist as a Young Man* (Ireland: 1916). Penguin Books 2003 (paper) 384pp. 0142437344 <u>S</u>

Stephen Dedalus narrates the story of his youth and the experience of his inner turmoil about faith and reality in turn-of-the-century Ireland. Church, school, family, friends, and society all pressure young Stephen to be a certain person when what he wants to be is an artist. Stephen is gifted and sensitive growing up in an environment hostile to his nature. Can he break free and live as himself, or will the past and the pressure of society make him conform?

Joyce's disjointed, subjective, impressionistic prose was revolutionary at the time it was written. Considered a breakthrough work of modernism, this novel shows Joyce striving to create a new style of fiction, which he further developed with *Ulysses.* The fact that we are reading his fiction one hundred years later must mean he succeeded.

**Audio:** Recorded Books cassette 1402598092. Read by Donal Donnelly.

**Film/Video/DVD:** *Portrait of the Artist as a Young Man* (1979) was filmed in Ireland.

**Similar Reads:** *Dubliners,* James's classic collection of short stories, is a good follow-up. Readers wanting an intense challenge can turn to Joyce's masterpiece, *Ulysses.* Maugham's *Of Human Bondage,* written at the same time, is also the coming-of-age story of a sensitive young man but told in a more traditional narrative style.

**Subjects:** Dublin; Ireland, 1882 to 1903; Family; Fathers and Sons; Catholics; Catholic Church; Stream of Consciousness; Modernism; Alienation; Autobiographical Novel

## Kerouac, Jack (1922–1969)

*On the Road* (USA: 1957). Penguin Books 1991 (paper) 307pp. 0140042598 **S**

Jack Kerouac's classic novel about the Beat generation and the adventure of finding yourself through spontaneity, improvisation, and just heading out and really experiencing whatever you encounter. Motivated by restless energy and a lack of anything else to do, narrator Sal Paradise and his buddy, the somewhat unstable Dean Moriarty, hit the road and crisscross America hopping trains and hitchhiking, looking for jazz, women, drugs, and authentic experiences. This book is like a jazz piece, it riffs and rolls, reaches out, comes back to its theme, then reaches out again. A unique piece of writing that expresses some universal truths about youth and energy and generational self-definition.

Its very freedom and lack of restraint make this a book that won't appeal to everyone. Truman Capote famously said about *On The Road,* "This isn't writing, this is typing."

**Audio:** Recorded Books cassette 1419328980. Read by Frank Muller. HarperAudio 2000 cassette 0694523615. Read by Matt Dillon.

**Similar Reads:** Readers interested in the Beat ethos may want to follow up with Kerouac's *Dharma Bums* or with *Howl,* Allen Ginsburg's famous poem about his generation. These works are for mature readers. *Zen and the Art of Motorcycle Maintenance* by Pirsig takes readers on another journey across America.

**Subjects:** Beats; Existentialism; Journey

## Kerr, M. E. (1927–)

*Dinky Hocker Shoots Smack* (USA: 1973). HarperTrophy/Harper Collins (paper) 198pp. 0064470067. **J Teen Q**

Dinky Hocker actually does not shoot smack. Her drug of choice is food—too much of it. Dinky eats and eats to stuff the pain of having a mother who has more compassion for recovering drug addicts than for her own daughter.

Although definitely a product of the 1970s, interesting characters make this a good read: Tucker's flaky uncle, Jingle; Natalia, the girl who rhymes when she is nervous; and P. John Knight, the overweight, ultra-conservative boy who calls Dinky by her real name, Susan, and tries to help her lose weight. This was M. E. Kerr's first YA novel.

**Film/Video/DVD:** *Dinky Hocker* was a 1978 TV movie.

**Similar Reads:** Kerr is an acclaimed YA author; try *Gentlehands* and *Deliver Us from Evie*. Also try her autobiography *Me, Me, Me: Not a Novel*. Judy Blume's *Blubber* or Robert Lipsyte's *One Fat Summer* may also interest readers.

**Subjects:** New York 1970s, Mothers and Daughters, Family; Friendships; Obesity; Margaret A. Edwards Award 1993

## Knowles, John (1926–)

*A Separate Peace* **(USA: 1959).** Scribner 2003 (paper) 208pp. 0743253973 **J**

Charming and irrepressible, Phineas is a natural athlete, not much of a scholar, a boy who can break rules and get away with it. Serious and levelheaded Gene is an excellent student, a decent athlete, and Finny's best friend. These sixteen-year-old boys attend the Devon School, an upper-class private boys school in New Hampshire. Ahead of them are World War II and the certainty of being drafted. But during this summer session of 1942, they are at school breaking rules, inventing new sports, and swimming in the river that runs through the school grounds. Throughout the novel, Gene struggles to comprehend his relationship with Finny—are they the best of friends or intense rivals? What hypnotic power does Finny possess that compels Gene (and others) to do everything Finny suggests? Can Gene ever be free of Finny's spell?

An elegant and moving story about an intense relationship and the complex, anxiety-producing world that awaits all teens as they mature to adults

**Audio:** Recorded Books cassette 155690469x; CD 0788746650. Read by Spike McClure.

**Film/Video/DVD**: *A Separate Peace,* a lame 1972 film, is not recommended (Leonard Maltin classed it a "Bomb"). There is also a 2003 TV movie.

**Similar Reads:** Other coming-of-age classics with male protagonists are *Catcher in the Rye* and *The Chocolate War.* Knowles wrote many books. *Peace Breaks Out* is about two other boys at the same school and is considered a companion to *A Separate Peace,* but it is not as widely read.

**Subjects:** New Hampshire, 1942; School Story; Boarding School; High School; Friendship; Rivalry

## Lee, Harper (1926–)

🏃 *To Kill a Mockingbird* **(USA: 1960).** Warner Books 1988 (paper) 288pp. 0446310786 **J**

Maycomb, Alabama, is the sleepy rural town where Jean Louise Finch and her older brother, Jeremy—nicknamed Scout and Jem, respectively—are being raised by their father, lawyer Atticus Finch. In easy, smoothly flowing prose, Scout tells us about her life from the ages of six to nine when she began school; when she, Jem, and their companion, Dill, were obsessed with getting their mysterious and reclusive neighbor Boo Radley to come out of his house;

and when, to the dismay of most of Maycomb, Atticus defended Tom Robinson, a black man, against a charge of raping a white woman. Honest and open-minded, innocent yet wise, Scout and Jem are guided in all things by their father who treats them as equals and by Cal, their housekeeper, who has been with them since their mother died.

Strong characters, a palpable setting, a social conscience, humor, and pervasive love have made this Pulitzer Prize–winning novel a favorite book for many readers. This was Harper Lee's only novel.

**Film/Video/DVD:** *To Kill a Mockingbird* (1962) stars Gregory Peck in a career-defining role as Atticus Finch.

**Similar Reads:** *A Tree Grows in Brooklyn* by Betty Smith tells a sensitive coming-of-age story set in New York. Other stories told from the perspectives of young narrators are *True Grit, Shane,* and *A Death in the Family.*

**Subjects:** Alabama 1930s; American South; Fathers and Daughters; Brothers and Sisters; Family; Trials; African Americans; Racism; Depression Era; Frequently Challenged; Pulitzer Prize 1961

## Lewis, Elizabeth Foreman (1892–1958)

🏆 *Young Fu of the Upper Yangtze* **(United States: 1932).** Yearling 1990 (paper) 288pp. 044049043x **M Teen**

The complexity and formality of traditional Chinese society is presented in the rags-to-riches story of Young Fu. After his father's death, Young Fu and his mother, Fu Be Be, move from the country to the big city of Chungking, where Young Fu will be apprenticed to a coppersmith and learn the business of making pots and vases. It is China in the 1920s, a time of social shift and movement away from traditional society and all of its trappings—women with bound feet, respect for the aged, absolute obedience, belief in the power of dragons—to the modern world of foreigners in China, Western medicine, soldiers, and revolutionaries.

Although Lewis's prose may feel awkward at first (perhaps she is attempting to represent the formalized speech of polite Chinese), the reader will fall into the flow of the prose and be swept along by the fast-paced story of a clever young protagonist as he outwits bandits, saves old people from a flood, learns to read, observes and is affected by life around him, and becomes a master at his craft.

**Similar Reads:** *Homesick: My Own Story* by Jean Fritz also depicts China in the 1920s. The classic novel about China for generations has been *The Good Earth* by Pearl S. Buck. Another apprentice who succeeds is *Johnny Tremain.*

**Subjects:** China; Family; Apprentices; Missionaries; Gentle Read; Historical Fiction; Newbery Medal 1933

## Lewis, Sinclair (1885–1951)

🏆 *Main Street* **(USA: 1920).** Signet 1998 (paper) 474pp. 0451526821 **S**

Gopher Prairie, Minnesota, is the unglamorous town that Carol Kennicott moves to as the wife of the town's doctor. But Carol is a modern woman—educated, progressive, energetic, and optimistic. Her attempts to bring culture, progress, and open-mindedness to the town that is satisfied with itself fail miserably. The people of Gopher Prairie, even her husband, have no desire to change their prejudices or embrace new ideas.

Lewis was a prolific writer. His realistic, descriptive, and satiric novels depict America in the first half of the twentieth century and provide social commentary of the times.

**Audio:** Recorded Books cassette 0788705725; CD 1419310798. Read by Barbara Caruso.

**Similar Reads:** Other Lewis classics featuring small-town America are *Babbitt* about a businessman questioning the emptiness of his life, *Arrowsmith* (1925 Pulitzer Prize winner) about an idealistic doctor, and *Elmer Gantry,* an expose of Evangelists and conmen.

**Subjects:** Minnesota; Marriage; Small-Town; Satire; Nobel Prize 1930

## Llewellyn, Richard (1906–1983)

*How Green Was My Valley* **(Wales: 1939).** Scribner 1997 (paper) 495pp. 0684825554 **J**

Huw Morgan narrates the story of his family of Welsh coal miners at the end of the 1800s.

Sentimental, poignant, lyrical, and slightly melancholy, the story of the Morgan's family is a wistful remembrance of times that are gone. Llewellyn was a prolific writer, but none of his other works are as well remembered today as *How Green Was My Valley.*

**Audio:** Chivers Audiobooks cassette 0745161065. Read by Phillip Madoc.

**Film/Video/DVD:** *How Green Was My Valley* (1941) stars Roddy McDowell and Maureen O'Hara in an Academy Award Best Picture winner.

**Similar Reads:** Llewelyn wrote three sequels that follow Huw as an adult working in South America: *Up, into the Singing Mountain*; *Down Where the Moon Is Small*; and *Green, Green My Valley Now.* Other nostalgic coming-of-age stories include *The Yearling, A Tree Grows in Brooklyn,* and *A Girl of the Limberlost.*

**Subjects:** Wales 1890–1910; Family; Coal Mining; Gentle Read

## Maugham, Somerset (1874–1964)

*Of Human Bondage* **(England: 1915).** Bantam Classics 1991 (paper) 656pp. 055321392X **S**

An obsessive love affair with the wrong woman is the centerpiece of this novel about finding one's path in life. Phillip Carey has many disadvantages. He is orphaned at an early age and raised by a remote uncle and his downtrodden wife; he has a lame foot, and a sensitive artistic nature. Phillip explores many modes of living—student, artist, doctor, Bohemian—before finding the path that will make him happy.

This coming-of-age story is set in London and Paris in the early years of the twentieth century.

**Film/Video/DVD:** *Of Human Bondage* was produced in 1934, 1946, and 1964 all focus on the mismatched love affair while omitting much that makes the book rich.

**Similar Reads:** Try Dreiser's *An American Tragedy. The Razor's Edge* by Maugham is another intriguing work.

**Subjects:** England early 1900s; London; Paris; Artists; Doctors

## McCullers, Carson (1917–1967)

*The Heart Is a Lonely Hunter* **(USA: 1940).** Bantam 1983 (paper) 320pp. 0553269631 <u>S</u>

The boardinghouse room of John Singer, a placid man who is a deaf mute, provides a gathering place for four other lonely people in a small Southern town in the late 1930s. Jake Blount, a worker with a rebellious streak; Mick Kelly, the gangly thirteen-year-old whose parents own the boardinghouse, who is passionate about music, and whose childhood is ending; Dr. Copeland, an African American doctor who has lived with pride through oppression and maltreatment; and Biff Brannon, owner of the local café, an observer of life. These people all come to Singer's room to talk, and though he cannot hear them, he listens sympathetically to each of them.

This is a book about isolation and loneliness. Eccentric characters and telling details of humanity combine to make *The Heart Is a Lonely Hunter* a character-driven read.

**Audio:** Recorded Books 1419302949. Read by Cherry Jones.

**Film/Video/DVD:** *The Heart Is a Lonely Hunter* (1968) with Alan Arkin is considered an ignored classic.

**Similar Reads:** McCullers's other classic coming-of-age story is *A Member of the Wedding. Winesburg, Ohio* by Sherwood Anderson tells of the loneliness and isolation people experience in a small Ohio town.

**Subjects:** Georgia 1930s; American South; Small Town; Depression Era; Family; Racism; Loneliness; Isolation; Alienation

*A Member of the Wedding* **(USA 1946).** Mariner Books (Houghton Mifflin) 2004 (paper) 176pp. 0618492399 <u>S</u> <u>Q</u>

There is minimal action but maximum turmoil in this novel about the moody summer when Frankie goes from twelve to thirteen. This is the summer when Frankie doesn't belong to anything, the summer "when Frankie was sick and tired of being Frankie," when she is "dirty and greedy and mean and sad." The summer when Frankie is suddenly tall, has no sense of humor, barks at everyone, throws knives, clings to and rejects her little cousin, makes a nuisance of herself, and grows up.

Frankie spends this summer in the kitchen at home playing cards with her six-year-old cousin, the wise and genial John Henry, and Berenice, the matriarchal cook who is also Frankie's surrogate mother. When Frankie's grown brother, Jarvis, returns home from military duty in Alaska to get married, Frankie hopes that the wedding will change her life, give her something to do, something to believe in, something to be a member of.

**Audio:** Available from LA Theatre Works (www.latw.org). Read by a full cast.

**Film/Video/DVD:** Filmed definitively in 1952 with Julie Harris and Ethel Waters, but modern YAs may be more drawn to the 1997 version with Anna Paquin and Alfre Woodard.

**Similar Reads:** For more McCullers, read *The Heart Is a Lonely Hunter.* Harper Lee's *To Kill a Mockingbird* is another coming-of-age classic set in the South.

**Subjects:** Georgia 1940s, Family; Small Town; Jealousy; Alienation

## Montgomery, Lucy Maud (1874–1942)

*Anne of Green Gables* (Canada; 1908) Bantam Starfire 1990 (paper, boxed set) 0553609416 <u>M</u> Teen

Needing help around the house, aging brother and sister Marilla and Matthew Cuthbert adopt a boy from the orphanage. But instead of a boy, they end up with Anne Shirley, an eleven-year-old girl with red hair, a quick temper, and a vivid imagination. Comical, unconventional Anne finds the home she has longed for in Avonlea, and she proceeds to get into one scrape after another. She finds a bosom friend in Diana Barry and a childhood enemy in Gilbert Blythe, and she never abandons her search for "Kindred Spirits." Easy, straightforward prose; beautiful, descriptive passages of the natural glories of Avonlea; and humorous episodes have made this book a beloved classic.

Anne is a phenomenon among girl heroines. In print for one hundred years, the series of Anne books by L. M. Montgomery has been translated into at least fifteen languages and is a very popular series in Japan. International tourists regularly make the pilgrimage to Prince Edward Island off the eastern Canadian coast to walk in Anne's footsteps. The books in the order that take Anne from a young girl to a woman with children of her own are as follows:

*Anne of Avonlea* **(1909)**

*Anne of the Island* **(1915)**

*Anne of Windy Poplars* **(1936)**

*Anne's House of Dreams* **(1917)**

*Anne of Ingleside* **(1939)**

*Rainbow Valley* **(1919)**

*Rilla of Ingleside* **(1920)**

**Audio:** Recorded Books cassette 1556900228; CD 0788795244. Read by Barbara Caruso.

**Film/Video/DVD:** *Anne of Green Gables* (1985) is the faithful and beloved Canadian production, followed by the equally good *Anne of Green Gables: The Sequel* (1987), and *Anne of Green Gables: The Continuing Story* (2000).

**Similar Reads:** Anne is also found in *The Chronicles of Avonlea* and *The Further Chronicles of Avonlea*. Montgomery also wrote *Emily of New Moon,* the first book in a trilogy of Emily stories. Other great girl heroines can be found in *Little Women, A Tree Grows in Brooklyn, A Girl of the Limberlost, Caddie Woodlawn, Pollyanna* by Eleanor Porter, *Heidi* by Johanna Spyri, and Kate Wiggins's *Rebecca of Sunnybrook Farm.*

**New Media:** The L. M. Montgomery Institute Web site is an interesting place to go for all things Anne www.lmmontgomery.ca.

**Subjects:** Canada late 1800s; Prince Edward Island; Orphans; Friendship; Family; Rural Life; Strong Heroine; Humor; Childhood Classic; Gentle Read

## Morrison, Toni (1931–)

🔖 *The Bluest Eye* **(USA: 1970).** Plume/Penguin 2000 (paper) 216pp. 0452282195 **S**

In a society where Shirley Temple is the mainstream idea of beauty, how can an abused little black girl fit in? Eleven-year-old Pecola Breedlove, growing up in Ohio in 1941, is everybody's victim—white people don't see her, the other black children taunt her, her mother prefers the orderly home and docile daughter of her white employers, and her father rapes her thinking he is tenderly expressing his love.

Morrison writes in a very distinctive, poetic, and self-consciously literary style. This book is powerful, graphic, and violent, although it also has humor and truth, it is a disturbing book best for mature readers.

**Audio:** Recorded Books, cassette 0788743546; CD 0788751581. Read by Lynne Thigpen.

**Similar Reads:** Reader's intrigued by Morrison's unique style will want to read *Beloved*. Other classics about African American women are *Their Eyes Were Watching God* by Zora Neale Hurston and *The Color Purple* by Alice Walker.

**Subjects:** Ohio 1940s; Family; Child Abuse; African Americans; Racism; Beauty; Mental Illness; Self-Esteem; Mature Read; Frequently Challenged; Nobel Prize 1993

## O'Hara, Mary (1885–1980)

*My Friend Flicka* **(USA: 1941).** Harper 1988 (paper) 304pp. 0060809027 **M Teen**

Ten-year-old Ken McLaughlin is a dreamy boy growing up on a ranch in Wyoming with a realist father and an understanding mother. Above all else, Ken wants to have his own horse. But is he ready for the responsibilities?

More than just a story about a boy and his horse, this is a coming-of-age novel about a boy and his father and the growth of responsibility and courage.

**Audio:** Harper Audio CD 006089931x. Read by Michael Louis Wells.

**Film/Video/DVD:** *My Friend Flicka* (1943) features Roddy McDowell. In 2006, a remake changed the boy protagonist to a girl.

**Similar Reads:** Other classic horse stories to revisit are *Thunderhead,* the story of Flicka's foal; *Black Beauty* by Anna Sewell; *National Velvet* by Enid Bagnold;

*Misty of Chincoteague* by Marguerite Henry; and *Smoky the Cowhorse* by Will James.

**Subjects:** Wyoming 1920s; Family; Fathers and Sons; Horses; Ranch Life; American West; Gentle Read

## Parks, Gordon (1912–2006)

*The Learning Tree* **(USA: 1963).** Fawcett 1987 (paper) 240pp. 0449215040 <u>S</u>
The segregated lives of blacks and whites are intertwined in the small rural town of Cherokee Flats, Kansas, where Newt Winger is growing up. From the haven of his home filled with a large and loving African American family, Newt explores the world and begins to discover his role in it. His mother, Sara, encourages him and has ambitions for him believing her youngest son to be intellectually gifted. A dramatic tornado opens the novel and events unfold rapidly through Newt's first love, a murder trial, and the violent exploits of Marcus Savage, the boy who hates Newt.

Author Gordon Parks was a famous photographer, poet, and film director (he directed the original *Shaft* in 1971). This autobiographical novel deals frankly with teenaged Newt's emerging sexuality. This is an exceptional and somewhat forgotten book about the strength of family and the challenges facing a young black man in the first part of the twentieth century. The book is permeated with deaths and peppered with racially motivated violence; it is a mature read.

**Film/Video/DVD:** See *The Learning Tree* (1969) directed by Gordon Parks.

**Similar Reads:** Try *To Kill a Mockingbird, Black Boy,* and books by Mildred Taylor.

**Subjects:** Kansas 1920s; Family; Mothers and Sons; Small Town; African Americans; Racism; Mature Read; Autobiographical Novel

## Potok, Chaim (1929–2002)

*The Chosen* **(USA: 1967).** Fawcett 1987 (paper) 304pp. 0449213447 <u>S</u>
The mysterious world of Hasidic Judaism is revealed in this novel about two American boys being raised in Jewish homes, one Hasidic and one Orthodox, and therefore very unlike each other. The boys, Danny Saunders and Reuven Malter, meet during a heated baseball game when Danny hits a ball into Reuven's eye. From then on, they are intellectual friends, both serious about their studies and both heavily influenced by their very different fathers.

World War II and the founding of the Jewish homeland provide the backdrop for this novel set in New York.

**Audio:** Books on Tape 0736691324. Read by Jim Weiss.

**Film/Video/DVD:** *The Chosen* (1982) stars Rod Steiger, Maximilian Schell, and Robby Benson.

**Similar Reads:** Potok's next book, *The Promise,* follows Danny and Reuven further in their careers; for other books about Jewish life in American try *The Bread Givers* by Anzia Yezierska; *The Romance Reader* by Pearl Abraham, or Pete Hamill's *Snow in August.*

**Subjects:** New York 1940s; Brooklyn; Family; Fathers and Sons; Friendship Jews; Hasidism; Zionism

## Rawlings, Marjorie (1896–1953)

🏆 *The Yearling* **(USA 1938).** Aladdin Books/Simon & Schuster, 2001 (paper) 513pp. 0689846231. **M**

The scrub country of northern Florida is the setting for this Pulitzer Prize–winning coming-of-age novel. Jody, a young boy growing up in the 1870s with a loving father and hardworking mother, befriends a deer and must then decide its fate when he comes to understand that the survival of his family and the natural instincts of the deer cannot coexist.

*The Yearling* is a story that is both regional and universal. It depicts the harsh reality of rural poverty and the painful choices humans are forced to make as they grow from children to adults. Filled with robust memorable characters, this is an old-fashioned novel full of descriptive passages of nature and concerned with the big issues of humanity, such as conducting yourself with honor, prizing loyalty and honesty, choosing to act nobly, and squarely facing reality, even when it hurts.

**Audio:** Recorded Books cassette 0788735306; CD 1402551916. Read by Tom Stechschulte.

**Film/Video/DVD:** Two touching versions of *The Yearling* have been produced: the 1946 family classic with Gregory Peck as the father and a TV version in 1994 with Peter Strauss in that role. Rawlings's 1942 autobiographical book *Cross Creek* about her years in Florida also made a fine movie, *Cross Creek* (1983), starring Mary Steenburgen.

**Similar Reads:** Some other great animal books include *Bambi, Old Yeller, Where the Red Fern Grows,* and *My Friend Flicka.* Other historical coming-of-age classics are *A Tree Grows in Brooklyn, A Girl of the Limberlost,* and *To Kill a Mockingbird.*

**Subjects:** Florida, 1870; Family; Rural Life; Poverty; Deer; Pets; Historical Fiction; Gentle Read; Pulitzer Prize 1939

## Salinger, J. D. (1919–)

*A Catcher in the Rye* **(USA: 1951).** Little, Brown 1991 (paper) 224pp. 0316769487 **S**

Holden Caulfield is the archetypal alienated teen. Kicked out of several fancy schools, trying to cope with the recent death of his brother, Holden is loosing his grip. New York City in the late 1940s is the setting where Holden Caulfield explores his own inner angst. Narrating in a flashback, Holden leads us through the story of his life so far, his impressions of all the "phonies" he encounters, and his anguished experience of the world.

Salinger is notoriously reticent and has never talked about his work, something that adds to the mystique of Holden Caulfield. It's as if the author is saying, "figure him out for yourself."

**Similar Reads:** The reclusive Salinger also wrote *Frannie and Zooey*, *Raise High the Roof Beams,* and a story collection, *Nine Stories*. Other works that feature the theme of teen alienation include *The Outsiders*, *The Chocolate War*, *A Member of the Wedding,* and *Lord of the Flies. Ordinary People* also involves the death of a brother.

**Subjects:** New York 1940s; Family; Teachers and Students; High School; Boarding School; Alienation; Frequently Challenged

## Shange, Ntozake (1948–)

*Betsey Brown* (USA: 1985). Picador USA 1995 (paper) 208pp. 0312134347 <u>S</u> Q

It is 1959, and thirteen-year-old Betsey has a challenge this year. She will be in the first racially integrated school in St. Louis. Betsey is the oldest of five children. Her father is a successful doctor, her mother a compassionate social worker, and her family lives in a nice neighborhood. They are proud of their African heritage; the father teaches his kids about black history and music. But will the pressures of this unusual year overwhelm clever, responsible Betsey?

**Similar Reads:** Consider *A Tree Grows in Brooklyn* and *To Kill a Mockingbird*; novels by Mildred Taylor.

**Subjects:** St. Louis, 1950s; Family; African Americans; Historical Fiction; Racism; School Integration

## Smith, Betty (1896–1972)

*Tree Grows in Brooklyn* (USA: 1943). Perennial Classics 1998 (paper) 496pp. 006092988X <u>J</u>

Francie Nolan is a serious girl who loves books and school and is growing up in Brooklyn, a small town within the big city of New York. Her father is a lovable but irresponsible drunk; her mother works hard to provide for the family and has little time for pleasure. Teachers, librarians, neighborhood characters, and her colorful extended family populate this famous and affecting coming-of-age classic.

Realism and lyricism mingle in this beloved story of growing up in material poverty and intellectual wealth. Readers have loved Francie and her take on life since this book was a bestseller in 1943.

**Audio:** Recorded Books cassette 1556905246; CD 1402567871. Read by Barbara Rosenblatt.

**Film/Video/DVD:** *A Tree Grows in Brooklyn* (1945) was directed by Elia Kazan.

**Similar Reads:** Smith wrote a passionate novel about the first years of a marriage called *Joy in the Morning* that is still in print and may interest

YAs. Two other classic coming-of-age stories with different settings but similar impact are *To Kill a Mockingbird* by Harper Lee and *The Yearling* by Marjorie Kinan Rawlings.

**Subjects:** New York, early 1900s; Brooklyn; Family; Historical Fiction; Alcoholism; High School; Poverty; Teachers and Students; Gentle Read

## Smith, Dodie (1896–1990)

*I Capture the Castle* **(England: 1948).** St. Martin's Griffin 1999 (paper) 352pp. 0312201656 **J**

In England during the 1930s, seventeen-year-old Cassandra Mortmain longs to be a writer. *I Capture the Castle* is her attempt to teach herself to write by recording the happenings of her life. Cassandra is a memorable character set among a cast of eccentrics: her father is a brilliant author who has never been able to write a second book; her stepmother, Topaz, a famous artists' model and free spirit who plays the lute and takes nude moon baths; her brother, Thomas, still in school; Stephen, the maid's son, the only one who earns any money to support the family; and Cassandra's sister, Rose, a young woman ready for a young man. And they do live in a castle with a tower and a moat—and no electricity, very little food, and never any new clothes. When Simon and Neil Cotton, two young brothers raised in the United States, inherit the neighboring manor and become landlords of the Mortmain's castle, the family embarks on a merry-go-round of social activity and interpersonal upheaval. Cassandra records it all with her straightforward, wise yet still youthful observations.

A rediscovered classic since J. K. Rowling acknowledged it as an influence. Dodie Smith also wrote *The Hundred and One Dalmatians* (1956).

**Audio:** Chivers Audio Books (www.chivers.co.uk/). Read by Jenny Agutter.

**Film/Video/DVD:** *I Capture the Castle* (2003) is a lovely adaptation.

**Similar Reads:** Jane Austen's *Pride and Prejudice* is a comic story of sisters looking for husbands. Stella Gibbons's *Cold Comfort Farm* depicts another eccentric English family. For more English comedy, try books by P. G. Wodehouse or *One Pair of Hands* by Monica Dickens, about an upper-class English girl who decides to work as a domestic.

**Subjects:** England, 1930s; Family; Sisters; Poverty; Writers; Creativity; Humor; Gentle Read

## Steinbeck, John (1902–1968)

*The Red Pony* **(USA 1945).** Penguin Classics 1993 (paper) 100pp. 0140177361 **J Q**

*The Red Pony* is four previously published short stories that Steinbeck compiled into a novel in 1945. All are about Jody, a ten-year-old boy growing up on a ranch in Central California in the early part of the 1900s. Jody is a boy who brings home toads in his lunch pail and sneaks out of the house in the middle of a cold night to check on a horse, a boy with a harsh father and a good friend in Billy Buck, the ranch hand. Each story relates an episode in Jody's journey to maturation; they deal with death and sadness and show us Jody's empathy, imagination, and curiosity. In "The Gift," Jody is given a pony and lovingly raises it until tragedy strikes. "The Great Mountain" tells the story of Gitano, an old *paisano* returning to his birthplace, now the ranch where Jody lives, to die. In "The Promise," Jody is promised a colt then must witness its anguishing birth. *The Leader of the People* finds Jody's aging and disappointed grandfather visiting the ranch.

Even though the protagonist Jody is ten years old, this is not a book for young readers, nor is it for the squeamish or readers who might be highly sensitive to its harsh realities. Steinbeck's trademark crystalline, understated prose gives the drama even more impact.

> **New Media:** www.steinbeck.org leads one to the National Steinbeck center.

> **Film/Video/DVD:** Steinbeck wrote the screenplay for the 1949 film *The Red Pony* starring Robert Mitchum as Billy Buck and Myrna Loy as the mother. Made again in 1973 with Henry Fonda and Maureen O'Hara.

> **Similar Reads:** Other Steinbeck classics are *The Pearl* and *Of Mice and Men*. Or try *Cannery Row* and *Tortilla Flats*. For a similar horse story with a gentler effect, try O'Hara's *My Friend Flicka*.

> **Subjects:** California, 1930s; American West; Horses; Family; Fathers and Sons; Nobel Prize 1962

## Swarthout, Glendon (1918–1992)

***Bless the Beasts and the Children*** (USA: 1970). Pocket 1995 (paper) 224pp. 0671521519. **J**

> At an elite cowboy camp in Arizona, six misfit boys find a mission that unites them. Dumped in the camp because their parents needed to put them somewhere for the summer, their common status as outsiders and losers bonds these boys into the last-place team known as the Bedwetters. When they witness a government-sponsored slaughter of a herd of buffalo, the bloody and traumatizing experience galvanizes them into a (mostly) functioning team with the mission of freeing the remaining buffalos.

> Very definitely a product of the sixties, this story nevertheless remains potent and engaging.

> **Film/Video/DVD:** *Bless the Beasts and the Children* (1972) was directed by Stanley Kramer.

> **Similar Reads:** Other dramatic coming-of-age stories include *The Outsiders* and *The Chocolate War, Catcher in the Rye,* and *A Separate Peace.*

> **Subjects:** Arizona 1970s; American Southwest; Friendship; Animal Cruelty; Buffalo; Alienation

## Twain, Mark (1835–1910)

***The Adventures of Huckleberry Finn*** (USA: 1884). Signet 2002 (paper, includes *Tom Sawyer*) 544 pp. 0451528646; Modern Library 2001 (paper) 304 pp 0375757376 **J**

> Huckleberry Finn is one of the landmark characters of American literature. Oppressed and uneducated but resourceful and wise, Huck is being raised by

the Widow Douglas, who is trying her best to make a civilized boy of him. When his drunk, abusive father, Pap, returns to claim him, Huck fakes his own death and, with the escaping slave Jim as a companion, sets out on a raft down the Mississippi River. Thus begins a uniquely American odyssey through the settings and characters of the American South in the years before the Civil War. Huckleberry himself narrates the tale of his journey, and Twain pulled out all the stops with his portrayals of the feuding, the larcenous, the genteel, the foolish, and the sincere.

Comical, sad, thought provoking, or merely an adventure on a raft, *Huckleberry Finn* is many books in one. Some scholars consider this to be the Great American Novel. Twain was a prolific writer whose satire helps define the American character.

**Audio:** Recorded Books cassette 1556900015; CD 1402519737. Read by Norman Dietz.

**Film/Video/DVD:** *The Adventures of Huckleberry Finn* (1939) featured Mickey Rooney. The book is also the basis for a tuneful Tony-winning Broadway musical called *Big River* (1985).

**Similar Reads:** *The Adventures of Tom Sawyer* is sort of the prequel to *Huckleberry Finn* and should not be missed.

**Subjects:** Mississippi River; American South, mid-1800s; Friendship; Slavery; Orphans; Journey; Humor; Frequently Challenged

***The Adventures of Tom Sawyer*** (USA: 1876). Signet 2002 (paper, includes *Huckleberry Finn*) 544pp. 0451528646 or Modern Library 2001 (paper) 304pp. 0375756817 **M**

One of the most well-known boys in American fiction, Tom Sawyer is the eternal American boy living in a world of perpetual summer where adventure, first love, constant mischief, danger, and opportunities for heroism all coexist. Tom is clever and playful, heroic and good, part con artist (the whitewashing the fence incident; the Sunday school tickets), and full of imagination fired by books. A natural leader of the other boys, Tom has one escapade after another with his pal Huck Finn and his sweetheart Becky Thatcher.

**Audio:** Recorded Books cassette 1556900058. Read by Norman Dietz. Audio Partners 1995 cassette 1572700106. Read by Patrick Fraley.

**Film/Video/DVD:** See *Adventures of Mark Twain* (1944).

**Similar Reads:** Older readers will naturally want to read *The Adventures of Huckleberry Finn,* although the two books are very different in tone. Some other classic "boy books" include *Toby Tyler: Or Ten Weeks with a Circus* by James Otis; Frances Hodgson Burnett's *Little Lord Fauntleroy; Summer of the Monkeys* by Wilson Rawls; and *Rascal* by Sterling North

**Subjects:** Missouri, mid-1800s; Boys; Orphans; Aunts; Humor; Childhood Classic; Gentle Read; Frequently Challenged

## Walker, Alice (1944–)

🏵 *The Color Purple* (USA: 1982). Harvest Books 2003 (paper) 300pp. 0156028352 <u>S</u> Q

Celie isn't pretty, and she isn't educated. She is abused by her stepfather and then by her husband. She puts the anguish about her harsh life and her growing self-awareness into the letters she writes to God and to her sister Nettie, a sister she hasn't seen in years—Celie doesn't even know if she is alive. Passive Celie finds a role model in Shug, the glamorous blues singer girlfriend of her own husband. With new confidence from her relationship with Shug, Celie grows into a creative force and turns a chore into a profitable business. She makes her own money and decisions and finds her true voice.

This historical novel set in rural Georgia in the first half of the twentieth century does not paint a big canvas with historical themes. It tells a narrow story of the life and times of one woman, her circle of family and friends, and her awakening to life. Celie's struggles for dignity, for love, for family, and for self-expression form the core of this small but potent novel that is filled with life, emotion, and hope.

> **Film/Video/DVD:** *The Color Purple* (1985): Steve Spielberg directed this blockbuster that stars Whoopi Goldberg and features Oprah Winfrey in a dramatic role. In 2005, the story became a Broadway musical.

> **Similar Reads:** See *Their Eyes Were Watching God, The Bluest Eye, and The Street* for other strong African American heroines living through difficult times. For younger readers, Mildred Taylor's books depict strong black families during the same time period.

> **Subjects:** Georgia; 1920–1940; Africa; Sisters; Self-Esteem; African Americans; Racism; Friendships; Sexuality; Epistolary Novel; Strong Heroine; Mature Read; Frequently Challenged; Pulitzer Prize 1983

## Wolfe, Thomas (1900–1938)

*Look Homeward, Angel* (USA: 1929). Scribner 1995 (paper) 500pp. 0684804466. <u>S</u>

Eugene Gant is the youngest of nine children, six of whom are still living. His father is a powerful stonecutter, a spirited man; his mother, who runs a boarding house, is an unhappy woman interested only in money. The Gant family dynamics are extreme, the tension ever present. Eugene, a lover of books and learning, grows to realize that he must break with his family to create himself. Written with passion, this book uses expansive prose to express loneliness and alienation, a theme of many nineteenth-century writers.

According to critics, Thomas Wolfe missed being one of the greatest writers of the twentieth century because he could not organize his writing. They accuse him of writing the same book four times, each about himself, and each a sprawling mass of words that were given shape by good editing.

> **Film/Video/DVD:** *Look Homeward, Angel* (1972) was filmed for TV.

> **Similar Reads:** *Time and the River* is the sequel; Wolfe's other books *The Web and the Rock* and *You Can't Go Home Again* cover the same territory. For big novels about other young men emerging from families in the first

part of the twentieth century, try *Of Human Bondage* by Somerset Maugham, *Sons and Lovers* by D. H. Lawrence, or Dreiser's *An American Tragedy*.

**Subjects:** North Carolina, early 1900s; Family; Autobiographical Novel

## Wright, Richard (1908–1960)

*Black Boy* (USA: 1945). Perennial 1998 (paper) 448pp. 0060929782 **S**

A large cast of characters populates this vivid and gritty story of an African American childhood in the poor South where racism and segregation are a way of life and poverty, hunger, anger, and ignorance are part of the typical experience. Richard Wright, a spirited but sensitive boy with a curious mind but limited opportunities, grew up in Mississippi and Tennessee in the early part of the twentieth century. He narrates his coming-of-age story with fluid details as he explains his expanding awareness of the world and his place in it.

Both an autobiography and a novel, this is the story of Wright's childhood. Wright was an artist and intellectual even as a child, and the alienation from his own people this created is also part of the story.

> **Audio:** Recorded Books cassette 078872164x; CD 0788767090. Read by Peter Francis James.

> **Similar Reads:** Wright's classic novel about entrenched racism is *Native Son*. Read *I Know Why the Caged Bird Sings* by Maya Angelou, *Go Tell It on the Mountain* by James Baldwin, *The Street* by Ann Petry, or *Invisible Man* by Ralph Ellison for other gritty depictions of the African American experience.

> **Subjects:** Mississippi; Tennessee; Early 1900s; New York; Family; Grandparents; Fathers and Sons; African Americans; Racism; Childhood; Abuse; Autobiographical Novel

## Yezierska, Anzia (1885–1970)

*The Bread Givers* (USA: 1925). Persea Books 2003 (paper) 336pp. 0892552905 **J**

Sara Smolinsky, the youngest daughter in a family of girls, struggles in the tenements of New York's Lower East Side at the turn of the century. She is struggling against her patriarchal, tradition-bound father who reads while his wife and daughters eke out a living for the entire family. He insists on the old ways even though he is in a new country, and Sara becomes determined to seek her own American life.

An immigrant herself, Yezierska came to America from Eastern Europe when she was fifteen. She worked hard to gain an education and devoted her life to writing about the Jewish immigrant experience, especially the experiences of women.

> **Similar Reads:** For other coming-of-age books with Jewish themes, try *The Romance Reader* by Pearl Abraham, *The Chosen* by Potok, or stories by Isaac Bashevis Singer.

> **Subjects:** New York, early 1900s; Family; Fathers and Daughters; Immigrants; Independence; Jews; Strong Heroine; Autobiographical Novel

### Zindel, Paul (1936–2003)

🐖 *The Pigman* (USA: 1968). HarperTrophy 2005 (paper) 192pp. 0060757353 **J Teen Q**

It all starts with a crank phone call.

Lorraine Jensen and John Conlan meet with their buddies after school for a session of telephone pranks. When Lorraine gets Angelo Pignati on the line, the game changes. Lorraine and John are smart, creative, bored high school sophomores who have miserable families. Mr. Pignati is a man with a generous heart, a huge smile, and the ability to laugh. This is a realistic story filled with humor and tragedy about alienated teens and a lonely man and what happens when they meet.

Zindel is a prolific YA writer who won a Pulitzer Prize for his play about a dysfunctional family, *The Effects of Gamma Rays on Man in the Moon Marigolds. The Pigman's Legacy* tells the further story of John and Lorraine and *The Pigman and Me* is Zindel's 1991 autobiographical work about his own unhappy youth.

> **Similar Reads:** Other classics about alienated teens are *Catcher in the Rye*, *The Outsiders*, and *The Chocolate War*.

> **Subjects:** New York, 1960s; Friendship; Betrayal; Alienation; Senior Citizen; Frequently Challenged; Margaret A. Edwards Award 2002

# Relationships

Where can we learn more about ourselves than in our relationships with other human beings—not just love relationships, but relationships with family and friendships? These interactions help define us, teach us, and make us human. Yet all can be rife with anxiety, doubt, and self-questioning. Good relationships and bad, exploitive and supportive, are included in this section. Generally, these novels are realistic, emotionally rich stories told with straightforward narrative and heavy doses of dialogue.

### Blume, Judy (1938–)

🐖 *Forever* (USA: 1975). Pocket Books, 1989 (paper) 224pp. 0671695304 **J Teen Q**

High school seniors Katherine and Michael meet at a New Year's party. From the moment they set eyes on each other, they are in love and believe that their relationship will last forever. Set in the context of their loving and supportive families, Katherine and Michael face the realities of first love, and the pain of promises that may not last.

Maybe not great literature but an important book and the first YA novel to deal graphically with a sexual relationship between two teens. When it was published, it was the only book of its kind. Today's sophisticated readers can turn to adult romance or any number of YA novels with this theme. Over the years,

Judy Blume has taken a good deal of heat for this one, but thirty years later, it is still in print.

**Film/Video/DVD:** *Forever* (1978) was a TV movie with Stephanie Zimbalist.

**Similar Reads:** For other teen love stories, try *Mr. and Mrs. Bo Jo Jones* and *Seventeenth Summer*. Some of Judy Blume's other teen novels are *Deenie*, *Tiger Eyes*, *Then Again Maybe I Won't,* and *It's Not the End of the World*.

**Subjects:** New Jersey, 1970s; First Love; Family; Sexuality; High School; Frequently Challenged; Margaret A. Edwards Award 1996

## Cleary, Beverly (1916–)

*Fifteen* **(USA: 1956).** Harper Trophy (paper) 208pp. 0380728044 <u>M</u> **Teen Q**

Walking to her babysitting job one summer afternoon, fifteen-year-old Jane Purdy hopes and hopes that she will meet a boy—and then she does! A really nice boy, but will he like her? Will her parents let her see him? Will she do everything wrong like always? Jane agonizes every detail of her first relationship with a boy. Only when she relaxes and starts to be herself does Jane see how nice having a boyfriend can be.

Although the details are dated (for example, Jane wears white gloves when she goes into town), the basic story of a girl's anxiety at her first relationship with a boy is valid today. Cleary's description of the agony of being young and unsure will speak to many.

**Similar Reads:** Cleary, best known for her books for younger readers, especially the <u>Ramona</u> series, has several other teenage books: *The Luckiest Girl, Sister of the Bride,* and *Jean and Johnny*. All are dated now, but each has moments of truth and is full of humor. Less sophisticated readers will always love Cleary's teen books because she gets the feelings right. Cleary fans will also love her autobiographical books, *A Girl from Yamhill* and *My Own Two Feet*.

**Subjects:** California 1950s; Family; Dating; First Boyfriend; Humor; Gentle Read

## Dreiser, Theodore (1871–1945)

*An American Tragedy* **(USA: 1925).** Signet 2000 (paper) 880pp. 0451527704 <u>S</u>

Clyde Griffiths is an awkward and naïve young man growing up in an itinerant family of street missionaries. Clyde learns that by working hard, he can have a chance at a better life, so he leaves his repressive family, and, after several false starts in the world, he goes to work for his rich uncle in the city. There he meets Roberta, a commonplace girl who is honest and simple, and Sondra, a wealthy, sophisticated girl who likes him. When Roberta becomes pregnant, Clyde sees that he will never achieve his ambitions of worldly success if burdened by Roberta and a baby. A boating trip and a deadly decision change everything for Clyde and his dreams of a future with Sondra.

*An American Tragedy* is a big novel written in the style of naturalism. It poses one of fiction's enduring moral questions: Was it murder?

**Audio:** Audio Book Contractors 1446857896. Read by Flo Gibson.

**Film/Video/DVD:** *A Place in the Sun* (1951) is a classic starring Montgomery Clift and Elizabeth Taylor.

**Similar Reads:** Try *Of Human Bondage* by Maugham.

**Subjects:** New York, early 1900s; Murder; Trials; Mature Read

## Flaubert, Gustave (1821–1880)

*Madame Bovary* **(France: 1857).** Bantam 1982 (paper) 512pp. 0553213415 **S**

Emma Bovary is bored, bored, bored with her small-town life in provincial France. She is bored with her simple husband, a barely competent country doctor who will never earn a large income; and she is bored with the general lack of glamour in her bourgeois existence. Although she glimpses the romantic and sophisticated life she longs for by reading novels and attending a memorable ball, Emma can never truly achieve it. Through adulterous affairs and ruinous money borrowing, she grasps at the good life, but her tragic yearning destroys her and everyone who loves her.

This nineteenth-century French novel shocked readers in its day and continues to have the power to upset. Written realistically, this is an intense depiction of self-destruction. Flaubert, a master stylist and artist who believed in precision and craft, famously said, "Emma Bovary c'est moi." Did he mean he identified with his own fictional creation? Or that we all have the capacity to make mistakes, as did Madame Bovary?

**Audio:** Blackstone Audiobooks. Read by Walter Zimmerman.

**Film/Video/DVD:** Frequently filmed; *Madame Bovary* (1991), a French film with Isabelle Huppert, is recommended.

**Similar Reads:** An American story with a similar theme is Kate Chopin's *The Awakening*. Tolstoy's *Anna Karenina* and Hardy's *Tess of the D'Urbervilles* are other doomed nineteenth-century heroines. *Nana* depicts the depredations of another French heroine. *Sister Carrie* shows a nineteenth-century woman who isn't destroyed when she defies society. Flaubert's other famous novel to consider is *A Sentimental Education*.

**Subjects:** France; Marriage; Adultery; Mature Read

## Garden, Nancy (1938–)

🏵 *Annie on My Mind* **(USA: 1982).** Farrar, Straus & Giroux 1992 (paper) 234pp. 0374404143 **S Teen Q**

New York high school seniors Liza and Annie meet at the Metropolitan Museum one day. Although they are from different economic and cultural backgrounds and attend different schools, they find in each other true friendship. As their friendship grows, they come to realize that they are in love with each other. This relationship tests Liza, Annie, their families, and their friends.

Frequently challenged because of the sympathetic depiction of gay relationships, this is a book about tolerance, understanding, and self-acceptance.

**Similar Reads:** Try *Deliver Us from Evie* by M. E. Kerr.

**Subjects:** New York; Friendship; High School; Gay Teens; Sexuality; Mature Read; Frequently Challenged; Margaret A. Edwards Award 2003

## Goethe, Johann Wolfgang von (1749–1832)

***The Sorrows of Young Werther*** **(Germany: 1774).** Penguin Classics 1989 (paper) 144pp. 014044503X <u>S</u> **Q**

How do you tell true love from obsession? In letters to a friend, young Werther narrates the story of a love triangle formed by himself, an intense and passionate young man of twenty; Lotte, the pretty nineteen-year-old who, after the death of her mother, is ably raising her younger brothers and sisters; and Albert, the man Lotte is engaged to marry. Werther, unsure of his own path in life, finds solace and sympathy with Lotte. His unrequited love for Lotte and his understanding that they will never be more than friends must, however, lead to misery and despair.

Goethe expresses the universal pain of unrequited love while depicting the sensitivity of the young artist in this eighteenth-century epistolary novel. *Werther* was an early work in the Romantic tradition of *Sturm und Drang,* an artistic reaction to the overly rational works of the Enlightenment, characterized by depictions of nature, passion, deeply felt emotions, and an examination of the tortured life of the genuine artist. This novel was a sensation when first published. It was banned early in its history because of the wave of suicides it inspired among passionate young people. Goethe is the German Shakespeare, a national literary figure who transcends his era and nation and contributed classics to world literature.

> **Similar Reads:** Other passionate and tragic love stories are *Madam Bovary* by Flaubert, *Anna Karenina* by Tolstoy, *The Awakening* by Kate Chopin, *An American Tragedy* by Dreiser, and *Of Human Bondage* by Maugham.

> **Subjects:** Germany, mid-1700s; Obsession; Suicide; Epistolary novel

## Hardy, Thomas (1840–1928)

***Tess of the D'Urbervilles*** **(England: 1891).** Penguin 2003 (paper) 517pp. 0141439599 <u>S</u>

Encouraged by her mother, lovely young Tess Durbeyfield reluctantly goes to work for her distant relations, the wealthy D'Urbervilles. There she is raped by Alec, the son of the house. Tess gives birth to a baby that soon dies. After a gradual recovery, Tess finds true love with Angel Clare, but when he learns about her past, he is unable to forgive, and he abandons her. Tess must now fend for herself in an unsympathetic world, but a chance meeting with Alec changes her life again.

Hardy's forte is tragic intensity. He depicts the inexorable defeat of his characters in the face of the bleak and malevolent forces of nature, their own impulses, and the social environment—*Tess* is no exception. Modern readers may not enjoy the long descriptive passages of nature and details of nineteenth-century agricultural practices, but this tragic and heartbreaking story remains a sobering read.

> **Audio:** Recorded Books. Read by Davina Porter.

> **Film/Video/DVD:** *Tess* (1979) starring Nastassja Kinski and directed by Roman Polanski is a beautiful and faithful film adaptation.

> **Similar Reads:** Hardy's bleak realism is evident in all his novels, fans will want to read *Far from the Madding Crowd*, *Jude the Obscure*, *The Return of the Native*, and *The Mayor of Casterbridge*.

**Subjects:** England, late 1800s; Country Life; Family; Murder; Mature Read

## Head, Ann (1915–)

*Mr. and Mrs. Bo Jo Jones* (**USA: 1967**). Signet 1968 (paper) 189pp. 0451163192 **J Teen Q**

Bo Jo Jones, a high school senior, is heading to college next year on a football scholarship. July Greher has another year of school and is then off to her mother's alma mater, a girl's college on the East Coast where she should meet an appropriate young man to marry. But all those plans change when July gets pregnant and the only option Bo Jo and July see is to quit school and get married.

Set in the 1960s, *Mr. and Mrs. Bo Jo Jones* presents a time when husbands earned a living and wives ran the homes, and when a pregnant girl's only option was to quit school. It also presents timeless issues such as family expectations, the difficulty of making life-affecting choices, and the real meanings of attraction, love, and commitment.

> **Film/Video/DVD:** *Mr. and Mrs. Bo Jo Jones* (1971) was made for TV movie with Desi Arnaz Jr.

> **Similar Reads:** Try *Forever* by Judy Blume and *Seventeenth Summer* by Maureen Daly.

> **Subjects:** High School; Family; Marriage; Pregnancy; Frequently Challenged

## Lawrence, D. H. (1885–1930)

*Sons and Lovers* (**England: 1913**). Signet 1985 (paper) 416pp. 0451518829 **S**

Unhappy in her marriage to a miner, a man beneath her class, Gertrude Morel puts all her love and attention into her sons—first her oldest son William and upon his death her younger son Paul. Pulled by his mother's love yet yearning for his own life, Paul never achieves an emotionally mature relationship with a woman. Although he has relationships with Miriam, a smart local girl, and Clara, a married woman, his intense relationship with his mother dominates, and perhaps destroys, his life.

This is the searing portrayal of the emotional crippling of a young man. Lawrence was a brilliant stylist, and readers may be familiar with his famous short stories. He was controversial in his lifetime for his own audacious private life and because his fiction boldly explored the complicated and often messy psychology of his characters and addressed adult themes such as relationships and sexuality. His works were often banned as obscene in their early days.

> **Audio:** Recorded Books cassette 1402538804. Read by Jenny Sterlin.

> **Film/Video/DVD:** *Sons and Lovers* (1961) starred Wendy Hiller as Gertrude and Dean Stockwell as Paul. British TV adaptations were made in both 1981 and 2003.

**Similar Reads:** Other classics of modernism that will interest readers are *To the Lighthouse* and *Mrs. Dalloway* by Woolf and *Portrait of the Artist as a Young Man* by Joyce. Other novels about complex men and their tortured relationships are *Of Human Bondage* by Maugham, *East of Eden* by Steinbeck, and *An American Tragedy* by Dreiser.

**Subjects:** England; Family; Mothers and Sons; Coal Miners; Autobiographical Novel; Modernism; Mature Read

## Steinbeck, John (1902–1968)

🌸 *Of Mice and Men* (USA: 1937). Penguin Books 1993 (paper) 107pp. 0140177396 S Q
George and Lennie are friends. They work as itinerant laborers on the farms and ranches of California, moving from job to job as the seasons demand. Together they share a dream of someday owning their own place where George can farm and Lennie can raise rabbits. But their dream is jeopardized by Lennie, a big man with the mentality of a child. He is a gentle-hearted person who seldom understands what is going on around him; he doesn't appreciate his own power or know how to control his own strength. George protects Lennie in all situations, until they get to a ranch where things go terribly wrong.

*Of Mice and Men* is a cogent piece of fiction where every detail propels the reader to the inevitable conclusion. Steinbeck wrote it as a novella but intended it to be a play, so the action is tight and the dialogue is purposeful. This tragic story is often found on banned book lists because of language, racism, sexual situations, and the portrayal of mental retardation.

**Audio:** Recorded Books CD 0788737244. Read by Mark Hammer.

**Film/Video/DVD:** Filmed many times, each version has powerful performances; 1939 with Lon Chaney and Burgess Meredith and 1992 with Gary Sinise and John Malkovitch are worth comparing.

**Similar Reads:** Two more Steinbeck short classics are *The Red Pony* and *The Pearl*. *Flowers for Algernon* by Daniel Keyes tells another story of a grown man with limited mental abilities.

**Subjects:** California 1930s; Friendship; Migrant Labor; Poverty; Mental Disability; Mature Read; Death; Frequently Challenged; Nobel Prize 1962

## Wharton, Edith (1862–1937)

*Ethan Frome* (USA: 1911). Pocket Enriched Classics 2004 (paper) 208pp. 0743487702 J Q
Ethan Frome is married to the dour and depressing Zeena. When her cousin Mattie moves in to help with the house, Ethan learns what love really is. Then a fateful decision creates enduring tragedy for this triangle. A classic story of "be careful what you wish for."

*Ethan Frome* is probably one of the most hated YA reads in history (*Silas Marner* being another). "A tragic waste of time" and " They all got what they deserved" were two recent Amazon.com reviews! Still the prose is exquisite, the setting is beautifully delineated, and the character study and situation depicted create a true tragedy. Serious and thoughtful readers will appreciate the beauty of this short novel.

**Audio:** Recorded Books cassette 155690813X; CD 1402549172. Read by George Guidall.

**Film/Video/DVD:** *Ethan Frome* (1993) with Liam Neeson and Patricia Arquette as the doomed pair.

**Similar Reads:** Try Wharton's short novel *Summer* about a young girl's first affair, a counterpart to this novel filled with snow.

**Subjects:** New England late 1800s; Marriage; Tragic Choices

## Woolf, Virginia (1882–1941)

*Mrs. Dalloway* **(England: 1925).** Harvest Books/HBJ 1990 (paper) 216pp. 0156628708 <u>S</u>

Clarissa Dalloway is giving a party tonight. She spends her day preparing for it. She buys flowers and mends a dress. She thinks about the past and takes delight in London. She is visited by her old love, Peter Walsh. Intertwining with Clarissa's story is the parallel story of the descent of Septimus Warren Smith, a shell-shocked World War I veteran also traveling through this June day in London with his Italian wife, Lucrezia.

The fluidity of time, the reality of past events in our current thoughts, relationships, expectations of youth, the realities of aging, love, and death are all explored in this brilliant novel. *Mrs. Dalloway* was a groundbreaking work of modernism and is narratively challenging. It all takes place in one day, and the narrative shifts among the minds of the characters.

**Audio:** Recorded Books CD 1402540590. Read by Virginia Leishman.

**Film/Video/DVD:** *Mrs. Dalloway* (1997) with Vanessa Redgrave. Also watch *The Hours* (2002).

**Similar Reads:** Continue exploring Virginia Woolf with *To the Lighthouse, Orlando,* and her famous essay from 1929, "A Room of One's Own." *The Hours* by Michael Cunningham was inspired by *Mrs. Dalloway* and has Virginia Woolf as a character.

**Subjects:** London, 1920s; Family; Friendships; Suicide; Modernism; Stream of Consciousness; Multiple Narrators

## Zola, Emile (1840–1902)

*Nana* (France: 1880) Penguin 1972 (paper) 480pp. 0140442634 <u>S</u>

Born in poverty, surrounded by alcoholism, Nana triumphs on the Paris stage not because of innate talent, but because she appears almost naked! Nana prostitutes herself to rich and powerful men, and although she achieves riches, she destroys everything in her path. Nana is a fascinating character without a soul or a conscience, a primal animal prowling through the most sophisticated social milieu of the time, upper-class Second Empire Paris.

Zola shocked everyone with *Nana*, and his depiction of moral corruption was considered pornography in its day. Zola was a naturalist who wanted to create

a record of the absolute realities of life—dirty, gritty, unseemly, and unsentimental.

**Similar Reads:** Zola wrote twenty novels in his famous <u>Les Rougon-Macquart</u> series. He wanted to show his times and his society through the members of an extended fictional family. Start with *L'Assomoir,* which explores alcoholism and poverty. *Germinal* is a harsh novel about a coal miner's strike. *La Bete humaine* centers around the railways. Readers may also want to explore novels by Balzac, who wrote French novels a generation before Zola, and by Flaubert.

**Subjects:** Paris; France; Theater; Prostitution; Poverty; Mature Read

# Family

Defined by some as "the primary social group," family is a prominent force in the life of a teen. Parents, siblings, extended members such as grandparents and "steps," all of these people contribute to identity. Some families nourish and support, some challenge and provoke. From ancient mythology where the gods can be seen as a bickering extended family through the loving warmth of Jo March's experiences, to the challenges faced by modern blended families, this primary social unit has been a popular subject of fiction for thousands of years

### Alcott, Louisa May (1832–1888)

*Little Women* **(USA: 1869).** Signet 2004 (paper) 456pp. 0451529308 <u>M</u>

Meg, the oldest, longs to be a great lady. Jo, unconventional and energetic, wants to be a writer. Beth, gentle and kind, is talented at music. Amy is the pretty baby of the family. These are the little women. With father away fighting in the Civil War, the girls, under the guidance of their loving mother, have adventures, romances, and insights that help them grow from girls into women.

One of the all time great girl books, this a charming depiction of a loving family and their endeavors in nineteenth-century America.

**Audio:** Recorded Books cassette 0788703277. Read by Barbara Caruso.

**Film/Video/DVD:** Every decade sees a new film version—a true indication of a beloved story. *Little Women* with Katherine Hepburn in 1933 and Winona Ryder 1994 as Jo are outstanding. A 1949 version with June Allyson as Jo and Elizabeth Taylor as Amy is glossy and colorful.

**Similar Reads:** Jo's story continues in *Little Men* and *Jo's Boys.* For the story of Alcott's real life, read *Invincible Louisa* by Cornelia Meigs (Newbery Medal 1934).

**Subjects:** New England; 1860s; Poverty; Writers; Sisters; Strong Heroine; Gentle Read

### Cleaver, Bill (1920–1981), and Vera Cleaver (1919–1993)

*Where the Lilies Bloom* **(USA: 1969).** HarperTrophy 1989 (paper) 224pp. 0064470059 <u>M</u> **Teen Q**

Fourteen-year-old Mary Call Luther has many burdens. Her mother is dead. Her father is dying. She has two younger siblings and a "cloudy headed" older sister to care for.

And Mary Call has promises to keep. Promises she made to Roy Luther, her dying father, promises to keep the family together, never to accept charity, never to allow her sister Devola to marry the neighbor Kiser Pease. Mary Call promised to always take care of everything. With their father gone and desperate for money, Mary Call devises a plan. She and the other children will become "wildcrafters" like their late mother. They will gather herbs, plants, and roots to sell to botanists and pharmacists. The abundant mountains, Old Joshua, and Sugar Boy will surely provide enough for a small family to stay together. But winter hits hard this year, and Mary Call's dogged insistence on honoring the promises she made to her dead father may destroy the family.

*Where the Lilies Bloom* tells a story about strength and stubbornness, the beauty, bounty and cruelty of nature, and the power of family and friends.

**Film/Video/DVD:** *Where the Lilies Bloom* (1974) is an adaptation of the book.

**Similar Reads:** *Homecoming* by Cynthia Voigt is another family trying to stay together without parents. *Christy* and *The Dollmaker* are books set in Appalachia.

**Subjects:** Appalachia; Brothers and Sisters; Strong Heroine; Gentle Read

## Conroy, Pat (1945–)

*Great Santini* (USA: 1976). Bantam 2002 (paper) 480pp. 0553381555 <u>S</u>

The Meechums are a military family directed in all endeavors by Marine colonel and father Bull Meechum. All of his children struggle to live with the abusive, volatile, larger than life colonel, but for oldest son Ben, life is particularly challenging with a tougher than nails father who can never be pleased.

Eminently readable, fast-moving, and filled with dialogue, Conroy's book depicts a world where love and brutality exist side by side. His books are best sellers with depth, rich characterizations, and lasting emotional impact.

**Film/Video/DVD:** *The Great Santini* (1979) starred Robert Duvall.

**Similar Reads:** *The Lords of Discipline* and *The Water Is Wide* are two other Conroy novels with appeal for YA readers.

**Subjects:** American South; U.S. Marines; Fathers and Sons

## Markandaya, Kamala (1924–2004)

*Nectar in a Sieve* (India: 1954). Signet 2002 (paper) 190pp. 0451528239 <u>J</u>

Village life in rural India is depicted with simplicity and power as we enter the story of Ruku and see her struggle to live well amid poverty and change. Her arranged marriage to a poor farmer turns into a love match, and together Ruku and Nathan raise a family and strive to build a life. But the capriciousness of the natural world—droughts, punishing rains, insect invasions—will always have an impact on their ability to succeed. As her town shifts from a gentle and slow-paced agricultural economy to an industrial economy, all the young men take jobs in the new tannery, leaving their fathers to work the fields alone.

Hope and fear, deep love of family, and a primitive (to Western eyes) life lived with a valiant spirit make this a touching and enlightening book about survival, endurance, and triumph.

**Similar Reads:** *The Good Earth* set in China tells a similar story of a family striving to escape poverty. *Nectar in a Sieve* is reminiscent of *Things Fall Apart* in its depiction of the modernization of traditional society and of *The Dollmaker* in the portrayal of urbanization and a strong mother figure.

**Subjects:** India; Poverty; Marriage, Gentle Read

## Paterson, Katherine (1932–)

🎗 *Jacob Have I Loved* (USA: 1980). HarperTrophy 1990 (paper) 256pp. 0064403688 **J Teen**

Louise Bradshaw narrates this story of two sisters growing up on a tiny island in Chesapeake Bay. Louise's twin sister Caroline has a special talent for singing and for making people love her, and the only person that hates Caroline is Louise. After much struggle, Louise comes to understand that she must create her own identity and her own happiness and rise above her jealousy of her golden sister.

Paterson is a prolific author of respected, serious fiction for young readers.

**Audio:** Recorded Books cassette 0788720805; CD 0788742175. Read by Christina Moore.

**Film/Video/DVD:** Wonderworks TV production from 1989 with Bridget Fonda.

**Similar Reads:** Other books by Paterson are *Lyddie, Bridge to Terabithia, Master Puppeteer,* and *Great Gilly Hopkins.*

**Subjects:** Chesapeake Bay, 1940s; Sisters; Island Living; Hurricane; Historical Fiction; Newbery Medal 1981

## Saroyan, William (1908–1978)

*The Human Comedy* (USA: 1945). Laurel Leaf 1988 (paper) 192pp. 0440339332 **J Q**

The Macauley home in the fictional town of Ithaca, California, is a safe haven in an uncertain world. Homer Macauley is growing up there in the shadow of World War II. Working as the night delivery boy for the telegraph office, Homer has an inside view of the lives of his neighbors as they deal with the realities of the war. His own brother is away fighting, and his father is dead. As his loving mother struggles to raise Homer, his little brother, and his sister, she continues to talk to her dead husband, believing that as long as he is remembered, he still exists in their lives.

Naïve and sentimental, gently humorous with acute character descriptions, this is a touching depiction of family life on the home front and the growth of a boy during World War II.

**Film/Video/DVD:** See *The Human Comedy* (1943) with Mickey Rooney.

**Similar Reads:** Try *How Green Was My Valley.*

**Subjects**: California; World War II; Home Front; Gentle Read

## Taylor, Mildred (1943–)

🏆 *Roll of Thunder, Hear My Cry* **(USA: 1976).** Puffin 2004 (paper) 288pp. 0142401129 **J Teen**

> Cassie Logan narrates this story about her strong resilient family as they work hard to keep their own land in an era of poverty. The realities of racism are battled by the defensive power of family in Taylor's works.

> **Audio:** Listening Library cassette 0807206210.
>
> **Similar Reads:** Try *Let the Circle Be Unbroken, The Friendship, The Road to Memphis*, and *Mississippi Bridge*. *The Land* is the prequel to the stories of the Logan family.

> **Subjects:** Mississippi 1933; Depression Era; Racism; Prejudice; Poverty; African Americans; Newbery Medal 1977

## Voigt, Cynthia (1942–)

🏆 *Homecoming* **(USA: 1981).** Simon Pulse 2002 (paper) 416pp. 0689851324 <u>M</u> **Teen**

> Resourceful thirteen-year-old Dicey Tillerman must shepherd her sister and two brothers after their unstable mother abandons them in the parking lot of a shopping mall. But Dicey is used to the responsibility, "Dump it all on Dicey, that was what Momma did, she always did." Dicey decides the best strategy for survival is to walk along U.S. Route 1 until they come to their Aunt Cilla's house, a woman they have never met. Dicey must find food and places to sleep and keep the family from being separated, all the while encouraging them onward. When they get to Aunt Cilla's house, they learn they have a grandmother living in Maryland, a grandmother they never met.

> **Audio:** Recorded Books 0307281728. Read by Lynne Thigpen.
>
> **Film/Video/DVD:** *Homecoming* (1996) stars Anne Bancroft as the grandmother.

> **Similar Reads:** The Tillermans story continues with the 1983 Newbery Award winner, *Dicey's Song*. Voigt also wrote several companion books to the series: *A Solitary Blue*; *The Runner; Come a Stranger; Sons from Afar*; and *Seventeen against the Dealer.*

> **Subjects:** Connecticut; Family; Brothers and Sisters; Grandparents; Historical Fiction; Mental Illness; Journey; Survival; Margaret A. Edwards Award 1995

# Extreme Mental States—Mental Illness and Drug Addiction

The books in this section are novels that depict mental illness and pose the question: What would it feel like to loose my mind?

Books about the negative effects of experimentation with drugs, an unfortunate rite of passage in the lives of many young Americans, are also included.

## Anonymous (Beatrice Sparks 1918–)

*Go Ask Alice* (USA: 1967). Simon Pulse 1998 (paper) 192pp. 0689817851 **J** Teen **Q**

Alice seems to be a typical teenager. She worries about her weight, her hair, her relationship with her mother, her popularity with boys, and her desire to have one true friend. Invited to a party with the "cool" kids, she unknowingly drinks a cola with LSD in it. Starting that night, she begins an odyssey of drug use, sexual exploitation, running away, and homecomings. Her life becomes a giant tug-of-war between addiction and staying clean. Her family loves but oppresses her, her friends help but exploit her. She spends time on the streets, she tries to live her old life at home, and she resides for a time in a mental hospital, all the while telling her diary everything.

Frequently challenged as objectionable because of drugs and sex, this is a blunt and gruesome story; and it doesn't have a happy ending. However, it's a morality tale as relevant for today as for the decade of the sixties that created it. Teens ignore the dated bits as they come to know Alice and share her anguish and slight triumphs. This controversial classic is a harrowing read, not appropriate for the highly sensitive.

**Audio:** Recorded Books cassette 078870690X; CD 1402550316. Read by Christina Moore.

**Film/Video/DVD**: *Go Ask Alice* (1973) with William Shatner as the father is very dated now; where is the contemporary remake of this emotional story?

**Similar Reads:** Beatrice Spark is the "anonymous" author of several angst-filled books for teens: *Annie's Baby: The Diary of an Anonymous, Pregnant Teenager*; *Jay's Journal* about suicide; and *It Happened to Nancy* about HIV infection. For another harrowing tale about drug abuse set in England, read *Smack* by Burgess Melvin. Other books in diary format are *Perks of Being a Wallflower* by Stephen Chbosky and *Don't You Dare Read This, Mrs. Dunphrey* by Margaret Peterson Haddix.

**Subjects:** 1960s; Runaways; High School; Peer Pressure; Mental Hospital; Diary Format; Frequently Challenged

## Childress, Alice (1920–1994)

*A Hero Ain't Nothin' but a Sandwich* (USA: 1973). Puffin Books/Penguin Group, 2000 (paper) 126pp. 0698118545. **M** Teen **Q**

Benjie Johnson is a thirteen-year-old heroin addict. We learn the story of Benjie from the perspectives of the many distinctive characters that populate his life: his mother, his stepfather, his teachers, and his friends.

Realistic, angry, funny, and controversial, this is 1970s social realism, African American history, and very good writing

**Similar Reads:** Other books about the inner-city experience include *Daddy Was a Number Runner* by Louise Meriwether, *Manchild in the Promised Land* by Claude Brown, and *Down These Mean Streets* by Piri Thomas. Other books with multiple narrators are *Bull Run* and *Seedfolks* by Paul Fleischman and *Spoon River Anthology* by Edgar Lee Masters.

**Subjects:** Addiction; Poverty; Inner City; African Americans; Teachers and Students; Multiple Narrators

## Greenberg, Joanne (1932–)

*I Never Promised You a Rose Garden* **(USA: 1964).** Signet 1989 (paper) 288pp. 0451160312. **J Teen**

How does it feel when reality slips away from you? When the concrete, three-dimensional, cause-and-effect world quivers and turns gray until you cannot see or hear or feel anything real and you must retreat to your secret made-up world to exist? Deborah Blau, age sixteen, has these experiences. When we meet her, her loving but baffled family has just placed her in a mental hospital. With the help of a compassionate doctor, Deborah will undertake the long and arduous journey back to wellness.

Sympathetic, fascinating, gripping, sobering, this is a glimpse into a an unknown world of mental illness seen from the victim's point of view.

> **Film/Video/DVD:** See *I Never Promised You a Rose Garden* (1977) with Kathleen Quinlan.
>
> **Similar Reads:** Try *Lisa Bright and Dark* by Neufeld and *The Bell Jar* by Plath.
>
> **Subjects:** Mental Hospital; Schizophrenia; Suicide; Psychiatrists; Therapy; Mental Breakdown

## Kesey, Ken (1935–2001)

*One Flew over the Cuckoo's Nest* **(USA: 1962).** Penguin USA (paper), 288pp. 014028334X; Signet (paper), 272 pp 0451163966 **S**

7

To avoid the work detail in the prison farm where he is serving six months for assault, inmate R. P. McMurphy gets himself committed to the mental ward where it's an easy life of orange juice for breakfast, card games all afternoon, and television in the evenings. McMurphy swaggers in expecting to rule. But Nurse Ratchet runs this mental ward, and she is a woman who dominates her patients with spirit-crushing effectiveness. McMurphy likes to sing, laugh, gamble, and play fair, and under his influence the other inmates begin to assert themselves—something Nurse Ratchet cannot allow. Narrated by Chief Broom, a fellow inmate whose grasp on reality comes and goes, the conflict between Nurse Ratchet and McMurphy unfolds as an epic battle of wills.

This is a raw and effecting story for mature readers about cruelty and freedom, rights and power, what constitutes sanity, the joy of individuality, and the resilience of the human spirit under dehumanizing conditions.

> **Audio:** Books on Tape 0736644997. Read by Jonathon Marosz.

**Film/Video/DVD:** *One Flew over the Cuckoo's Nest* (1975) is a blockbuster film starring Jack Nicholson in a career-defining role; it won six Academy Awards.

**Similar Reads:** Kesey's other novel, considered by some to be his best, is *Sometimes a Great Notion* about a family of loggers in the Pacific Northwest.

**Subjects:** Oregon, 1960; Nurses; Nonconformity; Mental Hospital; Mature Read

## Neufeld, John (1938–)

*Lisa Bright and Dark* (USA: 1969). Signet 1970 (paper) 144pp. 0451166841 **J Q**

Some days Lisa Schilling is the bright Lisa, smart and fun. Other days she is the dark Lisa, withdrawn, paranoid, violent, and suicidal. Lisa knows something is wrong. She begs and bullies her parents for help, but they think she is just acting up for attention. Eventually her boyfriend can't be with her anymore, and her teachers, unable to deal with her, agree to ignore her. But her three girlfriends—practical M.N.; sweet, Paul-Newman-obsessed Betsy; and cool, regal Elizabeth—recognize that something is radically wrong with Lisa. When they can't get any adults to be involved, they try to help Lisa themselves.

The 1968 setting is dated, but this is still a compelling story about mental illness, compassion, and friendship.

**Film/Video/DVD:** *Lisa Bright and Dark* (1973) was a Hallmark television movie starring Kay Lenz as Lisa and Anne Baxter as her mother.

**Similar Reads:** Other books about teen girls facing madness are *I Never Promised You a Rose Garden* by Greenberg and *The Bell Jar* by Plath. For more gritty realism, try *Go Ask Alice.*

**Subjects:** Friendship; Family; High School; Mental Breakdown

## Plath, Sylvia (1932–1963)

*The Bell Jar* (USA: 1963). Harper Perennial Classics 2005 (paper) 288pp. 0060837020 **S**

Nineteen-year-old Esther Greenwood is a girl to envy. She is smart and attractive. She has a scholarship to a prestigious women's college and is spending part of the summer of 1953 in New York City as an intern at a well-known ladies magazine. But things are not quite right with Esther. She has trouble reading, then writing, then sleeping. She doesn't bathe, she quits wearing clean clothes, and she explores different ways to kill herself. This is an intimate first-person account of Esther's journey through clinical depression, her stays at various mental hospitals, including treatments with electroshock therapy, and her subsequent journey back to independence and health.

Plath wrote a very personal account of mental disintegration based on her own experiences. She explores the themes of freedom and confinement, female sexuality, and societal pressure on women to conform to the roles of mothers and wives. Known as an accomplished poet, Sylvia Plath committed suicide a month after *The Bell Jar* was published.

**Audio:** Recorded Books, cassette 1556906560. Read by Christina Moore.

**Film/Video/DVD:** Readers may be interested in seeing *Sylvia* (2003) with Gwyneth Paltrow as Plath in a movie about her marriage to poet Ted Hughes.

**Similar Reads:** Plath's confessional poetry is highly recommended; try *Ariel*. Two stories of more modern young women experiencing mental difficulties are Elizabeth Wurtzel's *Prozac Nation* and *Girl, Interrupted* by Suzanna Kaysen.

**Subjects:** New York, 1950s; Depression; Suicidal Behavior; College; Mental Hospital; Mothers and Daughters; Mature Read; Mental Breakdown

# Death

One of the most dramatic experiences any of us will have is the loss of someone we love. By addressing this trauma through fiction, we can learn to cope with the reality of death and other losses in our own lives

## Agee, James (1909–1955)

🐾 *A Death in the Family* (USA: 1957). Vintage 1998 (paper) 320pp. 0375701230 <u>S</u>

Jay Follet leaves his sleeping family one night to travel to the bedside of his dying father. Ironically, his father recovers, but Jay is killed in a car crash on his way home. The Follet family must now struggle to accept the unexpected death of a vibrant and beloved young husband and father. Multiple viewpoints and elegiac impressionistic segments mixed with a strong simple narrative make this a beautiful and unforgettable story. Told mainly from the viewpoint of his six-year-old son, Rufus.

Lyrical and sad, this is a book about human emotion and the big ideas of life, love, and loss.

**Audio:** Recorded Books cassette 0788744011; CD 0788771647. Read by Mark Hammer.

**Film/Video/DVD:** *All the Way Home* (1963) with Robert Preston and Jean Simmons, is based on the Pulitzer Prize–winning play version. There was also a *Masterpiece Theatre* production in 2002.

**Similar Reads:** A classic memoir written by a father about the death of his son is *Death Be Not Proud* by John Gunther.

**Subjects:** Knoxville, Tennessee, 1915; Death; Grief; Family; Childhood; Gentle Read; Faith; Pulitzer Prize 1958

## Gipson, Fred (1908–1973)

🐾 *Old Yeller* (USA: 1956). <u>J</u> @ Q

*See* Chapter 2, "Historical Fiction," under the Western subgenre.

## Guest, Judith (1936–)

*Ordinary People* (USA: 1976). Penguin 1982 (paper) 272pp. 140065172 <u>S</u>

An accidental death, a suicide attempt, and a family imploding from the strain of unexpressed emotions are all to be found in *Ordinary People*. Seventeen-year-old Conrad Jarrett recently returned home from a hospital where he was recovering from attempted suicide. Now he must struggle to reconnect with Calvin, his concerned and loving father, and Beth, his lovely and distant mother who insists that she is healed from the accidental death of Conrad's brother.

A book about healing and recovery as much as about pain and loss.

**Audio:** Recorded Books cassette 1556903952. Read by Aviva Skell.

**Film/Video/DVD:** *Ordinary People* (1980) was directed by Robert Redford and stars Mary Tyler Moore, Donald Sutherland, and Timothy Hutton.

**Similar Reads:** Try *Catcher in the Rye* and *A Separate Peace.*

**Subjects:** Illinois; Family; Brothers; Depression; Suicide; Therapy; Fathers and Sons; Mental Illness; Friendship; Psychiatrists

## Masters, Edgar Lee (1868–1950)

*Spoon River Anthology* (USA: 1915). Signet 1992 (paper) 285pp. 0451525302 <u>SQ</u>

The deceased inhabitants of Spoon River, Illinois, narrate their lives through free-verse epitaphs. Every epitaph is a vignette that relates a moment in each life or delineates a character. Through the brief verses, we see how the lives in this town intertwined, how hopes were destroyed, and how brief happiness was lived. Because everyone is dead, they can be honest about their passions, disappointments, and dreams.

A unique work that is somber and fascinating. The reader experiences brevity of expression and depth of feeling.

**Audio:** Audio Partners cassette 1572702788. Read by full cast.

**Similar Reads:** Try Thornton Wilder's play *Our Town.*

**Subjects:** Illinois, early 1900s; Small Towns; Free Verse; Cemeteries; Multiple Narrators

## Peck, Robert Newton (1928–)

*A Day No Pigs Would Die* (USA: 1972). Random House 1994 (paper) 176pp. 0679853065 <u>M</u> Teen Q

The vivid realism of farm life shines through in Peck's autobiographical novel. Young Robert is given a pig as a reward for helping to birth a calf. He and his pig Pinky become companions on the Vermont farm in the 1930s. But Pinky proves unable to provide a litter of pigs, and the family can't support an unproductive farm animal.

Robert grows in his understanding of the harsh realities of life through his encounter with and acceptance of death.

**Audio:** Recorded Books cassette 0788703633. Read by Johnny Heller.

**Similar Reads:** Try *The Yearling.*

**Subjects:** Vermont, 1930s; Farm Life; Pigs; Fathers and Sons; Shakers; Pets; Frequently Challenged; Autobiographical Novel

## Rawls, Wilson (1913–1984)

*Where the Red Fern Grows* (**USA 1961**). Delacorte/Doubleday, 1996 (paper) 212pp. 0385323301 <u>M</u> **Teen Q**

It is a great day in the life of Billy Colman when he brings home his two new pups. He worked for two years picking berries and selling bait to save enough money to buy the only things in the world he desired: two hunting dogs, Little Ann and Old Dan. The dogs become his best companions and champion raccoon hunters. Many adventures and much growing up await Billy.

A simpler time is portrayed in this novel, a time when it took two years to save fifty dollars and country children only wore shoes when the weather got cold. This memorable tale of determination, love, and sacrifice has a strong rural setting and is narrated by the grown-up Billy.

> **Audio:** Recorded Books cassette 0788701851. Read by Frank Muller.
>
> **Film/Video/DVD:** *Where the Red Fern Grows* (1974) is a family classic with Beverly Garland and James Whitmore.
>
> **Similar Reads:** Try *Old Yeller* by Fred Gipson, *The Yearling* by Marjorie Kinan Rawlings, and Jack London's *The Call of the Wild*. Rawls's other memorable book is *The Summer of the Monkeys*.
>
> **Subjects:** Oklahoma, 1930s; Ozarks; Rural Life; Hunting: Dogs; Pets; Gentle Read

# Social Conflict

Fiction is all about conflict. The theme of men and women in conflict with their society is a topic of perpetual interest to authors and readers. Poverty, oppression, and cultural change are themes common to this subgenre. These books cover a wide geographic and historical range, and each shows people struggling with their society.

## Achebe, Chinua (1930–)

*Things Fall Apart* (**Nigeria: 1959**). Anchor 1994 (paper) 224 pp. 0385474547 <u>S</u>

This is the story of Okonkwo, a powerful and ambitious man, and of his wives, his children, and their tribal society in late-nineteenth-century Nigeria. The life they know is full of ritual and regulations, folklore, and prescribed ways of being. The arrival of foreign missionaries into this world leads to the disintegration of the traditional tribal life Okonkwo understands and loves.

Things Fall Apart is considered the first classic of modern African literature.

> **Audio:** Recorded Books cassette 0788708155. Read by Peter Francis James.
>
> **Film/Video/DVD:** A 1971 film was produced in Nigeria.

**Similar Reads:** *The Bride Price* by Buchi Emecheta also tells a story of Nigerian people, or try *Graceland* a coming-of-age novel set in Nigeria by Chris Abani.

**Subjects:** Nigeria; Africa, Late 1800s; Colonialism; Ibo Tribe; Tribal Life; Historical Fiction

## Forster, E. M. (1879–1970)

*A Passage to India* **(England: 1924).** Harvest Books 1965 (paper) 368pp. 0156711427 **S**

In 1922, Miss Adele Quested, a "queer, cautious girl," travels to exotic India in the company of her future mother-in-law, Mrs. Moore, a truly open-minded woman who espouses a pure love of mankind. Once there, both women want to experience the real India, but the cultural gap between East and West is great. They are discouraged in their explorations by everyone until kind and eager Dr. Aziz invites them on a trip to the famous Caves of Marabar. The British Mr. Fielding and the Hindu Professor Godbole are to accompany them on the trip, but at the last minute they miss the train. The trip is not successful and ends in humiliation and disaster when Adela accuses Aziz of attempted rape. As a courtroom drama plays out, tension between the cultures is greater than ever.

The flaws of Colonialism were on Forster's mind as he wrote *A Passage to India.* His depiction of the cultural differences and tense coexistence of the occupying British and the native Indians is memorable. Mrs. Turton, the wife of the local British official, sums up the Western arrogance when she tells Mrs. Moore, "You're superior to them, anyway. Don't forget that, you're superior to everyone in India." Lyrical prose and acute observations make this a powerful read.

**Audio:** Chivers Audio Books CD 0754053539. Read by Sam Dastor.

**Film/Video/DVD:** *A Passage to India* (1984) is a lush adaptation with Judy Davis and was director David Lean's last film.

**Similar Reads:** Other books about India include *Nectar in a Sieve* by Markandaya and *Kim* by Kipling. E. M. Forster's other works such as *Howard's End* and *A Room with a View,* are fine character studies. Another epic historical work about the British in India is Paul Scott's series of books called The Raj Quartet.

**Subjects:** India; British in India; Colonialism; Trials; Cultural Conflict

## Hugo, Victor (1802–1885)

*Les Miserables* **(France: 1862).** Signet 1987 (paper) 1463pp. 0451525264 **S**

Many story threads create the huge tapestry that is *Les Miserables.* Through it all is Jean Valjean, a poor but honest man who commits a noble crime: he steals a loaf of bread to feed his sister's starving children. As punishment, he is sent to prison, and his life is effectively ruined because he is now marked forever as a criminal. Years later, no longer in prison, Valjean's story intersects with Fantine, a prostitute, and her daughter, Cosette; Marius, an idealistic young man; and the unstoppable Javert, the man who wants to see Jean Valjean back in prison. Along the way, the Battle of Waterloo, the July Revolution of 1830, the Paris sewers, religious orders, and the criminal underworld of Paris all figure in this expansive novel.

One of world literature's "Big Books," this novel encompasses much of French society and history and the big issues of justice, love, and honor. Comparable to *War and Peace* in its scale and scope.

>   **Audio:** Blackstone Audio, available in abridged and unabridged versions, 078611035X (part 1), 0786110368 (part 2), 0786110376 (part 3). Read by Frederick Davidson.

>   **Film/Video/DVD:** This universal story has inspired many international filmed versions and a musical. The 1909 silent film is perhaps the oldest, and the 2000 French miniseries with Gerard Depardieu and John Malkovich is the most recent. The musical, often referred to as just *Les Mis* (1987), is very stirring and expresses the grandeur of the novel.

>   **Similar Reads:** Hugo's other classic is *The Hunchback of Notre Dame*.

>   **Subjects:** Paris; France; Justice; Retribution; Poverty; Historical Fiction

## Paton, Alan (1903–1988)

*Cry, the Beloved Country* **(South Africa: 1948).** Scribner 2003 (paper) 320pp. 0743262174 <u>S</u>

Humble and gentle Stephen Kumalo is a Zulu tribesman and an Anglican priest. To aid his sister and search for his son, he travels from his quiet and impoverished South African village to Johannesburg, the country's big and chaotic city. There his fate intersects with that of a wealthy white man, and he bravely faces tragedy.

Poetic and stylistically intriguing, this beautiful story is full of conflict among family members, races, generations, and classes. Paton was politically and socially aware; and this book addresses apartheid, poverty, crime, economics, education, and the effects of the societal shift from traditional tribal society to modern, impersonal, urban lifestyles.

>   **Audio:** Recorded Books cassette 1556906501. Read by Maggie Soboil.

>   **Film/Video/DVD:** *Cry, the Beloved Country* (1995) stars James Earl Jones and Richard Harris. An earlier 1951 version stars Sidney Poitier. The book is also the basis for a 1949 Broadway musical, *Lost in the Stars,* with music by Kurt Weil and book by Maxwell Anderson.

>   **Similar Reads:** *Kaffir Boy* by Mark Mathabane is the autobiography of a young man growing up under apartheid. Interested readers may also like to try Nelson Mandela's 1994 autobiography, *Long Walk to Freedom*.

>   **Subjects:** South Africa; 1946; Fathers and Sons; Apartheid; Clergyman; Family

## Rand, Ayn (1905–1982)

*The Fountainhead* **(USA: 1943).** Signet 1996 (paper, 50th anniversary ed.) 720pp. 0451191153 <u>S</u>

Howard Roark, intense, gifted, and passionate, is an architect with a pure vision, a man who will not compromise and who cannot be bought off with the temptation of easy money for inferior work. This is the story of his struggle to remain true to his vision.

Rand was a philosopher who developed a system of thought that she called Objectivism. She wrote fiction to express her philosophy of the primacy of the individual and of objectivity as the best way to deal with reality, the supremacy of capitalism as a political system, and the personal philosophy of "rational self-interest." Although sometimes criticized as ill-written fiction espousing a cruel and selfish philosophy, Rand's books have remained in print and continue to be a source of intellectual challenge for readers who like very big books.

> **Audio:** Books on Tape cassettes 0736630260 (part 1), 0736630279 (part 2). Read by Kate Reading.
>
> **Film/Video/DVD:** *The Fountainhead* (1949) with Gary Cooper and Patricia Neal, directed by King Vidor is histrionic but intriguing.
>
> **Similar Reads:** To further explore Rand's philosophy, try *We the Living* or *Atlas Shrugged*. Readers may want to start with her much shorter work *Anthem*.
>
> **Subjects:** New York; Individualism; Architecture; Objectivism; Mature Read

## Sinclair, Upton (1878–1968)

*The Jungle* (USA: 1905). Penguin Classics Deluxe 2006 (paper, with an introduction by Eric Schlosser) 464pp. 014303958x **S**

> Lithuanian immigrant Jurgis Rudkus is willing to work hard so his family can prosper in America. But as immigrants with little knowledge of the English language and American ways, his extended family is taken advantage of at every turn. When Jurgis's health is affected and he cannot work, their precarious world begins to topple.
>
> A heartbreaking story about an earnest, hopeful outsider reaching for a share of the American dream, this novel is often cited as an example of how literature can generate social change. President Theodore Roosevelt was prompted to create the first Food and Drug Act (1906) after reading Sinclair's vivid accounts of the inhumane meat industry of the early 1900s. Sinclair also depicts the cruel working conditions, abusive treatment of workers, blatant sexual abuse, and discrimination of the day.
>
> **Audio:** Recorded Books cassette 1556909772; CD 1402552211. Read by George Guidall.
>
> **Similar Reads:** Other novels that generated public awareness about social conditions include *Uncle Tom's Cabin*, *The Grapes of Wrath*, and *Cry, the Beloved Country*.
>
> **Subjects:** Chicago; Poverty; Meat Industry; Labor; Immigrants; Socialism; Family

## Steinbeck, John (1902–1968)

�$\bullet$ *The Grapes of Wrath* (USA: 1939). **S**

> *See* Chapter 2, "Historical Fiction," under The Great Depression heading.

*The Pearl* **(USA: 1948).** Penguin 2000 (paper) 96pp. 014017737X **J Q**

"And there it lay, the great pearl, perfect as the moon.. . . It was the greatest pearl in the world." And now it belongs to Kino, the poor pearl diver who hours earlier could not afford to pay a doctor to treat his son for a scorpion bite. Now, believes Kino, life will be different, better. He, his wife Juana, and their son Coyotito will live in peace and affluence. Coyotito will go to school and learn to read and the whole family will rise because of his knowledge. But as soon as news of the fantastic pearl spreads through the village, Kino and his family are under attack. Everyone wants a piece of Kino's new good fortune. The pearl promises a hopeful future, but it will bring only sorrow.

This is a fable of good and evil written in Steinbeck's eloquent and lucid prose. Kino's struggle against the greed, ambition, and violence unleashed by the valuable pearl creates a tragic universal story.

**Audio:** Highbridge Audio 0453008755. Read by Hector Elizondo.

**Similar Reads:** For more by Steinbeck, try *The Red Pony* or *Of Mice and Men*. For other earnest families struggling against poverty, read *The Good Earth* by Pearl S. Buck or *The Dollmaker* by Harriet Arnow.

**Subjects:** Mexico; Poverty; Family; Pearl Divers; Greed; Grief

# Chapter 8

## Romance Fiction

Romance fiction takes readers into the human heart and gives them front-row seats to the interaction of people in love.

The main appeal of this genre is emotional. The reader feels the story. The intense emotional involvement of the reader is crucial to the success of romance story. For a young adult reader, the vicarious participation in a relationship is a large part of the appeal, a young reader can "try on" relationship and romance.

According to the Romance Writers of American, a nonprofit genre writer's association, 51 million Americans read romance novels, and 93 percent of those readers are women. The poll also states that 71 percent of romance readers said they read their first romance at age sixteen or younger and 7 percent of current romance readers are between the ages of fourteen and nineteen. This is a genre that has great appeal to young female readers.

In the romance genre, the relationship is the story; the main characters are in love and must overcome adversity and obstacles—society, historical events, misunderstandings, their own prejudices, the meddling of others—to make their relationship work.

The main character of a romance novel is generally a strong and intelligent heroine. Romance Writers of America readers when polled ranked the top character traits of the heroine in a romance novel as "intelligence" and "strength of character."

Sadly, many classic romances end with the couple separated. Classic romances have a tendency to end in death, perhaps reflecting the greater mortality rates in earlier times. The reader, however, is often left with the belief that a future exists for the lovers—think of Scarlett scheming to get Rhett back or Cathy and Heathcliff united in death.

# Gothic Romance

Also called romantic suspense, these romances contain mystery, terror, and suspense. Sometimes there is an element of the supernatural in these stories as well. Mary Stewart, Barbara Michaels, and Victoria Holt are contemporary authors of Gothic romance.

## Austen, Jane (1775–1817)

*Northanger Abbey* **(England: 1818).** Modern Library 2002 (paper) 256pp. 0375759174 **J**

Seventeen-year-old Catherine Morland, naïve and unworldly but an avid reader of sensational novels, is invited to Northanger Abbey. There she hopes to find all the Gothic ingredients that she loves to read about—hidden passages, dark dungeons, mystery, murder, and family secrets. But the Tilney's family home is more prosaic than melodramatic, and Catherine's understanding of people, literature, and herself is in for revision.

This novel is a spoof of the rage for Gothic fiction in Austen's youth. Although not published until after Austen's death *Northanger Abbey* was written about twenty years earlier in 1798. It is a fast, almost breezy read full of humor, parody, and misunderstandings between young people looking for relationships. As in Austen's other novels, delusion eventually gives way to clarity, and the heroine's evolution leads to a happy ending.

> **Audio:** Tantor Media CD 1400102057. Read by Donada Peters.
>
> **Film/Video/DVD:** See *Northanger Abbey* (1986).
>
> **Similar Reads:** Try the Gothic granddaddies that Austen is spoofing: *The Castle of Otranto* by Horace Walpole, *The Monk* by Matthew "Monk" Lewis, and *The Mysteries of Udolpho* by Anne Radcliffe.
>
> **Subjects:** England, early 1800s; Family; Brothers and Sisters; Humor; Satire; Gentle Read

## Bronte, Charlotte (1816–1855)

*Jane Eyre* **(England: 1847).** Signet (paper) 480pp. 0451526554 **J**

Small, plain and serious, ten-year-old Jane Eyre is an orphan living with her nasty aunt and bratty cousins. Jane stoically endures abuse from these relations until she has a ghostly vision of her kind uncle when forced to stay in the room where he died. This episode causes Jane's rebellion and ultimate removal from the wicked Reed family to the Lowood Orphan Asylum, a charitable institution where students are barely fed and poorly sheltered. As time passes Lowood improves, and Jane becomes a star student and eventually a teacher there. One day she realizes that she must leave Lowood to create her own life. She advertises as a governess, her ad is answered, and she sets off for Thornfield Hall. There she encounters the housekeeper, kind Mrs. Fairfax; sweet Adele, her pupil, the malevolent Grace Poole; and the brooding and mysterious Mr. Rochester. Jane's life at Thornfield is happy and fulfilling. She enjoys teaching Adele; she longs for her interactions with the darkly handsome and deeply complex Mr. Rochester, and Mr. Rochester is attracted to Jane's independence and intelligence. But Thornfield Hall and Edmund Rochester have many secrets, and Jane will endure much before she can find lasting happiness.

**Audio:** Recorded Books cassette 1556902611. Read by Flo Gibson.

**Film/Video/DVD:** Filmed many times, teens will like the 1997 A&E version with Ciaran Hinds and Samantha Morton. It is passionate and brisk but excludes many episodes from the book. Film buffs will want to see the 1944 classic with Orson Welles and Joan Fontaine. *Jane Eyre* is also the basis for a well received though little performed Broadway musical.

**Similar Reads:** *Jane Eyre* rewards rereadings. Younger readers love the story of brave Jane as she quietly triumphs, and older readers see more depth to Jane and have an easier time with the Victorian language. Bronte's sister Emily's book *Wuthering Heights* is a natural next book for good readers. Charlotte's other books *Shirley* and *Villette* will interest avid readers.

**Subjects**: England, Early 1800s; Governess; Orphans; Mental Illness; Strong Heroine; Victorian Novel; Gentle Read

## Bronte, Emily (1818–1848)

*Wuthering Heights* (**England: 1847**). Signet (paper) 322pp. 0451529251; Scholastic Classics (paper) 406pp. 0439228913 <u>S</u>

*Wuthering Heights* is an amazing book. Most often described as the love story of Catherine and Heathcliff, it is really a novel full of violence, dysfunction, humiliation, cruelty, and all around bad behavior. When Catherine Earnshaw and her brother Hindley are young, their father, a kind and benevolent man, brings home to Wuthering Heights a little abandoned boy he found in the streets of Liverpool—the dark and unhappy Heathcliff. Hindley rejects Heathcliff as an intruder into his home and his father's affections, but Catherine finds a soulmate in Heathcliff, and they spend a childhood exploring the natural world of the moors around them. As they mature, Catherine is torn between her passion for the wild Heathcliff and her longing for a more civilized life. She chooses conventionality and marries her respectable neighbor, Edgar Linton. Linton and his sister Isabella have grown up at the refined and elegant Thrushcross Grange, a place that contrasts greatly with the rough and rustic Wuthering Heights. When Heathcliff hears Catherine say she will marry Edgar, he leaves the moors. Years later, Heathcliff returns to torment Catherine, Edgar, Isabella, and Hindley and to see that the next generation— Catherine and Edgar's daughter Cathy, Hindley's son Hareton, and Heathcliff's own son Linton—are tormented as well.

This was Emily Bronte's only novel, written while she was still in her twenties. It is a challenge—it's structurally complex, has multiple narrators, a convoluted timeline, and a fair amount of country dialect—but it is a must read.

**Audio:** Recorded Books cassette 1556905850. Read by Flo Gibson.

**Film/Video/DVD:** The Goldwyn classic of 1939 is wildly romantic and leaves the viewer with a very inaccurate understanding of the characters and their motivations. The 1992 film with Ralph Fiennes as Heathcliff follows the novel a little more accurately.

**Similar Reads:** Another gothic romance set in a big house is *Rebecca* by Daphne du Maurier. *Ethan Frome* by Edith Wharton is another story of unhappy and doomed lovers.

**Subjects:** England early 1800s; Family; Victorian Novel; Marriage

## du Maurier, Daphne (1907–1989)

*Rebecca* (England: 1938). Avon 1994 (paper) 384pp. 0380778556 **J**

"Last night I dreamt I went to Manderley again." So the second Mrs. de Winter begins her story of romance and terror. The handsome, tragic, and very rich Maxim de Winter meets his second wife in Monte Carlo. It is 1927. She is working as a ladies companion to a wealthy American, and even though she is half his age, Maxim falls in love with her. They marry and return to his home, the famous English estate, Manderley. But the honeymoon ends once they reach Manderley. This new Mrs. de Winter—we never do learn her name—is young and unsure of herself, and she lives totally in the shadow of the first Mrs. de Winter, the vibrant, beautiful, and accomplished Rebecca. Rebecca still inhabits Manderley. The sinister housekeeper Mrs. Danvers sees to it that Rebecca's orders are still carried out. Rebecca is there in the furnishings, the menus, the hearts of the servants, and the mind of Maxim—but Rebecca is dead! How can her power reach from the grave into the mind of her husband's new wife?

Readers have been swept away by this book since its publication in 1938—the naive and uncertain narrator has our sympathy and our attention from the intriguing opening line, and Manderley is a memorable place.

**Audio:** Recorded Books cassette 1556904355. Read by Alexandra O'Karma.

**Film/Video/DVD:** Hitchcock filmed this story brilliantly in 1939 with Laurence Olivier and Joan Fontaine. It won the Oscar for Best Picture. The *Masterpiece Theatre* production from 1997 is also recommended.

**Similar Reads:** du Maurier wrote many other period romances that will intrigue YA readers: *Jamaica Inn*, *My Cousin Rachel*, and *Frenchman's Creek*, for example. Other authors of romantic suspense are Mary Higgins Clark and Mary Stewart. Try *Nine Coaches Waiting*.

**Subjects:** England; Cornwall; Wealth; Marriage

# Historical

Romances set any time in history before the World Wars are considered historical. Many of the most memorable romance novels are set in the past. Perhaps it is the candle-light, or maybe it is the stricter societal conventions that governed the roles and interactions of men and women, but there is delicious tension inherent in historical romance.

## Blackmore, R. D. (1825–1900)

*Lorna Doone* (England: 1869). Oxford University Press (paper) 680pp. 0192836277 **J**

Oh those nasty, wicked Doones! Outlaws, thieves, and murderers, the Doone Clan are the wickedest people in English literature. Young Lorna is a child in the outlaw clan of the Doones. When she saves yeoman farmer John Ridd from them, he falls in love with her. Years later he returns to find her, and together they discover the secret of Lorna Doone.

A great love story with mystery and adventure all wrapped into a long-winded book—only the most motivated will stick with it—clever readers will skim over the dull bits and read for the story of John and Lorna.

> **Film/Video/DVD:** Almost a dozen film versions exist, starting with the 1915 silent film. The 2001 BBC/A&E version is very good—it tightens up the story and focuses on the romance.

> **Similar Reads:** Blackmore writes in the tradition of Sir Walter Scott; readers may want to turn to Scott's novels for more historical romance.

> **Subjects:** England, 1600s; Outlaws; Inheritance; Secrets

## Daly, Maureen (1921–)

*Seventeenth Summer* (USA: 1942). Simon & Schuster (paper) 360pp. 0671619314 **J Teen**

Angie Morrow and Jack Duluth undergo the universal experience of first love in Wisconsin in the summer of 1942. Angie narrates her inner turmoil and ultimate joy as her relationship with Jack progresses.

This is a wonderful "starter" romance. It was considered an up-to-date depiction of adolescence when it was first published. In 1942, it was really the only book of its kind—a book that presented an honest and emotional story of two young people falling in love. It retains a sweetness and depth of emotion that still appeals to readers.

> **Similar Reads:** Look for other stories about first love in *Forever, Fifteen, Pride and Prejudice, The Sound of Waves,* and *A Girl of the Limberlost*

> **Subjects:** Wisconsin, 1940s; First Love; Coming of Age; Dating; Family; Gentle Read

## Freedman, Benedict (1919–)

*Mrs. Mike* (USA: 1947). Berkley Books 2002 (paper) 320pp. 0425183238 **J**

Katherine Mary O'Fallon is a fiery, auburn-haired, sixteen-year-old Irish American girl from Boston who goes north for her health. While staying at her uncle's ranch (a two-day ride outside of Calgary), she meets a Canadian Mountie, the heroic Sergeant Mike—instant attraction! Kathy and Mike marry and travel even farther into the Northern Canadian wilderness to set up house and begin their lives together. Joy—babies, good friends, the beauty of the wilderness—and hardship—devastating forest fires, swarms of mosquitoes, sickness—come quickly one after another, and their love is tested.

This is one of the few romantic novels that puts the romance in the context of marriage. Kathy becomes Mrs. Mike very early in the book, and her love affair with her husband is played out in the dramatically beautiful and constantly challenging frozen Canadian north.

**Film/Video/DVD:** A 1949 film with Dick Powell and Evelyn Keyes very loosely follows the book; not highly recommended.

**Similar Reads:** *The Search for Joyful* tells the story of Kathy Flannigan's adopted daughter, and *Kathy Little Bird* follows Mrs. Mike's Grandaughter.

**Subjects:** Canada, early 1900s; Marriage; Family; Strong Heroine; Gentle Read

## Jackson, Helen Hunt (1830–1885)

*Ramona* (USA: 1884). Signet 2002 (paper) 376pp. 0451528425; Modern Library 2005 (paper) 416pp. 0812973518 **J**

Old California is the setting for this romance between the son of a wealthy landowning family and Ramona, the Native American girl who is patience, grace, and beauty personified.

Considered an ethical novel along the lines of *Uncle Tom's Cabin,* Jackson hoped her novel would bring awareness to the situation of Native Americans dispossessed of their lands.

**Film/Video/DVD:** D. W. Griffith made the first film version of this in 1910. There is also a 1936 film with Loretta Young and Don Ameche.

**Subjects:** California; Native Americans; Missions; Priests

## Marshall, Catherine (1914–1983)

*Christy* (USA: 1967). **J**

*See* the entry in Chapter 9, "Inspirational Fiction."

## Mishima, Yukio (1925–1970)

*The Sound of Waves* (Japan: 1954). Vintage 1994 (paper) 192pp. 0679752684 **S Q**

The small fishing village on an island off the coast of Japan is the setting for the story of Hatsue and Shinji, two hardworking, honorable young people who unexpectedly discover that they are in love. Modest and respectful Hatsue has returned to her island home after being raised in another town. She is the daughter of the wealthiest man in the village. Silent, diligent Shinji has spent his entire life on the island. He lives with his widowed mother and younger brother and works on a fishing boat. When they meet, it is love at first sight, but the gossipy neighbors on their small island home intrude. Will the couple overcome gossip, jealousy, tradition, and objections to fulfill their love?

A gentle, lyrical story that is uncharacteristic of Mishima's body of work. The unique island setting and Japanese cultural context make this an interesting book for adventurous readers. The love story of Shinji and Hatsue is chaste, but their story is filled with undeniable sexual tension.

**Similar Reads:** Other budding relationships can be found in *Seventeenth Summer, Fifteen, Pride and Prejudice,* and *A Girl of the Limberlost.*

**Subjects:** Japan; Family; First Love; Small Town; Island Living; Diving

## Mitchell, Margaret (1900–1949)

🌶 *Gone with the Wind* (**USA: 1936**). Scribner 1936 (hardcover) 1048pp. 068483068X; Warner Books 1993 (paper) 1024 pp. 0446365386 **J**

The antebellum South, the Civil War, and Reconstruction, all from the South's point of view. *GWTW* is a large, expansive novel that paints a panoramic picture of the culture of the South and the effects of the Civil War. As the world changes around her, heroine Scarlett O'Hara evolves from a spoiled and pampered Southern belle to a hardheaded businesswoman. She is willful, manipulative, and determined to survive, and she captures readers' imaginations the way few heroines do.

The blockbuster best seller of 1936, *GWTW* was one of the most beloved books of the twentieth century. It was Margaret Mitchell's first novel, and the only one she ever wrote.

**Audio:** Recorded Books cassette 0788749765. Read by Linda Stephens (50 hours long!).

**Film/Video/DVD:** *Gone with the Wind* (1939) was one of the highest moneymakers ever; it swept the 1939 Academy Awards and is a classic film.

**Similar Reads:** Other bold heroines who will stop at nothing to get their way can be found in *Forever Amber* by Kathleen Winsor and *Vanity Fair* by Thackeray. For more Civil War sagas, try *North and South* by John Jakes or Margaret Walker's *Jubilee*. Another sprawling historical novel, this one set in Australia, is *The Thorn Birds* by Colleen McCullough. A sequel to *GWTW* was written by Alexandra Ripley in 1991 called *Scarlett*. It is not as highly regarded as the original.

**Subjects:** Georgia; Atlanta; Civil War; Reconstruction; Antebellum South; Plantation Life; Family; Strong Heroine; Pulitzer Prize 1937

## Seton, Anya (1904–1990)

*Katherine* (**England: 1954**). Chicago Review Press 2004 (paper) 512pp. 155652532x **S**

Medieval England comes alive through this story of beautiful Katherine Swynford and her romance with John of Gaunt, the duke of Lancaster. Convent-bred Katherine arrives at King Edward the Third's court and becomes the object of obsession for the boorish knight Hugh Swynford. Given no alternative to this advantageous match, Katherine marries Hugh but loves the duke. As history unfolds around them, Katherine and her duke come together and part many times.

Still in print after fifty years, this novel has the elements of both classic romance and excellent historical fiction—a strong heroine, a tested relationship, a powerful sense of history and setting. *Katherine* is populated with fascinating historical figures—Chaucer, Froissart, Julian of Norwich, Wat Tyler, Henry of Bolingbroke—and is full of medieval events—jousting, banquets, the plague, the Peasants Revolt of 1381, pilgrimage.

**Similar Reads:** For another historical romance set in England, try *Forever Amber* by Kathleen Winsor. Other works by Seton include *Dragonwyck* and *That Winthrop Woman*. Seton was a master at atmosphere, setting, and historical accuracy. Interested readers may be tempted to read Chaucer's *Canterbury Tales* or Shakespeare's historical plays, especially *Richard the Second* or *Henry the Fifth;* both kings are characters in *Katherine*.

**Subjects:** Medieval England; London; Royalty; Knights; Strong Heroine; John of Gaunt; Edward the Third; Chaucer

## Speare, Elizabeth George (1908–1994)

🏅 *The Witch of Blackbird Pond* **(USA: 1958).** Yearling Newbery (paper) 249pp. 0440495962 **J Teen Q**

After the death of her grandfather, vibrant Kit leaves her sunny tropical home in the West Indies to go live with her aunt's family in chilly, Puritan New England. Although she works hard to contribute to her new family and fit into the stark Puritan surroundings, Kit is a free spirit living in a place where repression and suspicion are the norm. When she befriends Hannah Tupper, considered to be the town witch, and teaches the downtrodden little girl Prudence to read, trouble follows.

**Audio:** Listening Library cassette 0807207489. Read by Mary Beth Hurt.

**Film/Video/DVD:** No film version has been made—and why not?

**Similar Reads:** Explore the witch hunts of early New England with Ann Rinaldi's *A Break with Charity*. Older YAs may want to read Arthur Miller's famous play *The Crucible* or read works by Hawthorne.

**Subjects:** Connecticut, 1687; New England; Puritans; Witch Hunt; Family; Orphans; Strong Heroine; Newbery Medal 1959

## Stratton Porter, Gene (1863–1924)

*A Girl of the Limberlost* **(USA: 1909).** Indiana University Press 1984 (paper) 479pp. 0253203317 **J**

Elnora Comstock is one spunky girl. She is determined to have an education despite a lack of money and a mother that thwarts her every step of the way. To make the money she needs for school, she turns to the world she knows best—the swamp of the Limberlost in northeastern Indiana. There she earns money by collecting moths to sell as specimens. With the help of friends, both longtime and new, she makes her way in the world.

This is a long, leisurely story that espouses "old-fashioned" virtues such as honesty, loyalty, hard work, generosity, and self-reliance. Elnora's mother is one of the meanest moms in literature, and that makes her transformation and Elnora's triumphs even sweeter.

**Audio:** Recorded Books cassette 0788751069. Read by Christina Moore.

**Film/Video/DVD:** The 1990 Wonderworks production is not a very complete adaptation.

**Similar Reads:** *Freckles* from 1904 is Stratton Porter's prequel to this novel. Other memorable girl heroines: Jo in *Little Women*; Anne in *Anne of Green Gables*; and Francie in *A Tree Grows in Brooklyn*.

**Subjects:** Indiana; Nature; Education; Family; Mothers and Daughters; Secrets; Coming of Age; Strong Heroine; Gentle Read

## Webster, Jean (1876–1916)

*Daddy Long Legs* **(USA, 1912).** Puffin Classics 1995 (paper) 192pp. 0140374558 <u>M</u> Q

Growing up in an orphanage does not give a girl many advantages in life. But what if an unknown benefactor decides to send you to college with a liberal allowance and a new wardrobe? For Jerusha Abbott, this dream becomes a reality. But there is one stipulation: she must write to her benefactor every month to report her progress. There is also a mystery. Jerusha does not know who her benefactor is! She knows he is a trustee of the orphanage, she thinks she saw his shadow once, and it was so tall with such long arms and legs that she thought he looked like a spider, a Daddy Long Legs! Jerusha becomes Judy at college, and her story unfolds in the letters she writes to her Daddy Long Legs. She matures from insecure orphanage escapee to absorbed college girl to confident young woman and published author. Judy illustrates her letters with funny line drawings, and peppers them with good sense and much humor.

**Audio:** Recorded Books cassette 0788742434; CD 0788747363. Read by Kate Forbes.

**Film/Video/DVD:** *Daddy Long Legs* (1955), a musical, takes liberties but is delightful with Fred Astaire and Leslie Caron as a French orphan sent by a benefactor to an American college.

**Similar Reads:** A sort of sequel by Webster called *Dear Enemy* follows Judy's college roommate Sallie McBride when she goes to run Judy's old home, the John Grier orphanage. Also written as letters with little drawings, it is a humorous and charming read. Another beloved orphan is *Anne of Green Gables*.

**Subjects:** New England, Early 1900s; Orphans; College; Strong Heroine; Coming of Age; Humor; Gentle Read

## Winsor, Kathleen (1919–2003)

*Forever Amber* **(USA: 1944).** Chicago Review Press 2000 (paper) 976pp. 1556524048 <u>S</u>

Amber St. Clare is to England's Restoration what Scarlett O'Hara is to the American Civil War. Beautiful, willful, cunning, and ambitious Amber will survive no matter what it takes. We first meet Amber in a small English village, on the day a troupe of Cavaliers ride through. Amber is immediately smitten with Bruce, Lord Carlton. After a passionate afternoon together, she convinces him to take her along to London—and she never looks back. Follow Amber as she deftly navigates poverty, prison, poison, plague, the London fire, an affair with the king, gossip at court, and several marriages, all the while yearning for her one true love, Bruce, the father of most of her children but the man who refuses to marry her. Along the way, she meets many famous figures from Restoration London: actress Nell Gwynn, King Charles II, his glittering courtiers, and famous lovers. This book is a page-turner, full of passion and accurate historical detail.

This novel was an absolute scandal when published in 1944, so of course it was a best seller, too! Recently reissued with an introduction by romance genre master Barbara Taylor Bradford, it's still a little on the racy side. It's one of those big sprawling books a reader can get lost in.

> **Film/Video/DVD:** *Forever Amber* (1947) is a costume epic with Linda Darnell and Cornel Wilde that catches the spirit of the book.

> **Similar Reads:** Although readers demanded one, Winsor wrote no sequel. Other sprawling historical romances to try are Mitchell's *Gone with the Wind,* McCullough's *The Thorn Birds,* or Seton's Katherine.

> **Subjects:** London; England, 1600s; Restoration; Puritans; Cavaliers; Relationships; Plague; London Fire; Strong Heroine

## Wister, Owen (1860–1938)

*The Virginian* (USA: 1902). **J**
> *See* the entry in Chapter 2, "Historical Fiction," under Westerns.

# Regency Romance

Stories set in England in the early 1800s (1811–1820) during the reign of the Prince Regent. Although she didn't know it at the time, Jane Austen was establishing a romance subgenre with her six novels about manners, class, society, and marriage. Georgette Heyer, Marion Chesney, and Barbara Cartland have carried on the Regency tradition.

## Austen, Jane (1775–1817)

*Emma* (England: 1816). Bantam 1984 (paper) 432pp. 0553212737 **J**
> Beautiful, wealthy Emma Woodhouse can't help meddling in the affairs of other people. She sees herself as a capable matchmaker, but her endeavors in matters of the heart only lead to complications, misunderstandings, and pain. Emma convinces her friend, Harriet Smith (a girl with no social standing), to aspire to marry the eligible clergyman Mr. Elton (who really loves Emma) and reject the hardworking farmer, Robert Martin (a man more suited to Harriet's station in life), all the while defending her actions against the criticisms of her old friend Mr. Knightly (guess who he loves).

> Jane Austen does here what Jane Austen does best—precise observations of the foibles of humankind, graceful turns of phrase, depictions of a society impressed with appearance, and a young heroine learning about life and herself through her interactions with those around her. Happy endings abound in this elegant and wickedly witty novel of manners and society.

**Audio:** Recorded Books, cassette 1556901658; CD 1402540408. Read by Victoria Morgan.

**Film/Video/DVD:** *Emma* (1996) is a very witty film with Gwyneth Paltrow. The movie *Clueless* (1995) with Alicia Silverstone is a rendition of *Emma* set in 1990s Beverly Hills.

**Similar Reads:** Austen's other classics are *Sense and Sensibility, Pride and Prejudice, Mansfield Park, Northanger Abbey,* and *Persuasion.*

**Subjects:** England, early 1800s; Relationships; Marriage; Family; Manners; Strong Heroine; Humor; Gentle Read

*Pride and Prejudice* **(England: 1813).** Bantam 1983 (paper) 352pp. 0553213105 **J**

Her mother is a trial and her younger sisters a bother, but Elizabeth Bennet is lively, pretty, and very smart. When the proud, rich, handsome, and haughty Mr. Darcy comes to town, Elizabeth meets her match.

From the drawing room to the ballroom, from the card table to the tea table, Jane Austen depicts a small world where manners count for everything and a girl's best hope is to marry well. *Pride and Prejudice* is one of the most famous comic novels of all time, and Elizabeth Bennet one of literature's most endearing and enduring heroines.

**Audio:** Recorded Books 1980 cassette 155690424X; CD 0788749145. Read by Flo Gibson.

**Film/Video/DVD:** A 1940 MGM film has outrageously inaccurate costumes, but Laurence Olivier is a definitive Darcy and Greer Garson a lively Elizabeth. A&E's 1995 six-hour television production with Colin Firth and Jennifer Ehle is an excellent adaptation. The version released in 2005 with Kiera Knightley will appeal to today's teens. There was a rage in the filmmaking industry for Jane Austen in the mid-1990s *Emma, Sense and Sensibility, Mansfield Park,* and *Persuasion* were all filmed in creditable adaptations.

**New Media:** www.pemberley.com is a Web site devoted to Austen, with historical information, pictures, discussion, and the full text of each novel.

**Similar Reads:** Austen's writing can be a challenge to modern readers, but fans will want to read all six novels. *Sense and Sensibility* is an excellent next choice. A nice nonfiction companion to Austen is *What Jane Austen Ate and Charles Dickens Knew: From Fox Hunting to Whist—The Facts of Daily Life in Nineteenth Century England* by Daniel Pool. Fay Weldon's *Letters to Alice on First Reading Jane Austen* may also contribute to a reader's enjoyment of Austen.

**Subjects:** England, 1811; Relationships; Family; Manners; Sisters; Mothers and Daughters; Marriage; Strong Heroine; Humor; Gentle Read

### Heyer, Georgette (1902–1974)

*The Grand Sophy* **(England: 1950).** Harlequin 2003 (paper) 416pp. 0373835485 **J**

Sophia Stanton-Lacy is an unlikely Regency heroine, tall, forthright, capable—Sophy is definitely not demure. She doesn't even appear in this novel until the third chapter—and then she enters in a flamboyant coach with an entourage of servants, a dog, a parrot, and a monkey! But like other Regency girls, eligible men and advantageous marriages (preferably with love) are on her mind.

Heyer knew the period she writes about. Her mastery of historical detail, period language, and witty dialogue is never in doubt. Readers not yet ready for Austen may enjoy Heyer, and readers who have read all of Austen may also like to know Heyer!

**Similar Reads:** Try *Powder and Patch* also by Heyer.

**Subjects:** England; Relationships; Manners; Family; Strong Heroine; Gentle Read

# Chapter 9

## Inspirational Fiction

Readers choose inspirational stories to feel uplifted and to be instructed in and encouraged toward a better way of living. While Christian fiction predominates classics that express faith from a Protestant perspective, Catholic, Quaker, and Buddhist worldviews are also included here. In general, these books contain no sex or profanity and limited violence.

## Religious Scriptures

The sacred works of many religions make beautiful, enlightening, and culturally broadening reading for seekers wanting to deepen their own faith and explore the beliefs of others. These works are listed by title.

**The Bhagavad Gita (India: 500 B.C.).** Bantam 1986 (paper) 176pp. 0553213652 <u>S</u>

The *Bhagavad Gita* is a philosophical poem in the form of a dialogue between the warrior Arjuna and his charioteer, who is the god Krishna in disguise. Preparing for battle against his own kinsmen, Arjuna questions the meaning of existence. He is guided through an exploration of ideas by the Hindu god Krishna.

The *Bhagavad Gita* is contained in the national epic of India, *The Mahabharata*, one of the longest literary works in existence. Often referred to as just the *Gita* this is a good starting point for readers interested in the philosophy of the east. It has influenced many sages throughout history, including Thoreau and Gandhi.

> **Film/Video/DVD:** *The Mahabarata* (1989) is a miniseries (five hours long) that is hard to find, directed by Peter Brook with a huge international cast.

> **Similar Reads:** *Ramayana* is the other great Indian epic; readers interested in Eastern philosophies will also want to read *Siddhartha* by Hesse.

**Subjects:** India; Dharma; Hinduism; Krishna; Arjuna; Warriors; Caste; Conduct of Life

**The Bible.** Signet (paper, *The Bible's Greatest Stories* translated by Paul Roche) 512pp. 0451528212 **M**

Whether you turn to the Bible for religious inspiration or literary exploration, it is worthwhile to know the characters and stories that are found there. The Bible has served as the backdrop and inspiration for Western literature for more than two thousand years. *Bible,* in its most literary translation, simply means "book," and you can read the Bible as a compendium of ancient stories—histories, myths, family sagas, love stories, parables, poetry, and prophesy. The King James Version is considered one of the most beautiful and poetically rendered translations in existence, and serious students of world literature will want to be acquainted with it. Although other, perhaps more accurate translations exist, the King James has influenced the prose of many writers throughout history. Any collection of Bible stories can give readers the basics, but the Signet edition listed above is comprehensive and affordable.

**Audio:** Available from Recorded Books in many volumes.

**Film/Video/DVD:** The stories in the Bible have been the basis for many movies: *The Greatest Story Ever Told* (1965), *The Ten Commandments* (1956), *Samson and Delilah* (1949), the controversial *The Passion of the Christ* (2004), the Monty Python spoof *The Life of Brian* (1979); and musicals such as *Jesus Christ Superstar, Godspell,* and *Joseph and the Amazing Technicolor Dream Coat.*

**Similar Reads:** The religious writings and mythologies of other cultures also provide readers with a good literary base, and the stories are terrific: *Bulfinch's Mythology*, *Popol Vuh*, *The Bhagavad Gita*, and *The Norse Myths.*

**Subjects:** God; Christianity; Old Testament; New Testament; Conduct of Life

**The Koran (Arabia: A.D. 650).** Penguin 2004 (paper) 464pp. 0140449205 **J**

Followers of the Muslim religion believe that the Koran is the Word of God as revealed to the prophet Muhammad who lived in what is now Saudi Arabia between A.D. 570 and 632. Originally written in Arabic, the Koran is the holiest book for practitioners of Islam. It prescribes many aspects of the Muslim way of life still lived in much of the Arab world. Many personalities found in the Christian Bible and Jewish Torah are found in the Koran as well, including Adam, Noah, Moses, and Jesus, among others. It is also called Qur'an.

**Subjects:** Islam; Muslim life; Muhammad; Conduct of Life

*Tao Te Ching* **(China: 300 B.C.).** Penguin 1985 (paper) 131pp. 014044131x **S**

Also called the *Dao De Jing.* Attributed to a sixth-century B.C. Chinese sage known as Lao Tzu, the real authorship of the Tao is unknown. Comprising eighty-one very short chapters, the Tao is a collection of wise and enigmatic sayings that form the basis of Taoist philosophy and religion.

Tao can be translated as "the Way." It is an idea that, according to Taoists, permeates all of existence. The value of nature, of nonactivity, of "going with the flow," and being in harmony with reality are some of the lessons the Tao expresses in its perplexing yet poetic chapters.

> **Audio:** Recorded Books 1572703083. Read by Ralph Lowenstein.
>
> **Similar Reads:** See *The Analects* by Confucius and *The I Ching*.
>
> **Subjects:** China; Tao; Taoism; Ethics; Conduct of Life

# Early Christianity

Several famous epic historical novels depict the world at the time of Christ. These novels describe the Roman Empire in the early days of Christianity and often show faith triumphing over corrupt worldly politics. These books contain many of the elements that readers of historical fiction seek—a large canvas, diverse characters, a hero undergoing a personal crisis, and an absorbing, detailed depiction of life in a distant time and place

## Caldwell, Taylor (1900–1985)

*Dear and Glorious Physician* (USA: 1959). Out of print. <u>S</u>

> The life story of the Greek physician Luke is recounted in this imaginative historical novel. Luke meets Christ's mother Mary and becomes one of Christ's disciples.

> Caldwell was a prolific writer of big historical novels. Many of her books were best sellers. In addition to biblical histories, she also wrote lengthy family sagas about wealth and power, such as *The Captains and the Kings* (1972).
>
> > **Similar Reads:** *Great Lion of God* is Caldwell's account of St. Paul and the early Christian church.
> >
> > **Subjects:** Ancient Rome; Roman Empire; Historical Fiction; Gospel; Luke the Evangelist; Virgin Mary

## Douglas, Lloyd (1877–1951)

*The Robe* (USA: 1942). Mariner Books 1999 (paper) 520pp. 0395957753 <u>S</u>

> Young Centurion Marcellus Gallio is assigned to crucify Jesus, a job he is not eager to perform but an order he must obey. To pass the time until the crucified man dies, Marcellus plays in a game of dice with the other soldiers and wins Jesus' robe. The effect the garment has on Marcellus changes the course of his life.

> > **Audio:** Blackstone Audio cassette 0786123281. Read by Stuart Langston.
> >
> > **Film/Video/DVD:** The 1953 adaptation with Richard Burton and Deborah Kerr is famous as the first movie ever filmed in Cinemascope.

> > **Similar Reads**: Douglas also wrote a novel called *The Big Fisherman* about Saint Peter. *I, Claudius*; *The Bronze Bow*; and *The Silver Chalice* by

Thomas Costain are other stories that take the reader back to the ancient world near the time of Christ

**Subjects:** Ancient Rome; Roman Empire; Jesus Christ; Historical Fiction; Crucifixion; Caligula; Faith

## Lagerkvist, Par (1891–1974)

🏹 *Barabbas* **(Sweden, 1950).** Vintage 1989 (paper) 160pp. 067972544X **S**

Barabbas was a murderer and thief condemned to be crucified but released at the last minute so that Jesus Christ could be crucified in his place. The story of how Barabbas deals with the burden of being "the acquitted one" is told in this short and enigmatic, dark and understated novel by the Swedish Nobel Prize winner Par Lagerkvist. Barabbas is depicted as a miserable man, a loner who can never decide if he will put his faith in Jesus Christ or not.

A mature book for readers who like to think about what they read.

**Film/Video/DVD:** *Barabbas* is a 1962 film with Anthony Quinn and a young Jack Palance.

**Similar Reads:** A parallel story with a more traditional narrative style is *The Robe* by Lloyd Douglas.

**Subjects:** Ancient Rome; Jerusalem; Jesus Christ; Roman Empire; Historical Fiction; Mature Read; Nobel Prize 1951

## Sienkiewicz, Henryk (1846–1916)

🏹 *Quo Vadis* **(Poland: 1896).** Hippocrene Books 1997 (paper) 589 pp. 0781805503 **S**

The early years of Christianity within the Roman Empire are gloriously depicted by Polish author Sienkiewicz in this epic that pits pagan and licentious Romans against the poverty and morality of the early Christians.

Sienkiewicz was Poland's greatest novelist, and *Quo Vadis* was an international bestseller. This is the Nobel Prize–winning author's best-remembered work.

**Audio:** Blackstone Audiobooks cassette 078611732x. Read by Frederick Davidson.

**Film/Video/DVD:** *Quo Vadis* was first filmed in 1902; the MGM extravaganza with Robert Taylor and Deborah Kerr was made in 1951.

**Similar Reads:** Consider *Ben Hur* by Lew Wallace; *Spartacus* by Howard Fast; and *The Robe* by Lloyd Douglas.

**Subjects:** Ancient Rome; Faith; Martyrs; Pagans; Nero; Peter; Historical Fiction; Nobel Prize 1905

## Speare, Elizabeth George (1908–1994)

🏹 *Bronze Bow* **(USA: 1961).** Houghton Mifflin 1997 (paper) 256pp. 0395137195 **J Teen Q**

Hot-headed and angry eighteen-year-old Daniel lives in the hills above Palestine with a band of outlaws. Filled with hatred for the occupying Romans who murdered his parents, Daniel longs for the day when they will be driven out of his homeland. Two teachers influence Daniel, the outlaw leader Rosh, who uses force to achieve his ends, and Jesus the Nazarene, who counsels acceptance and love. Can the gentle teachings of this rabbi turn Daniel away from the violence he is so accustomed to? Could it be that love is more powerful than hate?

This exciting story about passion for freedom and the choice between violence and peace is great historical fiction. It has characters you come to care about, a vivid evocation of the harsh landscape of ancient Palestinian deserts and cities, and an exploration of the history and political milieu at the time of Christ.

> **Audio:** Recorded Books cassette 0788753639; CD 1402552335. Read by Pete Bradbury.

> **Similar Reads:** Reminiscent of *Ben Hur;* older readers may want to try Leon Uris's *Exodus* about the founding of modern Israel. Elizabeth George Speare was an accomplished author of YA historical fiction. Her other classics include *Calico Captive, The Witch of Blackbird Pond,* and *The Sign of the Beaver.*

> **Subjects:** Palestine; Roman Empire; Jesus Christ; Faith; Coming of Age; Historical Fiction; Newbery Medal 1962

## Wallace, Lew (1827–1905)

*Ben Hur* **(USA: 1880).** Signet 2003 (paper) 576pp. 0451528743 <u>S</u>

Young Judah Ben Hur is a noble Jew in the ancient Jerusalem of biblical times. Because of an accident, he is accused of the attempted assassination of a Roman official. His property is seized, his mother and sister are imprisoned, and he is sent to be a galley slave on a Roman war ship. His innate nobility and courage serve him well, however, even as a slave, and eventually, his fortunes ever increasing, he turns to the new religion of Christianity.

This is a grand Victorian novel, heavy on description and detail. Apart from a slow start, and some time spent philosophizing, the action is lively, the basic storytelling is exciting, the panorama of ancient Jerusalem is exotic and intriguing, and the battle scenes are vivid. Although some of the plot coincidences may cause today's readers to scoff, this is a book with sympathetic characters and a swift plot that is entertaining and vivid.

> **Film/Video/DVD:** Filmed as one of the biggest silent epics in 1925, the 1959 version with Charlton Heston won eleven Oscars, including Best Picture, Director, Cinematographer, and Best Actor for Heston.

> **Similar Reads:** *Quo Vadis, The Robe,* and *The Silver Chalice* by Thomas Costain all depict early Christianity. Also read *The Bronze Bow* by Elizabeth Speare.

> **Subjects:** Jerusalem; Gladiators; Family; Jesus Christ; Historical Fiction

# Christian Literature

The following are stories that show the world from the perspective of Christianity.

## Bunyan, John (1628–1688)

*Pilgrim's Progress* **(England: 1678).** Oxford University Press 2003 (paper) 368pp. 0192803611 **J**

Stalwart hero Christian travels on an allegorical journey from the Slough of Despond to the Celestial City in this classic work. On his trip he must pass through the Valley of the Shadow of Death; rest at the House Beautiful with the maidens Prudence, Piety, Charity, and Discretion; decline the temptations of Vanity Fair; and be imprisoned by the Giant Despair of Doubting Castle. His companions on the journey on whom he must rely are Faithful, Hopeful, and Evangelist. He must also guard against false friends such as Mr. Worldly-Wiseman and battle the fiend Apollyon, all the while carrying the burden of his sins upon his back.

An imaginative tour de force illustrating the Puritan tradition of nonconformist belief that arose in the sixteenth and seventeenth centuries, Christian is a Protestant Everyman fighting the good fight on the way to salvation. In Bunyan's time, God was certain, Hell was real, and Salvation was an ever-present concern. Bunyan's style is simple and vigorous, stout English prose. Written in two parts, the second part, less immediate and powerful, tells the story of Christian's wife and children who are aided on a similar journey by Mr. Great-heart. A consistent best seller for more than two hundred years, *Pilgrim's Progress* has influenced many other writers. Bunyan didn't start to write until he was jailed for twelve years for Nonconformist religious views and unlicensed preaching (because he was not ordained in the Church of England).

**Audio:** Blackstone Audio cassette 0786112735; CD 0786199318. Read by Robert Whitfield.

**Similar Reads:** Try C. S. Lewis *The Screwtape Letters*.

**Subjects:** Journey; Christian Allegory; Puritans; Religious Persecution; Protestantism; Gentle Read

## Lewis, C. S. (1898–1963)

### Chronicles of Narnia **(England: 1950). M**

*See* the entry in Chapter 4, "Fantasy," in the High Fantasy section.

*The Screwtape Letters* **(England: 1942).** Harper 2001 (paper) 224pp. 0060652934 **J**

Young Wormwood, a new devil, is being instructed by his uncle Screwtape, an assistant to Satan, in how to lure a man away from a life of faith and into temptation. In comic letters, Screwtape explains that many small sins will damn a soul just as effectively as one big sin.

**Audio:** Recorded Books cassette 1574532618. Read by John Cleese.

**Similar Reads:** Read *Pilgrim's Progress* and Lewis's Narnia books.

**Subjects:** Christianity; Satan; Conduct of Life; Repentance; Good and Evil; Satire; Epistolary Novel; Humor

## Marshall, Catherine (1914–1983)

*Christy* (**USA: 1967**). Avon 2006 (paper) 576pp. 0380001411 **J**

After nineteen-year-old Christy Huddleston hears a lecture about the need for teachers in the Appalachian Mountains, she is off for adventure. What begins as a selfish escape from her own predictable future as an upper-middle-class society lady becomes a journey to self-understanding and compassion through her interactions with the proud yet primitive mountain people of Cutter's Gap, her rapport with the forceful Quaker missionary Alice Henderson, and her relationships with two men.

Marshall based this novel on the real-life experiences of her mother. She created a grand story, memorable characters, a strong depiction of place, and a classic book about love and faith. This book could stand with *The Yearling* and *A Tree Grows in Brooklyn* as American coming-of-age classics. (In fact, it might be rediscovered as a classic if the publishers would provide it with a more appealing and inclusive cover.)

**Film/Video/DVD:** *Christy* (1994) was a made-for-TV movie with Kellie Martin and Tyne Daly that became a family classic. It spun off into a TV series.

**Similar Reads:** Marshall's other book about a determined young woman is *Julie*. *Mrs. Mike* is another resolute young woman facing hardship and finding romance. Two stories about teachers in unusual circumstances are *Tisha* by Robert Specht about a young teacher in the Alaska Wilderness of 1927 and Pat Conroy's *The Water Is Wide* the story of a young male teacher's year on an island off the Carolina coast. *Christy* is also reminiscent of *The Yearling* and *The Dollmaker* in its portrayal of rural poverty, hardship, and the endurance of the human spirit.

**Subjects:** Appalachia, 1912; Kentucky; Teachers; Romance; Strong Heroine; Gentle Read

## Stowe, Harriet Beecher (1811–1896)

*Uncle Tom's Cabin* (**USA: 1851**)

*See* entry in Chapter 2, "Historical Literature," in the section on slavery.

# Other Inspirational Stories

These stories have faith and compassion as their core.

## Cather, Willa (1873–1947)

*Death Comes for the Archbishop* (**USA: 1927**). Vintage 1990 (paper) 304pp. 0679728899 **J**

In 1848, French priest Father Latour is sent to be bishop of Santa Fe, the farthest outpost of American Catholicism, neglected by the Church for nearly three hundred years. There he will spend the next forty years living among Mexicans, Native Americans, other missionaries, scoundrels, and settlers, spreading his belief in God, building a Cathedral, and becoming part of the land.

In sincere, unpretentious prose that gives equal weight to human character as to physical landscape, Cather tells about a harsh environment where faith and compassion coexist with brutality and hardship. Although Father Latour (based on the real Bishop Lamy) is the focal character of the story, this novel is a collection of vignettes about the American Southwest, about how humans treat each other, and about the ultimate loneliness of all men.

**Similar Reads:** Cather's other classics that express the influence of landscape on character include *My Antonia; O, Pioneers!; Shadows on the Rock,* set in seventeenth-century Quebec; and *The Song of the Lark,* which has an episode in the cliff dwellings of Arizona.

**Subjects:** New Mexico, mid-1800s; Santa Fe; American Southwest; Catholic Church; Priests; Missionaries; Historical Fiction; Gentle Read

## Craven, Margaret (1901–1980)

*I Heard the Owl Call My Name* (USA: 1967). Laurel 1980 (paper) 160pp. 0440343690 **J Q**

Written in an understated and quiet style, this is a story with a strong sense of setting. A young priest, not knowing he has only a short time to live, is sent by his superiors to live and work among the Kwakiutl tribe in British Columbia. From these people, he learns eternal truths about life and death.

**Film/Video/DVD:** This classic was also a 1973 made-for-TV movie.

**Similar Reads:** *Death Comes for the Archbishop* by Cather is an equally touching story set in the Southwest. *A Light in the Forest* by Conrad Richter addresses the cultural conflict between whites and Native Americans during Colonial days.

**Subjects:** British Columbia; Kwakiutl Tribe; Native Americans; Cultural Conflict; Gentle Read; Missionaries

## Dante (Dante Alighieri) (1265–1321)

*Divine Comedy* (Italy: 1321). New American Library 2003 (paper, John Ciardi translation) 900pp. 0451208633 **S**

Travel through *Inferno,* hell; *Purgatorio,* purgatory; and finally *Paradiso*, heaven, as the poet Virgil leads Dante through these realms on a journey that depicts human suffering and human triumph.

The *Divine Comedy* is both universal and specific. Historical characters from Dante's times populate the poem, and many of the references to them are lost on modern readers. Dante's epic is best read with a study guide.

**Audio:** Recorded Books offers the Robert Pinsky translation, 1419328948. Read by George Guidall.

Similar Reads: Other epics Milton's *Paradise Lost* and Bunyan's *Pilgrim's Progress.*

Subjects: Paradise; Hell; Medieval Literature; Epic and Legend

## Hesse, Hermann (1877–1962)

❦ *Siddhartha* (Germany: 1951). Bantam Classics 1982 (paper) 160pp. 0553208845 S Q

The universal quest for enlightenment and self-knowledge is dramatized in Hesse's quiet, spiritual novel. Siddhartha, son of a wealthy Brahmin, rejects the material comfort his father can provide to search for enlightenment. With his friend Govinda, he follows a band of ascetics who reject all physical desires. There he does not find enlightenment. He meets the Buddha who has achieved Nirvana, but Siddhartha comes to understand that another's enlightenment is not ours. Next he becomes a businessman devoted to making money so he can take the beautiful courtesan, Kamala, as his lover, but even with physical and material wealth, he is spiritually empty. Eventually Siddhartha returns to the river where the peaceful ferryman Vasudeva seems already to have achieved what Siddhartha seeks. Can Siddhartha learn enlightenment from this simple man whose method is to sit and listen to the river?

The tone Hesse uses in this philosophical novel is hypnotic and calming. Hesse's works often include ideas from Eastern philosophy, religion, and psychoanalysis. He is a writer with a deep sympathy for humanity and the themes of self-discovery, the cultural conflict of the artist, and the search for a spiritual center, all of which are explored in many of his works. Hesse influenced American popular culture of the 1960s and 1970s: the Beat poets read Hesse, Timothy Leary was a fan, and the hippies turned to his philosophical books for inspiration.

Similar Reads: Explore *The Bhagavad Gita* for more insights into Hindu thought. Readers ready for a challenge may want to try other novels by Hesse such as *Steppenwolf* or *Demian.*

Subjects: India; Buddha; Buddhism; Hinduism; Enlightenment; Spiritual Quest; Nobel Prize 1946

## Milton, John (1608–1674)

*Paradise Lost* (England: 1667). Signet 2001 (paper, includes *Paradise Regained)* 384pp. 0451527925 S

"To justify the ways of God to men" was Milton's famous purpose for writing *Paradise Lost,* one of the grandest and most majestic epic poems in English. Taking Genesis as his basis, Milton retells the story of the creation, fall, and redemption of humankind beginning not with God or man, but with Satan. Newly banished from Heaven for starting a war, Satan and his second in command, Beelzebub, rally the other "rebel angels" to a council to decide whether to continue the war with heaven or dwell as kings in Hell, for as Satan defiantly asserts, "Better to reign in hell, than to serve in

heaven." The devils decide to stay in Hell and work to corrupt the new race of beings that God is planning, "some new race call'd Man."

To express his grand vision, Milton used vibrant imagery and created new words such as *Pandemonium*—Satan's new temple in Hell, a place of "all demons." This text requires slow and careful reading, with access to a dictionary and a study guide to help decipher classical allusions and arcane syntax (try Spark notes or www.paradiselost.org).

> **Audio:** Naxos Audiobooks Ltd. 1994 cassette 9626345020. Read by cast (slightly abridged). Also Blackstone Audio cassette 0786107340. Read by Frederick Davidson.

> **Similar Reads:** Another epic that takes on the big topics is Dante's *Divine Comedy*. John Bunyan's *Pilgrim's Progress* is a classic allegory of the Christian life.

> **Subjects:** Satan; Good and Evil; Creation; Redemption; God; Angels; Free Will; Christianity

## Werfel, Franz (1890–1945)

*The Song of Bernadette* (USA: 1941). St. Martin's 1989 (paper) 576pp. 0312034296 **J**
Gentle young Bernadette, growing up in poverty in France, is destined to see a miracle. Our Lady, the Virgin Mary, visits her. But who will believe a sickly, uneducated peasant girl?

Franz Werfel, born in Prague, wrote his books in German. He wrote *Song of Bernadette* to pay a debt. Passing through Lourdes on his escape from Nazi Germany, he learned about Bernadette and the miracle there. He vowed he would tell her story to the world when he reached America safely. Werfel was a prolific poet, playwright, and novelist at the forefront of the modernist expressionist movement in Europe in the early nineteen hundreds. *Song of Bernadette* is his best-known work. He is largely forgotten today.

> **Audio:** Blackstone Audiobooks cassette 0786111240. Read by Johanna Ward.

> **Film/Video/DVD:** *Song of Bernadette* (1945) stars Jennifer Jones, who won the Best Actress Oscar for her portrayal of pious Bernadette.

> **Subjects:** France; Lourdes; Catholic Church; Nuns; Visitations; Saints; Virgin Mary; Bernadette of Lourdes

## West, Jessamyn (1902–1984)

*The Friendly Persuasion* (USA: 1945) Harvest Books 2003 (paper) 228pp. 015602909X **J Q**
This collection of gentle stories is about a family of Quakers in Indiana at the time of the Civil War. Jess and Eliza Birdwell are raising their children and living their lives according to the principles of nonviolence set forth in their Quaker religion.

> **Film/Video/DVD:** A charming family film with Gary Cooper and Dorothy McGuire was made in 1956.

**Similar Reads:** *Christy* by Catherine Marshal also depicts a Quaker philosophy espoused by the character Miss Henderson. *Friendly Persuasion* is reminiscent of *Life with Father* or *Cheaper by the Dozen* in its depiction of family situations told in a gentle way.

**Subjects:** Indiana; Quakers; Family; Civil War; Pacifism; Gentle Read

# Chapter 10

## Humor

Light and amusing or serious and profound, a comic novel is distinguished by the response it generates in the reader. Readers who enjoy humorous fiction want to be amused, to feel happy or lighthearted, to follow the exploits of someone who will make them laugh.

Philosophers, linguists, anthropologists, and psychiatrists have tried for generations to explicate the humor impulse in mankind—what is funny, how do we know something is funny? Why do things written hundreds of years ago still strike us as funny? Often humor transcends its time and place. After all humans, their concerns, and their reactions to situations don't change all that much.

Originally, a comedy was any story with a happy ending, no matter how dark the story was. That is why Shakespeare's plays are divided into tragedy and comedy, even though the comedies are often serious with somber overtones (*A Winter's Tale,* for example).

What seems funny to one reader may or may not seem funny to another. There is also a scale of maturity in humor that relates to the age and experience of the reader. Younger readers often prefer physical humor, slapstick, gross-out humor, and very literal humor. As sophistication levels rise, readers often appreciate more subtle forms of humor such as satire, irony, parody, wit and verbal repartee, and funny ideas, not just comical characters or situations.

The main appeal of the genre is sheer entertainment and diversion. We all need a good laugh. Whether it makes you laugh out loud or just smile knowingly, to be considered a comedy, a book just has to be funny.

## Berger, Thomas (1924–)

*Little Big Man* (USA: 1964). Delta 1989 (paper, 25th anniversary ed.) 480pp. 0385298293 <u>S</u>

"Jack Crabbe was either the most neglected hero in the history of this country or a liar of insane proportions." From his nursing-home bed, 111-year-old Jack Crabbe narrates the outrageous and comical story of his life and times as both a white man and a Cheyenne Indian on the American frontier and the only living survivor of the Battle of Little Big Horn.

> **Audio:** Isis Audio 0753108631.

> **Film/Video/DVD:** *Little Big Man* (1970) with Dustin Hoffman was directed by Arthur Penn.

> **Similar Reads:** This book was followed by *The Return of Little Big Man*. *Bugles in the Afternoon* by Ernest Haycox also tells the story of Custer and the Battle of Little Big Horn.

> **Subjects:** American West; Native Americans; General George Armstrong Custer; Little Big Horn; Satire; Cheyenne Indians; Western

## Cervantes, Miguel de (1547–1616)

*Don Quixote* (Spain: 1605). Modern Library 2001 (paper) 1132pp. 037575699X; Signet 2001 (paper) 1050pp. 0451527860 <u>S</u>

Two of the most recognizable and memorable characters of world fiction, the would-be knight Don Quixote and his faithful companion Sancho Panza, travel through the countryside of Baroque Spain tilting at windmills and fighting armies of sheep.

This is a huge book and not so much a novel as a series of hilarious episodes that add up to a life experience. Harold Bloom says you don't read a novel like Don Quixote for the plot but rather to spend time with the characters in their world.

> **Audio:** Recorded Books cassette 1402563787. Read by George Guidall, Edith Grossman translation.

> **Film/Video/DVD:** *Don Quixote* (2000) was made for TV with John Lithgow and Bob Hoskins. The book is also the basis for a Broadway musical called *The Man of La Mancha* (1965) and for a ballet.

> **Subjects:** Spain, 1605; Knights; Chivalry; Mental Illness

## Chaucer, Geoffrey (c. 1343–1400)

*Canterbury Tales* (England: c. 1387–1400). Bantam 1982 (paper) 448pp. 0553210823 <u>S</u>

On a pilgrimage to the shrine of Thomas Becket in Canterbury, twenty characters pass the time while they travel by telling stories: heroic stories, bawdy tales, animal fables, morality tales. But more entertaining than the stories are the people who tell them. Chaucer gave us a cross-section of his own society with his band of pilgrims: the knight, the prioress, the monk, the Wife of Bath, the miller, and others, each a distinct and memorable medieval character.

Eternally dreaded by high school students, *The Canterbury Tales* needs to be appreciated for what it is: a bold celebration of story. Chaucer wrote about common people, as opposed to royalty or saints, and this was an astonishing idea for the time. He also wrote in the vernacular English of his day (as opposed to the more scholarly Latin typically used), and although it is archaic and obtuse to us now, it was the way the people talked at the time.

**Audio:** Recorded Books cassette 0788760904. Read by various narrators.

**Similar Reads:** *The Decameron* by Boccacio written in 1350 is also a cycle of tales told on a journey (to escape plague). *Katherine* by Anya Seton features Chaucer as a minor character.

**New Media:** The URL www.unc.edu/depts/chaucer/index.html will take you to a MetaPage on Chaucer that will refer you to other Web sites such as Harvard's Chaucer page and the Web site for the Chaucer Society.

**Subjects:** Medieval England; 1300; Middle Ages; Journey; Pilgrimage; Medieval Literature

## Dahl, Roald (1916–1990)

*Charlie and the Chocolate Factory* (**England: 1964**). Puffin 1998 (paper, with Quentin Blake's illustrations) 155pp. 0141301155 **M Teen Q**

Charlie Bucket lives a life of poverty and despair. But a chance to visit the marvelous Willy Wonka and his fabulous chocolate factory gives Charlie hope for the future.

Dahl's books are wickedly funny, full of playful language and populated with abominable adults, bratty children, and one virtuous and clever child protagonist who has the reader's sympathy from page one.

**Audio:** Recorded Books cassette 0060510641; CD 0060852801. Read by (Monty Python alum) Eric Idle.

**Film/Video/DVD:** *Willy Wonka and the Chocolate Factory* (1971) cult classic musical with Gene Wilder, remade in 2005 as *Charlie and the Chocolate Factory* with Johnny Depp as Wonka. Both movies are highly recommended.

**New Media:** Dahl's official Web site is www.roalddahl.com.

**Similar Reads:** Readers who love Dahl, LOVE Dahl. Charlie's adventures continue in *Charlie and the Great Glass Elevator. James and the Giant Peach, Matilda,* and *The Witches* will also be big hits with Dahl fans. Dahl's autobiographical work, *Boy,* will also interest fans.

**Subjects:** England; Poverty; Grandparents; Eccentrics; Childhood Classic

## Dennis, Patrick (1921–1976)

*Auntie Mame* (**USA: 1955**). Broadway Books 2001 (paper) 320pp. 0767908198 **J**

When his father drops dead in the steam room of his club, ten-year-old Patrick is sent to live with his maiden aunt in New York, a "fate I wouldn't wish on a

dog" according to his late father. But instead of a staid spinster, Patrick encounters the vibrant and eccentric woman who will teach him how to live. Mame Dennis embraces her newest project—raising her nephew—with all the enthusiasm, exuberance, and madcap energy that distinguishes her life.

A comic classic and best seller in its day, *Auntie Mame* has taught generations of people to relax and enjoy the best the world has to offer.

**Film/Video/DVD:** *Auntie Mame* (1958) with Rosalind Russell was based on the play adapted from Dennis's book. Also a successful Broadway musical, *Mame* (1966) and film musical (1974) with Lucille Ball as Mame.

**Similar Reads:** *Auntie Mame* followed by *Around the World with Auntie Mame*

**Subjects:** New York; Family; Orphans; Aunts

## Fielding, Henry (1707–1754)

*Tom Jones* **(England: 1749).** Oxford University Press 1998 (paper) 968pp. 0192834975 (1707–1754) **S**

Tom Jones is a foundling, a boy of mysterious parentage being raised as a gentleman by the kindly Squire Allworthy. Handsome, generous, and rowdy Tom Jones loves his neighbor Sophia Western, but her father will not allow their relationship to proceed because of Tom's low birth. Tom's predicaments are comic, sophisticated, and sexual, but he's a bad boy with a good heart.

One of the first English novels, this is a spirited story and a very long book. Critics have called the plot an example of architectural perfection where every detail contributes, all the supporting characters play an important role, and every plot line is resolved in the end.

**Film/Video/DVD:** *Tom Jones* (1963) is the Best Picture Oscar winner starring Albert Finney and directed by Tony Richardson.

**Similar Reads:** *Moll Flanders* by Defoe offers similar flavor. Fielding's other picaresque novel is *The Adventures of Joseph Andrews*.

**Subjects:** England; Picaresque; Family; Orphans; Romance

## Gilbreth, Frank (1911–2001) and Ernestine Carey (1908–)

*Cheaper by the Dozen* **(USA: 1948).** Perennial Classics 2002 (paper) 224pp. 006008460X **M Q**

Funny and touching, this is a family classic about the large Gilbreth clan living in the early 1900s. Father is an efficiency expert, and he rules his home and twelve children with organized tyranny.

**Audio:** Recorded Books cassette 0788700073. Read by George Guidall.

**Film/Video/DVD:** The classic film version made in 1950 starred Clifton Webb and Myrna Loy. The 2003 remake with Steve Martin has little relation to the original book, but it's a funny family movie.

**Similar Reads:** The Gilbreths followed *Cheaper by the Dozen* with *Belles on Their Toes*. For other classics about family life, try *Life with Father* by Clarence Day.

*Mama's Bank Account* by Kathryn Forbes is the basis for the play and film called *I Remember Mama.*

**Subjects:** New Jersey; Family; Fathers; Brothers and Sisters; Gentle Read

## Herriot, James (1916–1995)

*All Creatures Great and Small* **(England: 1972).** St. Martin's 1998 (paper) 448pp. 0312965788 **J**

Hard work, love of country life, respect for animals, and tolerance for others fill Herriot's books with warmth and honest emotion. James Herriot was a country veterinarian who had been in practice for more than twenty years when he began writing down the stories that had accumulated throughout his working years. The result was a series of best-selling, semi-autobiographical novels set in the English countryside.

These books are a great recommendation for readers who love animals or are interested in working with animals. Although sad things happen in these stories, their tone is one of gentle humor, perhaps due to the author's accepting nature.

**Audio:** Audio Renaissance 1559277734. Read by Christopher Timothy.

**Film/Video/DVD**: *All Creatures Great and Small* (1974) starred Anthony Hopkins and Simon Ward. The book was also made into a television series for the BBC in the 1970s.

**Similar Reads:** Herriot followed with several other volumes *All Things Bright and Beautiful, All Thing Wise and Wonderful, The Lord God Made Them All,* and *Every Living Thing.*

**Subjects:** England; Veterinarian; Farm Life; Animals; Autobiographical Novel; Gentle Read

## Irving, John (1942–)

*The World According to Garp* **(USA: 1978).** Ballantine Books 1997 (paper) 464pp. 0345418018 **S**

Being raised by his single mother, the redoubtable nurse Jenny Fields who wanted a child but no husband, T. S. Garp comes of age surrounded by eccentric and loving friends. Family, friends, creativity, and death all find a place in Garp's unconventional life as a writer, a father, and the son of a famous woman.

Comic and tragic, darkly hilarious, this is a book best recommended to mature readers. Dickensian in his inclusion of a wide range of eccentric characters, Irving is a grand storyteller who does not shy away from the violence or controversial issues of our times.

**Audio:** Random House Audio cassette 0375403841. Read by Michael Prichard.

**Film/Video/DVD:** A film was made in 1982 with Robin Williams as Garp and Glenn Close as Jenny Fields.

**Similar Reads**: Irving is a prolific writer whose work appeals to teens. Try *Cider House Rules* or *A Prayer for Owen Meany*.

**Subjects:** New England: Family; Nurses; Wrestling; Feminists; Coming of Age; Mature Read

## Kaufman, Bel (1911–)

***Up the Down Staircase*** (USA: 1965). Perennial 1991 (paper) 340pp. 0060973617 <u>S</u>
Naïve new teacher Sylvia Barrett begins her career at Calvin Coolidge High, an inner-city high school in New York where the teachers have to be tougher than the students if they hope to survive. The montage style makes this a lively read.

**Film/Video/DVD:** *Up the Down Staircase* (1967) was directed by Robert Mulligan.

**Similar Reads:** *To Sir, with Love* by E. R. Braithwaite is set in an urban school in London. For a gentler school story set in England, read *Goodbye, Mr. Chips*. For teachers in a rural settings, try *The Water Is Wide* by Pat Conroy or *Christy* by Catherine Marshal.

**Subjects:** New York; School Story; Teachers and Students; High School

## Marquis, Don (1878–1937)

***Archy and Mehitabel*** (USA: 1927). Anchor 1970 (paper) 192pp. 0385094787 **J Q**
A cockroach that can typewrite and a cat with a shady past make comical companions in this inventive and unique book. Archy the cockroach can use a typewriter but only by throwing his entire body on each key, hence no capital letters (he's unable to use the shift key). Mehitabel is an alley cat with a past (she was Cleopatra in a previous incarnation). These two unlikely friends philosophize about life and love with a pervasive sense of melancholy and Weltschmerz.

These stories, more accurately described as free verse poems, began as newspaper columns in 1916 and were collected into three books. Memorable illustrations by comic strip master George Herriman.

**Similar Reads:** Similar humor can be found in *The Pushcart War*.

**New Media:** See www.donmarquis.com.

**Subjects:** New York; Journalists; Talking Animals; Gentle Read

## McKenney, Ruth (1911–1972)

***My Sister Eileen*** (USA: 1938). Out of print. <u>M</u> **Q**
Growing up in the 1920s in Ohio, ambitious Ruth McKenney wants to be a writer; her sister Eileen wants to be an actress. Their misadventures as children include causing a riot at a movie and almost drowning during lifesaving class. Together the two sisters move to New York to fulfill their destinies. They rent a basement apartment that rattles every time a subway train goes by and has a perpetual fungus growing down from the bathroom ceiling.

The sketches were originally published in the *New Yorker*. They are episodic and hilarious, funny stories from a gentler time.

**Film/Video/DVD:** *My Sister Eileen* (1942) stars Rosalind Russell, and a musical film (1955) features Betty Garret and Janet Leigh. The book was also made into a Broadway musical called *Wonderful Town* (1953) with music by Leonard Bernstein and lyrics by Comden and Green.

**Similar Reads:** Other family comedies set in more innocent times are *Cheaper by the Dozen* by Gilbreth and *Life with Father* by Clarence Day.

**Subjects:** Ohio; New York; Sisters; Writers; Gentle Read

## Merrill, Jean (1923–)

*The Pushcart War* **(USA: 1964).** Yearling 1978 (paper) 222pp. 0440471478 <u>M</u> Teen Q

It's the little guys against the big in this comic story that takes place in New York City in 1976. This is the history of the war that erupted between the pushcarts and the trucks when the streets got too crowded for them to coexist. Learn about the bravery of Morris the Florist, the tactics of General Anna, and the accuracy of Harry the Hot Dog as he becomes Harry the Hot Shot in the infamous Pea Shooter Campaign. See the treachery of Big Moe, Louie Livergreen, and The Tiger, the leaders of the trucking industry, as they battle to control the streets of New York. Will peace ever return to the Big Apple? Will the traffic ever flow smoothly again?

Presented with high seriousness this is a mockumentary about a war that never happened. Illustrations add to the gentle humor.

**Audio:** Recorded Books cassette 0788701770. Read by Mark Hammer.

**Similar Reads:** *Animal Farm* by Orwell is another satire that can be read on multiple levels. Also reminiscent of Damon Runyan, try *Guys and Dolls: The Stories of Damon Runyan* (Penguin 1992).

**Subjects:** New York; Traffic; Conflict; Trucks; Peddlers; Gentle Read; Childhood Classic

## Swift, Jonathan (1667–1745)

*Gulliver's Travels* **(England: 1726).** Signet Book 1999 (paper) 311pp. 0451527321 <u>J</u>

Lemuel Gulliver is a restless soul, much in the mold of Robinson Crusoe. In four separate voyages, his ill luck takes him to lands never before visited by Englishmen, including Lilliput, the home of the very tiny people known as Lilliputians; Brobdingnag, inhabited by giants; Laputa, a flying island so full of scholars and deep thinkers that nothing practical exists; and at last to Houyhnhnmland, where horses are the enlightened masters and humans are the beasts of burden. On each of his voyages, Gulliver, the outsider, observes the strange ways and his own reactions to each new place.

A story with many levels, younger readers enjoy the first two voyages, where Gulliver is the giant in the land of Lilliput and miniaturized in Brobdingang. Swift's trademark satire becomes more biting in the final two voyages when politics and the ways of humanity are lambasted.

**Audio:** Blackstone cassette 0786105496. Read by Walter Cowell.

**Film/Video/DVD:** A 1939 animated classic was made to compete with Disney's *Snow White*. *The Three Worlds of Gulliver* (1960) is well known for its famous effects by Ray Harryhausen. *Gulliver's Travels* (1996), a TV movie with Ted Danson and Mary Steenburgen, is very good, although it adds elements not found in the book.

**Subjects:** England; Journey; Lilliputians; Satire

## Thackeray, William (1811–1863)

*Vanity Fair* **(England: 1847).** Modern Library 2001 (paper) 768pp. 0375757260 <u>S</u>

Becky Sharp, one of the least lovable heroines in fiction, connives and manipulates her way into increasingly better social positions in Regency England. With few connections and fewer scruples, Becky is able to manipulate society to her liking. As Becky's fortunes rise, the fortunes of her friend Amelia Sedley, daughter of a wealthy man, fall.

English satire at its finest. Thackeray was a master at depicting the viciousness of genteel society.

**Audio:** Blackstone cassette 0786115572 (Part 1), 0786115580 (Part 2). Read by Frederick Davidson.

**Film/Video/DVD:** *Vanity Fair* (2004) starring Reese Witherspoon has beautiful production values but some egregious character and plot alterations. The 1999 A&E/BBC production, at almost six hours long, is a more accurate adaptation and very entertaining.

**Similar Reads:** For other comic novelists writing in Victorian England, try Charles Dickens and Anthony Trollope. Jane Austen, writing earlier and with less venom than Thackeray, is another English author to try. Two other heroines who will stop at nothing are Scarlett O'Hara in *Gone with the Wind* and Amber St. Claire in *Forever Amber*.

**Subjects:** England; Satire; Waterloo; Society; Regency Period; Napoleonic Wars; Strong Heroine; Victorian Novel

## Trollope, Anthony (1815–1882)

*Barchester Towers* **(England: 1857).** Oxford University Press 1998 (paper) 328pp. 0192834320 <u>S</u>

The small, closed world of the Church of England clergy in Victorian England is a surprisingly vicious place. When there is an opening for a new bishop in the cathedral at Barchester, an epic battle for control plays out over the teacups. The odious Mr. Slope is one of the oiliest creatures in English literature, and the Signora Vesey-Neroni enchants and bewitches all the gentlemen.

Gentler than his contemporaries Dickens and Thackeray, Trollope is a comic master with a quiet touch. Trollope was famously prolific writing more than fifty other novels, as well as travel essays and a renowned autobiography, all the while working full time for the British Post Office (he invented the corner mailboxes).

**Audio:** Audio Partners 1999 cassette 1572701145. Read by Timothy West.

**Film/Video/DVD:** *Barchester Chronicles* (1984) is a *Masterpiece Theatre* production that combines *The Warden* and *Barchester Towers.*

**Similar Reads:** The prequel to *Barchester Towers* is *The Warden.*

**New Media:** www.victorianweb.org, originating from Brown University, is an interesting site for background on Victorian literature, personalities, and issues.

**Subjects:** Victorian England; Clergy; Church of England; Satire; Family; Small Town; Victorian Novel; Gentle Read

## Voltaire (1694–1778)

*Candide* (**France: 1759**). Penguin 1990 (paper) 144pp. 0140440046 <u>S</u> Q

Banished from his home for exchanging a kiss with the baron's daughter, our hero, sweet-natured, naïve Candide, begins his journey through the wide world. Always in his mind are the teachings of his professor, Dr. Pangloss, that we are living in the "best of all possible worlds." But the reality that Candide encounters on his travels makes him question Pangloss's theory. Along the way, Candide is conscripted into the Bulgarian Army, beaten, arrives in Lisbon just as the great earthquake destroys the city, survives an *auto de fe* and an encounter with cannibals, hears stories of cruelty and abuse from all the travelers he meets, is reunited and then separated again from his true love, and gains and loses a fortune. Through it all, Candide must struggle to reconcile reality with the theory that everything happens for the best in this best of all possible worlds.

A comedy with a bitter core, *Candide* is absurd and extreme. Voltaire, perhaps the most well-known writer of his own times, is today remembered mainly for *Candide.*

**Audio:** Recorded Books cassette 1556900864; CD 1419328891. Read by Donal Donnelly.

**Film/Video/DVD:** Basis for a Broadway musical (1956) composed by Leonard Bernstein.

**Similar Reads:** Swift's *Gulliver's Travels*, Rabelais's *Gargantua and Pantagruel, The Adventurous Simplicissimus* by Grimmelshausen, and *Don Quixote* are other early picaresque novels that are bawdy and thought provoking.

**Subjects:** Europe; Optimism; Picaresque

## Wilder, Thornton (1897–1975)

*Theophilus North* (**USA: 1973**). Perennial 2003 (paper) 448pp. 0060088923 <u>S</u>

The wealthy enclave of Newport, Rhode Island, where the super rich spend their summers in elaborate mansions they call "cottages" is where Theophilus North decides to pass his summer. After leaving his job as a teacher, he is looking for an adventure. He finds it in the summer of 1921 among the citizens of Newport. Part con artist, part rebel, part hero, part friend, Theophilus has a talent for solving other people's problems.

This was Wilder's last novel, a product of his late years. It is gentle and episodic, more like a collection of stories than a cohesive novel. Theophilus has an expansive, open-minded approach to life that is very appealing, and the novel is evocative of a certain time, place, and way of life that is gone.

**Film/Video/DVD:** *Mr. North* (1988) with Anthony Edwards is a flawed adaptation of parts of this novel.

**Similar Reads:** *Heaven's My Destination* is another sly comedy by Wilder.

**Subjects:** Newport; Rhode Island; Wealth; Domestic Servants; Gentle Read

## Wodehouse, P. G. (1881–1975)

*The Code of the Woosters* **(England: 1938).** Vintage 1975 (paper) 240pp. 0394720288 <u>S</u> **Q**
Bertie Wooster is a colossal twit; Jeeves is his brilliant and unflappable valet. Bertie gets in to trouble, and Jeeves gets him out. Aunt Dahlia, Gussie Fink-Nottle, Anatole the French chef, Stiffy Byng, "Stinker" Pinker, and a cow-shaped cream pitcher all contribute to the complications in *The Code of the Woosters*. But in the end, everything is put right by "the inimitable Jeeves." The absurd meanderings of Bertie are frothy, humorous nonsense.

Wodehouse was monstrously prolific. Often cited is his famous quote, "I know I was writing stories when I was five. I don't know what I did before that … just loafed, I suppose." Quintessentially British, these stories are great fare for anglophiles, lovers of language, and appreciators of the silly.

**Audio:** BBC Audio (www.bbcshop.com) Full cast radio production.

**Film/Video/DVD:** See the *Jeeves and Wooster* British television series starring Stephen Fry and Hugh Laurie from 1990 to 1993.

**Similar Reads:** Try the *Lucia* books by E. F. Benson; *One Pair of Hands* by Monica Dickens; or the works of Evelyn Waugh. Another well-known master-valet relationship found in Dorothy Sayers's Lord Peter Wimsey novels is Wimsey and his valet Bunter.

**Subjects:** England; London; Butlers; Gentle Read

# Resources

The reader's advisor has many resources for further information about classics, genres, literature in general, reader's advisory services, and teen reading. Following is a sampling of resources that are particularly helpful with both classics and teens.

## YA Reader's Advisory Resources

### Paperback Publishers

Paperbacks are vital to the success of a young adult collection. They should be continually updated and refreshed.

**Bantam** (www.randomhouse.com/bantamdell/classics): a division of Random House, Bantam's books are the comfortable-to-hold mass-market paperbacks with the lovely cover art that signifies "Classic."

**Barnes and Noble Classics** (www.barnesandnoble.com/classics): a new entry into the publishing of classics these are attractive editions with new introductions, biographical material, notes, and bibliographies.

**Dover Thrift Editions** (store.doverpublications.com): these books are appealing because of the low price and the wide range of titles. They are also incredibly thin because the text is crammed into as few pages as possible with barely any white space or paragraph demarcation which limits reading ease. Although a challenge to middle-aged eyes, these editions will appeal to cash-conscious teens wanting to purchase their own copies of classics.

**Harper Perennial Modern Classics** (http://www.harpercollins.com/features/perennial/modern.asp): an imprint of Harper Collins, the Harper Perennial Modern Classics are newly redesigned, large-format paperback editions of significant works of great modern authors. The Web site has reading guides with discussion questions for Harper publications.

**HarperTrophy** (www.harpercollins.com): Harper Collins's paperback imprint for children's books, HarperTrophy includes many Caldecott- and Newbery-winning books; it is the publishing home of Laura Ingalls Wilder, E. B. White, Beverly Cleary, Katherine Paterson, and others.

**Modern Library** (www.randomhouse.com/modernlibrary/pbclassics.html): elegant and oversized, these trade paperbacks are well-produced books that include reset and redesigned text with "generous type size and wide margins to facilitate easy reading and note taking." With "new and commanding introductions by today's leading writers," endnotes, biographical material, and reading guides. Many foreign classics are offered in new translations. Modern Library is the home of the Best 100 Novels of the Twentieth Century List, a controversial list that generated discussion and renewed interest in the classics when first published in 1998 (www.randomhouse .com/modernlibrary/100bestnovels).

**Norton Critical Editions** (www.wwnorton.com/college): definitive editions of the classics that include annotations, scholarly essays that place the books in historical and critical contexts, and bibliographies. Printed on acid free paper, these are often used as college textbooks.

**Oxford World's Classics** (www.oup.co.uk): these are the books with the distinctive red bar across the top. Oxford classics have been publishing for more than one hundred years. The publisher has a list of more than 700 world titles and a very informative Web site.

**Penguin** (www.penguinclassics.com): for years the major source of classics, Penguin has an extensive catalog and very high standards of textual scholarship. Its reading guides Web site (http://us.penguinclassics.com/static/html/readingguides.html) is a terrific resource with reading guides and author information

**Pocket Enriched Classics** (http://www.simonsays.com/content/browse.cfm?sid=33 &pid=499181): published by Simon and Schuster, these attractive mass market paperbacks provide an introduction to the work, biographical information about the author, explanatory notes, a list of other sources (including films) discussion questions, and even pictures. They are affordable with colorful covers and useful supplementary information.

**Signet** (www.signetclassics.com): providing paperback classics since 1948 these, along with Bantam Classics, will make up the bulk of any YA classics collection. Now a division of NAL/Penguin.

**Tor** (www.tor.com): known as a publisher of science fiction and fantasy, Tor presents a version of the classics with surefire young adult appeal. The cover art is slightly lurid, and the taglines are outrageously sensational. Tor makes the classics seem interesting. All editions are complete, unabridged, and printed in a "reader-friendly" type size.

**Yearling Newbery:** Newbery winners from Random House. Also be sure to check out www.randomhouse.com/teens for current young adult titles.

## Hardback Publishers

**Buccaneer Books** (www.buccaneerbooks.com): this publisher is committed to "keeping the best of Fiction and Non-Fiction in print." The house reprints hard-to-find classics with library bindings

**Everyman** (www.randomhouse.com): founded in 1905 and relaunched in 1991 by Alfred A. Knopf, now a division of Random House, these are the elegant little books made with acid-free paper, sewn bindings, and an attached silk ribbon place marker. It also publishes a line of children's classics and a line of contemporary classics. These are very appropriate hardback purchases for library collections.

**Library of America** (www.loa.org): "America's best and most significant writing in durable and authoritative editions" with the dramatic glossy black book jackets.

**Modern Library** (www.randomhouse.com/modernlibrary/backlist): These are distinctive hardbacks with the well-known running torchbearer emblem, printed on acid-free paper since 1927.

**Scribner Classics** (www.scribnerclassics.com): an imprint of Simon & Schuster, these illustrated, large-format hardbacks are excellent for younger readers.

## Online Editions

Because the copyright for many classics has expired, the works have reverted to the public domain, and the text of many classics can now be easily found online. A Google search of any title with the word "etext" or "ebook" (for example, "heart of darkness etext") will result in an array of online choices. Recommended sites include the following.

**Bartelby** (www.bartelby.com): the tagline for this Web site is "Great Books Online." It provides "students, researchers and the intellectually curious with unlimited access to books and information on the web, free of charge."

**Bibliomania** (www.bibliomania.com): text and study guides to more than two thousand classics, including reference books, nonfiction, drama, and more. Users need to register, but access is free.

**Eserver** (http://eserver.org): founded in 1990 and based at Iowa State University, Eserver seeks to provide an alternative publishing niche for works that the market-based publishing industry may ignore. This site has an emphasis on the Humanities and includes many diverse areas of interest such as Gender Studies, Film and Television, and Lectures on Demand.

**Electronic Text Center at the University of Virginia** (http://etext.lib.Virginia.edu): access to more than 2,100 publicly available e-books, as well as journals and access to manuscript collections of George Washington, Thomas Jefferson, and early American fiction.

**Literature.org: The Online Literature Library** (www.literature.org): find the full and unabridged text of many classic novels here.

**The Online Books Page** (http://digital.library.upenn.edu/books/aboutolbp.html): access to 25,000 texts from the well known (*Ulysses* by James Joyce) to the rather obscure (*Umboo the Elephant* by Howard Roger Garis).

**Project Gutenberg** (www.gutenberg.org): the originator of free online ebooks Project Gutenberg was started in 1971 and continues as an industry leader today.

## Downloadable Editions

The burgeoning field of downloadable books is changing by the day. Many of the sites listed above offer downloads of text, and many public libraries now offer free etext downloads. Sites that charge the user a general membership fee are also available—for example, www.booksdownload.org.

## Audio Book Sources

**Blackstone Audiobooks** (www.blackstoneaudio.com): has an inventory of more than 2,500-title with many classics.

**BBC** (www.bbcshop.com): a good source for British videos, audiobooks, and radio shows.

**Books on Tape** (www.booksontape.com): a division of Random House.

**Full Cast Audio** (www.fullcastaudio.com): a newer entry into the audio book field founded by children's author Bruce Colville and friends, this company presents unabridged full-cast readings of family-friendly books aimed mainly at middle graders. Full Cast Audio has an expanding list and plans to add at least one "classic" title every year. Teen books are marked with a "Teen Listening" logo.

**Listening Library** (www.randomhouse.com/audio/listeninglibrary): the division of Random House that offers their list of children's literature and young adult books in audio formats.

**Naxos AudioBooks** (www.naxosaudiobooks.com): this source has a good selection of classics including many poetry selections

**Recorded Books** (www.recordedbooks.com): the largest independent publisher and distributor of audio books—the go-to source for audio books.

**Downloads:** even as this is being written, the world of audio books is changing, and downloadable audio books are becoming more available. Just as the LP gave way to the cassette, and the cassette is giving way to the CD, both of these formats will eventually give way to downloadable books as technology races forward and the public catches up. Many libraries now offer downloadable audio books on their Web sites, the major recorded book companies offer downloads for a fee, and the number of pay sites is increasing (for example, www.audible.com).

## Graphic Novels and Comics

Comics and graphic novels are fun and entertaining and belong in the young adult collection of any library. It can be a short and successful series of steps from a Tarzan comic, to Edgar Rice Burrough's 1912 pulp classic *Tarzan the Apeman,* to Jules Verne's *Mysterious Island,* and on to Ray Bradbury and other writers.

**Dark Horse Comics** (www.darkhorse.com) is the home of Tarzan and Conan.

**Graphic Classics** (www.graphicclassics.com) publishes a series of classic fiction "illustrated by some of the best artists working today in the fields of comics, illustration and fine arts" authors include Mark Twain, Conan Doyle, Robert Louis Stevenson, H. P. Lovecraft, Poe, O. Henry, and others.

**Hodder Education** (http://www.hoddereducation.co.uk/TitlesList.aspx) is a publisher of curriculum materials in the UK publishes a series of graphic novels call Livewire Graphics.

**Puffin Books,** a division of Penguin, is putting out a series of classic novels in graphic formats. Titles include *The Wizard of Oz, Black Beauty, The Call of the Wild, Treasure Island,* and others.

## Books for Reader's Advisory with Teens

Bodart, Joni. *100 World Class Thin Books or What to Read When Your Book Report Is Due Tomorrow*. Libraries Unlimited, 2004
>     Arranged by "thinnest," "thinner," and just plain "thin," Bodart has compiled a list of very good books (not necessarily "classics") that could help readers out of a time crunch.

Bromann, Jennifer. *Booktalking That Works*. Neal-Schuman, 2001.
>     A lively book with practical tips for talking books to the most difficult of audiences—teen readers. Includes many sample booktalks of contemporary YA literature. Bromann advises booktalkers to avoid a hard sell when it comes to the classics: "Classics are the books that make reluctant teen readers hate reading."

Donelson, Kenneth, and Alleen Pace Nilson. *Literature for Today's Young Adults* (7th edition). Allyn and Bacon, 2004.
>     This is the standard textbook for working with young adults and YA literature.

Estell, Doug, with Michele L. Satchwell and Patricia S. Wright. *Reading Lists for College-Bound Students* (3d edition). Arco, 2000.
>     This volume provides recommended reading lists for precollege and first-year students from more than one hundred American colleges and universities with suggestions of how to create your own reading plan and an annotated listing of the "100 most recommended books."

Herald, Diana Tixier. *Teen Genreflecting: A Guide to Reading Interests* (2d edition). Libraries Unlimited, 2003
>     Popular titles for young adult readers sorted into genres and subgenres. Herald is a one of the founders of genre work with YA literature.

Herz, Sarah K., and Donald R. Gallo. *From Hinton to Hamlet: Building Bridges Between Young Adult Literature and the Classics*. Greenwood, 2005.
>     A book to help teachers guide their students from popular and familiar books to the classics.

Jones, Patrick, Patricia Taylor, and Kirsten Edwards. *A Core Collection for Young Adults*. Neal Schuman, 2003
>     More than one thousand titles with high appeal to teen readers are annotated; classics and contemporary titles are intermixed.

Kaywell, Joan F., editor. *Adolescent Literature as a Complement to the Classics* (four volumes). Christopher Gordon, 1992.
>     Intended for the classroom teacher, these accessible books pair young adult literature with classic books as a way to expand teen readers' literary world, for example "Friendships and Tensions in *A Separate Peace* and *Staying Fat for Sarah Byrnes*" by Lynn Alvine and Devon Duffy. Chapters are written by various authors.

Koelling, Holly. *Classics Connections: Turning Teens on to Great Literature*. Libraries Unlimited, 2004

Langemack, Chapple. *Booktalker's Bible: How to Talk about the Books You Love to Any Audience.* Libraries Unlimited, 2003.

> Great advice from a seasoned pro about booktalking to all ages, tips on how to select books, and prepare for the talks physically, emotionally, and intellectually.

Rosow, LaVergne. *Accessing the Classics: Great Reads for Adults, Teens and English Language Learners.* Libraries Unlimited, 2005

Schall, Lucy. *Booktalks and More: Motivating Teens to Read.* Libraries Unlimited, 2003

> Nice examples of booktalks and suggested activities for each book as well as related reads. Not a book that recommends classics but a good addition to the YA reader's advisory arsenal.

Young Adult Library Services Association. *Outstanding Books for the College Bound; Choices for a Generation.* ALA, 1996 and 2006.

> A list compiled every five years by the YALSA committee to recommend the current most important books those planning on college should know.

# General Books about Literature

*Benet's Reader's Encyclopedia* (3d edition). Harper and Row, 1987.

*Contemporary Authors.* Gale. (Ongoing series).

Seymour-Smith, Martin. *Novels and Novelists: A Guide to the World of Fiction.* St. Martin's Press, 1980.

*Something about the Author.* Gale. (Ongoing series).

Thomason, Elizabeth, editor. *Novels for Students.* Gale.

# Reader's Advisory Theory

Glossbrenner, Alfred, and Emily Glossbrenner. *About the Author.* Harcourt, 2000.

Saricks, Joyce. *The Reader's Advisory Guide to Genre Fiction.* ALA, 2001.

Saricks, Joyce, and Nancy Brown. *Reader's Advisory Service in the Public Library.* ALA, 1997.

Shearer. Kenneth D., and Robert Burgin, editors. *The Readers' Advisor's Companion.* Libraries Unlimited, 2001.

> A fine collection of well-documented essays by various authors about all aspects of Reader's Advisory, includes discussions of RA with young adult readers in schools.

# Journals and Magazines

*ALAN Review*: published three times per year by ALAN (see below).

*Booklinks* (http://www.ala.org/BookLinksTemplate.cfm?Section=booklinks): ALA publication of children's literature across the curriculum aimed at "adults interested in connecting children with high-quality books."

*Bookmarks* (www.bookmarksmagazine.com): A lively mass market magazine that provides excellent summaries of reviews for current releases and publishes articles about classic authors and their works.

*English Journal* (www.ncte.org/pubs/journals/ej): published by the National Council of Teachers of English aimed at the classroom.

*Horn Book* (www.hbook.com): A classy and thoughtful journal that has been promoting good books for children and young adults with critical essays and reviews since 1924.

*PW* (www.publishersweekly.com): Formerly called *Publisher's Weekly,* this is the industry source for information about the contemporary publishing, best sellers, upcoming books, and major promotions.

*School Library Journal* (www.schoollibraryjournal.com): focusing on libraries and media centers in schools from the same company that publishes *PW*, *Criticas* (an excellent source for Spanish language material information www.criticasmagazine.com), and *Library Journal.*

*Teen Ink* (www.teenink.com): a monthly print magazine written by teens for teens, in print for seventeen years.

*VOYA* (www.voya.com): published since 1978, this is a bimonthly journal for "librarians, educators and other professionals who work with young adults." Each issue has 150-plus reviews of books for YA readers

# Study Guides

Whether you call them academic aids or tools for cheating, they exist. Used intelligently they can actually expand the experience of literature—almost every guide includes a quiz that can cement a novel in the mind of the reader and offers study questions and essay topics. Teens will always want them. So make peace with them and offer them in your library. Yes, it's always better to read (and actually enjoy) the book itself, but hey, everyone needs a hand now and then, and sometimes the paper is due tomorrow and your patron "just couldn't get into" *Ethan Frome*. Provide them nonjudgmentally as a supplement, not a substitute.

**Sparknotes** (www.sparknotes.com): Barnes and Nobles blue and red entry into the study guide arena.

**Cliff's Notes** (www.cliffsnotes.com): the distinctive slim yellow and black study guides that we all used in high school.

# Web Sites

**Amazon** (www.amazon.com): Amazon is in the business to sell books (and everything else under the sun). But they have created an intellectually valuable Web site by opening it up to the public for reviews of books and reader-compiled booklists and by providing access to the content of the books they sell.

**Book a Minute Classics** (http://rinkworks.com/bookaminute/): offers the briefest plot descriptions imaginable.

**Bookrags** (www.bookrags.com): is a pay site with study guides, ebooks, and essays.

**Cliff's Notes** (www.cliffsnotes.com).

**Genreflecting** (www.genreflecting.com): a database devoted to reader's advisory and genre literature for adults and teens from Libraries Unlimited, the people who bring you the Genreflecting Advisory series of books.

**Guys Read** (www.guysread.com): a lively sight aimed at getting guys to read, this is the brainchild of author Jon Scieszka. Patrick Jones is a contributor.

**Pinkmonkey.com** (www.pinkmonkey.com): read more than four hundred study guides free online or pay for downloads. Good content but lots of ads.

**Reading Group Guides** (www.readinggroupguides.com): an adult site that has reading group guides for more than 1,800 books, many suitable for teens.

**Reading Rants—Out of the Ordinary Teen Booklists** (http://tln.lib.mi.us/~amutch/jen/).

**Sparknotes** (www.sparknotes.com): from Barnes and Noble, free access to study guides for literature and other subjects, this site has an extensive section devoted to test prep, college admission and first year survival.

**Teenreads** (www.teenreads.com): reviews books of interest to young adult readers. Part of The Book Report Network a group of Web sites that focus on book reviews, author profiles, interviews, and other aspects of the literary experience.

## Subscription Databases

These databases are generally purchased by a library and made available to registered patrons. Many times they are available from the state library for citizens whose local libraries cannot afford them. Generally a library card is required for access.

**Literature Resource Center**—online access to the biographical and critical essays from the Gale print reference sets.

**Magill on Literature**—home of the famous Masterplots, from Ebsco.

**Novelist**—a very helpful database from Ebsco for reader's advisory work and genre study. Search by author, title, keyword, or subject; create lists of books; find author read alikes; and have access to essays about books, reading group guides, and articles written by acknowledged experts in the world of reader's advisory work.

**Reader's Advisor Online**—the new readers' advisory tool from Libraries Unlimited, which is based on the guides in the Genreflecting series and has potent functionality for finding read-alikes.

**What Do I Read Next** —a reader's advisory database from Gale with thousands of titles, summaries, book lists, and searching capability by author, title, genre, series and more.

# Genre-Specific Print Sources, Online Sources, and Associations and Awards

## Fantasy

### *Print Sources*

Herald, Diana Trixier. *Fluent in Fantasy.* Libraries Unlimited, 1999.

Lynn, Ruth Nadelman. *Fantasy Literature for Children and Young Adults.* Libraries Unlimited, 2005.

Pringle, David, Editor. *The Ultimate Encyclopedia of Fantasy: The Definitive Illustrated Guide.* Overlook Press, 1999.

### *Online Sources*

**www.pantheon.org** is the home of *Encyclopedia Mythica* an online source for information about mythic characters and stories

**www.legends.dm.net/** has information and access to Web sites about legends from around the world.

## Associations and Awards

The Mythopoeic Society (www.mythsoc.org) gives awards for fantasy novels and works of scholarship on myth and fantasy. The society is a "non-profit international literary and educational organization for the study, discussion, and enjoyment of fantastic and mythic literature, especially the works of J. R. R. Tolkien, C. S. Lewis, and Charles Williams." Membership is open to scholars, writers, and readers. Awards are given for best adult fantasy novel and best children's (YA, children's, or picture book) fantasy novel in the tradition of *The Hobbit* or the Narnia books. Past YA winners have included *The Folk Keeper, Haroun and the Sea of Stories,* and *The Ropemaker.* The society was founded in 1967 and the children's award was started in 1992.

The World Fantasy Conference (www.worldfantasy.org) that meets every year also gives an award for fantasy novel. There is no separate YA award, but past nominees have included such YA-friendly authors as Neil Gaiman, Philip Pullman, and Diana Wynn Jones. They give multiple awards each year including awards for professional contributions to the fantasy field and fantasy art.

There is also a YA divisions for the Locus Award given by the reader's of Locus Magazine, and a new award debuting in 2006, the Andre Norton Award for Young Adult Fiction given by the Science Fiction and Fantasy Writers of America.

## Historical Fiction

### *Print Sources*

Adamson, Linda. *American Historical Fiction: An Annotated Guide to Novels for Adults And Young Adults.* Oryx, 1999.

Burt, Daniel S. *What Historical Novel Do I Read Next.* Gale, 1997.

Coffey, Rosemary K., and Elizabeth Howard. *America as Story: Historical Fiction for Middle and Secondary Grades*. ALA, 1997.

Gordon, Lee, and Cheryl Tanaka. *World Historical Fiction Guide for Young Adults*. Highsmith, 1995.

Johnson, Sara. *Historical Fiction: A Guide to the Genre*. Libraries Unlimited, 2005.

### *Awards*

**The Newbery Award** (http://www.ala.org/ala/alsc/awardsscholarships/literaryawds/ newberymedal/newberymedal.htm) has been given many times to a book with a historical focus, *The Door in the Wall, The Bronze Bow,* and *Sounder* are only three of the many historical fiction novels honored by the Newbery committee over the years.

**Scott O'Dell Award** (www.scottodell.com): Given for a meritorious book written for young people and depicting historical moments in the "New World." O'Dell, a prolific and honored YA author, established the award in 1982 to encourage other authors to focus on historical fiction. He hoped the interest of young readers in their historical past and the events that created the world they live in would be piqued through well-crafted historical fiction.

**Nobel** (www.nobelprize.org): International award for literature given for a distinguished body of work, not a specific title, since 1901. Famous for the Peace Prize, the Nobel committee also gives awards in physics, chemistry, economics, and medicine.

**Pulitzer** (www.pulitzer.org): given annually for journalism, letters, drama, and music. The winning novel should be "distinguished fiction by an American author preferably dealing with American life" An award for fiction has been given since 1918. Many of these titles are entirely appropriate for YA readers, *To Kill a Mockingbird, The Good Earth,* and *Lonesome Dove,* for example.

The Western subgenre has its own awards:

The **Spur Award** given by the Western Writers of America for the best novel with a western setting. Awards are also given for juvenile fiction, screenplays, short stories, and nonfiction (www.westernwriters.org).

The **Willa Award** (www. womenwritingthewest.org) is given at the Women Writing the West conference each year. Awards are given to outstanding adult, children's and young adult, nonfiction, memoir, and poetry which feature women's stories set in the West.

## Horror

### *Print Sources*

Barron, Neil. *Fantasy and Horror: A Critical and Historical Guide to Literature, Illustration, Film, TV, Radio, and the Internet*. Scarecrow Press, 1998.

Burgess, Michael, and Lisa R. Bartle. *Reference Guide to Science Fiction Fantasy and Horror*. Libraries Unlimited, 2002.

Fonseca, Anthony J., and June Michele Pulliam. *Hooked on Horror: A Guide to Reading Interests in Horror Fiction* (2d edition). Libraries Unlimited, 2003.

Fonseca, Anthony J., and June Michele Pulliam. *Read On . . . Horror.* Libraries Unlimited, 2006.

### *Associations and Awards*

The Horror Writer's Association (www.horror.org) gives the **Bram Stoker Award.** The award itself is a creepy haunted house sculpture. Past winners and nominees have included Clive Barker, Stephen King, Anne Rice, Thomas Harris, and Neil Gaiman. The HWA has given an award for a "Work for Young Readers" since 1998, Clive Barker's *Arabat: Days of Magic, Nights of War* and *Oddest Yet* by Steven Burt were tied winners in 2004.

# Inspirational

### *Print Sources*

Mort, John. *Christian Fiction: A Guide to the Genre.* Libraries Unlimited, 2002.

Walter, Barbara. *The Librarian's Guide to Developing Christian Fiction Collections for Young Adults.* Neal Schuman, 2005.

### *Associations and Awards*

**The Christopher Awards** (www.christophers.org) were founded in 1945 and are "rooted in the Judeo-Christian tradition of service to God and humanity" they "embrace people of every nation, religion and age level." The Christopher Award winners "celebrate the humanity of people in a positive way. Award winners encourage audiences to see the better side of human nature and motivate artists and the general public to use their best instincts on behalf of others." Awards are given to adult and young people's books, television shows and movies that "affirming the highest values of the human spirit."

**The Christy Awards** (www.christyawards.com) established in 1999 and named for Catherine Marshal's heroine seek to celebrate novels with a Christian worldview that entertain, educate, challenge and inspire readers. Jan Karon, Janet Oke, and Gilbert Morris are all past winners. No specific YA award is given, though most of the Christy winners would be appropriate recommendations for YA readers.

# Mysteries

### *Print Sources*

Keating, H. R. F. *Crime and Mystery: The 100 Best Books.* Carroll and Graf, 1987.

Niebuhr, Gary Warren. *Make Mine a Mystery: A Reader's Guide to Mystery and Detective Fiction.* Libraries Unlimited, 2003.

### *Online Sources*

**Mystery Net** (www.mysterynet.com) is a site for information about mystery books, online mystery games, and the history of the mystery

### Associations and Awards

The writer's group the Mystery Writer's of America (www.mysterywriters.org) gives out the **Edgar** awards. Named for Edgar Allan Poe, they have been awarded since 1946. An Edgar is also awarded to the year's best Young Adult novel and Best Juvenile novel. Past YA winners and nominees have included Katherine Patterson, Richard Peck, Kin Platt, Phyllis Whitney, Joan Lowery Nixon, and Avi.

The **Agatha Awards** (www.malicedomestic.org) honor the traditional mystery—books best typified by the works of Agatha Christie, mysteries with "no explicit sex, excessive gore, or gratuitous violence . . . usually featuring an amateur detective, they have a confined setting and characters who know one another." Although police procedurals are considered, nothing "hard-boiled" is allowed. In 2001, they began giving an award for Best Children's/Young Adult novel.

# Romance

### Print Sources

Carpan, Carolyn. *Rocked by Romance: A Guide to Teen Romance Fiction*. Libraries Unlimited, 2004.

Kristin Ramsdell. *Romance Fiction: A Guide to the Genre*. Libraries Unlimited, 1999.

### Associations and Awards

The Romance Writers of American give the **RITA** to adult fiction for excellence in the romance genre. The RITA has been awarded since 1982. From 1983 to 1996, a Young Adult award was also given.

# Science Fiction

### Print Sources

Baron, Neil. *Anatomy of Wonder: A Critical Guide to Science Fiction*. Bowker. 1997.

Clute, John, and Peter Nichols. *Encyclopedia of Science Fiction*. St. Martin's, 1995.

D'Ammassa, Don. E*ncyclopedia of Science Fiction*. Facts on File, 2005.

### Associations and Awards

The **Hugo** (http://worldcon.org/hugos.html) is named after Hugo Gernsback (1884–1967), founding editor of *Amazing Stories,* the first magazine devoted to science fiction. The Hugo originated in 1953 and is given to books nominated and chosen by fans. The awards are given each year at the Worldcon, the World Science Fiction Society's World Science Fiction Convention(http://worldcon.org/hugos.html).

**Locus Award** (http://www.locusmag.com/SFAwards/Db/Locus.html): voted by the reader's of *Locus* magazine since 1971.

**Nebula Award** (www.sfwa.org/awards/)—professional writers and critics who are members of Science Fiction and Fantasy Writers of America founded the Nebula Award in 1965.

# Films

## Print Sources

Ebert, Roger. *Roger Ebert's Movie Yearbook.* Andrews McMeel. Updated annually.

Maltin, Leonard. *Leonard Maltin's Classic Movie Guide.* Plume, 2005.

Maltin, Leonard. *Leonard Maltin's Movie Guide.* Signet. Updated annually.

## Online Sources

**Film Education** (www.filmeducation.org): a British site that has very interesting and usable information.

**Internet Movie Database** (www.imdb.com): aka "Earth's Biggest Movie Database," began as a Usenet bulletin board in the 1980s and is now an Amazon.com company. This is an easily searchable database for information about casts and crews, current releases. Also has user boards for critical commentary and film discussion.

**The Story of Movies** (www.storyofmovies.org): this site features an interdisciplinary curriculum designed to teach middle school students the "cultural, historical and artistic significance of film" using such classics as *To Kill a Mockingbird* and *The Day the Earth Stood Still.* Presented by the Film Foundation along with IBM and Turner Classic Movies.

# Young Adult Awards

**Alex Awards** (http://www.ala.org/ala/yalsa/booklistsawards/alexawards/alexawards.htm): Given by the ALA Alex committee to fiction and nonfiction adult works that have appeal for YA readers. The award is named for Margaret Alexander Edwards, a librarian renowned for her pioneering work with young adults at Baltimore's Enoch Pratt Free Library. Her famous book, *The Fair Garden and the Swarm of Bees* (1969), is still a classic.

**Coretta Scott King Award** (http://www.ala.org/ala/emiert/corettascottking bookawards/corettascott.htm): awarded since 1970 to "an African American author and an African American illustrator for an outstandingly inspirational and educational contribution. The books promote understanding and appreciation of the culture of all peoples and their contribution to the realization of the American dream. The Award is further designed to commemorate the life and works of Dr. Martin Luther King Jr. and to honor Mrs. Coretta Scott King for her courage and determination to continue the work for peace and world brotherhood." Past winners have included novels of interest to young adult readers such as *Bud, Not Buddy; Slam; The Land;* and *Miracle's Boys.*

**Margaret A. Edwards Award** (http://www.ala.org/ala/yalsa/booklistsawards/margaretaedwards/margaretedwards.htm): given to an author for lifetime achievement in young adult literature. The award was established in 1988, is given by YALSA, and is sponsored by School Library Journal. Past winners have included M. E. Kerr, Robert Cormier, Judy Blume, Gary Paulsen, and Chris Crutcher, among others.

**Newbery** (http://www.ala.org/ala/alsc/awardsscholarships/literaryawds/newberymedal/newberymedal.htm): Since 1921, this award has been the Academy Award of YA fiction. It is given to a "distinguished: book by an American author written for "children" defined as "persons of ages up to and including 14."

**Michael L. Printz Award** (http://www.ala.org/ala/yalsa/booklistsawards/printzaward/Printz,_Michael_L__Award.htm): First given in 2000, the Printz is intended to complement the Newbery with acknowledgment of excellence in books for older YA readers. Michael Printz was a Kansas school librarian who was active in YALSA and passionate about YA literature and authors.

**Pura Belpre Award** (http://www.ala.org/ala/alsc/awardsscholarships/literaryawds/belpremedal/belprmedal.htm): Presented every two years to a "Latino writer and to a Latino illustrator whose work best portrays, affirms and celebrates the Latino cultural experience" Pura Belpre was a librarian and storyteller in New York, originally from Puerto Rico. The award has been given since 1996. *Esperanza Rising* and *Parrot in the Oven* are two past winners.

## Associations

**YALSA** (www.ala.org/yalsa): the Young Adult Library Service Association, a division of the American Library Association. YALSA is the group behind many YA book awards such as the Alex, the Printz, and the Margaret Edwards. YALSA sponsors Teen Read Week and compiles the *Outstanding Books for the College Bound* list every five years. This is a great clearinghouse for information about young adults and libraries.

**ALAN** (www.alan-ya.org): the Assembly on Literature for Adolescents was founded in 1973 as a special interest group within the NCTE (National Council of Teachers of English; www.ncte.org). It is the "leading society dedicated to the study of Young Adult Literature" membership is open to anyone interested in YA literature. They give the ALAN award every November at their conference to "honor those who have made outstanding contributions to the field of adolescent literature." Past winners have been Walter Dean Myers, Madeleine L'Engle, and Mildred Taylor. They publish the ALAN Review.

## Listservs

**YALSA–BK** (www.ala.org/yalsa): Young adult librarians freely exchange ideas about YA books and service to teens on this active list. To subscribe, send message to listproc@ala.org saying "subscribe YALSA-BK"

## Events

**Banned Book Week** (www.ala.org/ala/oif/bannedbooksweek/bannedbooksweek): Begun in 1982, this event brings awareness to the issues of censorship and intellectual freedom, the guaranteed right we have in America to freely explore all ideas and opinions. This is a great week to do some consciousness-raising among teens and educate all readers about the issue of censorship and the American tradition of Freedom to Read. The weeklong celebration is usually in September and sponsored by the American Library Association. Many schools, libraries, and bookstores hold events or put up displays to commemorate the week.

**Teen Read Week** (www.ala.org/ala/yalsa/teenreading/trw/teenreadweek): a weeklong celebration, usually in October, that encourage teens to explore good books and their libraries. Past themes have been poetry slams, graphic novels, and horror fiction. It is sponsored by YALSA; a visit to its Web site will provide ideas on how to implement the program in your community.

# Banned Books

Books of all kinds get challenged in the United States. Books are challenged because, generally, someone or some group is trying to protect others, often children, from material that is difficult or upsetting in some way. Some of the reasons books get challenged in schools and libraries across the country is that they contain depictions of sexual activity, questionable religious content, disagreeable politics, offensive language, violent action, or the material is not age-appropriate for certain readers. Although challenges occur with some regularity, actually banning of materials and removal from shelves is rare.

No one who works with children and young adults would deny that young readers do need guidance and perhaps protection from situations and ideas they are not yet mature enough to comprehend. Age-appropriateness of material is critical for YA readers both in terms of difficulty of reading material and exposure to ideas. But making a book unavailable to all because of the objections of a few is considered unacceptable in our society. The First Amendment guarantees our access to all ideas and expressions no matter how offensive. In the United States, we have the freedom to read, view, and listen to all ideas and to form our own opinions without government or interest group interference.

The Office of Intellectual Freedom a section of the American Library Association makes it their job to monitor and report on challenges to materials that occur. They offer information and support for dealing with local challenges

Foerstel, Herbert. *Banned in the USA: A Reference Guide to Book Censorship in Schools and Public Libraries*. Greenwood, 1994.

Karolides Nicholas J., Margaret Bald, and Dawn Sova. *100 Banned Books: Censorship Histories of World Literature*. Checkmark Books, 1999.

*Hit List: Frequently Challenged Books for Young Adults*. Prepared by the Intellectual Freedom Committee of the Young Adult Services Association, a division of the American Library Association. ALA, 1996.

# Appendix A:

# Chronology of Titles

## B.C.

*Aeneid*
*Aesop's Fables*
*Bible*
*Gilgamesh*
*Iliad*

*Norse Myths*
*Odyssey*
*Popol Vuh*
*Tao Te Ching*

## A.D.

### 100

*Bhagavad Gita, The*

### 400

*Jataka Tales*

### 600

*Koran*

### 700

*Beowulf*

### 1000

*Song of Roland*

### 1200

*El Cid*
*Nibelungenleid*
*Saga of the Volsungs*

### 1300

*Divine Comedy*
*Sir Gawain and the Green Knight*
*Sundiata*

### 1400

*Arabian Nights*
*Canterbury Tales*
*Le Morte d'Arthur*

### 1600

*Don Quixote*
*Paradise Lost*
*Pilgrim's Progress*
*Tales (Perrault)*

### 1700

*Adventures of Tom Jones, The*
*Baron Munchhausen*
*Candide*
*Gulliver's Travels*
*Journal of the Plague Year*
*Moll Flanders*
*Robinson Crusoe*
*Sorrows of Young Werther*

### 1800

*Adventures of Huckleberry Finn, The*
*Adventures of Sherlock Holmes, The*
*Adventures of Tom Sawyer, The*
*Alice's Adventures in Wonderland*

*Anderson's Fairy Tales*
*Anna Karenina*
*Around the World in Eighty Days*
*Awakening, The*
*Barchester Towers*
*Ben Hur*
*Black Beauty*
*Brother's Karamazov*
*Bulfinch's Mythology*
*Captains Courageous*
*Christmas Carol*
*Collected Stories and Poems (Poe)*
*Count of Monte Cristo*
*Crime and Punishment*
*Daisy Miller*
*David Copperfield*
*Dead Souls*
*Dr. Jekyll and Mr. Hyde*
*Dracula*
*Emma*
*Flatland*
*Frankenstein, or the Modern Prometheus*
*Great Expectations*
*Grimm's Fairy Tales*
*Happy Prince, The*
*House of the Seven Gables, The*
*Hunchback of Notre Dame, The*
*Invisible Man (Wells)*
*Island of Dr. Moreau, The*
*Ivanhoe*
*Jane Eyre*
*Journey to the Center of the Earth*
*Jungle Books*
*Kalevala*
*Kidnapped*
*King Solomon's Mines*
*Last of the Mohicans, The*
*Legend of Sleepy Hollow*
*Little Women*
*Looking Backward*
*Lorna Doone*
*Madam Bovary*
*Man Who Would Be King, The*
*Merry Adventures of Robin Hood, The*
*Middlemarch*
*Miserable, Les*
*Moby Dick*
*Moonstone*
*Murders in the Rue Morgue*
*Norwegian Folktales*
*Oliver Twist*
*Picture of Dorian Gray, The*

*Pinocchio*
*Portrait of a Lady*
*Pride and Prejudice*
*Prince and the Pauper, The*
*Prisoner of Zenda*
*Quo Vadis*
*Ramona*
*Red Badge of Courage*
*Scarlet Letter, The*
*Secret Agent, The*
*Silas Marner*
*Swiss Family Robinson*
*Tale of Two Cities*
*Tess of the D'Urbervilles*
*Three Musketeers*
*Time Machine*
*Tom Brown's School Days*
*Treasure Island*
*Turn of the Screw*
*Twenty Thousand Leagues under the Sea*
*Uncle Tom's Cabin*
*Vanity Fair*
*War and Peace*
*War of the Worlds*
*White Company*
*Wuthering Heights*

# 1900

*1984*
*2001 A Space Odyssey*
*Across Five Aprils*
*Adam of the Road*
*Age of Innocence*
*All Creatures Great and Small*
*All Quiet on the Western Front*
*American Tragedy*
*And Then There Were None*
*Andersonville*
*Animal Farm*
*Anne of Green Gables*
*Annie on My Mind*
*April Morning*
*Archy and Mehitabel*
*Ashenden: or the British Agent*
*Auntie Mame*
*Autobiography of Miss Jane Pittman*
*Awakening Land, The*
*Barabbas*
*Beau Geste*
*Beauty*
*Belgariad, The*

*Bell for Adano*
*Bell Jar, The*
*Betsey Brown*
*Big Sleep, The*
*Black Boy*
*Bless Me Ultima*
*Bless the Beasts and the Children*
*Bluest Eye, The*
*Book of the Dun Cow, The*
*Brave New World*
*Bread Givers*
*Bridge of San Luis Rey*
*Bronze Bow*
*Caddie Woodlawn*
*Caine Mutiny, The*
*Call of the Wild*
*Canticle for Leibowitz, A*
*Carrie*
*Cat Ate My Gymsuit, The*
*Catch 22*
*Catcher in the Rye*
*Cay, The*
*Charlie and the Chocolate Factory*
*Charlotte's Web*
*Cheaper by the Dozen*
*Chocolate War, The*
*Chosen, The*
*Christy*
*Chronicles of Narnia*
*Clockwork Orange*
*Color Purple, The*
*Conan the Barbarian*
*Cruel Sea, The*
*Cry, the Beloved Country*
*Crystal Cave*
*Daddy Long Legs*
*Dark Is Rising Sequence*
*Darkness at Noon*
*Daughter of Time*
*Day No Pigs Would Die*
*Death Comes for the Archbishop*
*Death in the Family, A*
*Dinky Hocker Shoots Smack*
*Do Androids Dream of Electric Sheep*
*Door in the Wall, A*
*Dr. Zhivago*
*Dune*
*Eagle of the Ninth*
*Earthsea Cycle, The*
*East of Eden*
*Education of Little Tree, The*
*Enchantress from the Stars*

*Ender's Game*
*Ethan Frome*
*Exodus*
*Fahrenheit 451*
*Farewell to Arms, A*
*Farewell to Manzanar*
*Fifteen*
*Fighting Ground, The*
*Flowers for Algernon*
*Flowers in the Attic*
*Forever*
*Forever Amber*
*Forgotten Beasts of Eld*
*Forsyte Saga, The*
*Foundation*
*Foundation Trilogy*
*Fountainhead, The*
*Friendly Persuasion*
*Giants in the Earth*
*Girl of the Limberlost, A*
*Go Ask Alice*
*Go Tell it on the Mountain*
*Gone With the Wind*
*Good Earth, The*
*Good Night, Mr. Tom*
*Goodbye, Mr. Chips*
*Grand Sophy, The*
*Grapes of Wrath*
*Great Gatsby*
*Great Santini, The*
*Grendel*
Harper Hall Trilogy
*Haunting of Hill House, The*
*Have Spacesuit Will Travel*
*Heart Is a Lonely Hunter, The*
*Heart of Darkness*
*Hero Ain't Nothing But a Sandwich, A*
*Hero and the Crown*
*High Wind in Jamaica, A*
*Hitchhikers Guide to the Galaxy*
*Hobbit, The*
*Hound of the Baskervilles, The*
*House of Dies Drear, The*
*House of Mirth, The*
*House of Stairs, The*
*House on Mango Street*
*How Green Was My Valley*
*Human Comedy*
*I Am the Cheese*
*I Capture the Castle*
*I Heard the Owl Call my Name*
*I Know What You Did Last Summer*

*I Never Promised You a Rose Garden*
*I, Claudius*
*I, Juan de Pareja*
*I, Robot*
*Illustrated Man*
*In Cold Blood*
*Interstellar Pig*
*Invisible Man (Ellison)*
*Island of the Blue Dolphin*
*Italian Folktales*
*Jacob Have I Loved*
*Johnny Got His Gun*
*Johnny Tremain*
*Jubilee*
*Jungle, The*
*Katherine*
*Killer Angels, The*
*Kim*
*Kindred*
*King Must Die, The*
*King's Fifth*
*Kristin Lavransdater*
*Land That Time Forgot, The*
*Last Unicorn*
*Left Hand of Darkness*
*Light in the Forest*
*Lisa Bright and dark*
*Little Big Man*
*Little Prince, The*
*Lonesome Dove*
*Look Homeward Angel*
*Lord Jim*
*Lord of the Flies, The*
<u>Lord of the Rings Trilogy</u>
*Lost Horizon*
*Lost World*
*Magnificent Ambersons, The*
*Maigret and the Fortuneteller*
*Main Street*
*Maltese Falcon*
*Manchurian Candidate, The*
*Mark of Zorro*
*Martian Chronicles, The*
*Member of the Wedding*
*Metamorphosis*
*Mists of Avalon*
*Mr. and Mrs. Bo Jo Jones*
*Mr. Midshipman Hornblower*
*Mrs. Mike*
*Murder of Roger Ackroyd, The*
*Murder on the Orient Express*
*Mutiny on the Bounty*

*My Antonia*
*My Brother Sam Is Dead*
*My Friend Flicka*
*My Sister Eileen*
*Name of the Rose, The*
*Native Son*
*Nectar in a Sieve*
*Neuromancer*
*Neverending Story*
*Night*
*No Promises in the Wind*
*O, Pioneers*
*Of Human Bondage*
*Of Mice and Men*
*Old Man and the Sea, The*
*Old Yeller*
*On the Beach*
*On the Road*
*Once and Future King, The*
*One Day in the Life of Ivan Denisovich*
*One Flew over the Cuckoo's Nest*
*One Hundred Years of Solitude*
*Ordinary People*
*Outsiders, The*
*Ox Bow Incident*
*Painted Bird*
*Passage to India*
*Pearl, The*
*Peter Pan*
*Phantom of the Opera*
*Phantom Tollbooth*
*Pigman, The*
*Portrait of the Artist as a Young Man*
*Prince of Foxes*
*Princess Bride, The*
*Prydain Chronicles*
*Pushcart War*
*Ragtime*
*Rebecca*
*Red Pony*
*Riddle of the Sands, The*
*Riders of the Purple Sage*
*Rifles for Watie*
*Robe, The*
*Roll of Thunder Hear my Cry*
*Roots*
*Sarah Plain and Tall*
*Scaramouche*
*Scarlet Pimpernel*
*Schindler's List*
*Screwtape Letters*
*Searchers, The*

*Secret Agent, The*
*Secret Garden*
*Separate Peace, A*
*Seventeenth Summer*
*Shane*
*Shining, The*
*Siddhartha*
*Sister Carrie*
*Slaughterhouse Five*
*Slave Dancer*
*Something Wicked This Way Comes*
*Song of Bernadette*
*Sons and Lovers*
*Sophie's Choice*
*Sound of Waves*
*Sounder*
*Spell for Chameleon*
*Spoon River Anthology*
*Stars My Destination, The*
*Starship Troopers*
*Story of Doctor Doolittle*
*Stranger in a Strange Land*
*Stranger, The*
*Strangers on a Train*
*Street, The*
*Strong Poison*
*Summer of My German Soldier, The*
*Tailchaser's Song*
*Tarzan the Apeman*
*Theophilus North*

*Things Fall Apart*
*Thirty-Nine Steps*
*Time and Again*
*Tin Drum*
*To Kill a Mockingbird*
*Tree Grows in Brooklyn, A*
*Trial, The*
*Tripods Trilogy*
*True Grit*
*Tuck Everlasting*
*Up a Road Slowly*
*Up the Down Staircase*
*Upstairs Room*
*USA Trilogy*
*Virginian, The*
*Watership Down*
*We Have Always Lived in the Castle*
*When the Legends Die*
*Where the Lilies Bloom*
*Where the Red Fern Grows*
*White Fang*
*Wind in the Willows*
*Winnie the Pooh*
*Witch of Blackbird Pond, The*
*Witch World*
*Wonderful Wizard of Oz, The*
*World According to Garp, The*
*Worm of Ouroboros, The*
*Wrinkle in Time, A*
*Yearling, The*
*Z Is for Zacharia*

# Appendix B:

# Titles by Reading Level

## M (Grades 5–7, Ages 10–12)

Aesop, *Aesop's Fables* (Fantasy, Animal Fantasy and Fable)

Alcott, Louisa May *Little Women* (Life Issues, Family)

Alexander, Lloyd, Prydain Chronicles (Fantasy, High Fantasy)

Andersen, Hans Christian, *Andersen's Fairy Tales* (Fantasy, Fairy Tales)

Armstrong, William, *Sounder* (Coming of Age)

Asbjornsen, Peter, *Norwegian Folktales* (Fantasy, Folk Tales)

Avi, *Fighting Ground, The* (Historical, American Revolution)

Babbitt, Natalie, *Tuck Everlasting* (Fantasy)

Barrie, J. M., *Peter Pan* (Fantasy)

Baum, Frank, *Wizard of Oz, The* (Fantasy)

*Bible, The* (Inspirational, Religious Scripture)

Brink, Carol, *Caddie Woodlawn* (Historical, Settlers and Pioneers)

Bullfinch, Thomas, *Bulfinch's Mythology* (Fantasy, Mythology)

Burnett, Frances, *Secret Garden, The* (Historical, Victorian Novel)

Burnford, Sheila, *Incredible Journey, The* (Adventure, Nature)

Carroll, Lewis, Alice's *Adventures in Wonderland* (Fantasy)

Childress, Alice, *Hero Ain't Nothin' but a Sandwich, A* (Life Issues, Drugs)

Christopher, John, Tripods Trilogy (Science Fiction, Aliens)

Cleary, Beverly, *Fifteen* (Life Issues, Relationships)

Cleaver, Bill and Vera, *Where the Lilies Bloom* (Life Issues, Family)

Collier, James Lincoln, *My Brother Sam Is Dead* (Historical, American Revolution)

Collodi, Carlo, *Pinocchio* (Fantasy)

Cooper, Susan, Dark Is Rising, The (Fantasy, Arthurian)

Dahl, Roald, *Charlie and the Chocolate Factory* (Humor)

Danziger, Paula, *Cat Ate My Gymsuit, The* (Coming of Age)

de Angeli, Marguerite, *Door in the Wall, A* (Historical, Middle Ages)

Dickens, Charles, *Christmas Carol, A* (Fantasy)

Engdahl, Sylvia, *Enchantress from the Stars* (Science Fiction, Space Travel)

Forbes, Esther, *Johnny Tremain* (Historical, American Revolution)

Fox, Paula *Slave Dancer* (Historical, Slavery)

Gilbreth, Frank, *Cheaper by the Dozen* (Humor)

Gipson, Fred, *Old Yeller* (Historical, Western)

Grahame, Kenneth, *Wind in the Willows* (Fantasy, Animal Fantasy and Fable)

Greene, Bette, *Summer of My German Soldier* (Historical, World War II Home Front)

Grimm, Wilhelm, and Jacob *Grimm's Fairy Tales* (Fantasy, Folktales)

Harris, Joel Chandler, *Uncle Remus Tales* (Fantasy, Folk Tales)

Heinlein, Robert, *Have Spacesuit, Will Travel* (Science Fiction, Space Travel)

Hunt, Irene, *Across Five Aprils* (Historical, American Civil War)

Hunt, Irene, *No Promises in the Wind* (Historical, Great Depression)

Irving, Washington, *Legend of Sleepy Hollow, The* (Horror, Ghost Stories)

Juster, Norton, *Phantom Tollbooth, The* (Fantasy, Humorous)

Kipling, Rudyard, *Captains Courageous* (Adventure, Sea Story)

Kipling, Rudyard, *Jungle Book, The* (Fantasy, Animal fantasy and Fable)

L'Engle, Madeleine *Wrinkle in Time, A* (Science Fiction, Space Travel)

Le Guin, Ursula <u>Earthsea Cycle</u> (Fantasy, High Fantasy)

Lewis, C. S., <u>Chronicles of Narnia, The</u> (Fantasy, High Fantasy)

Lewis, Elizabeth Foreman, *Young Fu of the Upper Yangtze* (Coming of Age)

Lofting, Hugh, *Story of Doctor Dolittle, The* (Fantasy, Animal fantasy and Fable)

MacLachlan, Patricia, *Sarah, Plain and Tall* (Historical, Settlers and Pioneers)

Magorian, Michelle, *Good Night, Mr. Tom* (Historical, World War II Homefront)

McGraw, Eloise, *Golden Goblet, The* (Historical, Ancient Egypt)

McKenney, Ruth, *My Sister Eileen* (Humor)

Merrill, Jean, *Pushcart War, The* (Humor)

Milne, A. A., *Winnie the Pooh* (Fantasy, Animal Fantasy and Fable)

Montgomery, Lucy Maud, *Anne of Green Gables* (Coming of Age)

Nesbit, Edith, *Five Children and It* (Fantasy)

O'Dell, Scott, *Island of the Blue Dolphins* (Adventure, Survival)

O'Dell, Scott, *King's Fifth, The* (Historical, Spanish Colonies)

O'Hara, Mary, *My Friend Flicka* (Coming of Age)

Peck, Robert Newton, *Day No Pigs Would Die, A* (Life Issues, Death)

Perrault, Charles, *Tales by Perrault* (Fantasy, Fairy Tales)

Pyle, Howard, *Merry Adventures of Robin Hood, The* (Adventure, Swashbuckler)

Rawlings, Marjorie Kinan, *Yearling, The* (Coming of Age)

Rawls, Wilson, *Where the Red Fern Grows* (Life Issues, Death)

Reiss, Joanna, *Upstairs Room, The* (Historical, Holocaust)

Saint Exupery, Antoine de, *Little Prince, The* (Fantasy)

Salten, Felix, *Bambi: A Life in the Woods* (Fantasy, Animal fantasy and Fable)

Sewell, Anna, *Black Beauty* (Historical, Victorian Novel)

Stevenson, Robert Louis, *Kidnapped* (Adventure, Journey)

Stevenson, Robert Louis, *Treasure Island* (Adventure, Sea Story)

Sutcliff, Rosemary, *Eagle of the Ninth, The* (Historical, Roman Empire)

Taylor, Theodore, *Cay, The* (Adventure, Survival)

Tolkien, J. R. R., *Hobbit, The* (Fantasy, High Fantasy)

Trevino, Elizabeth Borton de, *I, Juan de Pareja* (Historical, Sixteenth, Seventeenth, Eighteenth Century)

Twain, Mark, *Adventures of Huckleberry Finn, The* (Coming of Age)

Twain, Mark, *Adventures of Tom Sawyer, The* (Coming of Age)

Twain, Mark, *Prince and the Pauper, The* (Historical, Sixteenth, Seventeenth, Eighteenth Century)

Unknown, *Jataka Tales* (Fantasy, Animal Fantasy and Fable)

Unknown, *Sundiata* (Fantasy, Epic and Legend)

Verne, Jules, *From the Earth to the Moon* (Science Fiction, Space Travel and Adventure)

Verne, Jules, *Journey to the Center of the Earth* (Science Fiction, Space Travel and Adventure)

Verne, Jules, *Twenty Thousand Leagues under the Sea* (Science Fiction, Space Travel and Adventure)

Vining, Elizabeth Gray, *Adam of the Road* (Historical Middle Ages)

Voigt, Cynthia, *Homecoming* (Family)

Webster, Jean, *Daddy Long Legs* (Romance, Historical)

White, E. B., *Charlotte's Web* (Fantasy, Animal Fantasy and Fable)

Wilde, Oscar, *Happy Prince, The* (Fantasy, Fairy Tales)

Wyss, Johann, *Swiss Family Robinson* (Adventure, Survival)

Yolen, Jane, *Favorite Folktales from around the World* (Fantasy, Folktales)

# J (Grades 7–9, Ages 12–14)

Abbott, Edwin, *Flatland* (Science Fiction, Space Travel and Adventure)

Adams, Douglas, *Hitchhiker's Guide to the Galaxy, The* (Science Fiction, Space Travel and Adventure)

Adams, Richard, *Watership Down* (Fantasy, Animal Fantasy and Fable)

Aldrich, Bess, *Lantern in Her Hand, A* (Historical, Settlers and Pioneers)

Anaya, Rudolpho, *Bless Me, Ultima* (Coming of Age)

Anonymous, *Go Ask Alice* (Life Issues, Drugs)

Anthony, Piers, *Spell for Chameleon, A* (Fantasy, Humorous)

Austen, Jane, *Emma* (Romance, Regency)

Austen, Jane, *Pride and Prejudice* (Romance, Regency)

Beagle, Peter, *Last Unicorn, The* (Fantasy, Animal Fantasy and Fable)

Blackmore, R. D., *Lorna Doone* (Romance, Historical)

Blume, Judy, *Forever* (Life Issues, Relationships)

Bradbury, Ray, *Something Wicked This Way Comes* (Horror, Supernatural/Weird Stories)

Bronte, Charlotte, *Jane Eyre* (Romance, Gothic)

Bunyan, John, *Pilgrim's Progress* (Inspirational, Christian Literature)

Burroughs, Edgar Rice, *Land that Time Forgot, The* (Adventure, Lost World)

Burroughs, Edgar Rice, *Tarzan the Apeman* (Adventure, Survival)

Calvino, Italo, *Italian Folktales* (Fantasy, Folk Tales)

Card, Orson Scott, *Ender's Game* (Science Fiction, Aliens)

Carter, Forest, *Education of Little Tree* (Coming of Age)

Cather, Willa, *Death Comes for the Archbishop* (Inspirational)

Cather, Willa, *My Antonia* (Historical, Settlers and Pioneers)

Cather, Willa, *O, Pioneers!* (Historical, Settlers and Pioneers)

Chandler, Raymond, *Big Sleep, The* (Mystery, Private Eye)

Christie, Agatha, *And Then There Were None* (Mystery, Suspense)

Christie, Agatha, *Murder of Roger Ackroyd, The* (Mystery, Detectives)

Christie, Agatha, *Murder on the Orient Express* (Mystery, Detective)

Cisneros, Sandra, *House on Mango Street, The* (Coming of Age)

Clark, Walter van Tilburg, *Ox-Bow Incident* (Historical, Western)

Cooper, James Fenimore, *Last of the Mohicans, The* (Historical, Colonial America)

Cormier, Robert, *Chocolate War, The* (Coming of Age)

Cormier, Robert, *I Am the Cheese* (Mystery, Suspense)

Crane, Stephen, *Red Badge of Courage, The* (Historical, American Civil War)

Craven, Margaret, *I Heard the Owl Call My Name* (Inspirational)

Crossley Holland, Kevin, *Norse Myths* (Fantasy, Mythology)

Daly, Maureen, *Seventeenth Summer* (Romance, Historical)

Defoe, Daniel, *Robinson Crusoe* (Adventure, Survival)

Dennis, Patrick, *Auntie Mame* (Humor)

Dickens, Charles, *David Copperfield* (Coming of Age)

Dickens, Charles, *Great Expectations* (Coming of Age)

Dickens, Charles, *Oliver Twist* (Historical, Victorian Novel)

Dickens, Charles, *Tale of Two Cities, A* (Historical, Sixteenth, Seventeen, Eighteenth Century)

Doyle, Sir Arthur Conan, *Adventures of Sherlock Holmes, The* (Mystery Detective)

Doyle, Sir Arthur Conan, *Hound of the Baskervilles, The* (Mystery, Suspense)

Doyle, Sir Arthur Conan, *Lost World, The* (Adventure, Lost World)

Doyle, Sir Arthur Conan, *White Company, The* (Historical, Middle Ages)

Du Maurier, Daphne, *Rebecca* (Romance, Gothic)

Dumas, Alexandre, *Count of Monte Cristo, The* (Adventure, Swashbuckler)

Dumas, Alexandre, *Three Musketeers, The* (Historical, Swashbuckler)

Duncan, Lois, *I Know What You Did Last Summer* (Mystery, Suspense)

Eddings, David, Belgariad, The (Fantasy, High Fantasy)

Eliot, George, *Silas Marner* (Historical, Victorian Novel)

Ende, Michael, *Neverending Story, The* (Fantasy, High Fantasy)

Fast, Howard, *April Morning* (Historical, American Revolution)

Forester, C. S., *Mr. Midshipman Hornblower* (Adventure, Sea Story)

Freedman, Benedict, *Mrs. Mike* (Romance, Historical)

Gaines, Ernest, *Autobiography of Miss Jane Pittman, The* (Historical, Slavery)

Golding, William, *Lord of the Flies* (Adventure, Survival)

Goldman, William, *Princess Bride, The* (Fantasy, Humorous)

Greenberg, Joanne, *I Never Promised You a Rose Garden* (Life Issues, Mental Illness)

Grey, Zane, *Riders of the Purple Sage* (Historical, Westerns)

Haggard, H Rider, *King Solomon's Mines* (Adventure, Journey)

Haley, Alex, *Roots* (Historical, Slavery)

Hamilton, Virginia, *House of Dies Drear, The* (Mystery, Suspense)

Hawthorne, Nathaniel, *House of the Seven Gables* (Horror, Haunted Houses)

Head, Ann, *Mr. and Mrs. Bo Jo Jones* (Life Issues, Relationships)

Hemingway, Ernest, *Old Man and the Sea, The* (Adventure, Sea Story)

Herriot, James, *All Creatures Great and Small* (Humor)

Heyer, Georgette, *Grand Sophy, The* (Romance, Regency)

Hilton, James, *Goodbye, Mr. Chips* (Historical, Victorian Novel)

Hilton, James, *Lost Horizon* (Adventure, Journey)

Hinton, S. E., *Outsiders, The* (Coming of Age)

Homer, *Iliad, The* (Fantasy, Epic and Legend)

Homer, *Odyssey, The* (Fantasy, Epic and Legend)

Hope, Anthony, *Prisoner of Zenda, The* (Adventure, Swashbuckler)

Houston, Jeanne, *Farewell to Manzanar, A* (Historical, World War II Homefront)

Howard, Robert, *Conan the Conqueror* (Fantasy, High Fantasy)

Hughes, Thomas, *Tom Brown's School Days* (Historical, Victorian Novel)

Jackson, Helen Hunt, *Ramona* (Romance, Historical)

Keith, Harold, *Rifles for Watie* (Historical, American Civil War)

Kerr, M. E., *Dinky Hocker Shoots Smack* (Coming of Age)

Keyes, Daniel, *Flowers for Algernon* (Science Fiction, Science Gone Awry)

Kipling, Rudyard, *Kim* (Adventure, Espionage)

Kipling, Rudyard, *Man Who Would Be King, The* (Adventure, Journey)

Knowles, John, *Separate Peace, A* (Coming of Age)

*Koran, The* (Inspirational, Religious Scripture)

Lee, Harper, *To Kill A Mockingbird* (Coming of Age)

LeMay, Alan, *Searchers, The* (Historical, Western)

Leroux, Gaston, *Phantom of the Opera, The* (Horror, Gothic)

Lewis, C. S., *Screwtape Letters* (Inspirational, Christian Literature)

Llewellyn, Richard, *How Green Was My Valley* (Coming of Age)

London, Jack, *Call of the Wild, The* (Adventure, Nature)

London, Jack, *White Fang* (Adventure, Nature)

Lovecraft, H. P., *Call of Cthulhu and Other Weird Stories* (Horror, Supernatural/Weird Stories)

Malory, Sir Thomas, *Morte d'Arthur, Le* (Fantasy, Arthurian)

Markandaya, Kamala, *Nectar in a Sieve* (Life Issues, Family)

Marquis, Don, *Archy and Mehitabel* (Humor)

Marshall, Catherine, *Christy* (Inspirational Christian Literature)

McCaffrey, Anne, Harper Hall Trilogy (Fantasy, High Fantasy)

McCulley, Johnston, *Mark of Zorro, The* (Adventure, Swashbuckler)

McKillip, Patricia, *Forgotten Beasts of Eld* (Fantasy, High Fantasy)

McKinley, Robin, *Beauty: A Retelling of Beauty and the Beast* (Fantasy, Fairy Tales)

McKinley, Robin, *Hero and the Crown, The* (Fantasy, High Fantasy)

McMurtry, Larry, *Lonesome Dove* (Historical, Westerns)

Mitchell, Margaret, *Gone with the Wind* (Romance, Historical)

Neufeld, John, *Lisa, Bright and Dark* (Life Issues, Mental Illness)

Nordhoff, Charles, and James Hall, *Mutiny on the Bounty* (Adventure, Sea Story)

O'Brien, Robert, *Z is for Zachariah* (Science Fiction, Dystopias and Alternative Futures)

Orczy, Baroness Emma, *Scarlet Pimpernel, The* (Adventure, Swashbuckler)

Orwell, George, *Animal Farm* (Fantasy, Animal Fantasy and Fable)

Paterson, Katherine, *Jacob Have I Loved* (Life Issues, Family)

Pearl Poet, *Sir Gawain and the Green Knight* (Fantasy, Arthurian)

Poe, Edgar Allan, *Murder in the Rue Morgue* (Mystery, Detective)

Poe, Edgar Allan, *Poe's Collected Stories and Poems* (Horror, Gothic)

Portis, Charles, *True Grit* (Historical, Western)

Raspe, Rudolph, *Baron Munchhausen* (Fantasy, Humorous)

Richter, Conrad, *Light in the Forest, The* (Historical, Colonial America)

Saroyan, William, *Human Comedy, The* (Life Issues, Family)

Sayers, Dorothy, *Strong Poison* (Mystery, Detective)

Schaefer, Jack, *Shane* (Historical, Western)

Scott, Sir Walter, *Ivanhoe* (Historical, Middle Ages)

Shelley, Mary, *Frankenstein, or the Modern Prometheus* (Horror, Science Gone Awry)

Sleator, William, *House of Stairs* (Horror, Science Gone Awry)

Sleator, William, *Interstellar Pig* (Science Fiction, Aliens)

Smith, Betty, *Tree Grows in Brooklyn, A* (Coming of Age)

Smith, Dodie, *I Capture the Castle* (Coming of Age)

Speare, Elizabeth George, *Bronze Bow, The* (Inspirational, Early Christianity)

Speare, Elizabeth George, *Witch of Blackbird Pond, The* (Romance, Historical)

Steinbeck, John, *Pearl, The* (Life Issues, Social Conflict)

Steinbeck, John, *Red Pony, The* (Coming of Age)

Stevenson, Robert Louis, *Dr. Jekyll and Mr. Hyde* (Horror, Science Gone Awry)

Stewart, Mary, <u>Arthurian Saga</u> (Fantasy, Arthurian)

Stoker, Bram, *Dracula* (Horror, Vampires)

Stratton Porter, Gene, *Girl of the Limberlost, A* (Romance, Historical)

Swarthout, Glendon, *Bless the Beasts and the Children* (Coming of Age)

Swift, Jonathan, *Gulliver's Travels* (Humor)

Taylor, Mildred, *Roll of Thunder, Hear My Cry* (Life Issues, Family)

Tey, Josephine, *Daughter of Time, The* (Mystery, Detective)

Tolkien, J. R. R., <u>Lord of the Rings</u> (Fantasy, High Fantasy)

Twain, Mark, *Roughing It* (Historical, Western)

Unknown, *Beowulf* (Fantasy, Epic and Legend)

Unknown, *Nibelungenlied* (Fantasy, Epic and Legend)

Unknown, *Song of Roland* (Fantasy, Epic and Legend)

Verne, Jules, *Around the World in Eighty Days* (Adventure, Journey)

Wangerin, Walter, *Book of the Dun Cow, The* (Fantasy, Animal Fantasy and Fable)

Wells, H. G., *Time Machine, The* (Science Fiction, Time Travel)

Wells, H. G., *Invisible Man, The* (Horror, Science Gone Awry)

Werfel, Franz, *Song of Bernadette, The* (Inspirational)

West, Jessamyn, *Friendly Persuasion* (Inspirational)

Wharton, Edith, *Ethan Frome* (Life Issues, Relationships)

Wiesel, Elie, *Night* (Historical, Holocaust)

Wilde, Oscar, *Picture of Dorian Gray* (Horror, Supernatural/Weird Stories)

Wister, Owen, *Virginian, The* (Historical, Western)

Wren, P. C., *Beau Geste* (Adventure, Swashbuckler)

Yezierska, Anzia, *Bread Givers, The* (Coming of Age)

Zindel, Paul, *Pigman, The* (Coming of Age)

# S (Grades 10–12, Ages 15–18)

Achebe, Chinua, *Things Fall Apart* (Life Issues, Social Conflict)

Agee, James, *Death in the Family, A* (Life Issues, Death)

Andrews, V. C., *Flowers in the Attic* (Horror, Gothic)

Arnow, Harriet, *Dollmaker, The* (Historical, Urban Realism)

Asimov, Isaac, *Foundation* (Science Fiction, Space Travel and Adventure)

Asimov, Isaac, *I, Robot* (Science Fiction, Dystopias and Alternative Futures)

Baldwin, James, *Go Tell It on the Mountain* (Coming of Age)

Bellamy, Edward, *Looking Backward* (Science Fiction, Time Travel)

Berger, Thomas, *Little Big Man* (Humor)

Bester, Alfred, *The Stars My Destination* (Science Fiction, Space Travel and Adventure)

Unknown, *Bhagavad-Gita, The* (Inspirational, Religious Scriptures)

Borland, Hal, *When the Legends Die* (Coming of Age)

Bradbury, Ray, *Fahrenheit 451* (Science Fiction, Dystopias and Alternative Futures)

Bradbury, Ray, *Illustrated Man, The* (Horror, Supernatural/Weird Stories)

Bradbury, Ray, *Martian Chronicles, The* (Science Fiction, Space Travel and Adventure)

Bradley, Marion Zimmer, *Mists of Avalon, The* (Fantasy, Arthurian)

Bronte, Emily, *Wuthering Heights* (Romance, Gothic)

Buchan, John, *Thirty-Nine Steps, The* (Adventure, Espionage)

Buck, Pearl S., *Good Earth, The* (Historical. Family Saga)

Bulgakov, Mikhail, *Master and Margarita, The* (Historical, Russian Novel)

Burgess, Anthony, *Clockwork Orange, A* (Science Fiction, Dystopias and Alternative Futures)

Butler, Octavia, *Kindred* (Science Fiction, Time Travel)

Caldwell, Taylor, *Dear and Glorious Physician* (Inspirational, Early Christianity)

Camus, Albert, *Stranger, The* (Coming of Age)

Capote, Truman, *In Cold Blood* (Mystery, Crime)

Cervantes, *Don Quixote* (Humor)

Chaucer, Geoffrey, Ca*nterbury Tales, The* (Humor)

Childers, Erskine, *Riddle of the Sands, The* (Adventure, Espionage)

Chopin, Kate, *Awakening, The* (Coming of Age)

Clarke, Arthur C., *2001: A Space Odyssey* (Science Fiction, Space Travel)

Clarke, Arthur C., *Childhood's End* (Science Fiction, Aliens)

Collins, Wilkie, *Moonstone, The* (Mystery, Detective)

Conrad, Joseph, *Heart of Darkness* (Adventure, Journey)

Conrad, Joseph, *Lord Jim* (Adventure, Journey)

Conrad, Joseph, *Secret Agent, The* (Adventure, Espionage)

Conroy, Pat, *Great Santini, The* (Life Issues, Family)

Dante, *Divine Comedy, The* (Inspirational)

Defoe, Daniel, *Journal of the Plague Year, A* (Historical, Sixteenth, Seventeenth, Eighteenth Century)

Defoe, Daniel, *Moll Flanders* (Historical; Sixteenth, Seventeenth, Eighteenth Century)

Dick, Phillip K., *Do Androids Dream of Electric Sheep?* (Science Fiction, Dystopias and Alternative Futures)

Doctorow, E. L., *Ragtime* (Historical, Gilded Age)

Dos Passos, John, USA Trilogy (Historical, Jazz Age)

Dostoevsky, Fyodor, *Brothers Karamazov* (Historical, Russian Novel)

Dostoevsky, Fyodor, *Crime and Punishment* (Mystery, Crime)

Douglas, Lloyd, *Robe, The* (Inspirational, Early Christianity)

Dreiser, Theodore, *American Tragedy, An* (Life Issues, Relationships)

Dreiser, Theodore, *Sister Carrie* (Historical, Gilded Age)

Eco, Umberto, *Name of the Rose, The* (Mystery, Detective)

Eddison, Eric Rucker, *Worm Ouroboros, The* (Fantasy, High Fantasy)

Eliot, George, *Middlemarch* (Historical, Victorian Novel)

Ellison, Ralph, *Invisible Man* (Coming of Age)

Ferber. Edna, *Cimarron* (Historical, Settlers and Pioneers)

Fielding, Henry, *Tom Jones* (Humor)

Finney, Jack, *Time and Again* (Science Fiction, Time Travel)

Fitzgerald, F. Scott, *Great Gatsby, The* (Historical, Jazz Age)

Flaubert, Gustave, *Madame Bovary* (Life Issues, Relationships)

Forster E. M. *Passage to India* (Life Issues, Social Conflict)

Garden, Nancy, *Annie on My Mind* (Life Issues, Relationships)

Gardner, John, *Grendel* (Fantasy, Epic and Legend)

Gibson, William, *Neuromancer* (Science Fiction, Dystopias and Alternative Futures)

Galsworthy, John, *Forsyte Saga, The* (Historical, Family Saga)

Goethe, Johann Wolfgang von, *Sorrows of Young Werther, The* (Life Issues, Relationships)

Gogol, Nicholai, *Dead Souls* (Historical, Russian Novel)

Grass, Gunter, *Tin Drum, The* (Historical, World War II - Home Front)

Graves, Robert, *I, Claudius* (Historical, Roman Empire)

Guest, Judith, *Ordinary People* (Life Issues, Death)

Hammett, Dashiell, *Maltese Falcon, The* (Mystery, Private Eye)

Hardy, Thomas, *Tess of the D'Urbervilles* (Life Issues, Relationships)

Hawthorne, Nathaniel, *Scarlet Letter, The* (Historical, Colonial America)

Heinlein, Robert, *Starship Troopers* (Science Fiction, Aliens)

Heinlein, Robert, *Stranger in a Strange Land* (Science Fiction, Aliens)

Heller, Joseph, *Catch-22* (Historical, World War II)

Hemingway, Ernest, *Farewell to Arms, A* (Historical, World War I)

Herbert, Frank, *Dune* (Science Fiction, Space Travel)

Hersey, John, *Bell for Adano, A* (Historical, World War II)

Hesse, Hermann, *Siddhartha* (Inspirational)

Highsmith, Patricia, *Talented Mr. Ripley, The* (Mystery, Crime)

Hughes, Richard, *High Wind in Jamaica, A* (Adventure, Journey)

Hugo, Victor, *Hunchback of Notre Dame, The* (Historical, Middle Ages)

Hugo, Victor, *Miserables, Les* (Life Issues, Social Conflict)

Huxley, Aldous, *Brave New World* (Science Fiction, Dystopias and Alternative Futures)

Irving, John, *World According to Garp, The* (Humor)

Jackson, Shirley, *Haunting of Hill House, The* (Horror, Haunted Houses)

Jackson, Shirley, *We Have Always Lived in the Castle* (Horror, Haunted Houses)

James, Henry, *Daisy Miller* (Coming of Age)

James, Henry, *Portrait of a Lady* (Historical, Gilded Age)

James, Henry, *Turn of the Screw, The* (Horror, Ghost Story)

Joyce, James, *Portrait of the Artist as a Young Man* (Coming of Age)

Kafka, Franz, *Metamorphosis* (Horror, Psychological)

Kafka, Franz, *Trial, The* (Horror, Psychological)

Kantor, MacKinlay, *Andersonville* (Historical, American Civil War)

Kaufman, Bel, *Up the Down Staircase* (Humor)

Kelton, Elmer, *Day the Cowboys Quit* (Historical, Western)

Keneally, Thomas, *Schindler's List* (Historical, Holocaust)

Keruouc, Jack, *On the Road* (Coming of Age)

Kesey, Ken, *One Flew over the Cuckoo's Nest* (Life Issues, Mental Illness)

King, Stephen, *Carrie* (Horror, Psychological)

King, Stephen, *Shining, The* (Horror, Haunted Houses)

Koestler, Arthur, *Darkness at Noon* (Historical, Russian Novel)

Kosinski, Jerzy, *Painted Bird, The* (Historical, Home Front)

Lagerkvist, Par, *Barabbas* (Inspirational, Early Christianity)

Lawrence, D. H., *Sons and Lovers* (Life Issues, Relationships)

Le Guin, Ursula, *Left Hand of Darkness* (Science Fiction, Space Travel)

Lewis, C. S., *Out of the Silent Planet* (Science Fiction, Space Travel)

Lewis, Sinclair, *Main Street* (Coming of Age)

Lonnrot, Elias, *Kalevala* (Fantasy, Epic and Legend)

Mann, Thomas, *Buddenbrooks: The Decline of a Family* (Historical, Family Saga)

Marquez, Gabriel Garcia, *One Hundred Years of Solitude* (Historical, Family Saga)

Masters, Edgar Lee, *Spoon River Anthology* (Life Issues, Death)

Maugham, Somerset, *Ashenden: Or the British Agent* (Adventure, Espionage)

Maugham, Somerset, *Of Human Bondage* (Coming of Age)

McCullers, Carson, *Heart Is a Lonely Hunter, The* (Coming of Age)

McCullers, Carson, *Member of the Wedding, A* (Coming of Age)

Melville, Herman *Moby Dick* (Adventure, Sea Story)

Miller, Walter, *Canticle for Liebowitz, A* (Science Fiction, Dystopias and Alternative Futures)

Milton, John, *Paradise Lost* (Inspirational)

Mishima, Yukio, *Sound of Waves*, The (Romance, Historical)

Monsarrat, Nicholas, *Cruel Sea, The* (Historical, World War II)

Morrison, Toni, *Beloved* (Historical, Slavery)

Morrison, Toni, *Bluest Eye, The* (Coming of Age)

Norton, Andre, <u>Witch World Chronicles</u> (Fantasy, High Fantasy)

Orwell, George, *1984* (Science Fiction, Dystopia)

Parks, Gordon, *Learning Tree, The* (Coming of Age)

Pasternak, Boris, *Dr. Zhivago* (Historical, Russian Novel)

Paton, Alan, *Cry, the Beloved Country* (Life Issues, Social Conflict)

Petry, Ann, *Street, The* (Historical, Urban Realism)

Plath, Sylvia, *Bell Jar, The* (Life Issues, Mental Illness)

Potok, Chaim, *Chosen, The* (Coming of Age)

Rand, Ayn, *Fountainhead, The* (Life Issues, Social Conflict)

Remarque, Erich, *All Quiet on the Western Front* (Historical, World War I)

Renault, Mary, *King Must Die, The* (Historical, Ancient Greece)

Richter, Conrad, <u>Awakening Land, The</u> (Historical, Colonial America)

Rolvaag, Ole, *Giants in the Earth* (Historical. Settlers and Pioneers)

Sabatini, Rafael, *Scaramouche* (Adventure, Swashbuckler)

Salinger J. D., *Catcher in the Rye, The* (Coming of Age)

Seton, Anya, *Katherine* (Romance, Historical)

Shaara, Michael, *Killer Angels, The* (Historical, American Civil War)

Shange, Ntozake, *Betsey Brown* (Coming of Age)

Shellabarger, Samuel, *Prince of Foxes, The* (Historical; Sixteenth, Seventeenth, Eighteenth Century)

Shute, Nevil, *On the Beach* (Science Fiction, Dystopia)

Sienkiewicz, Henryk, *Quo Vadis* (Inspirational, Early Christianity)

Simenon, Georges, *Maigret and the Fortuneteller* (Mystery, Detective)

Sinclair, Upton, *Jungle, The* (Life Issues, Social Conflict)

Solzhenitsyn, Alexander, *One Day in the Life of Ivan Denisovich* (Historical, Russian Novel)

Steinbeck, John, *East of Eden* (Historical, Family Saga)

Steinbeck, John, *Grapes of Wrath* (Historical, Great Depression)

Steinbeck, John, *Of Mice and Men* (Life Issues, Relationships)

Stowe, Harriet Beecher, *Uncle Tom's Cabin* (Historical, Slavery)

Styron, William, *Sophie's Choice* (Historical, Holocaust)

*Tao Te Ching* (Inspirational, Religious Scripture)

Tarkington, Booth, *Magnificent Ambersons, The* (Historical, Gilded Age)

Tedlock, Dennis, *Popol Vuh* (Fantasy, Mythology)

Thackeray, William, *Vanity Fair* (Humor)

Tolstoy, Leo, *Anna Karenina* (Historical, Russian Novel)

Tolstoy, Leo, *War and Peace* (Historical, Russian Novel)

Trollope, Anthony, *Barchester Towers* (Humor)

Trumbo, Dalton, *Johnny Got His Gun* (Historical, World War I)

Turgenev, Ivan, *Fathers and Sons* (Historical, Russian Novel)

Undset, Sigrid, *Kristin Lavransdatter* (Historical, Middle Ages)

Unknown, *Arabian Nights* (Fantasy, Fairy Tales)

Unknown, *Cid, El* (Fantasy, Epic and Legend)

Unknown, *Gilgamesh* (Fantasy, Epic and Legend)

Unknown, *Saga of the Volsungs* (Fantasy, Epics and Legends)

Uris, Leon, *Exodus* (Historical, Holocaust)

Virgil, *Aeneid, The* (Fantasy, Epic and Legend)

Voltaire, *Candide* (Humor)

Vonnegut, Kurt, *Slaughterhouse Five* (Science Fiction, Time Travel)

Walker, Alice, *Color Purple, The* (Coming of Age)

Walker, Margaret, *Jubilee* (Historical, Slavery)

Wallace, Lew, B*en Hur* (Inspirational, Early Christianity)

Waltari, Mika, *Egyptian, The* (Historical, Ancient Egypt)

Wells, H. G., *War of the Words, The* (Science Fiction, Aliens)

Wells, H. G., *Island of Dr. Moreau, The* (Horror, Science Gone Awry)

Wharton, Edith, *Age of Innocence, The* (Historical, Gilded Age)

Wharton, Edith, *House of Mirth, The* (Historical, Gilded Age)

White, T. H., *Once and Future King, The* (Fantasy, Arthurian)

Wilder, Thornton, *Bridge of San Luis Rey, The* (Historical, Spanish Colonies)

Wilder, Thornton, *Theophilus North* (Humor)

Williams, Tad, *Tailchaser's Song* (Fantasy, Animal Fantasy and Fables)

Winsor, Kathleen, F*orever Amber* (Romance, Historical)

Wodehouse, P. G., *Code of the Woosters* (Humor)

Wolfe, Thomas, L*ook Homeward, Angel* (Coming of Age)

Woolf, Virginia, *Mrs. Dalloway* (Life Issues, Relationships)

Wouk, Herman, *Caine Mutiny, The* (Historical, World War II)

Wright, Richard, *Black Boy* (Coming of Age)

Wright, Richard, *Native Son* (Historical, Urban Realism)

Zola, Emile, *Nana* (Life Issues, Relationships)

# Author/Title Index

Indexed here are the main entries for authors and titles, adaptations, and authors and titles listed in the Similar Reads sections. Book titles are in *italics*. Films are listed with their date of release.

# Subject Index

Fighting Ground, The, 39–40
Five Children and It, 111
Flowers in the Attic, 151–52
Forever, 199–200
Forsyte Saga, The, 73
Friendly Persuasion, The, 242–43
Girl of the Limberlost, A, 228–29
Giants in the Earth, 50
Go Tell It on the Mountain, 176–77
Gone with the Wind, 227
Good Earth, The, 72–73
Good Night, Mr. Tom, 69
Grand Sophy, The, 232
Grapes of Wrath, The, 61
Great Expectations, 181
Great Santini, The, 207
Have Spacesuit, Will Travel, 99–100
Heart Is a Lonely Hunter, The, 188
Homecoming, 207
House of Dies Drear, The, 172
House of the Seven Gables, The, 149–50
House on Mango Street, The, 62, 179
How Green Was My Valley, 187
Human Comedy, The, 208
I Am the Cheese, 171
I Capture the Castle, 194
Jacob Have I Loved, 208
Jubilee, 46–47
Jungle, The, 218
Kidnapped, 8
Kristin Lavransdatter, 31
Lantern in Her Hand, A, 47
Learning Tree, The, 191
Light in the Forest, The, 39
Lisa, Bright and Dark, 212
Little Women, 206
Look Homeward, Angel, 197–98
Magnificent Ambersons, The, 57
Member of the Wedding, A, 188–89
Metamorphosis, 156
Mr. and Mrs. Bo Jo Jones, 203
Mrs. Dalloway, 205
Mrs. Mike, 225–26
My Brother Sam Is Dead, 40
My Friend Flicka, 190
Nectar in a Sieve, 207–8
No Promises in the Wind, 60
Northanger Abbey, 222
O, Pioneers!, 48–49
Odyssey, The, 126
Old Yeller, 51–52
One Hundred Years of Solitude, 176

Ordinary People, 213–14
Outsiders, The, 182
Pearl, The, 219
Peter Pan, 108–9
Pinocchio, 110
Portrait of a Lady, 56–57
Portrait of the Artist as a Young Man, 183
Pride and Prejudice, 231
Ragtime, 55–56
Red Pony, The, 194–95
Roll of Thunder, Hear My Cry, 209
Roots, 45
Sarah, Plain and Tall, 50
Searchers, The, 52–53
Secret Garden, The, 75, 75
Seventeenth Summer, 225
Shane, 54
Shining, The, 151
Silas Marner, 76
Sons and Lovers, 203–4
Sound of Waves, The, 226
Sounder, 176
Street, The, 62
Summer of My German Soldier, The, 67–68
Swiss Family Robinson, 17–18
Tess of the D'Urbervilles, 202–3
To Kill a Mockingbird, 185–86
Tom Jones, 248
Tree Grows in Brooklyn, A, 193
Tuck Everlasting, 108
Upstairs Room, The, 70–71
War and Peace, 80
We Have Always Lived in the Castle, 150–51
Where the Lilies Bloom, 206–7
Witch of Blackbird Pond, The, 228
World According to Garp, The, 249–50
Wrinkle in Time, A, 101
Wuthering Heights, 223
Yearling, The, 192
Young Fu of the Upper Yangtze, 186

**Family Curse**
Hound of the Baskervilles, The, 172

**Family Saga**
Buddenbrooks: The Decline of a Family, 73
East of Eden, 74
Forsyte Saga, The, 73
Good Earth, The, 72–73
One Hundred Years of Solitude, 176

**Generational Differences**
Fathers and Sons, 80–81

**Genetic Engineering**
Ender's Game, 86, 86

**Genetic Manipulation**
Flowers for Algernon, 94–95

**Gentle Read**
Adam of the Road, 32
Adventures of Tom Sawyer, The, 196
Alice's Adventures in Wonderland, 110
All Creatures Great and Small, 249
Anne of Green Gables, 189
Archy and Mehitabel, 250
Around the World in Eighty Days, 8
Awakening Land, The, 38–39
Bambi: A Life in the Woods, 142
Barchester Towers, 252–53
Black Beauty, 78
Bridge of San Luis Rey, The, 36–37
Charlotte's Web, 143
Cheaper by the Dozen, 248–49
Christmas Carol, A, 111
Christy, 239
Code of the Woosters, 254
Daddy Long Legs, 229
Daisy Miller, 183
Death Comes for the Archbishop, 240
Death in the Family, A, 213
Door in the Wall, The, 29
Education of Little Tree, 178
Emma, 230–31
Fathers and Sons, 80–81
Fifteen, 200
Five Children and It, 111
Flatland, 95–96
Friendly Persuasion, The, 242–43
Girl of the Limberlost, A, 228–29
Golden Goblet, The, 26
Goodbye, Mr. Chips, 77
Grand Sophy, The, 232
How Green Was My Valley, 187
Human Comedy, The, 208
I Capture the Castle, 194
I Heard the Owl Call My Name, 240
I, Juan de Pareja, 34–35
Jane Eyre, 222–23
Jungle Book, The, 140
Lantern in Her Hand, A, 47
Last Unicorn, The, 139

Little Prince, The, 112
Little Women, 206
Lost Horizon, 6
Mrs. Mike, 225–26
My Friend Flicka, 190
My Sister Eileen, 250
Nectar in a Sieve, 207–8
Northanger Abbey, 222
Old Yeller, 51–52
Peter Pan, 108–9
Pilgrim's Progress, 238
Pride and Prejudice, 231
Pushcart War, The, 251
Sarah, Plain and Tall, 50
Secret Garden, The, 75
Seventeenth Summer, 225
Silas Marner, 76
Sound of Waves, The, 226
Story of Doctor Dolittle, The, 140–41
Swiss Family Robinson, 17–18
Theophilus North, 253–54
Tree Grows in Brooklyn, A, 193
Tuck Everlasting, 108
Where the Lilies Bloom, 206–7
Where the Red Fern Grows, 215
White Company, The, 30
Wind in the Willows, 139–40
Winnie the Pooh, 141
Yearling, The, 192
Young Fu of the Upper Yangtze, 186

**Geometry**
Flatland, 95 96

**Georgia**
Color Purple, The, 196–97
Gone with the Wind, 227
Heart Is a Lonely Hunter, The, 188
Jubilee, 46–47
Member of the Wedding, A, 188–89

**Germany**
All Quiet on the Western Front, 105
Baron Munchhausenm, 145
Buddenbrooks: The Decline of a Family, 73
Grimm's Fairy Tales, 133
Nibelungenlied, 126
Night, 72
Riddle of the Sands, The, 3
Schindler's List, 70
Sorrows of Young Werther, The, 202
Tin Drum, The, 67

**World War II**
Bell for Adano, A, 65–66
Caine Mutiny, The, 67–68
Catch-22, 65
Cay, The, 18
Cruel Sea, The, 66
Exodus, 71–72
Farewell to Manzanar, A, 92
Good Night, Mr. Tom, 69
Human Comedy, The, 208
Night, 72
Painted Bird, The, 69
Schindler's List, 70
Slaughterhouse Five, 105
Sophie's Choice, 71
Summer of My German Soldier, The,
     67–68
Tin Drum, The, 67
Upstairs Room. The

**Wrestling**
World According to Garp, The, 249–50

**Writers**
I Capture the Castle, 194
Little Women, 206
My Sister Eileen, 250
Sophie's Choice, 71

**Wyoming**
My Friend Flicka, 190
Shane, 54
Virginian, The, 55

**Xanth**
Spell for Chameleon, A, 144

**YA Classics**
Across Five Aprils, 42
Adam of the Road, 32
Anne of Green Gables, 189
Annie on My Mind, 201–2
Beauty: A Retelling of Beauty and the
     Beast, 135–36
Bronze Bow, The, 236–37
Caddie Woodlawn, 48
Cat Ate My Gymsuit, The, 180
Cay, The, 18
Charlie and the Chocolate Factory, 247
Charlotte's Web, 143
Chocolate War, The, 179–80
Chronicles of Narnia, The, 116–17

City of Gold and Lead, 86
Daddy Long Legs, 229
Dark Is Rising Sequence, The, 129
Day No Pigs Would Die, A, 214
Dinky Hocker Shoots Smack, 184–85
Door in the Wall, The, 29
Eagle of the Ninth, The, 28
Earthsea Cycle, 139–40
Enchantress from the Stars, 99
Ender's Game, 86
Farewell to Manzanar, A, 92
Fifteen, 200
Fighting Ground, The, 39–40
Forever, 199–200
Girl of the Limberlost, A, 228–29
Go Ask Alice, 210
Golden Goblet, The, 26
Good Night, Mr. Tom, 69
Harper Hall Trilogy, 117–18
Have Spacesuit, Will Travel, 99–100
Hero Ain't Nothing but a Sandwich, A,
     210–11
Hero and the Crown, The, 118
Homecoming, 207
House of Stairs, 158–59
House of Dies Drear, The, 172
I Am the Cheese, 171
I Know What You Did Last Summer, 173
I Never Promised You a Rose Garden, 211
I, Juan de Pareja, 34–35
Incredible Journey, The, 10–11
Interstellar Pig, 88
Island of the Blue Dolphins, 10–11
Jacob Have I Loved, 208
Johnny Tremain, 41
Kim, 3–4
King's Fifth, The, 36
Light in the Forest, The
Lisa, Bright and Dark, 212
Merry Adventures of Robin Hood, The, 22
Mr. and Mrs. Bo Jo Jones, 203
My Brother Sam Is Dead, 40
Neverending Story, The, 114
No Promises in the Wind, 60
Old Yeller, 51–52
Outsiders, The, 182
Phantom Tollbooth, The, 145
Pigman, The, 199
Pool of Fire, The, 87, 87
Prydain Chronicles, 112–13
Pushcart War, The, 251
Rifles for Watie, 43

# About the Author

Tina Frolund is a librarian in Las Vegas, Nevada. She has worked a children's librarian and a young adult librarian, as well as a reference librarian in university and community college libraries. She is an active member of YALSA and a reviewer for *VOYA: Voice of Youth Advocates*.